FOCUS: IRISH TRADITIONAL MUSIC

Focus: Irish Traditional Music, Second Edition introduces the instrumental and vocal musics of Ireland, its diaspora in North America, and its Celtic neighbors while exploring the essential values underlying these rich musical cultures and placing them in broader historical and social context. With both the undergraduate and graduate student in mind, the text weaves together past and present, bringing together important ideas about Irish music from a variety of sources and presenting them, in three parts, within interdisciplinary lenses of history, film, politics, poetry, and art:

I. **Irish Music in Place and Time** provides an overview of the island's musical history and its relationship to current performance practice.
II. **Music Traditions Abroad and at Home** contrasts the instrumental and vocal musics of the "Celtic Nations" (Scotland, Wales, Brittany, etc.) and the United States with those of Ireland.
III. **Focusing In: Vocal Music in Irish-Gaelic and English** identifies the great songs of Ireland's two main languages and explores the globalization of Irish music.

New to this edition are discussions of those contemporary issues reflective of Ireland's dramatic political and cultural shifts in the decade since first publication, issues concerning equity and inclusion, white nationalism, the Irish Traveller community, hip hop and punk, and more. Pedagogical features—such as discussion questions, a glossary, a timeline of key dates, and expanded references, as well as an online soundtrack—ensure that readers of *Focus: Irish Traditional Music, Second Edition* will be able to grasp Ireland's important social and cultural contexts and apply that understanding to traditional and contemporary vocal and instrumental music today.

Sean Williams is Professor of Ethnomusicology at The Evergreen State College in Olympia, Washington.

FOCUS ON WORLD MUSIC

Series Editor: Michael B. Bakan, Florida State University

The **Focus on World Music Series** is designed specifically for area courses in world music and ethnomusicology. Written by the top ethnomusicologists in their field, the Focus books balance sound pedagogy with exemplary scholarship. Each book provides a telescopic view of the musics and cultures addressed, giving the reader a general introduction to the music and culture of the area and then zooming in on different musical styles with in-depth case studies.

FOCUS: IRISH TRADITIONAL MUSIC

Second Edition

Sean Williams

Routledge
Taylor & Francis Group

NEW YORK AND LONDON

Second edition published 2020
by Routledge
52 Vanderbilt Avenue, New York, NY 10017

and by Routledge
2 Park Square, Milton Park, Abingdon, Oxon, OX14 4RN

Routledge is an imprint of the Taylor & Francis Group, an informa business

First edition published by Routledge 2010

Library of Congress Cataloging-in-Publication Data
Names: Williams, Sean, 1959- author.
Title: Focus: Irish traditional music/Sean Williams.
Other titles: Irish traditional music
Description: Second edition. | New York: Routledge, 2020. |
Series: Focus on world music | Includes bibliographical references and index.
Identifiers: LCCN 2019052623 (print) | LCCN 2019052624 (ebook) |
ISBN 9780367244019 (hardback) | ISBN 9780367244026 (paperback) |
ISBN 9780429282256 (ebook)
Subjects: LCSH: Folk music–Ireland–History and criticism.
Classification: LCC ML3654 .W56 2020 (print) | LCC ML3654 (ebook) |
DDC 781.62/9162–dc23
LC record available at https://lccn.loc.gov/2019052623
LC ebook record available at https://lccn.loc.gov/2019052624

ISBN: 978-0-367-24401-9 (hbk)
ISBN: 978-0-367-24402-6 (pbk)
ISBN: 978-0-429-28225-6 (ebk)

Typeset in Minion
by Deanta Global Publishing Services, Chennai, India

Visit the companion website: http://cw.routledge.com/textbooks/focusonworldmusic/

Contents

Figures

All photos by Sean Williams unless otherwise noted.

Series Foreword

Recent decades have witnessed extraordinary growth in the arena of ethnomusicology and world music publishing. From reference works such as the *Garland Encyclopedia of World Music* and *Grove Music Online* to a diverse array of introductory world music textbooks, and an ever-growing list of scholarly monographs and hefty edited volumes, the range of quality published sources for research and teaching is unprecedented. And then there is the Internet, where YouTube, Spotify, websites, blogs, social media, and countless digital platforms for music delivery, multimedia production, and music-related metadata have fostered a veritable revolution in the realm of all things musical, from production and reception to public access, commodification, and practices of listening, reading, and viewing.

Yet for all that has come along and all that has been transformed, there has long been a conspicuous gap in the literature. For those of us who teach entry-level area courses in world music and ethnomusicology subject areas—the kinds of courses that straddle the divide between the introductory world music survey and the advanced graduate seminar, the ones that cater to upper-division undergraduates or to new graduate students who have a basic foundation in the field but are not yet ready for the highly specialized studies of, say, a Chicago Studies in Ethnomusicology-based reading list—available options for appropriate core texts have remained slim at best.

It is to the instructors and students of these types of courses that the Routledge *Focus on World Music* series is primarily directed. *Focus* books balance sound pedagogy with exemplary scholarship. They are substantive in content yet readily accessible to specialist and non-specialist readers alike. They are written in a lively and engaging style by leading ethnomusicologists and educators, bringing wide interdisciplinary scope and relevance to the contemporary concerns of world music studies. While each volume is unique, all share a commitment to providing readers with a "telescopic" view of the musics and cultures they address, zooming in from broad-based surveys of expansive music-culture areas and topics toward compelling, in-depth case studies of specific musicultural traditions and their myriad transformations in the modern world.

When you adopt a *Focus* book for your course, you can count on getting a work that is authoritative, accessible, pedagogically strong, richly illustrated, and integrally linked to excellent online musical and multimedia supplementary resources. Threading the needle between pedagogical priorities and scholarly richness, these are texts that make teaching specific topics in world music and ethnomusicology meaningful, valuable, and rewarding. I am delighted to be part of the team that has brought this exciting and important series to fruition. I hope you enjoy reading and working with these books as much as I have!

Michael B. Bakan
The Florida State University
Series Editor

Preface

Aithníonn ciaróg ciaróg eile ~ One beetle recognizes another.

I first encountered recorded Irish music in the form of a lullaby on an old Sam Hinton LP. Called "The Eagle's Lullaby," it included some soothing lyrics about birds falling asleep, and what I took to be just vocables, written as follows in the liner notes: "sho-ho-een, sho-ho-een, ay-nee-nee, ay-nee-nee." At the time my mother told me that it was probably from some unspecified Native American language. Years later, when I was studying Modern Irish with Breandán Ó hÉithir at UC Berkeley, I was startled to discover the true lyrics: *seoithín, seoithín, éiníní, éiníní*: "hush, hush, little birds, little birds." I had known some Irish since I was a kid! Between that early encounter and my enjoyment of the gory Appalachian murder ballads such as "Lord Thomas and Fair Ellender" that I heard (and sang) throughout my childhood and teenage years, I began to seek out recordings of the Clancy Brothers and Tommy Makem, then the Bothy Band and Planxty. The "beetle recognizing another" of the proverb, above, describes me fairly accurately as I began veering toward Irish music more and more. My path toward traditional Irish music in Ireland became clearer each year.

Having regularly performed on the (five-string) banjo in an all-girl high school bluegrass band, I began to seriously pursue Irish music on the (four-string) tenor banjo and (eight-string) mandolin in college. I also performed ballads and other Irish songs in English, accompanying myself on the guitar. I finally had the chance in 1982 to spend a significant amount of time in Ireland. I do wish that my experience had *not* been identical to that of so many other Americans who first arrive in Ireland: I felt as if I had come "home" for the first time. My later research on Ireland as a type of fictive homeland revealed to me some of the cultural reasons for my powerful initial reaction to being there. Now that I have been to Ireland many times, I recognize my then-typical American reaction as a combination of excellent marketing, familiarity with the descendants of Irish (and Scots-Irish) music in traditional Appalachian and popular American song, and a city girl's need for some kind of connection to the rural past. While the banjo, mandolin, and other instruments had offered me some satisfaction, I finally picked up the fiddle in 2002 because I decided to transcend the belief that if you haven't been playing since the age of four, you'll never play. I can play.

The Goals of *Focus: Irish Traditional Music*

This book is intended to clarify and contextualize Irish music for those who are interested in studying it, or perhaps those who already play and/or sing it, and to reveal the distinctiveness of the music of Ireland compared to related musics in other cultures. The reader will come to understand why it is that one cannot correctly call Irish music "Celtic," why "When Irish Eyes Are Smiling" and "Danny Boy" are more popular in the United States than in Ireland, and what essential values underlie the powerful vocal traditions in Irish-Gaelic and English.

Focus: Irish Traditional Music will help the reader to distinguish a jig from a reel from a hornpipe, *uilleann* pipes from highland pipes, and a macaronic (bilingual) song from one in either Irish or English. It brings together important ideas about Irish music from a rich variety of resources, and adds interdisciplinary elements of history, film, politics, poetry, and images to give a deeper context to the music outside of the (public) pub music session. Readers with the ability to understand sheet music will find transcriptions of each of the major Irish forms (reel, jig, hornpipe, highland, slide, etc.) to try out, as well as lyrics and notation to bring the transcribed songs to life. Some of the transcriptions are of tunes and songs included on the online soundtrack.

How This Book is Organized

Focus: Irish Traditional Music is grouped into three parts. Part I, "Irish Music in Place and Time," gives an overall sense of the island's musical history and its relationship to the sound and context of current performance practice. Part II, "Music Traditions Abroad and at Home," gets closer to the music of the region by contrasting the instrumental musics of the non-Irish "Celtic Nations"—Scotland, Wales, Brittany, Galicia, etc.—with Irish instrumental music. When many regions share instruments, the similarities and differences can be striking. Part III, "Focusing In," calls the reader's attention first to the great songs of Ireland's two main languages, then concludes with an examination of the globalization of Irish music and its superstars, and the increasing importance of computer technology in music marketing, distribution, and consumption. Throughout the book, the text brings together the past and the present, moving back and forth across time in ways that are similar to a typical conversation in Ireland.

History and context are crucial aspects of Irish culture, and therefore of Irish music. Irish people pay very close attention to their history, and weave their music into it rather tightly; hence the presence in this textbook of not just one but *two* chapters on history and culture. Even in contemporary Irish punk, country, and hip hop, references to what seems like the distant (and therefore, forgettable?) past are common. Poetry and film are also important in understanding the lenses through which Irish people view themselves. Finally, Ireland and North America are so completely interwoven—because of the continuous interplay between families, histories, politics, religions, and any number of other factors—that an Ireland with no North America in its past (or future) is unthinkable.

The second edition of *Focus: Irish Traditional Music* includes new sections dedicated to the contemporary issues in Irish culture, society, and music that affect people *now*. It has been ten years since the first edition was published; Ireland's dramatic political shift (reflected by its landslide vote for marriage equality, among other changes) has had an impact on musicians and the music they play. Those changes are reflected in the new material published here; for example, the second edition includes sections on equity and inclusion, white nationalism, Ireland's Travelling people, the enduring popularity of "Danny Boy" in North America, and other features that bring the volume up to date. Interested readers will find both a historical timeline and a set of recipes for a full Irish meal! Note that every chapter begins with an Irish-language proverb. Why? Because these proverbs offer subtle clues to the way Irish people think, and what they believe. It is worth your while to ponder these proverbs—such as *Ní ghabhann dorn dúnta seabhac ~ A closed fist won't catch a hawk*—and to imagine their relationship to the people, the music, and the social context of each one.

If you are a student, pay attention to the way that this book moves from the general to the specific, and cycles repeatedly through the past and present. Try to understand all the major points and be able to discuss them with others. Note the discussion questions at the end of each chapter. Consider what the concept of "cyclic time" means in this context. Search online for examples of Irish music and dance; watch a few Irish films too. If you are a professor, the same principles apply, but take note of the interdisciplinary aspects of the book as well. The back matter includes essential resources (glossary, bibliography, web resources, etc.) to help make your students' exploration of Irish music more effective and long-lasting. Finally, the series website is at **http://www.routledge .com/focusonworldmusic**, which will take you to quizzes and essay questions.

Acknowledgements

It has been a pleasure to write this book. My own students in Irish Studies have needed such a book for years, and it is at least partly because of them that I developed the materials and did the necessary research to create this book. No one ever writes a textbook alone, however; in the process of writing *Focus: Irish Traditional Music* I consulted the works (and opinions) of many scholars, whose own books and articles were of great help to me and can be found in the References section.

I owe a debt of gratitude to my friend and ethnomusicology colleague Michael B. Bakan, the series editor of Routledge's *Focus on World Music*. Constance Ditzel selected me to write the book and helped to shepherd it through to completion, for which I am very grateful. The editorial team for the first edition deserves my thanks. Denny Tek is an exceptionally talented editorial assistant, without whose dedicated help the book would have taken much longer. Susan Dunsmore painstakingly copyedited the manuscript, braving Irish-language words and ethnomusicological jargon at each step. The Production Editor Mhairi Baxter worked long and hard to turn the manuscript, photographs, maps, and musical transcriptions into an actual book. In the second edition, I have been fortunate to work with Peter Sheehy on editing, Stephen Riordan's Dublin team at Deanta Global Publishing doing the copyediting, and Lauren Ellis in production. The result is always one of teamwork, and I am lucky to have a great team.

Joe Heaney was an extraordinary singer and storyteller from Connemara in the west of Ireland; he was widely considered the best *sean-nós* ("old style") singer of his generation. While I was a graduate student at the University of Washington I worked with him for several years prior to his death in 1984, and he—perhaps more than any other musician or singer—profoundly shaped and guided my understanding of Irish song in both Irish and English. My gratitude to him, and my respect for his exceptional abilities, extend beyond what I can express in words.

My husband, David Nelson, is a champion in his support of my research, musical endeavors, and writing; my daughter Morgan Black is one of the most interesting and creative people I know, and I am so grateful that she was present for significant portions of my initial research for the first volume. My love goes out to both of them, now and always. My friends Gloria Hatch, Lillis Ó Laoire, Sonia Seeman, Tomie Hahn, Tes Slominski, Adrienne Asher, and Martine van Buuren continue to be both a solid support system and a reality check for me. My brother Guy Williams and his spouse Antonio Navas-Rufino refined my discussion of Galicia. My colleagues at The Evergreen State College, especially those participating in the summer faculty development institute called "Write That Book," have been very supportive of this project.

It is a joy to include musical examples on the online soundtrack for this volume. I am so appreciative of the musicians who graciously gave permission to use their playing and singing on the accompanying CD for this volume (in alphabetical order): Randal Bays, Philip and Pam Boulding, Karan Casey, Valerie Casey, Deirdre Chawke, Tim Collins, Pauline Conneely, Kevin Conneff, Steve Cooney, Elaine Cormican, Síle Denvir, Claire Dolan, John Doyle, Lawson Dumbeck, Séamus Egan, Denny Hall, Damian Harrigan, Joe Heaney, Winifred Horan, James Keane, Seán Keane, James Kelly, Laoise Kelly, Anthea Lawrence, Joanie Madden, Catherine McEvoy, Róisín McGrory, Susan McKeown, Dana Lyn, Mick Moloney, Garry O'Briain, Mick O'Brien, Mick O'Connor, Lillis Ó Laoire, Eamon O'Leary, Caoimhín Ó Raghallaigh, Peadar Ó Riada, Audra Poor, Eilís Ní Shúilleabháin, Dáithí Sproule, John Williams, and Sarah Jane Woods. The responsibility for any errors or flaws of content in this book rests, of course, with me. To the members of the various and diverse Irish music communities around the world who are too numerous to mention but who have contributed, one way or another, I send my heartiest *go raibh míle maith agaibh*.

Sean Williams
The Evergreen State College
Olympia, Washington

PART I

Irish Music in Place and Time

CHAPTER 1

Looking In from the Outside

Is glas iad na cnoc i bhfad uainn ~ Distant hills look green.

Ireland seems so familiar to those who have never visited. A high-functioning tourist machine generates powerful and alluring images of castles, rocky shorelines, rolling green hills, and remarkably good-looking people. A never-flagging set of factories feeds a never-ending desire on the part of foreigners for Irish-themed clothing, tea towels, shot glasses, leprechauns, shamrock pins, and other signifiers of Irish heritage. In a cultural climate where red hair is enough to (erroneously) proclaim one as "Irish," and where being descended from one Irish grandparent (along with Muhammad Ali, Che Guevara, and Mariah Carey) allows one to gain Irish citizenship, it should not be surprising that Ireland's economic upswing of the late 1990s and early twenty-first century should have brought a corresponding upswing in the international popularity of all things Irish.

This second edition of *Focus: Irish Traditional Music* brings the traditional music of Ireland as it is played and sung today together with the essential interdisciplinary features that make Irish music still so important in Ireland and abroad. Divided into three main parts, *Focus: Irish Traditional Music* covers the historical context, the cultural context, and the important details of Irish instrumental and vocal music. Chapter 1, "Looking In from the Outside," approaches Ireland from a foreign, particularly diasporic, perspective. It locates Ireland not only as part of Europe but as the homeland of the Irish diaspora, engages the reader in understanding musical processes such as texture, variation, and modes, and discusses what happens at a performance of Irish music in Ireland.

Chapter 2, "Roots and Branches of Gaelic Ireland," has as its concentration the historical context of Irish traditional music and culture, from the establishment of settlements on the island to the development of the bards as powerful culture-bearers.

Chapter 3 begins with Queen Elizabeth I's 1603 proclamation to "hang all harpers where found," and brings the reader up to the present, to the establishment of what is now considered "Irish traditional music." Chapter 4, "Music of the 'Celtic' Nations," explores the related musics of Scotland, Wales, Northumberland, Cornwall, Brittany, Galicia, and Cape Breton in eastern Canada. It examines the problematic nature of the linguistic term "Celtic" in its application to music. It also focuses on instruments, contexts, languages, and related cultural issues that both join and separate the various traditions. Chapter 5, "The Green Fields of America," explores not only the reasons for the Irish diaspora around the globe, but also the rich music that resulted from their experiences in emigration and exile. The chapter also discusses authenticity in the context of how foreigners, particularly Americans, have created for themselves a vision of Ireland and celebrated that vision primarily in song. Chapter 6, "Irish Instrumental Music," is entirely devoted to the instruments, forms, and playing styles of the bagpipes, fiddles, flutes, accordions, and other common instruments heard in traditional contexts.

Chapters 7 ("Vocal Music in Irish-Gaelic") and 8 ("Vocal Music in English") are the heart of this book. These chapters introduce the reader to *sean-nós* ("old style") singing, often considered (particularly by its practitioners) to be the soul of Irish music and among its most ancient forms. These chapters cover *sean-nós* together with other songs in Irish, the great English-language ballads, and Irish macaronic (bilingual) songs. These chapters are the book's primary focus because few published works reach into the vocal tradition. Chapter 9, "New Contexts for Music and Dance," looks at the current excitement and attraction toward Irish (and, more broadly, "Celtic") music, highlighting the nation's dramatic economic growth and the easing of tensions in Northern Ireland. The chapter concludes with a sense of how Irish music is developing into an international language for people from all over the world who know how to play and sing it, and what listeners can expect to hear from Irish music and musicians in the future.

The second edition—which includes updated and relevant current information—features specific short articles, each with a discussion question. These topics, such as the use of "Celtic" signifiers by white nationalists, issues of equity and inclusion in Irish music, the enduring popularity of "Danny Boy" *outside* of Ireland, and the intersection of films, music, and culture, connect Irish traditional music with what is happening today. Ireland is very much embedded in the twenty-first century—regardless of promotional efforts to keep it looking the way it did in the nineteenth century—and it should come as no surprise to find a dozen different mobile phones scattered among the pints of Guinness and cider on the tables at a typical music session.

At the end of the book the reader will find: a glossary of Irish terms; a set of additional resources (for reading and web surfing); a listening guide to online music tracks; references; and an index. All of these resources are intended to directly connect the reader with little previous knowledge of Ireland, its culture or music, to what is most essentially *Irish* in the country's music.

Locating Ireland in Place and Time

The island of Ireland comprises two countries: the Republic of Ireland in the south, and Northern Ireland (part of the United Kingdom of Great Britain and Northern Ireland) in the northeast. As a two-nation island, Ireland is a very small place compared to, for example, Russia, China, Canada, or the United States. It is approximately the same size as Indiana in the United States, and its entire population of over 6.6 million people (4.8 million in the Republic; 1.8 in Northern Ireland) would easily fit inside the five boroughs of New York City with room to spare. It is in close proximity to the mainland of Europe (Figure 1.1), and it is part of the European Union, making it subject to laws and treaties voted on by the EU member states. With the looming upheavals regarding the United Kingdom's decision to leave the EU ("Brexit"), Northern Ireland may become more politically separate from the Republic than it has been for two decades. Ireland— the island—is also a homeland for the more than 70 million descendants of its people around the world.

Ireland is also a kind of fictive homeland for the people with no heritage connection, but who are profoundly attracted by its music. It might be worth asking why it is that thousands of non-Irish visitors descend on the village of Doolin in Ireland's County Clare each year. In spite of its small size, Doolin is one of several centers of Irish instrumental performance, geared toward the tourism industry that brings busloads of foreigners into the town every day. People can enter a pub, drink a pint, listen to a performance, and get back on the bus, confident that they have experienced the "true Ireland" of their imaginations. The fact that many of the instrumentalists in the Doolin pubs are not local and perhaps not even Irish is, to the average visitor, irrelevant. What is important is the array of visual, aural, and other experiential indicators proclaiming that the scene is "just right" in its authenticity and sense of welcome. Indeed, to some

Figure 1.1 Ireland as a part of Europe

extent, the context *is* an Irish pub, Irish music *is* being played, and the beer *is* flowing. What more does anyone need?

American Images of the Irish

Of all the roads into Irish culture, surely one of the most well-worn takes listeners through "Danny Boy," "When Irish Eyes are Smiling," and other hits of the late nineteenth and early twentieth centuries. Or perhaps the reader has encountered green beer on St. Patrick's Day, or carefully studied—as a child—cartoon images of leprechauns while consuming a bowl of Lucky Charms™ breakfast cereal. The friendly Irish cops in the classic children's book *Make Way for Ducklings* (McCloskey 1941) and Huck Finn's no-good drunken absent father (Twain 1884) are but two examples of Irish-themed character types that non-Irish-born children encounter early on. Certain films highlight particular traits ascribed to the Irish. *Mary Poppins*, for example, includes a sneaky Gaelic-speaking fox; *Singing in the Rain* presents two "reformed" huckster stage Irishmen with hearts of gold; numerous cartoons and even a few *Star Trek* episodes feature periodically drunken but attractive Irishmen that serve to cement images in the hearts and minds of North Americans in particular.

How did Irish imagery give rise to such an array of stereotypes, as far as the non-Irish view the Irish? Think of these images of Irishness, reinforced since the 1850s in American popular culture: the drunken father, weak son, sweet colleen, saintly mother, valiant soldier, noble priest, scatter-brained maid, jovial-but-slightly-corrupt cop, and gangster. We have all likely seen images on public television of *Riverdance* (or *Celtic Woman*, or *Celtic Thunder*) and heard the lush, vague, echoey sounds of Enya's New Age recordings. Some of us, or our sisters or daughters, may have taken classes in Irish stepdance, complete with heavy, embroidered, expensive dance outfits, wigs with dozens of tiny ringlets, and hordes of anxious hovering stage mothers at competitions.

Those of us who play and sing Irish music in the United States know well the annoyed looks directed at people who stray too far from the Irish-American hit repertoire of songs like "Too-Ra-Loo-Ra-Lay" as sung by Bing Crosby. It is not out of the question, after playing a set of jigs, to be asked to "play an Irish jig" (meaning "The Irish Washerwoman," whose title alone reinforces more Irish stereotypes in the American mind). Similarly, singing a song in Irish-Gaelic frequently leads to the request for a "real Irish" song (in other words, an Irish-themed American song). The ubiquitous St. Patrick's Day accessories, together with the license to drink to excess, did not develop in a vacuum. Irish-American songs, images, stereotypes, marketing gimmicks, and musical sounds all have historical precedent resulting from Irish immigrants' transitions into American society. Since the reader is beginning this book by looking into Irish musical culture from the outside, it is reasonable to assume at least a little familiarity with the outer trappings of Irishness.

My own early encounters with Irish music occurred when I was a teenager in Berkeley, California. I used white chalk and a mechanical pencil (perfectly, thanks to being an architect's daughter) to alter the date on my driver's license so that I could get into Irish bars in the San Francisco Bay Area to listen to music sessions. I was delighted to hear the Irish and Scottish antecedents to my mother's Kentucky ballads. As a bluegrass musician, I began carefully picking my way through the notated jigs and reels of various Irish music resources on the four-string tenor banjo, the mandolin, and the guitar. I sang songs learned from recordings of the Clancy Brothers, and tried to accompany a few songs on the guitar using "open" chords and DADGAD tuning (see Chapter 6, "Irish Instrumental Music"). I signed myself up for several years of studying Modern Irish, Middle Irish, and Old Irish as a music major at the University of California at Berkeley, took folklore classes, translated songs and folktales from Irish into English, and generally immersed myself even as I pursued a degree in classical guitar performance. What I discovered in college, and much more so after graduate school, was that the further I ventured into Irish music, the further behind I left the Ireland of Irish-American fantasy.

Ireland's history is tightly bound up with that of North America, and the two chapters of history in regard to music included in this book comprise the minimum of what one needs to know to carry on a normal conversation in Ireland (with musicians or without). Ireland's history *is* its present, and its history lives in such places as the slabs of prehistoric tombs surrounded by cows and half-buried in the bog; a photograph of John F. Kennedy enshrined next to one of the Pope in pubs and homes; and band names that recall historical figures, events, and concepts: the Wolfe Tones, Black 47, and Lúnasa.

What's in a Name?

Ireland has two national languages: Irish-Gaelic and English. Irish-Gaelic is radically different from English, and to speak Irish-Gaelic is not to simply speak English with an Irish accent. It belongs in the Gaelic branch of the Celtic family of Indo-European languages. English, in contrast, belongs in the Germanic family. In Ireland, the Irish-Gaelic word for the language is *Gaeilge*, pronounced "**guail**-i-gya." The English word for the same language is *Irish*! Because this book is in English, you will find the word "Irish" used to refer to Irish-Gaelic. Most people in Ireland speak English as their primary language for a variety of reasons, though Irish is taught in all the schools and has recently experienced a resurgence in popularity among native Irish. Many Irish people also learn Irish at home, then learn English at school, particularly in the Gaeltacht (Irish-speaking) districts. In contrast to the English-speaking, uniformly white, traditional "Ireland of the Welcomes" presented by *Bord Fáilte* (the Irish Tourism Board), Ireland's newest immigrants also speak Mandarin, Polish, Hindi, Brazilian Portuguese, Burmese, Latvian, and multiple languages of African origin. Ireland has become a polyglot nation because of its membership in the European Union, and the barista who makes your espresso in Dublin just might speak English with a Polish-inflected Irish accent. In addition, some of Ireland's second-generation immigrant offspring, whose parents might have come from Cameroon or India or Mongolia, speak *Irish*.

Scotland is the home of the Scots: of Scotsmen and Scotswomen. Scotch, on the other hand, is both a drink (a type of whiskey) and a verb ("to put an end to"), and is a long-outdated and inappropriate word for Scottish people used only by outsiders. Scottish music is what Scottish (and Irish, and British, and North American, and Australian, and other) people play. The words Scots and Scottish come from the old word *Scottis*, originally used to describe the Irish (!) who migrated to what is now Scotland around the end of the fifth century C.E. The version of Gaelic spoken by the Scots (in some parts of the highlands and on some of the outer Hebridean islands) is locally pronounced

"Gallic." In addition, the Scots dialect of English—unintelligible to outsiders, made famous by the poet Robert Burns, and spoken to varying degrees by many Scots—is referred to as Scots, as in "the Scots word for 'from' is *frae*."

The Welsh occupy part of the western portion of the island of Britain. They speak a language from a different branch of the Celtic language family than the Gaelic branch of Irish- and Scots-Gaelic. Many Welsh people speak both English and Welsh, among other languages learned in school, though the majority speak only English. The word "Welch" is, like "Scotch," an outdated and somewhat offensive term. After a number of Welsh immigrants came to North America and clashed with the people in power, the words "welsh" and "welch" fell into popular usage to refer to someone who backs out of an agreement. "Welsh," "Welshman," or "Welshwoman" are the only appropriate ways to refer to someone from Wales.

The North American Protestant "Scots-Irish" are the descendants of Scottish borderlands people who migrated to the Ulster (northern) region of Ireland in the sixteenth and seventeenth centuries, and whose descendants (some 200,000 people) then emigrated to North America in the "Great Migration" of the eighteenth century. Many Scots-Irish later settled in the southern mountains of the United States. Compared to the millions of Irish Catholics who settled in North America, 200,000 Scots-Irish seems like a paltry number. However, their impact on American history was significant, and their presence in North America has included both positive and negative contact with the Catholic Irish at home and abroad.

The Celts made their first set of appearances in Central Europe in the late Bronze Age. Their gradual arrival in Ireland over the first millennium B.C.E. appears to stem primarily from the Iberian Peninsula and the Atlantic coast, however, not from Central Europe. Ireland was populated prior to the arrival of the Celts, but the term "Celtic" has come to be applied, inaccurately, to *all* the Irish (and indeed, to those who spoke related languages such as Welsh and Breton). The word "Celtic" is itself a linguistic term that refers to a branch of the Indo-European language family, as in Germanic, Indic, Celtic, Iranian. Each of these linguistic groups includes a number of local languages. The earliest written record of the Celts includes the Greek word *Keltoi*. Notice the letter K in *Keltoi*; Celtic is always pronounced "**Kel**-tic," not "**Sel**-tic." "Seltic" is correct only when referring to certain sports teams (in Boston and Glasgow); it is never correct to say "Seltic" otherwise, no matter what your dictionary (or mine) says. Note to self: "Scotch," "Welch," and "Seltic" bad; "Scottish," "Welsh," and "Celtic" (with a hard C) good.

The Celtic languages include the Gaelic languages (Irish-Gaelic, Scots-Gaelic and Manx, the latter from the Isle of Man) in one branch, and Brythonic languages (Welsh, Cornish, and Breton) in the other branch. Galego, a language spoken in the northwest region of Spain—Galicia, often referred to as "Celtic Spain" with its many Celtic place names and archaeological sites—is believed to have once carried multiple examples of Celtic root words (see Chapter 4, "Musics of the 'Celtic' Nations"). Galego, however, is actually closer to Portuguese in some ways than to, say, Breton. Because the term Celtic is at once primarily a linguistic designation and a handy—and highly contested—marketing term for some types of New Age music, Irish musicians shun it as inappropriate to describe what they do. Lastly, instrumental tunes are not songs; only a piece with lyrics is a *song*, and an instrumental piece is a *tune*.

Irish Musical Processes

Coming to Irish instrumental music from the world of bluegrass required a shift in my own musical orientation. Both bluegrass and Irish music require considerable skill on a melody instrument. Both genres involve men and women playing tunes from memory, sometimes with other people, in ways that enable a careful listener to note the pleasing differences between a melody played on a fiddle and one played on a banjo (in bluegrass) or a fiddle and a button accordion (in Irish music). My background as a bluegrass banjo and mandolin player took me that far readily, but I was still very much an outsider to Irish music. At a bluegrass session, many tunes start off with one or two repetitions of the entire tune. After that, players can take turns soloing while the others play chords or offer subtle background texturing through the use of filler patterns or instrumental flourishes. Collective shifts in body language (especially in performance) indicate to the audience that attention should be paid to the mandolin player, for example, followed by the guitarist. By the end of the tune, everyone is playing the tune together again. You might see this same arrangement in a jazz ensemble, or in a rock band just before the "breakdown," when the guitarist and drummer improvise dramatically prior to the song's conclusion. The essential contrast in these bands, then, is between soloists and ensemble, with a clear indication—through body language, spoken words, and musical signals—as to whose "turn" it is to solo, and when the tune is coming to an end. This structure of sequential solos is not common in Irish traditional music, but it is essential to bluegrass.

All of this linkage between Irish music and bluegrass or jazz is well and good when one considers Irish music as an ensemble tradition. However, Irish traditional music is not so much "band music" as it is a solo instrumental tradition that *sometimes* includes playing in groups for the good times and camaraderie. Playing a bluegrass instrument in a band or playing a jazz instrument in combination with just a few other people is itself the height of the genre; it is the musical give-and-take that adds so much power to the experience. If I play bluegrass banjo alone, it is certainly fun for a while, and my playing improves; however, it's clear in my mind that I'm practicing for the chance to play with others. In contrast, if I pick up the fiddle and start in on the jigs and reels and slides, I can go for hours with no expectation that I'll take the fiddle down to the local session now that my playing has improved. It's enough to play the instrument on its own, and deeply fulfilling to me as a musician. And so it is with many other musicians who play Irish music.

Here is another way of looking at the issue: between Irish music, bluegrass, and jazz, the three genres *can* be performed by a group of players all playing at the same time. In Irish music, that scenario would be at an evening session or festival; in bluegrass, at festivals that routinely draw thousands of spectators and participants; in jazz, in a big band with its rows of horns. In that unwieldy context, the chance for individual expression is minimal. It is normal for smaller groups of musicians at festivals to break away from the multitudes and jam. Once a small group of players with, for example, just one person on each type of instrument—one fiddle, one button accordion, one wooden flute, or in the case of bluegrass, one fiddle, one banjo, one dobro—is playing together, the individual artistry soars. In a small jazz combo of keyboard, bass, drums, and melody instrument, the individuals come together to create something greater than the sum of their musical parts. It is precisely this smaller-group configuration—regardless of *where* it happens—in which the "magic" of the group emerges. But in Irish music, the magic can and does happen also with a single instrument or singer, alone.

Musical Textures

In an Irish music session, whether it is at a pub (a relatively new context) or at a home, the players face each other, not the audience if there is one, because Irish music does not require an audience. Instead of taking turns soloing, Irish musicians playing in a group all play the tune together at the same time in a texture called *heterophony* (hetero-, "different," phone, "sound, voice"). Now picture in your mind a solo singer or melody instrumentalist: when that person is performing alone, unaccompanied, the texture of the music is *monophonic*, "one voice." Adding in the multiple instruments of Irish music, however, means that the melody of the fiddle might not be precisely the same melody as it is when played on the tin whistle, the flute, the button accordion, or any other instrument. Because, for example, a tin whistle in D cannot be played below the pitch of D, when the notes of the melody stray into the lower octave, the whistle player must choose notes from an octave up, or play ornaments, or make do when the instrument's limitations prevent the player from following the tune's descent into the lower register. In another example, a button accordion player performing a melody can also use chords as both an accompaniment to the melody and as a percussive element; in addition, the keys of the accordion are fixed and unable to slide across pitches the way a fiddle can. Each instrument has its advantages and drawbacks, and listening to them all fit together despite their differences is part of the fun.

An image that might help clarify the practice of heterophony is that of a small marching band. Picture the scene: six players all headed in the same direction, but on separate parallel trails. Some players have to negotiate the equivalent of tree stumps, children on tricycles, or possibly a slip-n-slide! Others march on paving stones with guardrails; their steps are easy to follow. Everyone arrives at the street corner at the right time (ideally), free of injuries (ideally), and they all start marching on the next block. An Irish music session could include a handful of musicians, all "marching" (or reeling, or jigging) on the same well-known trails, but the player of each instrument has an individual trail to negotiate. The place in an Irish instrumental tune with the most variation between instrumental "trails" is often the last two bars of a section, in which players mix and match melodic lines from various tunes to finish the section. In time, if the players perform often together, the group settles, more or less, on one particular variant.

Coming back to monophony ("one voice"), if you spend time in Ireland, sooner or later you will hear someone sing a song unaccompanied, or play a solo tune. The solo player, or the solo singer, is central to the Irish tradition. While many people enjoy playing a guitar while singing, or listening to someone play a guitar and sing, particularly those influenced by the American folk scene, the solo singer or instrumentalist is special. At a pub or in an otherwise noisy kitchen, when a lone voice or instrumental line rises above the crowd, everyone is supposed to fall silent. To be able to hear a pin drop while one is singing or playing solo is high praise indeed, because silence toward the solo performer is a sign of respect. In a noisy session, the solo player of a slow instrumental "air" should be able to expect silence from the crowd as well. In practice, of course, it only sometimes works out that way for either a solo instrumentalist, or a singer.

What is it about monophony and heterophony that is so characteristic of Irish music? Perhaps it is worth considering that Irish music operates in two musical contexts: singing (monophony) and dancing (both monophony and heterophony). Instrumental music, for the greater part of its history in Ireland, has been played solo to accompany dancing. Its steady tempos have provided the musical backdrop for hundreds of thousands of dancers. Only recently—since the 1970s, for specific reasons—have instrumental music sessions begun to speed up beyond danceable tempos. In contrast, the solo singer or instrumentalist might be performing to an almost-breathing rhythm. Without a dancer, the singer or player is free to linger on notes, insert ornaments and variations, and allow space for the silences between the notes; this can happen even when playing for an attentive dancer. It is a luxury to perform solo to an appreciative audience. Should you happen to be in such an audience, you will recognize from the actions of those around you that the full force of your attention should be on the soloist.

Between monophony and heterophony, where is the harmony singing, or the orchestral playing of musicians performing different notes in harmony with each other? Harmony has not been a major textural focus of Irish traditional music. Certainly people will sing in harmony for an English-language song with a chorus, and Ireland has just as many orchestras and choir ensembles as any other European country. For traditional music, though, what you will hear most is the soloist or the group; when it's a group, they tend to all play the version of the chosen melody that suits their instruments the best. When it's a soloist, the tune is a carefully chosen melody that suits the context, the instrument, and the player, and both reflect years of listening, practice, and playing in just such a context as the one you might have the chance to attend.

Harmony *is* manifest in any instrument that plays more than one note at a time. The drones of the pipes, which establish a continuous "floor" against which the melody is played, reinforce the notion of a "home pitch" to which the melody returns; it offers a glimpse at functional harmony. *Uilleann* pipers can and do use chordal accompaniment, and so do the button accordionists, the piano accordionists, and concertina players. Guitarists use chords to accompany the melody players, though often their chords rely on pitches one and five of each chord. Although the general assumption about the music is that it is entirely monophonic or heterophonic, harmonizing does happen.

Regional Identities

Ireland's 32 counties are divided into four major provinces: Ulster (north, including the six counties of Northern Ireland and three counties of the Republic), Connacht (middle west), Munster (southwest), and Leinster (east). The division of these provinces reflects historical differences, but it also currently reflects linguistic and musical differences as well (Figure 1.2).

In fact, many Irish jokes (told by Irish people *to* Irish people) refer to differences in character (and accent, and sports playing ability) between the people of Ireland's regions, and extend into differences between counties, sections of counties, and even

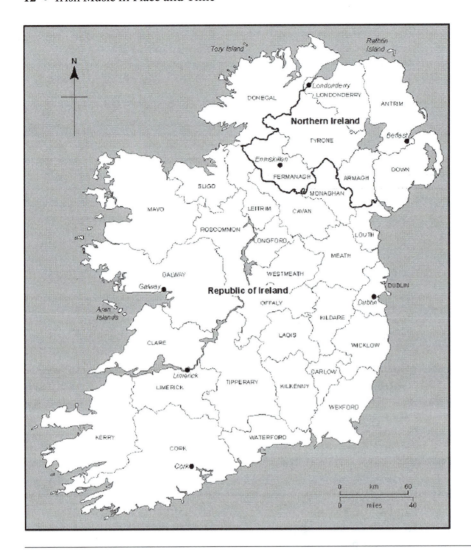

Figure 1.2 The provinces and counties of Ireland

parishes. Every county has its own special flag, which flies from houses and barns on sporting days. Stereotypes abound within as well as outside Ireland, and "slagging," or jovial and artful teasing, is a favorite conversational pastime of many Irish people. Musicians are particularly adept at slagging one another in good fun.

In music, particular districts are known for being the home of regional styles. Connemara, for example, is famous for having produced many fine singers of *sean-nós* or "old style" Irish singing (see Chapter 7). One can easily find first-rate *sean-nós* singers in Donegal (to the north), in Cúil Aodha (to the south), and in many other parts of Ireland, but Connemara happens to be best known for this type of singing. Similarly, the fiddle players of East Clare, of Sligo, of Sliabh Luachra—and of other places—are often held up as *the* standard of excellence. However, keep in mind that each region of

Ireland has its own set of musical elements and standards. In some regions, tourism, the Irish media, and marketing have made individual musicians justly famous and internationally known. In other regions, much of the finest performing is done privately, in the close intimacy of a pub or a kitchen, with only the neighbors and family members as the appreciative audience.

Chapter 6 examines each of the forms of Irish instrumental music, including jigs and reels. Yet Irish music includes many more forms, including polkas, slides, and barndances. Some areas of Ireland are best known for polkas, while others favor highlands. The regional variation extends outward, in fact, to reflect the varying emphases of the Irish diaspora. For example, musicians in Chicago might favor a particular set of musical forms over others, and that emphasis is likely to be different from what musicians playing Irish music in Perth, Tokyo, or St Petersburg are doing. This kind of regional variation, both within Ireland and the diaspora, is one of the things that makes Irish instrumental music so interesting and complex.

Musical Variation

In addition to the variation that develops over decades, separating tunes and populations into their multiple constituencies, another kind of musical variation takes place. This variation occurs in the context of multiple repetitions within the same tune or song, rather like the idea of never being able to step into the same river twice. The twelfth-century writer Giraldus Cambrensis ("Gerald of Wales") wrote with eloquence in his landmark work, *Topographica Hibernica*, about subtlety and musical variation in Irish harp music.

> They introduce and leave rhythmic motifs so subtly, they play the tinkling sounds on the thinner strings above the sustained sound of the thicker string so freely, they take such secret delight and caress [the strings] so sensuously, that the greatest part of their art seems to lie in veiling it, as if 'That which is concealed is bettered – art revealed is art shamed.' Thus it happens that those things which bring private and ineffable delight to people of subtle appreciation and sharp discernment, burden rather than delight the ears of those who, in spite of looking do not see and in spite of hearing do not understand; to unwilling listeners, fastidious things appear tedious and have a confused and disordered sound.
>
> (Giraldus Cambrensis, cited in Rimmer 1977: 29)

That Giraldus noticed both subtlety and the use of variation as far back as the twelfth century should tell us that they were at least as important then as they are now. Reading his words, all these years later, may help you to recognize that the musicians aren't just playing the same tunes over and over. The best elements of an evening's music might reveal themselves only through repeated attendance, participation, and careful listening.

Some Irish singers feel strongly that each verse of a twenty-verse song has to be different from all the others. In fact, they are correct: the lyrics do have an impact on the melody to a certain extent, so some natural variation will occur. Yet even if most of the verses one sings—especially toward the end of a song—follow roughly the same melody, the fact that there is a sense of insistence about variation points to a larger cultural value of variation. In other words, there is a deeper meaning to this point: variation doesn't just keep people interested in the melody. A song with twenty verses has the potential to lose its audience, particularly an uninformed audience. Variation in the melodic line can help hold the audience. However, adding or subtracting small ornaments, lingering on a particular word, and using other vocal techniques adds meaning and depth to a song in ways that reading the lyrics out loud as a poem cannot.

Singers are essentially storytellers who sing their stories; they are humans who laugh, love, and lament in song. They vary their verses not to show off, but to deliver greater emotional impact. Variation also engages attentive audience members at the level of the song's poetic rhythm; depending on the stressed syllables in a particular line, one might need to creatively add several decorative notes to reach the end on the right pitch. This skill is particularly well known and utilized in Connemara, in the west of Ireland. Musical variation also highlights the creative skills of the performer, allowing him or her to reveal a personal relationship to the song or the tune. Respect for a singer or instrumentalist carries over to respect for the strength of that relationship. Does the singer mean what she sings? Is the fiddler profoundly involved in his tune? How did the singer perform over twenty notes just in delivering one syllable?

Some of Ireland's musical communities are small, and while the store of songs and tunes might be large, everyone in a community knows each other's favorites, abilities, and ways of doing a song or tune. There is considerable pleasure taken in enjoying the differences between two musicians' versions of a song or tune. Note that a version of a song is different from a variation of a song, which would indicate a strong departure from the original. For example, contrast the Beatles' 1967 performance of "With a Little Help from My Friends" with Joe Cocker's gospel-tinged version of 1968. The Beatles' (note the Irish last names of Lennon and McCartney, by the way) wellspring of creativity and performance skills did not include the gospel sound. Joe Cocker's performance covers the same melody and lyrics, and the way he performed had to do with his own unique "take" on, and personal relationship to, the song. Compare also Elton John's "Your Song" from 1970 with Lady Gaga's 2018 version of the same song. Each recording has its own unique musical characteristics, and each will draw its admirers. One Irish singer doing a version of a song will have his or her own life story, experience, and personal relationship to bring to the song, which will automatically be different from that of another Irish singer. Exploring, discussing, and evaluating versions of performances from one person to the next is just as Irish as listening to a fiddle and a flute doing the same melody and appreciating the differences between them.

The "Irishness" of an Irish Melody

Much of American folk and rock'n'roll has at least a few roots in the musics of Ireland and Scotland. It is easy to listen to a ballad from Appalachia, then one from Ireland or Scotland, and mark the musical similarities. But what are they? Specifically, Irish and Scottish music use a set of pitches arranged into *modes*. The ancient Greeks first discussed modes, though they have existed in performance practice since before Aristotle ever considered music as an object of study. Modes comprise a set of notes, but also an order that they fall into (like a scale) as well as an individual set of emphasized notes that mark how the mode works in that particular tune or song.

If you were to sit down at a piano, find middle C, and play (left to right) only the white keys from C to the next C, you would have played a C major scale. Were you to sing it using *do-re-mi-fa-so-la-ti-do*, you would have sung a C major scale. The word "scale" comes from the Latin *scala*, "ladder." Pitches are played up the scale in steps like those in a ladder or staircase. Some steps are smaller ("half steps") while others are bigger ("whole steps"). It is the arrangement of half steps and whole steps that determines a mode in Western music, including Irish music. A major scale is also called Ionian mode: same notes in the same order, different name.

In most Western classical music, composers and musicians use the major scale (Ionian mode) and variants of the minor scale (Aeolian mode). You can find the Aeolian mode on the piano by returning to middle C, then counting down two white keys until you reach A. If you play from that A to the next A up, using only the white notes again, you will have played a "natural minor" scale. Melodies played using that scale are in Aeolian mode. You can test out the difference between major and minor easily: sing "Happy Birthday" normally, then again using Aeolian mode in the key of C (which means you would play the notes E, A, and B as flattened notes). One's birthday song will suddenly sound far less "happy."

Ionian (major) and Aeolian (natural minor) modes are the building blocks of plenty of Irish tunes and songs, but two more also loom large in importance, not only for the Irish, but for the Scottish and American folk and popular musicians as well. These two modes are Dorian and Mixolydian. To sound out a Dorian scale, sit back down at the piano and start on D this time. Walk slowly up the white notes, moving from low D to high D. It sounds different, even though it's the same notes that you played before! The reason it sounds different is because the arrangement of half steps and whole steps determines the overall sound and feel of each mode; it's like starting up an uneven ladder on the second step instead of the first.

The final mode to explore in Irish and Scottish music is Mixolydian. It is like Ionian mode (a major scale) but with a flatted seventh degree. You can hear its sound by starting on the pitch of G at the piano again, then walking up to the higher G playing only the white keys. You will hear it progressing like a major scale at first, and then the F *natural* (just before the high G) changes the entire feel of the scale. These four modes determine the nature of Irish melodies.

One of the most important things to know about modes is that they are not limited by the white keys where you found them on the piano. You might hear a D tune in Dorian mode, but you could just as easily hear a C, or G, or A tune in Dorian. Remember how you were able to sing "Happy Birthday" in both Ionian and Aeolian modes, starting on the same pitch? That is because you were using two different modes, which started on the same pitch, not necessarily a particular scale fixed to a single pitch like D.

> The four most common modes of Irish music are Ionian, Aeolian, Dorian, and Mixolydian. Not every Irish musician knows the names and patterning of these modes, of course, but they know what sounds culturally appropriate and "Irish."

Choosing from one of the three remaining modes (Phrygian, Lydian, or Locrian) would result in a tune that would sound emphatically *not* Irish. Because the majority of Western classical tunes are in either Ionian or Aeolian mode, those two modes do not necessarily sound particularly Irish. As soon as Mixolydian or Dorian modes are incorporated, however, Western classical music begins to sound much more Irish or Scottish.

Ionian mode starting on C: C, D, E, F, G, A, B, C
Aeolian mode starting on C: C, D, E flat, F, G, A flat, B flat, C
Dorian mode starting on C: C, D, E flat, F, G, A, B flat, C
Mixolydian mode starting on C: C, D, E, F, G, A, B flat, C

What happens when the tune sometimes includes a sharp and sometimes includes a natural on the same pitch at different points in the tune? Irish music is *rich* with these kinds of tunes. In Irish songs, which—to make a rank generalization—are often both happy and sad in mood, the "wandering pitch" is used to actually *enhance* a sense of instability of mood. In Chapter 5 you will encounter the full text of the song "The Green Fields of America." The lyrics are full of anguish about leaving Ireland and its dark conditions, yet full of optimism for the times to come in America. In the following transcription (Figure 1.3), the confluence of major and minor sounds appear in the first two lines as the song shifts back and forth between D Dorian (D–E–F–G–A–B–C–D) and D Mixolydian (D–E–F#–G–A–B–C–D). Note that the word "shamrock" includes the F#, but the syllable "well" of "farewell" leans on the F natural. Similarly, "farewell" with its F natural is followed by "girls" with an F sharp, which is followed by "Ireland" with an F natural.

For a guitarist unsure of how to accompany a song like this one, or a tune such as "Moran's Fancy" (see Chapter 6), the path is perilous! Many tunes and songs are fluid in mode, and require that the guitarist walk the fine line between modes by occasionally playing neither a major nor a minor chord behind the melody. No wonder so many Irish guitar players adopted the DADGAD tuning on the guitar (originally developed by English guitarist Davey Graham), which uses neither major nor minor thirds in the chords. As Fintan Vallely writes, "Chords need to be as 'open' as possible so that the 'mobile' notes can move about unimpeded" (Ní Chathasaigh 1999: 244).

Figure 1.3 First phrases of "The Green Fields of America"

Another aspect of the Irish modal system is "gapped" modes, in which a particular tune might leave out a crucial indicator of the mode. In Chapter 6, one of the slip jig examples ("Elizabeth Kelly's Favourite") simply does not include the sixth degree of the scale at all. Listening to (or playing) the tune, it is impossible to tell whether it is in Aeolian (minor) or Dorian mode. Combine the mode with the form (jigs, reels, etc.), instrumentation (fiddles, tin whistles, pipes, accordions), texture (heterophony or monophony), stylistic playing features connected to specific regions (East Clare, Donegal, Sliabh Luachra), and the various melodic patterns within the tunes, and you know you're playing Irish music.

Attending an Irish Music Event

Irish music wasn't always performed in pubs or on stages (and it still isn't always). In fact, the pub session so often lauded as "traditional" is a fairly recent development in music history. When large numbers of Irish men sought work as laborers in England in the early twentieth century, they often took cramped lodging at inexpensive boarding houses. The pub was a place of congregation and socializing, and it was there that musicians could safely play their instruments without disturbing lodgers next door or having to move their furniture out of their rooms. A few pubs included sessions by the 1930s, but the kind of session you might see today was not a national phenomenon before the 1950s; it certainly wasn't "traditional." Pub sessions have had a flexible existence since that time, with music springing up spontaneously in some places, and carefully planned (down to printed set lists and specific hours of performance) in others.

In the Ireland of the nineteenth century and before, music often occurred in homes, around a turf fire in an intimate room that functioned as both kitchen and living room. People would go "céilí-ing"—visiting friends and family members at their homes, at which each person present would be expected to contribute a "party piece." It is still common to have a particular tune, song, poem, or story for performance, and to offer that party piece at an event of this kind. Depending on where the gathering was taking place, a singer might follow a fiddler, or a piper might stop by for the night. Dances could occur spontaneously; either a solo dancer or a small set (or half set) of dancers, sometimes with only one musician providing all the music for the evening.

Another older context for music might be the crossroads dance, in which young men and women would meet and dance at a crossroads (single country roads being too narrow to accommodate full sets of dancers). This practice continued until it was banned by the Dance Halls Act of 1935, which mandated—right through to the present—that all dances should be licensed, and ought to take place in the parish hall under the watchful eyes of the priest. Please keep in mind, though, that these are generally older—not twenty-first-century—contexts for traditional music performance practice.

Many towns have Irish music sessions, not just in Ireland but abroad. If you live in a town with one or more Irish music sessions, they are likely to occur in pubs or, if you are lucky, an all-ages venue such as a restaurant, so that teenagers can join the adults in playing, listening, and socializing. As at any social gathering, the participants follow an array of unwritten rules. And, because the traditional Irish session is a relatively recent phenomenon that has spread around the world, every one of these "rules" is heavily contested, affirmed, denied, debated, proven, and disproven. Being a first-rate musician with excellent knowledge of your instrument and hundreds of local tunes within your grasp does not necessarily qualify you for instant membership in a session's fragile and changeable social order, as frustrating as that might be. Your status, gender, country of origin, social circle, sexual orientation, age, race, class, language, clothing, and other variables can count either for or against you, often simultaneously (Slominski 2020). Nonetheless, should you hope to join a session, follow these general rules:

1. Listen first. Attend the session a few times and start bringing your instrument (in its case). Set the case down, unopened. Observe who starts the tunes. Generally, the ones starting tunes are the leaders of the group. The leader is the one who will invite you to play if you come with a melody instrument. Do not attempt to take the lead; it is not a race to see who can reach the end of the tune first (though it may feel like it to you if the tunes are unfamiliar). When an unfamiliar tune comes up, do not try to fake your way through it. It is normal to sit and listen patiently, holding your instrument, while others are playing. You might quietly ask what the title of the tune was so that you can learn it for next time (with the caveat that musicians usually know more tunes than tune titles).

2. Some instruments are more welcome than others. More than one guitar is, generally, too many guitars. Similarly, if you have a *bodhrán* (a round-frame drum, pronounced "BOW-rawn"), you may not be welcome at all! Enough beginner *bodhrán* players have spoiled sessions by pounding away too loudly (or using inappropriate rhythms, or messing with the tempo) that you may receive glares instead of welcoming smiles. Fiddles, tin whistles, flutes, button accordions, and tenor banjos are often quite welcome indeed. But you will be most welcome if you play well.

3. You might know a hundred tunes, but if the tunes you learned are from a different region (see above), your fellow players may know none of yours. It is your job to conform to the group. If you are asked to lead a tune, choose a well-known tune such as a regional jig, not an obscure one such as a barndance from a tiny village far away from the session.

4. If you are a singer, consider singing an actual Irish song, not (necessarily) one of the Irish American hits. Conversely, you may be asked to sing a song from your part of the world or your heritage. The average instrumental session can accommodate only a couple of songs in an evening, so do not push for more. Once you have done your song, you are done altogether unless you are specifically invited to sing another, later in the evening. It is appropriate to ask if anyone has already sung the song you plan to do. A very brief (single-sentence) explanation of where you learned the song is a nice thing to do.

It is relatively easy to tell who is an insider and who might be an outsider. The insiders are often the ones playing for enjoyment instead of in competition with the others. They might start tunes a little more slowly and then warm up in speed, or they might offer more variation in the tune forms they choose. They don't jump in instantly to start "their" tunes when a set has finished. These musicians are highly unlikely to present you with a list of acceptable tunes at the door! Instead, they let the evening unfold according to the desires of the group; if the session devolves into talk about politics or sports, so be it. Similarly, if the group gets started on a whole series of polkas (unusual in some areas of Ireland), people might bring out their favorite polkas just for the variation of it. Do not be surprised if you do not get asked to play at all; some sessions have great music but suffer from rigid hierarchies, strict codes of behavior, and clashing personalities (see O'Shea 2006–7: 7).

People attending pub sessions as listeners have fewer restrictions on etiquette, and their attentive presence outside the circle of players is quite welcome. Sometimes the pub owner will have the television going with the sound turned off, so that patrons can enjoy whatever sports event is being broadcast. It is normal for the non-listening people in a pub to chat informally while music is being played. As a good observer, you will notice that musicians in a pub usually gather in a circle with their backs to the pub patrons. This is not rude behavior on their part; it is a way to hear the music well, and to make the session be about the music and the *craic* (camaraderie), as opposed to providing a formal performance for audience members. If there is a tip jar for the musicians, it is good form to put a euro or two in the jar. You are expected to order something from the bar, but it does not have to be alcohol. Should someone sing or play a solo on an instrument, be quiet.

Having read and understood all of that, keep in mind that the "rules" are flexible, moving targets, and that the session-in-a-pub is only one of multiple venues and types of musical performance. So much of this music started out as, and has continued to thrive as, solo instrumental music; thousands of players all over the world get an instrument down off the wall or shelf, play a few tunes for enjoyment, and put it back. Many of these people never (or almost never) "play out" in public, for a variety of reasons (modesty, the desire not to compete with others, playing for fun instead of for public performance, skill level, time limitations, the lack of childcare or a good session nearby, irritation with the "session rules," etc.). In fact, complaining about one's local session can be a favorite pastime among Irish musicians, especially those who travel outside of their hometown!

The solo instrumental tradition is also key to the development of decent musicianship. This term—musicianship—can encompass a wealth of ideas about what it means to become a good musician. In an Irish context, good musicianship implies that you have listened to so much music that you have internalized the *blas* or "feel" or "taste" of the music. It means, for example, that if you were to encounter a new jig, you would not play the six eighth notes in each measure using precisely the same amount of time for each note. Instead, you would slightly lengthen and shorten the time value of certain notes; you might slur the notes across particular barlines; you might start varying the tune immediately. You might group the phrases with your breathing, your fingering, or your bowing. You might throw in a roll instead of a dotted quarter note. Why? You would do it because it would be the right thing to do in *Irish* music, and exactly the wrong thing to do in *classical* music. Because musicianship develops over time, and with considerable solo practice, it is worth considering that for every Internet-listed pub session with a whole bank of fiddlers sawing away, dozens more musicians may be working on the jigs, reels, hornpipes, and slides in the privacy of their own homes, with no intention of *ever* playing at a pub session.

Singing in Ireland is another matter altogether. While there are singers' clubs in many Irish towns, most people simply sing without the expectation of performance. Ireland's reputation as "The Land of Song" is founded at least partly on the concepts that one does not have to be a trained singer to perform, and that singing is for everyone.

In practice, Irish people do *not* tend to burst into song for any public occasion. Instead, people sing along with the radio, sing to their children, sing in school or a pub with friends, and very occasionally sing for competitions and performances. Singing tends to be a more personal and private affair; in fact, it is much more difficult to locate singers performing in public venues than it is to locate sessions in pubs. People singing in Ireland—as opposed to Irish traditional singers—cross genres quite easily. The result is that the same person singing a song in *sean-nós* style (free rhythm, unaccompanied singing, using challenging poetic content across many verses) in an evening of singing might well be humming along to opera the next day, or belting out the lyrics to "Old Town Road" on the radio, or writing a new song accompanied by the guitar... or all of the above. Singer-songwriters of the past forty years are, generally, held in high esteem, regardless of where they originated. It is just as normal to hear songs by international stars such as Bob Dylan or James Taylor as it is to hear a song by any of the contemporary Irish songwriters.

Some institutions sponsor public concerts and festivals of Irish traditional music, for which tickets are sold. These institutions might include universities, hotels, or concert halls. Ireland has its share of superstars who perform traditional music either solo or in groups, and enough traditional music enthusiasts live in the larger cities to make such concerts viable for the artists and promoters. Even when a group comes to a smaller town, however, people from the region are generally willing to drive an hour or so to see someone whose playing they respect and enjoy. Doing a "tour" of Ireland is a short-term proposition because of Ireland's small size, but it is common for the major players to return to festivals year after year, or to the same town in which a successful concert took place in previous years.

One of the liveliest venues for the public performance of Irish music is the summer music schools. The most influential and famous of all the summer schools is the Willie Clancy Summer School in Miltown Malbay, County Clare. Held every July since 1973 (in honor of the great piper Willie Clancy), the summer school draws Irish music enthusiasts from all over the world and from across Ireland. Well over a thousand people attend each year, and the numbers are increasing. Although the week features classes for all levels in every "normal" Irish traditional instrument, dance, and vocal style, many people come for the packed, high-energy instrumental music sessions that seem to blossom everywhere, day and night. The town itself is overwhelmed with visitors during the week, and the social scene is quite festive. At the end of the week a large *céilí* (music and dance party) celebrates the closure of the event.

One way in which Ireland celebrates its great musicians and dancers is through the development of festival weekends to honor notable individuals. Festivals are held throughout the year in honor of people such as the concertina player Elizabeth Crotty (August, in Kilrush), tin whistle player Micho Russell (February, in Doolin), *sean-nós* singer Joe Heaney (May, in Carna), fiddler Pádraig O'Keeffe (October, in Castleisland), and others. Many more are one-time festivals, or occur only occasionally. Usually these weekends feature classes, late-night sessions (often with set dancing), and concerts. It is in the best interest of the future of Irish traditional music for young people to be encouraged to play, sing, and dance, and some festivals highlight participation by young people.

The Fleadh Cheoil na hÉireann (pronounced "flah khyol na hairrin") is an annual festival and competition featuring young people; it was created by Comhaltas Ceoltóirí

Éireann, the international organization of Irish music enthusiasts. Held every August, the Fleadh Cheoil celebrates the winners of all the regional competitions from the previous year and engages them in competition. The winners of the competitions then have the honor of being called the "All-Ireland" champion player, dancer, singer, duo, trio, band, or other configuration. The designation "All-Ireland" is inclusive not only of *all of Ireland* (both the Republic of Ireland and Northern Ireland), but is also inclusive of people from outside of Ireland. In 1984, for example, two Irish American women (Joanie Madden and Eileen Ivers) became All-Ireland champions on the tin whistle and fiddle, respectively.

The Fleadh Nua in Ennis, County Clare (in May), is just one more of dozens of festivals held all over Ireland, particularly in the summer season. As with the other summer schools and festivals, a relatively small town packs in hundreds of people, pub sessions and singers' clubs fill up with players, singers, and listeners, and people renew acquaintances, play tunes, and sing songs. It might be useful to keep in mind that in the middle of the twentieth century, Irish traditional music was experiencing quite a decline; it was unfashionable to listen to (or play), and few young people were bothering to learn to play or sing. For reasons you will learn in this book, however, those days are over. Going off to a weekend festival with friends for "the *craic*" (great tunes, fun times) is a fun way to spend one's time! Proportionately speaking, the healthy numbers of young people attending festivals such as the Fleadh Nua or a weekend honoring one of the great musicians of the past is fairly recent. Compared to the situation in the 1940s and 1950s, however, the sight of dozens of teens at sessions playing fiddles, pipes, flutes, and button accordions right alongside people in their thirties, fifties, and seventies is a dramatic development in inter-generational musical practice.

The home is a frequent venue for Irish traditional music playing. In a kitchen or living room the setting is informal, there are fewer listeners and more participants, and songs are much more frequent than in the pub or other settings. The drink of choice is often tea instead of a pint of beer, and children and neighbors are welcome to join in. Rather than an exclusive session of rapid-fire instrumental tunes, a home session can feature lively stories, poetry, jokes, conversations, and questions in addition to instrumental music and songs. The host—called the *fear a tí* (pronounced somewhat like "fair-a-tee," "man of the house") if it's a man or the *bean a tí* ("bann-a-tee," "woman of the house") if it's a woman—is responsible for the congenial atmosphere, the rotating participation of the guests, the fluid shifting of genres from songs to stories to tunes, and the overall success of the event. Everyone is expected to contribute something to the enjoyment of the event, including the outsider. What would you bring to contribute to a gathering of this kind?

If the pub session is a collective public performance, the home session is still collective, but it is much more private. Many more solo tunes are performed in the home, and people are much more attentive, respectful, and dedicated to the tunes and songs as a powerful expression of their relationships as family and community members. Whereas in a pub anyone can show up, a home session is much more likely to include those who have been invited or who know that they will be welcome, particularly family members of the hosts. This more selective sensibility reflects another aspect of Irish social life, which is that many Irish people spend a considerable portion of their free and social time on weekends with the members of their own extended families, rather than exclusively with friends. Friends and neighbors come over and are folded into an existing family structure, regardless of whether that family is functional or flawed, fractured or congenial.

The Travelling Community

Ireland has, for centuries, been home to a group of Irish people who call themselves Travellers (spelled with two ll's) or Pavees. Numbering approximately 30,000, members of this very close-knit group are often separated, one way or another, from the mainstream Irish. At least partly because of their long history of severe discrimination from the "settled" Irish and partly because of their history of nomadism, many tend to live on the outskirts of towns at what are called "halting sites" where they can camp. They mainly speak English, but also have an English-based creole language of their own, Shelta, which occurs in two dialects: Gammon (near Galway) and Cant (in the Southwest). Of those people belonging to the Travelling communities, just 35 surnames—including McDonagh, Ward, O'Connor, O'Brien, Cash, Dooley, and others—belong to 70% of the families. Travellers tend to live their lives outside the primary institutions of education, medicine, and religion in Ireland, resulting in a low life expectancy and high rate of illiteracy.

Historically, the Travelling community were associated with the repair of pots and pans made from tin. Repairing tin pans required them to move frequently to stay employed, and their service was required again and again because the fragile tin broke through as part of its regular use. They were known for their songs and stories, because they were often brought to a community from elsewhere, and for their poetry and artwork. The large, gentle draft horse now known as the "Gypsy Vanner" or "Irish Cob" is a central symbol of the Travellers; the horses tow caravans from place to place, and figure prominently in social/commercial events that include horse trading. The Ballinasloe Horse Fair, held at the end of September in County Galway, is the biggest such event of the year. Because the Travellers moved around so much, they were outsiders to the communities for whom they performed their important services; their outsider status led to them being distrusted and shunned. A derogatory name developed in connection to their tin work: "tinkers."

The problem with an exonym—a name given to a group of people by outsiders—is that it usually doesn't reflect the way people view themselves. Examples of exonyms include "Oriental" and "Gypsy." "Oriental" referred to people and objects and ideas from the East, where the sun rises; for the people who have always lived there, though, it isn't "east." The term "Gypsy" developed from the word for Egyptian, and was used by Europeans to describe the (mostly nomadic) Romani people whose ancestors came from North India. The Romani people were never Egyptian, but it was a handy—if wholly inaccurate—European way of describing the way they looked. In the United States, the term "Gypsy" has frequently been appropriated to refer to a free-spirited hippie type; it is often used as a name for animals, and as an insult: "I've been gypped." Stereotypes abound in popular culture about "Gypsies." All of these same stereotypes abound in Ireland about the Irish Travelling community.

Though the Irish Travellers are sometimes mistakenly called "Gypsies," they are unrelated to the Romani people (or the Egyptians!) and have been officially recognized as an indigenous ethnic minority in Ireland and the United Kingdom since 2017. A decades-long movement advocating for official recognition in the face of diminishment and severe discrimination ultimately led to this breakthrough. Playwright Rosaleen McDonagh notes that standard practice for Travellers has been "Hiding your surname, changing your accent, feeling insecure and always having to worry you'll lose that job, that place in school, that sense that you are going to be found out, singled out, and eventually pushed out" (McDonagh 2017). The Travelling people are genetically different from the mainstream Irish, and were known as a separate group by the twelfth century. Approximately half of the Travellers live in public assistance housing (and are referred to as "settled"), while others live in trailer parks in halting sites or on public land. In the United Kingdom about 15,000 Irish Travellers live and travel, among other communities of Travellers. In the United States, another 15,000 people descended from Famine-era Traveller immigrants live in communities in South Carolina, Texas, Ohio, Georgia, and Mississippi. As a group subject to broad discrimination in the realm of housing, education, and medicine, the Irish Travellers are also known for having a strong moral code, deep-seated beliefs, and rich folkloric traditions specific to their individual communities.

While some contemporary Irish Travellers are renowned for their skills in car and road repairs, painting, herbal medicine, tool sharpening, bare-knuckle boxing, and tree surgery, a number of Travellers are celebrated for their exceptional musical skills, particularly as *uilleann* pipers. Often caught between "settler culture" and life on the road, these musicians have had a significant impact on the development of Irish traditional music, even as the members of the new Irish nation struggled to define what an independent Ireland might look like in the mid-twentieth century. As part of the celebration of what is called "the Travelling style" of *uilleann* piping, authors Tuohy and Ó hAodha (2008: 2) describe the ways in which a unique individual piper (in the case of their book's subject, Johnny Doran) can work within the system of a piping family, and the ways in which a single piping family can influence a whole community of musicians. Johnny Doran (1907–1950) and his younger brother Felix Doran (1915–1972) of County Wicklow made names for themselves in the 1940s and 50s, respectively; Johnny Doran's celebrated playing (along with his career) was cut short by an accident, but his brother Felix won first prize at the Fleadh Cheoil na hÉireann, in 1963. Each brother has the legacy of a single recording (Johnny Doran: *The Master Pipers, volume 1* and Felix Doran: *Last of the Travelling Pipers*).

Finbar Furey (b. 1946), a neighbor of Paddy Keenan in the 1950s, studied the pipes with John Keenan (father of Paddy Keenan, below), and lived with the Keenan family in Ballyfermot for a time. He won several All-Ireland medals for his fine playing, which established his reputation early on. Touring with his brothers as "The Fureys," a string of studio recordings and two #1 hits made the family a household name in Ireland, with tenor banjo player Davey Arthur, by the 1970s and 1980s. In 2013, Finbar Furey won first prize on the Irish talent show series *The Hit*, and a Lifetime Achievement Award from the Gaelic Players Association in 2018.

Paddy Keenan (b. 1950) was a founding member of The Bothy Band, one of Ireland's most important revival groups in the 1970s. Sometimes referred to as "the King of the Pipers," he was raised in County Meath, and began studying the *uilleann* pipes with his father John Keenan by the time he was ten years old. The family moved to Ballyfermot, a Dublin suburb, where they established a musical household visited by many of Ireland's best-known musicians. Growing up in a climate of deep anti-Traveller discrimination in the 1950s and 1960s, he joined other musicians from the Traveller community to perform and tour as a young man. As an adult, Paddy Keenan has toured around the world and won awards, including Musician of the Year in 2002 and a Lifetime Achievement Award for his exceptional work in Irish traditional music.

Johnny Doherty (1900–1980) was a famous Donegal fiddler who flourished locally when Donegal fiddling was not nearly as well-known as the fiddling of counties farther south. His lineage includes the famous nineteenth century Donegal piper Turlough MacSweeney, himself descended from nobility. Doherty traveled throughout the county offering lessons and playing for dances; one of the main features of his playing, however, is that he specialized in using many different types of melodic ornaments and stylistic features that Donegal fiddling is well known for now. The recorded collection of his playing titled *The Floating Bow* continues to influence fiddlers today; his brother Mickey Doherty was recorded by Alan Lomax.

Margaret Barry (1917–1989) was Ireland's best-known Traveller to make her living through singing; she had a distinctively strident voice and, unusually, played the five-string banjo. She left Ireland for London in the 1950s and performed in folk clubs and on the street. Her first album, *Songs of an Irish Tinker Lady,* made unapologetic use of the word "tinker," and features her most famous song, "She Moved Through the Fair." She is said to have mentioned in an interview that she learned the song (discussed in detail in Chapter 8) from a recording by the famous Irish tenor, John McCormack. She performed at the 1965 Newport Folk Festival, and learned songs from people everywhere (including on recordings). As a Traveller, the entirety of several national songlists were hers to choose from.

Thomas McCarthy is a traditional singer related to the Doran family (above); in addition to performing songs in English (and occasionally Irish) internationally, he works as an activist to halt anti-Traveller discrimination. Awarded the Gradam Ceoil Singer of the Year award in 2019 by the Irish-language television station TG4, he is the first Irish Traveller to receive the award. He performs and records the songs of the Travelling Community that he had in his own family (from County Offaly) and gives talks, sings, and tells stories to both Traveller and settled communities. Note that the musical influences of the Travellers run deeply through the traditional spectrum of Irish musicianship at home and abroad; see more in the "Resources" section of this book.

The changes taking place in contemporary Ireland include serious discussions of what it means to be a nation that simultaneously legalizes marriage equality, but still discriminates against perceived outsiders of all types. These issues have historical reasons for their establishment, and there is a larger paradox: Ireland simultaneously carries a sense of tolerance *and* exclusion, and its progressive legislation contrasts with anxieties about difference; see the following section for more insights.

Equity and Inclusion in Irish Music at Home and Abroad

Imagine these scenes:

- a festival at which every featured performer is male, except for one female singer
- a celebration of Irish music that includes only English speakers
- a panel on equity and inclusion comprising straight white men only
- a music session on a second floor, without wheelchair access
- a stage (with a male emcee) featuring "women's traditions" far from the main stage

All kinds of people play and sing Irish music of all kinds, all over the world. The concept of intersectionality, coined by critical race theorist Kimberlé Crenshaw, reminds us that no one ever claims just one identity. People's skill sets, ages, instrument choices, abilities (both physical and mental), races, genders, classes, religions, sexual orientations, native languages, and philosophies all come into play both in Irish music circles and in their own lives. One can hear Irish music performed in many different contexts, from a command performance at an embassy or as part of a therapy session several thousand miles away from Ireland. The expectations of who plays or sings in Irish music, and the features that constitute the boundaries of Irish music and dance, are frequently up for debate, even in the twenty-first century. Not every player is an able white male straight Catholic fiddler, though media presentations of Irish music often seem to lean on exactly that characterization.

Equity in Irish music is not just about being in the room where people are playing, but about who sits in the few seats at the center of the session circle. Equity is also about considering who isn't in the room to begin with, and thinking about what maintains such a status quo. Moving from the image of the session as primarily a place for straight white men to a more open one requires small steps not just of invitation and welcome, but of people who don't look like those particular players walking in and sitting down to play, in session after session and festival after festival, all over the world.

Most of the work on equity in Irish music has been on the subject of gender; less so on race and disability. Most nations tend to have gendered personifications ("fatherland" or "motherland"). The inherently gendered nature of the perception of Ireland—named for the goddess Éiriú—has led, over time, to linkages between nationhood and womanhood. Those linkages shifted over the centuries from a fluid and highly localized distribution of power and participation between men and women to a severely patriarchal and newly nationalist system. This dramatic shift was particularly acute after the Devotional Revolution of 1850, which saw a strong upswing in public and private Catholicism in comparison to participation rates of perhaps 30% of the Irish people before the Famine of 1845–1850. During the 1910s and early 20s, women participated alongside men in the fight for Irish Independence, but despite an active suffragist movement, gender equality took a back seat to political self-determination. Through the creation of the new Constitution of 1937, women were allowed to vote, but could not work for pay after marriage, work in any kind of industry, or serve on a jury. This set of prohibitions was established in spite of the fact that women had served in all the major conflicts that resulted in Irish Independence.

Part of the erasure of women from the public sphere, and the historical narrative, has been a concurrent erasure of women from the ranks of composers and performers within Irish music. Music scholar Tes Slominski, who describes Irish traditional music as "simultaneously liberatory and confining," has documented a broad system of erasure as the result of a combination of larger societal forces that have historically aligned women with the domestic realm and denied female musicians recognition outside their relationships with their husbands, fathers, sons, and students. Female musicians, if they were mentioned at all, often had their legitimacy *as women* highlighted in that they were loving mothers or supportive spouses or reverent daughters of men before their merits as musicians or composers were ever mentioned (Slominski 2013: 4).

The Irish organization FairPlé (Irish *plé*, "discussion") is dedicated to achieving "gender balance in the production, performance, promotion, and development of Irish traditional and folk music." Through the use of discussions, advocacy, performance events, political activities, and development of a global support network and directory, FairPlé is raising awareness and effecting change precisely by *not* being silent. Founded in late 2017 and comprising both women and men interested in matters such as equal representation, equal working conditions, and equal pay for *all*, the organization notes the barriers to equality and inclusion, and works to break them down. The reaction against their efforts has been strong and swift; usually it has been by men who insist that no structural inequities exist, or that problems of sexism have been addressed by the occasional inclusion of women in performance. Criticism has also arisen—from women—about the treatment of female musicians who are not professionals.

Although both the Irish government and the Catholic Church played very strong roles in determining that women should stay out of the public eye in the early- to mid-twentieth century, no one disputed the existence or importance of women. However, when it comes to queer members of the traditional music ("trad") communities of Ireland and the diaspora, silence tends to prevail. Disrupting or interrogating the very public ethos of "just being in it for the tunes" at sessions is, most of the time, just not done, and differences are minimized in favor of enforcing a very specific heteronormative scene.

> Most women musicians do not talk about gender, queer musicians do not 'out themselves,' and non-white musicians do not mention race in the context of a session, thus maintaining the illusion that everyone in the scene is happy with the current arrangements, and that differences in race, gender, and sexuality are of no consequence.
>
> (Slominski 2018: 3)

By continually reinforcing a central narrative of white heteronormativity in instrumental music, then, any variation in that sphere can lead to a musician or a dancer being made to feel unwelcome. The result might be fewer playing opportunities, fewer gigs, and fewer festival invitations. However, the international community supporting Irish traditional music and dance includes thousands of people who—for various reasons—don't conform to the mainstream. The 2003 film *The Boys from County Clare*, for example, includes an African *céilí* band performing in competition with other bands. In 2011 a *céilí* band from Japan, led by flute player Kozo Toyota, performed at the Fleadh Cheoil—a major instrumental music festival—in Ennis, County Clare. Some of the greatest players at sessions across the world speak no English or Irish at all. In other words, musicians of color, queer musicians, disabled musicians, and female musicians are playing this music, participating in its communities, and maintaining and innovating in traditions labeled "Irish" worldwide.

As for those who sing in Irish or in English, the situation is somewhat different from instrumental session or festival contexts. Women are widely acknowledged and celebrated as great singers, equal to men, both historically and in the present, in both Irish and English. Part of the difference between the acclaim accorded to women who sing is that singing has, historically, been much more of a private affair than playing instrumental music. A woman might have been looked at with surprise or dismay if she ventured into the male section of the pub with a fiddle—pubs were divided between the front, public, section and the "snug" in the back for women. But if a woman sings in the snug, or the kitchen, or a singing club, or in a friend's home, it has always been right and normal because those moments are private. The occurrence of a song in a pub session is still a once- (or twice-) a-night experience, because sessions are for instrumentalists.

In an interview about performing songs that might reflect one's orientation, American performer Brían Ó hAirt pointed out the importance of highlighting the song, rather than the self. He notes that "the nature of song in the Irish tradition, while not void completely of a gender/sexual viewpoint, is one that cloaks the singer from ties to the song itself" (Léger 2012). Regardless of the pronouns used in the songs, the key feature of many Irish songs and the attraction of those songs to the singers has to do with their emotional content rather than the listed pronouns. As a result, singers may choose to leave the pronouns as is, regardless of their own orientation.

Having witnessed, multiple times, young men in various pubs leap to their feet to physically carry a wheelchair and its occupant into and out of an otherwise-inaccessible pub session, it appears that physical disability may now be less of a hindrance to session participation than it once was. People with physical disabilities in Ireland were often placed in institutions rather than cared for at home, but in 2018, Ireland joined the United Nations Convention on the Rights of Persons with a Disability (UNCRPD), legalizing some of the changes that were already occurring within the society.

As Ireland changes from within, and as social changes in the rest of the world reach Ireland, its future looks much more equitable than its past. In 2015, the Republic of Ireland became the first nation in the world to vote for marriage equality by popular acclaim (rather than by top-down decree). Practices of Catholicism have changed dramatically in Ireland, and Mass attendance has plummeted to about 20% (2% in some working-class urban neighborhoods). In a very short time, Ireland has become one of the most politically liberal places in Europe. Irish America as a whole has not directly followed suit, for various reasons reflecting regional and historical differences in a very large country. Change happens in fits and starts, in both positive and negative ways.

All of Ireland's Music

Lest the reader get the impression that every Irish home or pub hosts a music gathering nightly, or that Irish traditional music is all that is played on the radio or in the concert hall, let us expand our understanding of music in Ireland! In the twenty-first century, every musical current that develops in North American popular culture has its place in Ireland. Country music, for example, is quite popular, and the country singer Garth Brooks (among many others) has filled stadiums with screaming fans. In fact, the genre of "country Irish" (Irish songs written in American country music style in both English and Irish) has a large fan base. Most of the larger cities have multiple nightclubs where people dance to hip-hop, trance, industrial, and other American- or Euro-tinged genres. All the well-known American and English pop music and film stars are household names in Ireland, and some of the film stars most familiar to North American audiences—Daniel Day Lewis, Pierce Brosnan, Cillian Murphy, Peter O'Toole, Richard Harris, Liam Neeson, and Colin Farrell, for example—are Irish. Cell phones (called "mobiles"), digital cameras, computers, and other evidence of high-tech living are ubiquitous. In fact, several multinational corporations (Intel, for example, and an array of pharmaceutical companies) have established a base in Ireland because of the extremely high rate of both literacy and English fluency within its workforce. The Celtic Tiger (the economic boom of the 1990s) brought luxury goods to Ireland in full force, and even though the economy currently suffers from the same malaise that has affected the rest of the world, parts of Dublin in particular are awash in new construction, late model luxury cars, and high fashion.

Both rock and pop music have a strong foothold in Ireland. U2, Van Morrison, the Pogues, and other popular international rock acts are Irish and maintain homes in Ireland. Jazz has been performed in Ireland since the 1930s, and has a devoted following. Though it initially scandalized some members of the Church leadership, jazz persisted across the difficult economic years of the 1940s and 1950s, emerging in the 1990s as a symbol of new-found hip sophistication. Ireland's long history of proximity to the mainland of Europe has led to a rich interchange of classical composers, musicians, and other artists. Handel's *Messiah* received its world premiere in Dublin in 1742, an important event for the Irish aristocracy of the time and something of a coming-out party for Dublin. The prevalence of choirs, chamber orchestras, and other classical music ensembles offers testament to the fact that "Irish music" is much more than its traditional music. The traditional music is, however, that which is most characteristically Irish, and that which is the subject of this volume.

Most Irish radio stations (and there are many) tend to duplicate precisely what one would hear in the United States, or Australia, or England. The majority of stations focus on top-40 hits, followed by classic rock, talk shows, jazz, "light" rock, and classical music. Raidió Téilifís Éireann ("Irish Radio [and] Television," or RTÉ), the national public broadcasting corporation, has an Irish-language branch called Raidió na Gaeltachta ("Radio of the Gaeltacht"). RnaG broadcasts in Irish from multiple Irish-speaking regions in the country. In fact, Raidió na Gaeltachta has played an important role in both highlighting and blurring the linguistic distinctions between the different Gaeltacht regions because it broadcasts from each region to a national (and international) Irish-speaking audience. It can be heard via live streaming webcast at http://www.rte.ie, and it is fascinating to listen to if you have never heard the Irish language spoken before. RnaG also broadcasts *sean-nós* singing competitions, Irish language songs, and world music of various kinds.

Yet the radio airwaves in Ireland are not restricted to the English- and Irish-speaking audience alone. Since 2004, when 15 countries (primarily in Eastern Europe) entered the European Union on 1 May, Ireland has drawn thousands of people from Poland, Romania, Latvia, Estonia, and other former East Bloc nations. Ireland now has a Polish-language radio station, as Polish people form the majority of Eastern European immigrants to Ireland. Furthermore, the increase of immigrants from Asia has led to the creation of a Mandarin Chinese radio station, and more stations are in development. All of these changes in the media are reflections of an Ireland that is increasingly international, cosmopolitan, wealthy, and wired to the Internet. The "Additional Resources" section of this book includes the web addresses of various Irish radio stations, all of which are worth pursuing for their different perspectives on the spectrum of Irish music.

It should be clear at this point that Ireland, while never actually remote from the mainland, other islands, or the Mediterranean, is no longer remote at all. Alongside the recent economic boom and subsequent bust, Ireland has experienced many of the same issues as North America: a widening gap between the very wealthy and the very poor; problems with racism and gang violence; and a dramatic increase in drug use. On a positive note, and for the first time since the era of the bards, professional musicians are once again able to make something of a living exclusively from music. In addition, the Irish government has paid increasing attention to the traditional arts through funding, publicity, and other forms of support.

This chapter has introduced the concepts underlying this book, some of the basic musical ideas, and offered a sense of contemporary contexts for traditional music. In order to understand how Irish traditional music came to be the way it is today, it is appropriate for us now to explore some of its earliest developments in the context of Irish history. Just remember that Ireland's present is profoundly interwoven with its past.

Discussion Questions

1. What do you know about Ireland right now, and how much of your understanding of it is based on American stereotypes?
2. How much of a choice do you believe you have in choosing which aspect of your own heritage to celebrate? Do you need to be mostly or entirely of Irish descent to claim Irish heritage for yourself?
3. Are there certain unwritten rules about who may join in, and what instrument they may play, for genres besides Irish music? What are those rules, and where do they apply?
4. What other kinds of folk and popular music use heterophony as their primary texture? What about monophony?
5. Why is it that this book isn't about Irish classical, jazz, rock, or pop music?

Roots and Branches of Gaelic Ireland

Níl aon tinteán mar do thinteán féin ~ There is no hearth like your own hearth.

Ireland has always had something of an international flavor to it. From its earliest days as an inhabited island, Ireland saw frequent commerce with the island of Britain and the European mainland. The "sea roads" between Ireland and the Mediterranean have always been well traveled; travelers' accounts have noted Spanish ships in Galway Bay. Sea roads to the north were commonly traveled as well. Some of the first inhabitants of Iceland were Irish monks called *papars* ("fathers"), practicing what they called "white martyrdom." Between the seventh and eighth centuries C.E. a few select monks climbed into small boats called *currach*s and allowed themselves to be carried away from Ireland with no oars to guide their journey, trusting in God to take them to a new place. Enough of these monks survived to establish a foothold in Iceland and elsewhere, to which others came (Crawford 2002). The names of some of Iceland's oldest-named natural features (such as *á*, pronounced "aw," "river") bear a similarity to certain Irish words (*abhainn*, pronounced "awin," "river"). The Irish monks are said to have left Iceland when the Norse arrived in the ninth century C.E. (Harding and Bindloss 2004: 20), but their peripatetic ways were by that time legendary.

Even earlier than the Christian monks of Ireland, however, were the very first inhabitants of Ireland. From 9,000 B.C.E. the archaeological record reveals traces of Mesolithic people scattered throughout the island. They first established a foothold on the Derry coast in the north of Ireland, where shell middens and stone tools attest to their existence. What did Ireland look like in the earliest days of human settlement? The last Ice Age ended 15,000 years ago, and as the ice melted it submerged the land bridges that had connected many of today's islands to the nearest mainland. Ireland's land bridge with Scotland was submerged about 6,000 years ago (Andrews 1995: 32), though it did not become isolated because of the submersion. Animals and plants had crossed the land bridge as well, establishing a strong presence and enabling people to find food when they came to Ireland. Protein sources for the early Mesolithic people were abundant, including birds (and their eggs), fish, venison, pork, crabapples, and hazelnuts (Flanagan 2000: 17). Britain, too, was connected to the mainland via a plain (Sykes 2006: 16). Today one can stand on the Antrim coast in northeast Ireland and easily see Scotland, a mere 17 miles away and an easy boat ride on a fine day.

Antrim's proximity to the land bridge to Scotland gave rise to the legend of the Giant's Causeway (Figure 2.1); hexagonal basalt formations extend from the land into the sea, emerging at the nearest point in Scotland. Early Irish people envisioned the step-like formations as a crossing point for the giants of both sides. To this day, the

Figure 2.1 The Giants' Causeway

site is a fascinating, windswept viewpoint along the coast, not far from where *Game of Thrones* and other television, film, and literary features have been set.

Prehistoric Ireland

Away from the immediate seashore, the bogs of the early post-Ice Age dominated the landscape, to be grown over with bushes and, eventually, the mighty oak forests. Though many of the oak trees were cut down during the colonial era, place names attesting to their existence are scattered across Ireland (Derry, Edenderry, Derryaghy, Derryconor, etc.), and "bog oak"—the stumps of the great forests—are covered only thinly by the bogs. To this day, the lush inland regions contrast markedly with the now-treeless coastal areas.

The Proto-Indo-European word for tree, *deru*, appears in Irish as *doire*, "oak," anglicized as "derry." The city of Derry in Northern Ireland is named for its oak. This word is also the root for such English words as true, truth, troth, trust, and truce. Consider the possibility that in the presence of one of the great oak trees, where legal cases were once presided over by judges called *brehons*, one had to speak the truth. Do you ever touch wood to make something true? Conflicting theories explain that one touches wood (symbolic of the Christian cross) to make one's desires come true, or that one touches wood because "tree" = "true" and they literally share the same root.

According to DNA evidence, the people of Ireland and Scotland are not closely related to the Celts who migrated from Central Europe; instead, waves of people came north from the Iberian peninsula and along the Atlantic coast, shifting the population from hunter-gatherers, over time, to farmers in family-based settlements (Sykes 2006: 281). Mesolithic peoples of Irish antiquity were joined by groups of Celts who intermarried. While some Irish identity is bound up in the idea of an alleged "Celtic race," that identity developed only in the past few hundred years, and did so because of trends in philosophy, literature, and the arts.

The people living in Ireland prior to the arrival of the Celts possessed exceptional technological skills when it came to the movement of stone. Ireland is rich in megalithic tombs of various kinds, at least two hundred stone circles, and dozens of standing stones. If you know only of England's Stonehenge, then Ireland will seem like an archaeologist's dream come true. The tombs of Ireland (see Figure 2.2) are divided into multi-chambered court tombs (mostly in the north), single-chamber table-shaped portal tombs (also called dolmens, and also mostly in the north), and passage tombs (one reaches a central chamber through a long passage underground).

One of Ireland's most famous monuments is Newgrange, a Neolithic passage tomb, built well before the Pyramids at Giza in Egypt. Figure 2.3 shows not just the opening in Newgrange that allows the midwinter sun to illuminate the central chamber of the tomb, but also the spectacular stone with its spirals that lies prone in front of the

Figure 2.2   The 5,000-year-old Poulnabrone dolmen in County Clare

Figure 2.3   The opening at Newgrange

entrance. Today some of the stone circles, dolmens, standing stones, hillforts, and other structures are maintained as a part of Dúchas, the Irish Heritage Commission. Most of them are unexcavated, and are partly or wholly obscured by the encroaching bog, or lie in a farmer's field untended, surrounded by farm animals, and marked on a map with only a tiny symbol of a dolmen.

By about 200 B.C.E., Ireland was home to approximately 150 structured, small-scale kingdoms called *tuath*. These small kingdoms were centered on ring forts (circular earthen forts that provided some protection to the people, goods, and animals within). Thousands of these unmistakable earthworks still exist in Ireland, though—as with the megalithic structures—they are largely unexcavated and unmarked. Local rulers governed the small kingdoms, and they in turn were generally answerable to a provincial ruler (Cronin 2001: 3). Although Ireland was home to a series of High Kings who ruled from Tara in County Meath from before the Celts arrived, the balance of power shifted continually among royal family members, between areas large and small, and according to shifts in political allegiance. Tara is the best known of the royal sites (Raftery 1994: 65); not far from Dublin, it is on a hill with commanding views, earthworks, and a standing stone called the *Lia Fáil*, often translated as the "Stone of Destiny," that was the location of rites leading to the accession of the kingship at Tara.

Telling the Early Stories

At this point in Ireland's history (1st millennium B.C.E.), people were still clearing land and settling down to farming life. In addition to unearthing stone axes, archaeologists have found bronze beakers, flint tools, and pottery made by hand; people also built walled enclosures with rectangular and circular houses inside. The people managed cattle (an essential source of early wealth) and grew grains (protected from rodents by cats).

Cows (*bó*, as in "bovine") and bulls (*tarbh*) in particular feature prominently in early Irish mythology, most dramatically in the epic *Táin Bó Cuailnge*, the Cattle Raid of Cooley. Published versions of the *Táin* (pronounced "*taw*-yn" or "*toyn*") represent selections from a much larger oral tradition, originally transcribed in Old Irish. Each chapter represents an individual tale that would have been told over a series of evenings, and each tale was told to a Christian scholar-monk, who wrote that tale down in weeks or even months. Sometimes the monks changed the story so that it had a Christian feel to it; other times they changed it to punish women for being warrior-like or for being too sexual. Sometimes they wrote their own comments in the margins. Many of the inconsistencies in the *Táin* can be easily resolved by remembering that oral tradition is highly localized, and that Christian scholar-monks, too, were individuals with their own needs and interests.

These and other stories often begin with a question, followed by the answer in the form of a story; it is a classic narrative device from oral tradition. Other features of early Irish oral tradition (as transcribed in the earliest texts) include women serving as prophetesses and bards, lists of people, places, and names, and the use of stories about kings and queens to discuss gods and goddesses. Many of the earliest transcriptions from oral tradition include sections of poetry, which could possibly have been chanted to accompaniment. Hugh Shields points out that the performance of the stories did not necessarily include reference to singing, but rather to "reciting," and often with harp accompaniment (Shields 1993: 17).

Story types in Old Irish include *scél* (tidyings), *tochmarc* (courtship), *tógáil* (destruction), *acallam* (conversation), *macgnímartha* (boyhood deeds), *aided* (slaughter), *aisling* (vision), *compert* (begetting), *immram* (rowing to the otherworld), *echtra* (adventures in the otherworld), and *táin bó* (cattle raid). Some of these are explanations of life cycle issues, while others describe pilgrimage or war and death. At the time in which the *Táin* was set (several hundred years B.C.E.), the pre-Celtic and Celtic peoples were intermeshed through trade and intermarriage.

In the *Táin Bó Cuailnge*, partners Medb ("Maeve") and Ailill brag about their respective wealth. Ailill describes an extraordinary bull in his possession, and Medb has to find one to match it. She sends her armies north to Ulster to steal their magnificent bull, thousands of warriors die, many side-plots occur, and eventually the two bulls fight a glorious battle. The story is complex and fascinating, and includes passages of both oral prose and poetry. In reciting the story out loud, the poetic sections would have been chanted. The mighty warrior Cú Chulainn ("coo KHULL-in") is a part of this battle, and at one point he chants the following in the *Táin*:

> This great deed of mine outshines
> The brilliant spectral army
> Thunderstruck by my attack
> Lightning is the war I wage
> Against the hidden squadrons
> Likewise Ailill likewise Medb
> Unfostering their dark arts
> Through women conspirators
> Who stalk with cold treachery
> Over the true warrior
> And his words of brave advice
> That shine all the more brilliant
> Because of his true deeds.

(Carson 2007: 97)

Descriptions of the Irish warriors and their behavior in the *Táin* precisely match those of the chariot-riding warriors in the *Iliad* of Homer as well as the *Mahabharata* of India (Byrne 1995: 43). The *Táin* is considered by many to be the great Irish epic, and many of its smaller stories are still a part of oral tradition. Like most epics from oral tradition, the *Táin* has many versions, and each new telling of it reflects important local priorities, figures of speech, and stylistic differences from storyteller to storyteller.

Ireland's bogs, earthworks, and many ancient tombs have yielded up extraordinary treasures of bronze and gold. The National Museum in Dublin houses a set of bronze trumpets and rattles from the Late Bronze Age (ca. 700 B.C.E.), discovered in County Offaly. The Irish government does not automatically begin excavation on every newly found archaeological site (indeed, it is not good archaeological practice to excavate more than ten percent of any site because techniques improve over time), but many more instruments could still be buried. Decorative designs at this time included spirals, chevrons, diamonds, and suns. The figure of a cross inside a circle, which appears on more recent high crosses (Figure 2.4), is often held up as a symbol of the dialogue between pagan (the circle—cycles of seasons, representing the sky god Lúgh in the form of the sun, and other concepts) and Christian (the cross); however, its roots are pre-Christian. To this day, Irish brown bread is shaped in a circle and marked with a cross; see the recipe for an Irish meal in Appendix 2. Some people believe that the circle of the cross (and the bread) is a reference to the cyclic nature of Irish time, to the symbol of the snake with its tail in its mouth, and to other Irish (or Irish-American) beliefs.

Because the first actual writing in Ireland came with the Christians in the fifth century, we have no written record of what kind of music, exactly, was being played and sung in Ireland in the years prior to their arrival; however, we have some clues from oral tradition, written down centuries later. We also have some ideas from old stone carvings, but their clues are inexact. And since the Romans never conquered Ireland, neither their arrow-straight roads (or perfect bridges, or still-functional aqueducts) nor their detailed descriptions of the people they encountered can enlighten us very much about

Figure 2.4 High cross with the cross inside a circle

Ireland. What the Romans did, though, was to give the island a name based on limited trade in the Irish southeastern corner, and on what they knew about it: Hibernia, the place of winter.

Ireland in the millennium before Christianity was a warrior culture, and in the context of war, one's good name was paramount. One could even say that the word of the deed was more important than the deed! To be shamed in public was worse than death, and words held a great deal of power. It should come as no surprise, then, that the right words at the right time could make or break someone's reputation (or break someone's nose, as in the proverb *Is minic a bhris béal duine a shrón*, "It's often a person's mouth broke his own nose"). The Irish word for both warrior deeds and words about those deeds is *gaisce* (pronounced "*gesh*-ka"); being able to praise one person, or shame another, made the speaker, reciter, or singer very powerful indeed. An Irish song or story about a battle brings honor not just to the battler, but to the singer or storyteller as well.

Epic or heroic songs—referred to as lays (Irish: *laoithe*)—were not restricted to Ireland, but were also performed in Scotland and the Isle of Man. These were story songs providing a long form of oral literature, and are almost entirely gone from the Irish narrative landscape.

> The lays were basically heroic song and they compare, in spite of differences of length, style or form, with the heroic song of Homer, medieval France, the Russian court of Kiev, or the West African Sunjata epic. All these describe heroic deeds modeled upon the ethos of a class of nobility while at the same time they address society at large.
>
> (Shields 1993: 4)

Lays include the rich mythology of Ireland, now told mostly through stories and read in books. Lays celebrate characters such as Fionn MacCumhaill (pronounced "Finn MacCool"), his son Oisín ("*Ush*-een"), and his rival Diarmaid ("*Der*-mwid"), but they also celebrate the lives of saints such as Patrick and Brigid (see below). Like a good story, a lay can present fantastical creatures, eclipse time, and bring impossible-seeming conclusions. The following story, about the birth and upbringing of Fionn MacCumhaill, was transcribed from the storytelling of Joe Heaney of Carna (Connemara); it gives a sense of the great deeds ascribed to mythological warriors of the past.

> Fionn MacCumhaill's mother was a Dé Danann. And therefore she had great power. And it was forecast that the night that Fionn MacCumhaill would be born, his father would be killed by another clan, the Morna clan. The Morna clan was trying to take over chieftains of the Fianna Éireann. And to qualify to be a member of the Fianna Éireann, your minimum height had to be seven foot six. Otherwise, they made an envoy of you. And they reckon, there was never any invasion of Ireland while they lived, until the Milesians of course came, and that's another story.
>
> However, when Fionn MacCumhaill, the night he was born, right enough, Goll mac Morna, who was the strongest of the Morna clan, killed Cumhaill, who was the father of Fionn. The reason he was called Fionn is because he had fair hair. Now they say when Fionn MacCumhaill was born, and the news came

to his wife that he [the father] was killed, she threw the little child out through the window, and the child fell into the river, and he was only about six hours old. And they saw, the Morna clan came, and they saw this happening, and they went home, convinced he was dead. And his mother ran out to the river, crying, and what do you know? She saw Fionn MacCumhaill as a six-hour-old baby coming out of the river, with a salmon in each hand and one in his mouth. And she said, 'You'll do.'

Ah, she took him with her then, and she took him down, all the way to the south of Ireland, where there was two old women, that she relied on, to keep the secret about him being alive. But she did, they did keep the secret, and Fionn MacCumhaill started growing up to be very good at everything. Because at that time, the old witches, there were two old witches, they could beat a blow as good as a man. They could do every trick in the book, they could use a sword, they could hunt, they could throw the arrow, they could do anything. And they taught Fionn everything he should know before he set out on his own.

In this story (and in many stories about hero-warriors), showing early promise is essential. If Fionn MacCumhaill could already catch three salmon (note the magic number three) as a six-hour-old baby (a multiple of three), he could hardly show earlier promise! Prowess in fishing is important for coastal people; salmon are among the "power animals" of ancient Ireland (MacKillop 1998: 332). To catch salmon so early marks the hero as a gifted person indeed. Heaney then discusses Fionn's training with "the witches." It was common in the early stories for Irish hero-warriors to be trained to fight by older women, who were themselves mighty warriors. "And they taught Fionn everything he should know" is a nod to the power and training ability of older women. Note that when his first major test comes, he is eighteen, another multiple of three. The story continues:

And when he was eighteen years of age, one of the old women told him, 'Now we'll call you Fionn, because you have fair hair, but you should go to Tara.' Well, this was the seat of the Fianna, Tara, in County Meath. That's where the Fianna had their court. At that time it was called court, not palace, everything was court, *cúirt*.

So he was saddling along, till he came to a river. And there was an old man with a fishing rod, fishing and sitting on a chair. And without looking behind him, the old man said, 'For fifty years I've been fishing for a certain salmon. And I was told that I wouldn't get it until Fionn MacCumhaill came up to where I was fishing.' And at that very minute he caught the salmon, the salmon of knowledge, they called it. Anybody who tasted the salmon would have the gift of all knowledge, to see the future, and everything that was going to happen to himself, or to any friends of his.

And he took the salmon and put it on a spit, and he asked Fionn, he lit the fire under it and he told Fionn MacCumhaill, 'Keep turning the salmon. I'm going to lie down for awhile, and when I wake up, I want you to have the salmon ready for me. But I don't want you to eat any of that salmon till I get up.' And Fionn was getting the salmon, turning it around, and a big air bubble appeared on the side of the salmon. And Fionn thought to himself, 'Ah, the old man'll be angry with me now for spoiling the salmon,' and put a thumb on the bubble and he burned his thumb, and he put his thumb in his mouth. And that's where they said, he got the voice spoke to him. 'Now, Fionn MacCumhaill, you're the one that's got the gift. But since you didn't eat the salmon, when you want to find out something, you'll have to chew your thumb to the bone, and from the bone to the marrow, before you can get any knowledge you're looking for.'

And when the old man came out, he said to Fionn, 'What happened?' and he told him the truth. 'Well now,' he said, 'you may as well eat the salmon altogether, because I can't eat it now,' but because he didn't do that first, because he touched the bubble he still couldn't have the information he looked for until he chewed his thumb. And anytime he wanted to do it, it caused him so much pain, it's the last thing he wanted to do was chew his thumb. *You* try chewing your thumb into the marrow.

Salmon reappears in the next stage of the story, again as a power animal and conveyor of knowledge. Fionn MacCumhaill is actually alleged to have caught two different salmons of knowledge: at Linn Féic (on the Boyne river) and at Assaroe (on the Erne river). The salmon themselves gain wisdom by eating hazelnuts and berries, which are themselves imbued with magical power (MacKillop 1998: 332). This section of the tale incorporates some of the standard elements of the helper figure (whose name is Finnéces), the hero breaking a taboo, and the hero suffering to obtain information. In the last part of the story, Fionn becomes a full-fledged adult warrior by performing a heroic deed and saving the lives of people at court:

So the old man said to him, 'You should go to Tara—*Temhair na Rí*, Tara of the Kings—and try to get your father's job back, as chief of the Fianna Éireann.' So away he goes, and he came to Tara. And he hit the battle drum. In all these courts there was a battle drum outside, now something like a *bodhrán*, like a tambourine, there's plenty of them around. You hit that once if you wanted to be let in. You hit it twice if you wanted to challenge somebody.

But an old man came up to him, and he said, 'You're Fionn MacCumhaill, you're Cumhaill's son.' He said, 'I am.' He said, 'I won't tell anybody. But I'll give you this sword. While you have this sword, you can see everybody, and nobody can see you. While you hold this cloak I'm going to give you, over you, you'll keep awake when everybody else is asleep. Because tonight,' he said, 'there's going to be a big challenge here. Every first of May—and this was the first of May again—there's a magician comes to Tara. And he destroys all the crops, all the coach horses, he kills all the cattle, and everybody falls asleep when he blows his horn. So the morning after, everything is dead except the people inside the court. They're alive, when they wake up, the damage is done, and he's away.' And he said to Fionn, 'If you want to get your father's seat back, you'll do what I tell you to do: wear the cloak at midnight, and then you'll stay awake. Wear this sword, and you can see the fellow when he's coming to do the damage, he cannot see you. And when the time is right, throw the sword, and the sword will never miss the target.'

So at night they all prepared because they knew this fellow was coming, and the king, King Cormac said, 'The person who can save Tara can have anything he wants. If I find one man in my court who'll save Tara,' and Cumhaill's son Fionn stood up and said, 'I'll save it.' He still didn't know who he was. The old man did, but the king didn't.

So at midnight, the bugle sounded; everybody fell asleep. And Fionn MacCumhaill put on the cloak and he woke, he stayed awake and he walked outside. And it wasn't long till he saw this terrible whirlwind coming toward him. And this fellow, he had four horns and two wings. And he coming blowing, blowing flames out of his mouth, burning everything before him, killing everything before him, and Fionn saw him, but he didn't see Fionn. And when he came near enough, Fionn threw the sword right through the heart, and he fell down, and a big pool appeared where he fell. And anything that went near that pool afterward, died before they ever reached the pool.

Following morning, everything was safe when they all woke up and the king came to him and he said, 'You saved Tara. Now, you can have anything you want. But first of all, I want to know your name.' 'I'm the son,' he said, 'of Cumhaill, that was killed by Goll mac Morna. I want my father's job as leader of the Fianna Éireann. And I want Goll mac Morna to promise to be loyal to me from now on.' And it was there and then they did that, and that's how he got the job as leader of the Fianna Éireann back. And he controlled them, and you see, they were awful good people, the Fianna, they were terrible respect—*gallant*, as they called it—respectful toward women.

This story, together with a few songs dealing with similar material, are still a part of oral tradition. Fionn MacCumhaill is considered one of the great Irish hero-warriors, but many more men and women make up the pantheon of characters celebrated in stories and lays. Note that this event occurs at the eve of 1 May, the feast of Bealtaine. Bealtaine, one of the four major ancient Irish festivals, represents the official beginning of summer (see below). Each of the helper figures in this particular story is elderly ("and then an old man... "), and Fionn's motivation for saving the people of Tara is to regain the seat at court that was usurped by his father's rival. Setting standards for respectful behavior toward one's elders is often an aspect of Irish storytelling. At the end of each of the three sections of this story, Joe Heaney interjects something of his own: the "you'll do" comment from Fionn's mother, the suggestion that the audience members try chewing their thumbs to the marrow, and the commentary about the Fianna Éireann being *gallant* toward women. In each case, he elicited a laugh from the audience and brought them back to themselves while giving a nod to the mundane.

Cú Chulainn, Fionn MacCumhaill, Oisín, Deirdre of the Sorrows, and other characters fascinated the members of the Anglo-Irish literary movement at the turn of the twentieth century. Like many Irish people before and after them, the poet William Butler Yeats, writer Lady Augusta Gregory, and others used these heroes and heroines in poetry, short stories, and plays to spur the youth of Ireland to great deeds (see Chapter 3). While stories about early Irish mythological characters are still told out loud, and written versions of them appear by the ninth century, nothing was written down in Latin (or Irish) until the arrival of St. Patrick and his cohorts. Yet even St. Patrick's story was woven into oral tradition, which would have him in dialogue with Fionn's son Oisín (Shields 1993: 13). The real St. Patrick might have been surprised to find himself in such a conversation with a mythological person!

Brigid and Patrick

Irish spirituality, which has figured so prominently in the production, support, and condemnation of music over the centuries, was both rich and complicated prior to the arrival of Christianity, and it has continued thereafter into the present. Early religious activity was localized, not nationalized, and revolved around multiple goddess figures, particularly Brigid (pronounced "Bridget") and her various manifestations. The goddess Brigid, for whom the later Saint Bridget was named, is related to Brigantia, for whom Britain as well as Bregenz in Austria, Bragança in Portugal, and Brigetio in Hungary were named. Gods included Lúgh, the sun god (represented in other European cultures as Loki, Luke, Louis, and Lucifer among others, and represented in place names such as Lugos, Luzern, and Lyons). What we know of ancient Irish religious practices was notated by scholar-monks as late as the ninth century (four centuries after the arrival of Christianity).

In the first millennium C.E., priests could and did marry and raise children; celibacy was not an essential aspect of early monastic living; and some of the earlier, goddess-based traditions co-existed smoothly with some of the later, patriarchal traditions for centuries. Furthermore, men and women were not always separated in monastic centers, nor were men the exclusive holders of power and knowledge in the Church. In the early years, women had reason to embrace the Church for its shift away from warrior culture, which had resulted in so much death for lovers, husbands, brothers, and sons. It represented a new way of living in which people, especially men, could live in peace. The Church that came to dominate Irish religious, educational, and political life by the late nineteenth and twentieth centuries had changed slowly but dramatically over the centuries from one that closely linked with existing local traditions to one that determined, regulated, and sometimes abolished them.

It is possible to piece together some ideas about what may have been important to the early Irish, understanding of course that oral traditions change over time, that power lies in the hands of those who transcribe, and that history is written by the victors. For several centuries, however, the beliefs of the early Irish spiritual leaders were not incompatible with those of the Christian missionaries. Both traditions held the natural world in reverence, for example. Rivers carried the names of goddesses (the Rivers Shannon, Boyne, Liffey, and others), in keeping with Indo-European traditions linking women and water. Living as a hermit was a common practice, except that the earliest Christians were not really alone. "Green martyrdom" was a state of human solitude in nature, in which one's companions were birds and other creatures. While someone today might consider having only birds and small animals for company to be terribly lonely or even frightening, the early Christians considered themselves to be in excellent company. Consider the following poem, written anonymously in the ninth century:

The Scribe

Dom-fharcaí fidbaide fál	A hedge of trees surrounds me
Fom-chain loíd luin, lúad nád cél;	A blackbird sings to me
Húas mo lebrán ind línech	Above my lined booklet
Fom-chain trírech inna n-én.	The birds chant their songs to me.
Fom-chain coí menn, medair mass,	The cuckoo sings to me lovely and clear
Hi mbrot glass de dindgnaib doss	In a grey cloak from the ramparts of bushes.
Debrath! Nom-Choimmdiu coíma,	Well indeed does the Lord look after me
Caín-scríbaimm fo roída ross.	As I write with care in the woodland shade.

Christian beliefs wove their way gradually into existing beliefs, linking the important pagan celebrations with Christian ones, and replacing gods and goddesses with saints. The most important holidays among the Irish were those marking the seasons of the year, and included music and dance. Notice that in each case, a Christian religious holiday is now in place of an older pagan celebration. Such celebrations, particularly Lúghnasa, were times of great gatherings, feasting, and music. All the native Irish holidays begin in the evening before and run through the following day; Christian tradition begins the day with the rising of the sun in the morning.

> *Samhain*: New Year's Eve (31 October, evening)–All Soul's Day (1 Nov.)
> *Imbolc*: Brigid's Day and the start of Spring (31 January, evening)–Candlemas (2 Feb.)
> *Bealtaine*: the start of summer (30 April evening)–Mary's feast day (1 May)
> *Lúghnasa*: festival of Lúgh, the harvest time (31 July, evening)–Lammas (1 Aug.)

Brigid the saint was rumored to have been born in a doorway, born of a nobleman and a slave. Both of those elements related to her birth place her in liminal or in-between status, and indeed she was partly connected to her namesake the goddess Brigid, and partly connected to Christianity. In addition to becoming an ordained abbess, she also kept the sacred fire (symbolic of the goddess Brigid) burning in Kildare, a place whose name translates as "church of the oak" (remember the significance of oak!). Folkloric accounts place her at about the time of St. Patrick and include arguments and discussions between them, but she (and several other religious figures also named Brigid) actually lived later, in the sixth century. She is characterized as performing miracles consistent with the goddess, and of being "the healer, the wise woman, speaking with animals and controlling the forces of nature" (McCaffrey and Eaton 2002: 117). The following is a poem attributed to her, and reveals much about the early Irish value of hospitality:

The Heavenly Banquet

I would like to have the men of Heaven
in my own house;
with vats of good cheer
laid out for them.

I would like to have the three Marys,
their fame is so great.
I would like people
from every corner of Heaven.

I would like them to be cheerful
in their drinking.
I would like to have Jesus, too,
here amongst them.

I would like a great lake of beer
for the King of Kings.
I would like to be watching Heaven's family
drinking it through all eternity.

St. Patrick, Ireland's most famous saint, was born into a Welsh noble family but was captured and served as a slave before escaping. He later returned to Ireland, and is best known for having been the primary spearhead for the Christianization of the island. Many others were evangelizing in Ireland too, but Patrick is given the bulk of the credit and is, for many Irish, a beloved saint. While this information might disappoint legions of American schoolchildren, Patrick did *not* drive the snakes out of Ireland; there were no snakes! However, the serpent is a common representative image of the goddess across Indo-Europe, and it is safe to say that because of Patrick and his contemporaries—and the generations of Christians that followed—the serpent was, in fact, shown the door over time. Compare the poem attributed to Brigid, with its celebration of beer and everyone drinking in companionship, with this poem attributed to St. Patrick:

Saint Patrick's Breastplate

I arise today
Through a mighty strength, the invocation of the Trinity,
Through the belief in the threeness,
Through confession of the oneness
Of the Creator of Creation.

I arise today
Through the strength of Christ's birth with his baptism,
Through the strength of his crucifixion with his burial,

Through the strength of his resurrection with his ascension,
Through the strength of his descent for the judgment of Doom.

I arise today
Through the strength of the love of Cherubim,
In obedience of angels,
In the service of archangels,
In hope of resurrection to meet with reward,
In prayers of patriarchs,
In predictions of prophets,
In preaching of apostles,
In faith of confessors,
In innocence of holy virgins,
In deeds of righteous men.

I arise today
Through the strength of heaven:
Light of sun,
Radiance of moon,
Splendor of fire,
Speed of lightning,
Swiftness of wind,
Depth of sea,
Stability of earth,
Firmness of rock.

I arise today
Through God's strength to pilot me:
God's might to uphold me,
God's wisdom to guide me,
God's eye to look before me,
God's ear to hear me,
God's word to speak for me,
God's hand to guard me,
God's way to lie before me,
God's shield to protect me,
God's host to save me
From snares of devils,
From temptations of vices,
From everyone who shall wish me ill,
Afar and anear,
Alone and in multitude.

I summon today all these powers between me and those evils,
Against every cruel merciless power that may oppose my body and soul,
Against incantations of false prophets,

Against black laws of pagandom
Against false laws of heretics,
Against craft of idolatry,
Against spells of witches and smiths and wizards,
Against every knowledge that corrupts man's body and soul.

Christ to shield me today
Against poison, against burning,
Against drowning, against wounding,
So that there may come to me abundance of reward.
Christ with me, Christ before me, Christ behind me,
Christ in me, Christ beneath me, Christ above me,
Christ on my right, Christ on my left,
Christ when I lie down, Christ when I sit down, Christ when I arise,
Christ in the heart of every man who thinks of me,
Christ in the mouth of everyone who speaks of me,
Christ in every eye that sees me,
Christ in every ear that hears me.

I arise today
Through a mighty strength, the invocation of the Trinity,
Through belief in the threeness,
Through confession of the oneness,
Of the Creator of Creation.

Patrick's poem is significantly more Christian than Brigid's, yet his also has elements of reverence toward nature (the sun, moon, fire, lightning, wind, sea, earth, rock). It is incorrect to imagine that the early Christians in Ireland were single-minded in their pursuit of countrywide conversion, yet it is also important to notice that Patrick effectively surrounds himself with Christ as protection against what are clearly pagan elements. In addition to raising families, studying the arts and music, writing, noting down lively stories from oral tradition, and other activities, some of the monks were warriors themselves, defending their own monastery against other monasteries (McCaffrey and Eaton 2002: 134).

Patrick and the other Christians were operating in a region where power was centered in people, places, things, and ideas. Among the people who wielded power were the druids, the Irish priestly class. As a stratified group of people, the Irish lived with a range of hierarchies of class, knowledge (both esoteric and practical), and skill. Both men and women were respected authorities of different domains, and the historical texts generally present male druids in the role of gifted advisors to kings. They were also responsible for the perpetuation of Irish ritual life. No verifiable verses from druids exist, but they appear frequently in sources of early Irish mythology. Women prophetesses also appear (for example, in the great epic *Táin Bó Cuailnge*); while both men and women had the gift of prophesy, only men could bear the title of druid. In addition, druids were associated with both magical capability and with trees; the name druid itself can be drawn from either *draiocht*, "magic," or the proto-Indo-European *deru-, "tree," in combination with *wid*, "wise": "tree-wise." Like those of the many other culture-bearers of the first millennium C.E., the functions of the druids were gradually taken over by the church and other institutions.

Amairgin (a name ascribed to several people—real and mythological—in Irish history) is known as a poet, a druid, *and* a judge in early Irish legends (MacKillop 1998: 13). He is often compared to the Welsh poet Taliesin, and may have served as a model for stories about Taliesin (or vice versa). Compare St. Patrick's poem, above, with the well-known "Song of Amairgin." How different is Patrick's "I arise today" refrain from Amairgin's "I am… "?

> I am the wind that breathes upon the sea
> I am the wave of the ocean
> I am the murmur of the billows
> I am the ox of the seven combats
> I am the vulture upon the rocks
> I am a beam of the sun
> I am the fairest of plants
> I am a wild boar in valour
> I am a salmon in the water
> I am a lake in the plain
> I am a word of science
> I am the point of the lance of battle
> I am the God who created in the head the fire
> Who is it who throws light into the meeting on the mountain?
> Who announces the ages of the moon?
> Who teaches the place where couches the sun? (If not I?)

Another great bearer of cultural power was the *brehon*, a type of early Irish judge. The *brehons* wielded their own type of power in that they were responsible for dispensing justice and mediating between individuals and communities:

> One of the most informative of these tracts is *Crith Gabhlach*, which was written down towards the end of the eighth century. Focusing on social status, it refers explicitly to the legal standing of the *cruitire* or harper and places him above all other musicians in the social pyramid. Beneath him was a rabble of unfree musicians referred to as 'singers of *crónán*,' jugglers, mummers and buffoons, who had no legal franchise beyond that of the patrons who kept them.
>
> (Ó hAllmhuráin 1998: 15)

Laws also governed the use of the harp's tuning key and the legal status of various musicians. The *brehons* also documented their opinions on the disposition of property, restitution for crimes committed, various types of marriage into which the population could enter, inheritance laws, and land disputes. They are among the oldest written laws in Western Europe, and are still discussed among members of the contemporary legal system in Ireland, particularly for their rulings on restorative justice.

Given the importance of the warrior deed, Patrick emerged as a kind of warrior in Ireland because of one particular moment. He chose a hilltop near the Hill of Tara (the seat of the High Kings) and lit a bonfire on Bealtaine eve, the night that all the fires were supposed to be extinguished and lit anew. In doing so he successfully challenged the authority of the druids by laying claim to one of the most important pagan rituals. The celebration of St. Patrick's Day was until recently a fairly muted and personal affair in Ireland; however, because of the tremendous influence that North America has on Ireland, St. Patrick's Day in Ireland is now celebrated with parades, pipers, dancing, and general festivities.

Ireland's prehistoric standing stones serve as memorials, but also as important Christian pilgrimage and courtship sites. Even though their use has changed dramatically over time (shifting from pagan to Christian, for example), standing stones are still treated with some respect in Ireland. In Figure 2.5 one of a handful of standing stones in Glencolumbkille (Co. Donegal) has served as a station on the pilgrimage trail in honor of the valley's patron saint, Columba. Note the cross carved into the upper portion of it, later than the original work. These stones belong to a much earlier period, and in fact the valley is home to untold riches of stone monuments, most of which are several thousand years old. In keeping with the Irish tendency toward blending the old with the new, however, the inclusion of a carved standing stone from the Neolithic Era (ca. 2,000 B.C.E.) in twenty-first-century Catholic pilgrimage rituals is not particularly unusual. What might be even more unusual would be the enactment of a contemporary Catholic pilgrimage ritual that *ignored* the enduring presence of older beliefs represented by the presence of that standing stone.

Figure 2.5 Standing stone in Glencolumbkille

The monastic center of Clonmacnoise, not far from Galway, powerfully represents the strength of the Catholic Church in the first few centuries after Christianity arrived in Ireland. Developed in the seventh century, it has fortifications, round towers (tall, narrow bell towers, unique to Ireland), an excellent water and transportation source in the River Shannon, grain fields, and other amenities. Just outside the gates of Clonmacnoise is the women's church, an example of the incorporation of goddess-based traditions with Christianity. A typical Romanesque entrance, upon closer examination, reveals that the entrance is dotted with stone carvings in the shape of vulvas, and inside each one—at one time, prior to the church's Victorian-era "restoration"—was a small *sheela-na-gig*, a stone figure of a woman's face dominating a tiny body with legs spread open above her head. Only one *sheela-na-gig* remains at the site (barely visible in Figure 2.6); the rest of the *sheelas* have been deliberately shattered. Surrounding the door is the characteristic shape of a serpent, but with two nipples visible on the left side of the entrance, just in case the goddess symbolism was unclear! That this symbol-rich place of Christian worship should exist right next to—and in conjunction with—Clonmacnoise explains some of the ways in which the two traditions could, and did, combine.

The monasteries were great centers of learning, music, and art. Some of the monasteries had workmen devoted to creating what are now the justly famous high crosses—stone crosses twenty feet high or more—dating from the ninth century, with illustrations of scenes from the Bible to teach those who could not read. In addition, some of the stonework reveals musicians playing instruments—a harp, for example, or a set of pipes. The historians who documented the music, dance, and other aspects of Irish traditional culture focused entirely on male musicians; however, based on

Figure 2.6 Doorway of the women's church at Clonmacnoise

other elements such as the quasi-evidence discussed in mythological transcriptions, women had a more important role than some of the male scribes might have wished to admit.

Some of the larger monasteries held scriptoria, where copyists would painstakingly make duplicate pages of the great works of the time. The Book of Kells—a copy of the Four Gospels of the Bible—is one such famous work, with its dazzling illuminations of letters, human figures, and animals. It rests in muted light in the library at Trinity College in Dublin, close to one of the oldest harps in Ireland and surrounded by stunning first editions of books from hundreds of years ago. Though the text is neither Irish nor *in* Irish (it is in Latin), a number of features reveal it to be more thoroughly Irish than any other copy of the Four Gospels. For example, stylized animals in the margins of certain pages of the text run, leap, reveal their intimate body parts, yawn, vomit, run off with a communion wafer, have sex (both gay and straight), and skid to a halt in front of letters. The "Irish" aspect of this detail is that the Irish monks, who were often themselves poets well versed in Irish tradition, wove the natural world into their artwork as well as their writing. In addition to being gorgeously illustrated, decorated with the most extraordinary details, and quite revealing of the highest artistic standards of the time, the Book of Kells (available for viewing online) includes elements that are also delightfully funny. Although they were consummate artists, scholars, and devoted Christians, the monks of the scriptorium were also thoroughly human.

Some of the Irish monasteries were as large and diverse as cities, and they were rich in musical activity. The high crosses—designed as a visual aid to spreading the story of the Gospels—included depictions of music. Though the stone carvings have blurred over time (Figure 2.7), one can still see the image of a piper.

Plainchant (monophonic singing of religious texts) became an established practice. Most melodies and lyrics derive from continental (and English) sources, but neither place developed hymns for Irish saints, so when feast days were celebrated, local melodies were used. Some of these may have been a root source for some of the *sean-nós* (old-style song) melodies of the Gaeltacht. About 20 percent of the melodies from early Irish hymnals came neither from England nor from the Continent, and were quite possibly of Irish origin (Brannon 1993: 36). Furthermore, though the harp is associated with the bards (see below), written records describe Irish clergy playing the harp to accompany the psalms, as in the tradition of King David (Ní Riain 1993: 191; Ralls-MacLeod 2000: 54).

In Irish mythology the use of music as a magical weapon appears in several of the oldest texts. Gearóid Ó hAllmhuráin mentions the Battle of Magh Tuireadh, in which a harper plays in such a way as to disable his listener, allowing him (and his instrument) to escape; he cites passages from other tales in which music plays a strong and effective role in helping secure a victory, defy death, or shame an enemy (Ó hAllmhuráin 1998: 18).

The Arrival of the Vikings and the Normans

By the time the first Vikings arrived in County Antrim at the end of the eighth century, the coastal communities lay completely unprotected from attack by sea or river. Monasteries, with their rich collections of silver and gold metalwork, were raided repeatedly by successive waves of Vikings. The monastic center of Clonmacnoise, for

Figure 2.7   A piper on the Cross of the Scriptures at Clonmacnoise

example, was raided seven times. In Figure 2.8 one can see that the River Shannon is quite close to the monastery and provided an easy way for Viking ships to come right up to the door of the monastery from the ocean, year after year. One possible reason for the fact that so many gold items have been found buried (and so many lay as yet undiscovered) could be that they were tucked in a corner of the bog to hide them from the Vikings.

It is easy to imagine a monk of the ninth century, writing in the evening this oft-cited verse of his immense relief that the winter storms are too fierce to allow Vikings to come (de Paor 1995: 93):

A Stormy Night

Is aicher in gaíth innocht	The wind is rough tonight
Fu-fúasna fairge findfholt;	Tossing the white-combed ocean;
Ní ágor réimm mora mind	I need not dread fierce Vikings,
Dond láechraid lainn ua Lothlind.	Crossing the Irish Sea.

The Vikings began staying in Ireland during the winters by the mid-ninth century; in addition to their raids, they were also responsible for considerable trading, building, and settling, and for the establishment of walled cities. In fact, many Irish place names attest to a Viking past: Waterford, Wexford, Limerick, Cork, and Dublin.

Figure 2.8 Clonmacnoise monastery next to the River Shannon

Dublin in particular is deeply layered in Viking history; more artifacts, ships, and structures are unearthed each year as Dublin undergoes continuous development. The Viking raiders included both men and women, but they also intermarried with locals (McCaffrey and Eaton 2002: 204). Surnames such as McAuliffe, McLaughlin, and McIvor (and variants thereof) attest to Viking heritage. Whatever they may have done for Ireland in terms of developing the cities and adding variety to its genetic pool, however, there is no way to downplay their role as raiders and plunderers. The arts and music underwent a sharp decline during the time of the Vikings, as the wealth of the monasteries collapsed.

The warrior Brian Boru eventually defeated the Vikings in 1014 at Clontarf; the battle resulted in the deaths of over seven thousand people. Boru then became, briefly, the High King of Ireland, but was murdered shortly after his accession to the kingship. From that point onward, the center of Ireland was Dublin, not Tara; its position as Ireland's economic center, as well as its proximity to the ocean, was essential to commerce. Brian Boru is still revered as a mighty warrior; though the Vikings had been defeated, their settlements (and population, for the most part) remained in Ireland.

For the Anglo-Normans who followed, however, a different story emerges. The Normans (descendants of Vikings who had established a base in Normandy in what is now Western France) had taken over England in 1066 under the leadership of William the Conqueror. A little over a hundred years later, the (combined) Anglo-Normans invaded southeastern Ireland and gradually took control over much of the island, though it was not until the time of Henry VIII that the English held complete control. Over a period of several hundred years, the Anglo-Normans intermarried, assimilated, learned the Irish language, patronized Irish artists and musicians, and famously became "more Irish than the Irish themselves" (Ó hAllmhuráin 1998: 24). They brought with them historians and keepers of written records, and left an extraordinary legacy of large castles dotting the countryside (many of which are now in ruins, but others of which have been turned into rather impressive inns and hotels). In spite of the best efforts of the English to prevent the assimilation of the Anglo-Normans (including passing the Statutes of Kilkenny in 1366, forbidding the various Irish customs, language, and music patronage, along with intermarriage), the Anglo-Normans were there to stay. All the surnames beginning with *fitz-* (Fitzgerald, Fitzpatrick, etc.) connect the Norman French *fils* ("son") with the Irish.

With the twelfth-century reforms of the Church in Rome, Irish religious life (and the culture that it had developed) was dramatically and permanently altered. Before the twelfth century, the Irish Church had roughly followed the pre-Christian *Brehon* laws, which allowed divorce and a variety of options in marriage, among many other differences from Rome. In other words, the Church in Ireland was very much directed toward its own needs, not the needs of Rome. Once Rome gained control over Irish Catholicism, the great monastic centers of learning saw their power and influence reduced significantly, and everyone became answerable to Rome. Instead of remaining as centers of great teaching and learning, composition and creation of the arts, the monasteries eventually fell into ruin.

> The reform was a triumph for the administrators and a disaster for Irish literature and general culture. The reformers destroyed the social, economic, and cultural base of Irish learning. Nothing replaced the greater monasteries with their schools and learned cadres, which were now robbed of their resources and their status.
>
> (Donnchadh Ó Corráin, quoted in
> McCaffrey and Eaton 2002: 254)

Fortunately for Irish society and its culture, the collapse of the artistic patronage of the Church did not affect the concurrent secular patronage of the arts. The Anglo-Normans, in their movement toward assimilation with "Gaelic Ireland," continued the tradition of royal patronage by supporting poets, musicians, and other artists. The Welshman Giraldus Cambrensis, whose comments about musical variation we encountered in Chapter 1, was one of the historians who came to Ireland with the Anglo-Normans. He had this (and many other, largely disparaging, things) to say about the Irish:

> I find among these people commendable diligence only on musical instruments, on which they are incomparably more skilled than any other nation I have seen. Their style is quick and lively. It is remarkable that, with such rapid fingerwork, the musical rhythm is maintained and that, by unfailingly disciplined art, the integrity of the tune is fully preserved throughout the ornate rhythms and the profuse intricate polyphony.
>
> (cited in Ó hAllmhuráin 1998: 23)

Our Welsh historian would not have noted Irish musicianship with such admiration (particularly compared to how little he appreciated other elements of Irish society and culture) were it not already developed to a very high level. By the thirteenth century, when the Continent's musical development had shifted from monophony (single melody) toward polyphony (multiple melodies occurring simultaneously, particularly in vocal music), Ireland was experiencing a kind of Golden Age—a flowering of music, art, and literature similar to that which had taken place in the Arab world several centuries earlier.

The Time of the Bards

From the time that Ireland's people began to specialize in various activities according to skill and community needs, music and musicianship accrued value. In any stratified society, it is normal for certain people to have a stronger ability to focus, to remember, and to create. Such people might be raised in a family of like-minded members, or have a special aptitude, or they might be steered in that direction because other factors (for example, being visually impaired) prevented more physical activity. Over time, these people developed into a kind of living information storage and retrieval technology for their communities. The Old Irish word for them was *bard*.

A bard functions as a genealogist, accountant, geographer, political advisor, musician, and many other roles. Some of our earliest recorded acknowledgments of bards appear in the writings of the Christian monks, who notated a large number of stories from oral tradition. Think about what the many roles of a bard could be. The genealogist would keep track of your family lineage and who, in a society that favored fostering children and extended families, you might be related to through kin groups. The accountant would track your possessions, like a bank account except focusing on livestock (especially cattle) and acreage. The geographer would be able to discuss the origin of a place name or its history. A political advisor would remember what had taken place in previous battles with a neighboring kingdom, and make effective suggestions based on past experience. The musician would be able to provide varying entertainment over the very long, cold winter months. The Golden Age of the bards lasted for several hundred years, from the thirteenth to the early seventeenth century.

Culture bearers, in general, divided into multiple levels of status and position in society. Druids, poets, reciters, bards, and musicians were all kept separate by strict social rules involving patronage, hereditary lineages, and established rules about what could be done and said by whom. The ideal warrior or leader needed to be extremely brave in deeds, so as to be distinguished from other warriors. A mighty deed or warrior act won great praise. However, the highest priority was on the *word* of the deed, the *recounting* of the deed.

> It was the obligation of the poet to have this knowledge ready at call, and if faced by a demand to relate the associations of some deserted rath or lonely pillar stone he failed to render an exact and credible account, he was shamed to the very roots of his being.
>
> (Flower 1947: 1)

Some of the classes included druids, who were shamans charged with gifts of sight, hearing, and prophecy. *Breitheamhain* (often spelled and pronounced *brehon*) were knowledgeable about laws. *Oirfidigh* were musicians. The *filí* (singular *fileadh*) were very high-status professional poets. They were employed or patronized by select wealthy families throughout Ireland. Their job was to recite histories and genealogies, and to explain the names of people, places, and things. Bards were born into hereditary bardic families, but had to attend special schools to attain one of seven levels of expertise.

Ollamh was the highest level, which could be reached only after years of intensive study; think of it as a PhD or other high-level degree. Training was rigorous and included tests of one's abilities in improvisation, among other skills. However, the bardic schools (open to men and women) were not connected to the monastic schools. The bardic schools were secular, and their roots are believed to extend back before the entry of Christianity (Bergin 1913: 19). Part of what makes Ireland unique from the European mainstream in the medieval period is, for example, the idea that knowledge was not concentrated entirely in the monasteries, but existed concurrently in a secular body. In addition, the subjects taught included history, law, language, and literature (Corkery 1924: 80).

> As every Professor, or chief Poet, depended on some Prince or great Lord, that had endowed his Tribe, he was under strict ties to him and Family, as to record in good Metre his Marriages, Births, Deaths, Acquisitions made in war and Peace, Exploits, and other remarkable things relating to the Same. He was likewise bound to offer an Elegy on the Decease of the said Lord, his consort, or any of their children, and a Marriage Song when there should Occasion.
> (Memoirs of the Marquis of Clanricarde 1722, quoted in Bergin 1913)

The *fileadh*-in-training had to perform tasks such as composing in darkened rooms on specific subjects, and then presenting the compositions the following day. *Filí* were poets, but were neither songwriters nor singers. *Bards* were a step down from the *filí* or professional poet; they were nonprofessional verse-makers and singers with sixteen different levels of training and status. Each level of bard had its own limited number of syllabic verse forms to which it was restricted; bards were not allowed to compose in the more difficult poetic meters belonging to those in a higher category. Bards were not restricted to singing about a particular topic, however, as the *filí* were. Bards could sing about anything they wanted to. Also, they generally were not tied to a particular patron—being nonprofessionals—which freed them up for greater use of satire and shame. Bards could easily use some of the same techniques of praise or shame to manipulate a patron into offering payment of some kind: money, food, clothing, or lodging.

Visual impairment has rarely stopped people from becoming musicians. Some of the earliest depictions of musicians in the world, whether in paintings or temple carvings, have shown blind musicians playing some sort of plucked instrument, often a harp or a zither. Musicians who are relied upon to remember great epics, layers of facts, accounting of possessions, and the like, tend to play their instrument with an *ostinato* or basic repeating pattern. An *ostinato* provides a supportive background texture and can serve as a memory aid to the performer. The Five Blind Boys of Alabama, Stevie Wonder, Ray

Charles, Andrea Bocelli, and other musicians from many styles have been renowned performers who happen to be blind. In non-European cultures, these bards are also revered for their ability to praise, and feared for their equal ability to destroy a reputation. They are said to be able to "see" what isn't obvious.

Because the bards had to be extremely good with words and poetic forms, they paid close attention to special kinds of rhyme. This care extended to, and included, English-language songs. There were special names for each poetic type and rhyme scheme. The admiration, fear, and suspicion accorded people with such powerful memories and skills to praise and shame made the bards stand out in society. In general, the division of roles between poet, reciter, and musician meant that you might hear one person playing the harp (the *cruitire*) but another person reciting the poetry (the *reacaire*).

The Harp

The harp was one of the most favored instruments of the bards. In English we distinguish between a harper (one who performs vernacular music, including that of the Irish) and a harpist (a classical musician who performs solo or with other Western classical instrumentalists). The oldest evidence of the harp in Ireland is from about the ninth century, with all indications being that it had been there much longer. The basic shape of both the Irish and Scottish harps was and is that of a triangle, including metal strings and a resonating chamber with a crossbar to hold the strings. The earliest harps could fit on one's lap; they had about thirty strings. In the last several centuries, harps have been made successively larger. Harp makers continued to make a variety of harp sizes through the nineteenth century, at least partly because of the harp's connection to classical music and the expanding technical skill needed to play.

The Welsh and Irish were quite competitive about harping. Irish harpers were imported to Wales for several centuries to train the Welsh, who then took the basic concept of the harp and expanded it (see Chapter 4). Irish metal-strung harps were popular in Wales at first, but over time the Welsh harpers began to focus their attention on the local (gut-string) harp.

Many of the "big houses" (ones that patronized poets and harpers) included a poet and a harper in their retinue. The education of the harper was similar to that of the bardic schools, in which one studied rigorously, composed, improvised, and worked with the masters. Being a harper was a privilege that carried with it great responsibility to one's patron. For example, a harper might assist in some ceremonial duty, or take part in competitions between patrons, or simply escort the household into sleep each night. The term *planxty*, or praise tune, refers to melodies composed in honor of someone—a patron, a lover, a household guest—and some of them are still performed by harpers today (see Chapter 3).

> Harpers enjoyed a privileged position, receiving land, stock and protection free of rent and military obligation from their chieftain patrons in return for helping the patron fulfill ceremonial, ritual and social obligations by accompanying the intoning of clan genealogy and praise, lament and heroic poetry in addition to performing instrumental preludes, laments and salutes.
>
> (Heymann 1999: 172)

The harp music repertoire was categorized in terms of three main types. The first type, *goltraí*, refers to laments and melodies for crying. *Geantraí* is lighthearted music—for laughter and entertainment. *Suantraí* is gentle music for sleeping and, according to the renowned Belfast harper Janet Harbison, lovemaking. Harping performance practice at this time did not include Western functional harmony (chords, for example) because it did not exist yet on the Continent. Instead, Irish harping included basic melodies reinforced with lower strings plucked on the first and fifth degrees of the scale, decorated with multiple melodic ornaments. While classical harping has changed since this time (particularly with the inclusion of pedals instead of tuning levers), much of contemporary Irish harping builds on the earlier style. The crucial aesthetic in each style of Irish harping is—just as Giraldus Cambrensis stated—one of subtlety and decoration rather than of bluntness.

During the entire Anglo-Norman period, Ireland was engaged in trade, missionizing, battles, intellectual exchanges, and other frequent connections with the rest of Europe. Its continuous contact with the Continent and with England ensured that any European musical developments found their way to Ireland at approximately the same time they were evolving in Europe. Western functional harmony—with its sensibility of vertical consonance and forward movement toward a consonant conclusion—became established in Europe only in the late fifteenth century, and even then it was not uniformly spread across the continent.

The harp has been a powerful symbol for the Irish since its earliest appearances in Irish iconography. King Henry VIII is believed to have chosen the harp as the symbol of Ireland, though it had already appeared on monastic stone carvings. In the American Civil War, Irish immigrants on both sides (the Irish Brigade of the North, and the Georgia Regiment of the South) each fought under a flag depicting a harp. Because Ireland did not yet exist as a nation—at the time it was still a colony of England—the United States was the first place to fly an Irish flag as a national symbol. Once the Republic of Ireland gained its independence, the harp was chosen as the official symbol of the new nation. Its appearance on Irish coinage, on the covers of hundreds of sheets of nineteenth-century printed music, and on tourist bric-a-brac all reveal its importance as a unique representation of nationhood. No other country uses the harp as its national symbol, though the harp, as a musical instrument, is found everywhere from Burma to Peru to Africa. Only the Irish connect the historical reality of the silencing of the harp by the English with the metaphor of silencing a nation.

It is worth asking yourself who or what holds the functions of a bard in your own life. Some of this information you have in writing, because you have the ability to read and write. But do you know exactly how much is in your bank account, or even your wallet, right now? Perhaps not; perhaps you trust the bank to take care of things. Do you know why your hometown, neighborhood, or local natural feature, has its particular name, and what that name means? Maybe you can look it up on the Internet. Could you entertain a community of people over six months, night after night, without necessarily repeating yourself (and no written reminders of what you've done so far)? It is easy for us to get this information and entertainment because of our access not only to writing and reading, but also (and for some of us, especially) because of our access to the Internet. Now imagine if that access were taken away permanently at the same time that your native language was declared illegal. Could you remember the lyrics to all the songs on your cell phone? Could you tell your children, twenty years from now, what the name of a nearby natural feature means? What would happen in your life if the contents of every known library, bank, and computer were destroyed, and all the teachers were silenced, in just a short time? The historic equivalent of that potential contemporary disaster occurred in Ireland in 1603.

Discussion Questions

1. Why is it that the Celts are always the most celebrated of the early Irish, when they were comparatively late to arrive on the scene?
2. How do you reconcile the Catholicism of contemporary culture with the fifth-century nature-based spirituality that seems to characterize early Catholicism in Ireland? Is that a recognizable form of Catholicism to you?
3. The Vikings brought considerable development to Irish cities, but at what cost?
4. What does being visually impaired mean for musicians? Have you ever closed your eyes to play music? Do you think that visually impaired musicians have a greater gift for memorization and creativity, or is it just practice and free time?
5. Is there any one instrument (besides the harp) that symbolizes for you a nation—any nation—and its people? What would that be, and why?

CHAPTER 3

"Hang All Harpers Where Found"

Ní tír gan teanga ~ There is no country without [its own] language.

Queen Elizabeth I came into power in 1558, inheriting all of the Empire's colonial entities. Both she and King Henry VIII have been justly celebrated for their contributions to English court music in terms of patronage, and singers still perform the famous madrigals and motets of Elizabethan England. Elizabeth's work regarding Ireland, however, reveals a different relationship to the musical arts. The government, in general, felt that Irish musicians were "seditious and dangerous persons" (Rimmer 1977: 39). Shortly before she died in 1603, Elizabeth I is alleged to have issued a proclamation to "Hang all harpers where found and burn the instruments" (O'Boyle 1976: 10). The upper-class bards who had been such an important part of Gaelic Irish life were killed. Some escaped by going "underground," and a few were left to carry on the tradition, but nowhere near the numbers that had existed before. Ireland collectively underwent an upheaval as the society that had supported the culture bearers, upon whom many people depended, was shattered.

In 1541, England's King Henry VIII had declared himself to be "King of Ireland," and his influences on the island included the obligation of his Irish subjects to work within the new context of English laws and language. As part of a larger pattern of recognizing the ability of musicians and poets to build cultural unity, Henry VIII ordered in 1553 the suppression of most musical activity—with the exception of the pipers who accompanied his Irish soldiers—and the destruction of musical instruments (Ó hAllmhuráin 1998: 29). By the time Elizabeth was nearing the end of her reign at the beginning of the seventeenth century, most of the land belonged to English colonists, the shift away from old-style patronage of musicians was almost complete, and a number of

Ireland's most important leaders were about to flee into exile in Europe (often referred to as "the Flight of the Earls").

Only two harps of this era were saved from destruction, and serve as models for many contemporary harps (Figure 3.1). They served as the model for the harp on the back of both the former Irish pound and the modern Irish euro (Figure 3.2), and one of them stands in a glass case near the Book of Kells (see Chapter 2) in the library of Dublin's Trinity College. Musical activity continued in spite of the active suppression of the most elite aspects of tradition. Bards and verse-makers continued to ply their trade, and the shift of patronage from upper-level bards of the "big houses" of the Gaelic aristocracy to itinerants seeking charity was nearly complete.

The English government planned—in 1609—the Plantation of Ulster (in the north of Ireland) with the Plantation of Virginia, with the intention of ridding both areas of the "natives." The plan was to confiscate land and grant subsequent land plots to English and lowlands Scottish settlers, so that Protestants would populate the region. The settlers in the northern region of Ireland cut down forests, cultivated the land, and built villages with schools, markets, churches, and small industries (Clarke 1995: 191–2). All of this was in contrast to the native Irish in the region, whose activities had been primarily pastoral, and who lived in small clusters of rural dwellings. These clusters were called *clachans*, and were cooperative units that functioned effectively right up until the mid-nineteenth century to feed and support the majority of the rural Irish.

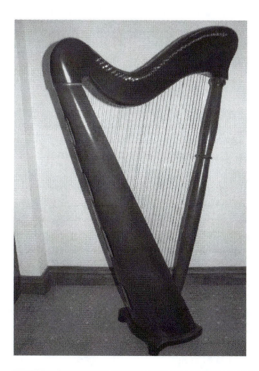

Figure 3.1 A contemporary Aoyama Irish harp, made in Japan. Photo courtesy of Helen Gubbins

Figure 3.2 The "Brian Boru" harp on the old Irish pound and the new Irish euro

Completing the Conquest

In 1649, Oliver Cromwell (Lord Protector of England, Scotland, and Ireland during the Commonwealth Period) arrived in Ireland with his Puritan armed forces, whose expressed aim was to complete the suppression of Catholicism and the takeover of Ireland's land. People were sent into exile and banished from towns, priests were executed, and many were driven from the fertile inland areas of Ireland out west to the barren rocky coasts of Clare and Connacht. One of the results of this forced migration is that the social strata of Gaelic society, already weakened by the Flight of the Earls in 1607 and various incursions from the English, were almost completely leveled. Aristocrats and commoners shared similar fates, as their music, religion, language, customs, dances, and other essentials of life were systematically suppressed. By 1652—several years after Cromwell had left Ireland—the last Irish city (Galway) had succumbed to the English. Cromwell's famous curse against the Catholic Irish—"To Hell or Connacht!"—is clearly remembered to this day; whereas in England some songs hail him as a hero, his reputation in Ireland is less than stellar. The returning curse—*mallacht Cromail ort* ("the curse of Cromwell on you")—is still in use.

In the seventeenth and eighteenth centuries Irish music continued to be performed in both instrumental and sung form in spite of the strictures placed against the people. Laments (both religious and individual), ballads and lays (about historical and mythological figures), and love songs were all part of the song lexicon, and were sung—by this time—in both Gaelic and English. In addition, a set of rich storytelling traditions continued unabated. The *seanchaí* (storyteller) became, for many, the solid link to the past as well as a binding force for the present. In an era of profound disorientation, cultural suppression, and fear, the old man or woman sitting by the fire in a cottage—creating love stories, heroic deeds, and great battles with words—was a source of strength, unity, and solace. Mythological heroes and heroines had thrived in local memory for centuries. The suppression of the Irish did nothing to dissuade people from reliving their past through stories and songs in the intimate context of the cottage. Indeed, storytellers around the world have long used their art to speak—in an oblique way—about contemporary political and social conditions, offering potential solutions to listeners.

By the end of the seventeenth century and through most of the eighteenth century, most of the Irish lived under the strict Penal Code, which—in brief—included laws against both Catholics and Presbyterians ("Dissenters"), aimed at keeping them out of positions of either wealth or power. Under such laws, they were not allowed to own a horse worth over five pounds, enter parliament or hold public office, teach school, build Catholic churches out of anything but wood, carry weapons, or inherit land owned by Protestants. While the English are often blamed for virtually every bad thing that ever happened in Ireland, many of the difficulties experienced by rural Irish men and women had much to do with the Irish agents employed by absentee English landlords.

The outward banning of Catholic religious practice led to the development of a deeply personal, individualized spirituality that included song, transmitted orally (Ní Riain 1993: 193). Some of these songs were Gaelic laments about the death and resurrection of Jesus, for example, or metaphoric songs that attempted to communicate about the faith in a type of musical code. Others were imported English-language carols: strophic folksongs having to do with seasonal aspects of Christianity, including Christmas, Easter, and Advent.

Lamenting in Ireland has tended to be the job of women, sometimes literally. Certain women in a community were known as the ones to attend the grieving family and perform a kind of stylized mourning known as "keening" (from the Irish *caoine*, "lament") on behalf of the deceased. In the lyrics of the following lament, titled "Caoineadh na dTrí Muire" (Lament of the Three Marys), notice how much the focus is on the grieving of the women (especially the mother of Jesus), as opposed to the suffering of Jesus himself. The word *óchón* ("alas"), part of the lexicon of lamenting words, appears in this song at the end of each line (see the musical transcription of this in Figure 3.3). The song itself first was mentioned in print in the thirteenth century, so it predates the period of strongest suppression of Irish traditional culture. However, it also serves as a metaphor to remind people that in a time of great hardship, they have much to lament. The three Marys of the lament are the Virgin Mary, Mary Magdalene, and Mary the mother of James and John.

Figure 3.3 "Caoineadh na dTrí Muire"

Caoineadh na dTrí Muire (Lament of the Three Marys)

A Pheadair a aspail, an bhfhaca thú mo ghrá bán?	Ochón, is ochón ó.
Chonaic mé ar ball é dhá chéasadh ag naimhid.	Ochón, is ochón ó.
Cé hé an fear breá sin ar Chrann na Páise?	Ochón, is ochón ó.
An é nach n-aithníonn tú do Mhac, a Mháithrín?	Ochón, is ochón ó.
An é sin an Maicín a d'iompar mé trí ráithe?	Ochón, is ochón ó.
An é sin an Maicín a rugadh in sa stábla?	Ochón, is ochón ó.
An é sin an Maicín a hoileadh in ucht Mhaire?	Ochón, is ochón ó.
A mhicín mhuirneach, tá do bhéal 's do shróinín gearrtha.	Ochón, is ochón ó.
Is cuireadh calla rúin ar le spídiúlacht óna naimhid	Ochón, is ochón ó.
Is cuireadh an chóroin spíonta ar a mhullach álainn	Ochón, is ochón ó.
Crochadh suas é ar guallaí arda	Ochón, is ochón ó.
Is buaileadh anuas é faoi leacrachaí na sráide.	Ochón, is ochón ó.
Cuireadh go Cnoc Chailbhearaí é ag méadú ar a Pháise	Ochón, is ochón ó.
Bhí sé ag iompar na Croiche agus Simon lena shála.	Ochón, is ochón ó.
Buailigí mé fhéin, ach ná bainidh le mo mháithrín	Ochón, is ochón ó.
Marómuid thú fhéin agus buailfimid do mháithrín.	Ochón, is ochón ó.
Cuireadh tairní maola thrí throithe a chosa agus a lámha	Ochón, is ochón ó.
Cuireadh an tslea trí na bhrollach álainn.	Ochón, is ochón ó.
Éist a mháthair, is ná bí cráite	Ochón, is ochón ó.
Tá mná mo caointe le bre fós a mháthairín.	Ochón, is ochón ó.

Translation (understanding that the refrain, *ochón*, means "alas"):

Who is that fine man on the Cross of Passion?
Don't you recognize your own son, mother?

Is that the son I carried for three trimesters?
Is that the son that was born in the stable?

Is that the son that was nursed at Mary's breast?
My dearest little son, your mouth and nose are bleeding.

They dressed him in purple and spat on him with scorn
They put a spiny crown on his beautiful forehead.

They lifted his mother up high on their shoulders
And threw her down on the flagstones of the street.

He was taken to Calvary Hill to hasten his Passion
He carried the cross and Simon helping him

Beat myself, but do not touch my mother
We'll kill yourself and we'll beat your mother

There were blunt nails put through his hands and feet
There was a sword put through his beautiful chest.

Listen, Mother, and don't be grieving
The women who'll weep for me have yet to be born.

This song belongs to the great *sean-nós* repertoire, about which you will read in much greater detail in Chapter 7. *Sean-nós* (pronounced "shan-nos") means "old style," and—ironically—refers to the Irish-language songs, poetry, and dances that were current during the seventeenth and eighteenth centuries *after* Cromwell and others had effectively eradicated the oldest of the songs, music styles, and poetic meters for which the bards had been so justly famous. In other words, once the instruments had been burned and the bards silenced, what was left was the vernacular music and poetry of the people. Since that time, it has come to be elevated as the most aristocratic and important form of the many kinds of traditional music in Ireland. "Caoineadh na dTrí Muire" bears many of the musical hallmarks of certain *sean-nós* songs (including decorative melodic ornaments such as turns and grace notes). If you look at the musical transcription of just the *óchón* line, you can see multiple notes above a single syllable (a musical phenomenon known as melisma). Not all *sean-nós* songs include this type of musical ornamentation, but a large proportion of them do (particularly those sung in the region of Connemara). The Irish-language lament, then, is a sub-category of *sean-nós*.

While it is hard to imagine that musical activity could have continued publicly during the difficult times of the Penal Laws, the laws were not enforced consistently, and depended on local conditions and fluid political currents. The musical proof of this variance can be seen in the life of Turlough Ó Carolan (1670–1738), the most famous of the Irish harpers (Figure 3.4). He was living and working very publicly from the time that he was in his late teens. Having been blinded by smallpox when he was 18, Ó Carolan was fortunate to be connected with a patron (a Mrs. MacDermott Roe) who set him up with lessons, a harp, a horse, and a guide. He was a prolific composer and performer who spent decades traveling and performing at many of Ireland's "big houses" (homes of the gentry). Many of his compositions were dedicated to—or named after—various patrons that he encountered on his travels, and are among the favorites of contemporary harpers. A composition in praise or honor of someone of that era is called a planxty (Irish *plancstaí*), so many of Ó Carolan's tune titles begin with the word planxty, as in "Planxty Mrs. McDermott" or "Planxty Irwin."

Ó Carolan is said to have composed his "Farewell to Music" (Figure 3.5) at the end of his life. You can listen to harper Laoise Kelly's performance of this beautiful harp tune online; it is a first-rate example not only of one of the finest harping tunes, but also of how a sensitive harper accompanies a melody in the old way: through doubling the octaves and playing arpeggios underneath the main melody.

TRACK 1

In contrast to the wire-strung harp music used in Ireland's preconquest era, Ó Carolan's harp music compositions were strongly influenced by musical currents of the European mainland, particularly the Italian Baroque. In some cases, he adapted local melodies to suit his style, while in other cases he developed entirely new works. Harpers such as Ó Carolan and others had to compete not only with the introduction of the pianoforte in 1709 (Ó hAllmhuráin 1998: 50), but also with the growing popularity of "foreign" music in general. On the mainland, the musics of Antonio Vivaldi,

Figure 3.4 Statue of Ó Carolan in Mohill, Co. Leitrim. Photo courtesy of Anna Sutton

Johann Sebastian Bach, and George Frideric Handel (whose "Messiah" saw its 1742 world premiere in Dublin) were current during the early years of the eighteenth century (White 1998: 30). People living in the big houses of Ireland were not in the least isolated from the social and musical events of the mainland of Europe, and with the increasing Europeanization of the upper classes in Ireland, the opportunities for itinerant harpers to continue plying their trade from house to house diminished over time.

The Soul of a Nation

Romantic nationalism, a philosophical trend developing in Europe toward the end of the eighteenth century, had a significant impact on Irish music. Based on the ideas of the German philosopher Johann von Herder (1744–1803), Romantic nationalism suggested

Figure 3.5 "Farewell to Music"

that nationhood was determined by the soul of its people (*Volksgeist*), and that a kind of inherent unity and originality was to be found in the indigenous culture of each nation. The Irish reaction to von Herder's (and others') ideas was multifaceted; among other things, an interest in the preservation of traditional culture developed among the aristocracy. In reference to the harp, several patrons hosted gatherings and festivals of harpers during the latter decades of the eighteenth century, as it became clear that the tradition was not just diminishing, but perhaps vanishing.

In 1792, the Belfast Harp Festival marked the culmination of early attempts to preserve (through performance and patronage) what was assumed to be a dying tradition; simultaneously, it marked the beginning of serious attempts to notate and collect Irish music from oral tradition. Ten harpers were gathered in Belfast for several days. Of these ten, most were blind, very elderly, and male. A 19-year-old church organist named Edward Bunting was asked to notate the music of the harpers, and the project resulted in the publication of several major works that have served, collectively, as an essential reference and touchstone of the sound and repertoire of the eighteenth century harp. Bunting's publications of 1796, 1809, and 1840 have recently been collected in the book *The Ancient Music of Ireland: The Bunting Collections* (Bunting 2002). As Bunting himself notes,

> The compiler of this Volume was appointed to attend on that occasion, to take down the various airs played by the different Harpers, and was particularly cautioned against adding a single note to the old melodies, which would seem from inferences, that will afterwards be drawn, to have been preserved pure and handed down unalloyed, through a long succession of ages.
>
> (ibid.: Preface)

Pay attention for a minute to what Bunting says: *to have been preserved pure and handed down unalloyed*. His introduction to the collection, then, sets the idea in stone that music does not change either over time or in the hands of individual musicians. As we know now, music is never fixed in time or place when living humans perform it. Even a digital film recording could not have fully captured the experience of attending the Belfast Harp Festival. Bunting's exceptional service to Irish musical history, though, was to make available to future generations of musicians, scholars, and enthusiasts a reasonable written facsimile of the music performed during the festival. It was, in many ways, a "last chance" moment.

The Belfast Harp Festival was just one manifestation of the currents of cultural preservation and revival that began to sweep Ireland, along with the rest of Europe, and which gained momentum during the nineteenth century. As the Penal Laws were slowly lifted, other laws replaced them (including those aimed at the suppression of the Irish language). The Acts of Union in 1800 finally and officially established the "United Kingdom of Great Britain and Ireland" (which already included Wales and Scotland). This development came on the heels of the 1798 Rebellion that—it was hoped—would unite both Protestants and Catholics ("the United Irishmen") in an attempt to form an Irish nation independent of England. The songs created to commemorate the 1798 Rebellion would themselves alone fill multiple recordings (cf. Doyle and Folan 1998).

Thomas Moore, a contemporary of Edward Bunting, was responsible for the creation of *Irish Melodies*, a five-volume compendium of songs that—together with the songs of the American composer Stephen Foster—were among the most popular and most-sung songs of the English-speaking nineteenth-century world (Hamm 1983: 44). These songs were gathered from various sources (oral and written, including from Bunting's own transcriptions), regularized so that they could fit into expected compositional forms of the time, and cleansed of what Moore himself regarded as "tasteless decorations"—the very same melodic ornaments often favored by *sean-nós* singers (White 1998: 47). They were also set to piano accompaniment, so that they could entertain the ladies and gentlemen of a particular class in their parlors. In fact, the contract that Moore held with his publisher included the requirement that he himself perform the songs in English parlors (Davis 2006: 14).

The publication (between 1807 and 1834) of Moore's *Irish Melodies* simultaneously rendered traditional Irish song acceptable for English (and North American) parlor tastes, and made a case—through the lyrics—for attention to be paid to Ireland's conditions under colonialism. Moore had been a student at Dublin's Trinity College, had been a supporter of the United Irishmen, and wrote eloquently of his sense of Irish music's potential: "Surely, if music ever spoke the misfortunes of a people, or could ever conciliate forgiveness for their errors, the music of Ireland ought to possess these powers" (quoted in White 1998: 46).

Compare the raw emotion of "Caoineadh na dTrí Muire" of folk tradition with the flowery sentiment of one of Moore's most popular compositions: "Believe Me, If All Those Endearing Young Charms." This song is intended to reassure a young woman that her lover will still appreciate her when she has aged. Considering that Moore was (and thousands of others were) performing his songs in the female-dominated context of the parlor soirée, it is no wonder that at least some of Moore's compositions were targeted to a particular demographic.

Believe Me, If All Those Endearing Young Charms

Believe me, if all those endearing young charms
Which I gaze on so fondly today

Were to change by tomorrow and fleet in my arms
Like fairy gifts fading away
Thou wouldst still be adored as this moment thou art
Let thy loveliness fade as it will
And around the dear ruin each wish of my heart
Would entwine itself verdantly still.

Now compare what you have just read with "The Harp That Once Thro' Tara's Halls," another popular Moore composition which is frequently brought up in reference to musical expressions of nationalism. In each case, the lyrics engage the listener with a sense of longing for a beautiful (but irretrievably lost) past. Yet in the case of "The Harp," Moore uses the harp—a potent symbol of Ireland—and the image of Tara—the former seat of the High Kings of Ireland—to make a statement about contemporary Irish politics of the early nineteenth century. Remember that it is often easier (and in many cases, politically safer) to comment obliquely about current political issues by evoking cultural points from the past. Given the Irish tendency to speak in metaphor (in both poetry and prose), political sentiment thinly veiled in comments about silenced harps is more culturally appropriate than simply objecting to colonialism.

The Harp That Once Thro' Tara's Halls

The harp that once thro' Tara's halls
The soul of music shed
Now hangs as mute on Tara's walls
As if that soul were fled;
So sleeps the pride of former days
So glory's thrill is o'er
And hearts, that once beat high for praise
Now feel that pulse no more.

Together with Bunting's collection and many local songs in both English and Irish, Moore's published works were a part of a larger trend of sometimes-chaotic nation-building that deeply divided those working on its behalf: politicians, poets, artists, writers, teachers, and many others. In the context of colonialism, some felt that armed revolution was the only way to independence, while others argued that working with the English was more appropriate. As the currents of nationalism began to take stronger political shape by the end of the 1830s, Ireland was stricken with a crisis that altered it beyond all expectation.

The Great Hunger

Ireland's terrible Famine of 1845–1850 was not its first, nor its last; the island had been struck by at least a dozen previous famines in the eighteenth and early nineteenth centuries alone (Harris 1999: 16). *An Gorta Mór* ("The Great Hunger") was a history-making event, however, for its enormous scope and its impact on Irish and American histories, musical and otherwise. From a pre-Famine population of over eight million, Ireland's post-Famine population had plummeted to a mere three and a half million by 1850, and held relatively steadily at (or around) four million for over a hundred years.

Figure 3.6 Dublin's Famine memorial, set right next to the downtown River Liffey

Ireland's population was not cut in half by starvation alone; diseases such as typhus and cholera carried off many people, and the rest emigrated to England, North America, and elsewhere (Figure 3.6). While it is easy to imagine that over-dependence on a single nutritious crop—the potato—was a mistake of monoculture, a view of the Famine from several different angles reveals a somewhat more complicated picture.

> A woman with a dead child in her arms was begging in the street yesterday and the Guard of the Mail told me he saw a man and three dead children lying by the roadside … nothing can exceed the deplorable state of this place … On Saturday, notwithstanding all this distress, there was a market plentifully supplied with meat, bread, fish, in short everything.
>
> (Major Parker, Relief Inspector of the Board of Works, December 1846)

Ireland had plenty of food before, during, and after the Famine. As many as eighteen ships left Ireland's ports every day, full of grain and livestock to be sold abroad for profit. This bounty of food, however, was out of reach of the rural and urban poor, which comprised the majority of Ireland's population. Furthermore, the fungus that blighted the Irish potato also infected crops in the mainland of Europe, and small famines occurred there as well. That the Irish suffered disproportionately in comparison with the mainland Europeans has much more to do with the political and economic policies of the English—which led to the disastrous dependence on a single crop—than with mismanagement or poor planning by the Irish themselves. The Irish planted potatoes in isolated areas all over the country in the hope of finding a place where the blight would not reach, a plan that met with very limited success.

Relief efforts came, as year after bleak year passed with no solution to the blight, in various forms. Catholics were offered food under the condition that they convert to Protestantism; to this day, being accused (or having one's Famine-era ancestors accused) of having "taken the soup" (Figure 3.7) is a terrible insult. Ships with food came from North America and elsewhere (shipping from America was free of charge for boxes marked "Ireland"), and the Choctaw Nation of Oklahoma sent money for Famine relief—a fact warmly remembered by the Irish. In Dublin, an ill-conceived plan to offer up a watery broth to the starving public was publicized as a spectacle to be viewed by the upper classes (Strang and Toomre 1999: 76).

Charles Trevelyan had been placed in charge of Famine relief; it was under his watch that the soup kitchens were closed and the Famine declared at an end several years before its actual conclusion. In 1846, in only the second year of the Famine, he declared the following anti-Catholic, anti-Irish sentiment: "The great evil with which we have to contend is not the physical evil of the famine, but the moral evil of the selfish, perverse and turbulent character of the people" (Mulcrone 1999: 219).

As a place so rich in musical expression, with a people so accustomed to reacting to political and cultural changes with corresponding developments in music, Ireland's musicians practically fell silent. Villages were depopulated; the people were evicted for their inability to pay the rent with nonexistent crops, or they died from starvation and disease in their cottages, which were simply pulled down around them. Among the

Figure 3.7 Famine-era Protestant soup pot in Glencolumbkille, Donegal

dead were some of the great musicians and poets. Others emigrated and found work abroad, in many cases abandoning their musical instruments altogether. Instrumental music does not bear the record of the Famine; in fact, potatoes appear in tune titles ("The Gander in the Pratie ['potato'] Hole," for example) but without the connotation of anguish experienced in the late 1840s. Songs and poems about the Famine existed, though many more were created *after* the Famine was over. During the Famine itself, the extra energy required for creativity combined with material support for poets and musicians was in short supply.

> [People] starve in the midst of plenty, as literally as if dungeon bars separated them from a granary. When distress has been at its height, and our poor have been dying of starvation in our streets, our corn [grain] has been going to a foreign market. It is, to our own poor, a forbidden fruit. – Dominic J. Corrigan, *On Famine and Fever as Cause and Effect in Ireland*, Dublin 1846.
>
> (Ellis 2004: 171)

Songs in both English and Irish reference the Famine. Gearóid Ó hAllmhuráin indicates the perspective of the Irish-language songs particularly in the west: they all "voice the gruesome themes of hopelessness, disease, and deprivation from the internal perspective of suffering communities" (1999: 118). Yet few are still sung today. The way that the Irish regarded the Famine until quite recently—with a mixture of shame, horror, and a desire to banish it from memory—led people to avoid even mentioning it. Musically, Irish-language Famine songs such as "Johnny Seoighe" nearly disappeared, reappearing only toward the end of the twentieth century as Ireland shifted into its fairly recent position as an economic powerhouse. Musicians in the 1990s began playing "Johnny Seoighe" as an instrumental air (see Chapter 9) because it was still too difficult to openly sing Famine songs. In the recent past, though, this and other songs have regained some of their old currency.

As an alternative to expressing memories of the Famine in other musical ways, the experience of the Famine is now most often recreated musically through a very popular English-language song, "The Fields of Athenry" (frequently referred to as a kind of "second national anthem" or even a "people's national anthem" when it comes up on the radio). "The Fields of Athenry" is a modern composition from the 1970s by songwriter Pete St. John, and it refers to a young man in prison having a conversation with his wife through the prison walls. The lyrics explain that he is being sent on a prison ship to Australia for having stolen "corn" (grain) to feed his family. Note the reference to Charles Trevelyan, the man in charge of Famine relief; the themes of loyalty and dignity are also reminiscent of songs of an earlier era.

The Fields of Athenry

By a lonely prison wall, I heard a young girl calling
Michael, they are taking you away
For you stole Trevelyan's corn, so the young might see the morn
Now a prison ship lies waiting in the bay.

CHORUS:
Low lie the fields of Athenry

Where once we watched the small free birds fly
Our love was on the wing, we had dreams and songs to sing
It's so lonely round the fields of Athenry.

While few Irish-language Famine songs have regained currency, "The Fields of Athenry" is played frequently on the airwaves, in pubs, on CDs, and in concert (with entire audiences joining the performers with enthusiasm on every word). One can find many examples of it, together with complete lyrics, online. Various recordings of it, including a dance remix and disco version, are still current. In 2012, Irish football (soccer) fans famously sang the chorus, over and over, as they lost the final European match with Spain that was held in Gdansk, Poland. The video (you can find it yourself) went viral to the point that "The Fields of Athenry" chorus is now routinely sung at matches. But why this particular song? The answer lies in how the Irish have processed their Famine memories. The Irish-language songs are heartfelt and direct; they detail the immediate problems of hunger and the terrible loss of joy, and often place blame. They are in a language that most Irish people do not speak. They are also difficult to sing. "The Fields of Athenry" has an easy-to-sing melody, and the theme is much broader: crimes were committed to save one's family members, a point which no one is willing to argue. Furthermore, there is no call to arms; the young woman plans to wait for the hero's return (itself a popular theme in Irish song, with the young woman acting as a metaphor for Ireland and the young man representing Ireland's heroes in exile).

Over a million people left Ireland during and immediately after the Famine, either by choice or because their landlords paid their passage in an effort to clear the land for grazing. Many of the ships used for transport were not seaworthy, earning the nickname "coffin ships" for their tendency to go down in the rough weather of the Atlantic crossing. Over a period of several decades, hundreds of thousands more arrived on the east coast of North America. The array of emigration songs offers a variety of perspectives, from despairing to hopeful. Similarly, songs of the New World that mention Ireland run the gamut from longing to bitterness; Chapter 5 ("The Green Fields of America") covers Irish-American vocal and instrumental music more thoroughly.

An important aspect of music during this period, but also more generally in the eighteenth and nineteenth centuries, is the prevalence of songs of rebellion. The names of some of the classic rebel songs read—to the modern, post-sectarian gaze—like a set list at a performance of discontented Irish-Americans: "The Wearing o' the Green," "Erin's Green Shore," "The Croppy Boy," "The Rambler from Clare," and many others. Still more developed during the twentieth century, particularly after the 1916 Easter Rebellion and the War of Independence. Symbolism is critical to most of these songs. In some cases, symbols might refer to the heroes and heroines of ancient Ireland, or they might link humans with the land, or with animals or birds. A favorite theme is the *aisling* ("ashling") poem in which a woman is met in a dream. The more political *aislingí* tend to portray women as passive symbols of Ireland, with names such as Granuaile or Róisín Dubh. Men are often referred to as birds: Bonnie Prince Charlie, for example, is called "the blackbird," Napoleon is "the linnet," and Daniel O'Connell is "the eagle."

"Erin's Green Shore," a nineteenth-century broadside ballad, is a classic example of the *aisling* or vision poem, in which a young man stumbles upon a woman, often dressed in traditional "magic" colors of green, red, and/or white. Upon closer questioning, he discovers that she is Ireland, in distress over her oppression by the English. She tells her sad story to him, but he wakes up and vows to protect her, or blesses her. Often, in *aisling* songs, the young man sees the vision of Ireland-as-a-young-woman while walking next to a river or the ocean shore. This custom is echoed in many other countries in which women with access to a particular gift are associated with water (sirens and courtesans among them). In the following lyrics, note the use of power symbols: flowers, jewels, clothing, water, and colors (Zimmerman 2002: 27). "Erin" is the Anglicization of the Irish word for Ireland ("Éireann"). This version is taken from the singing of Joe Heaney.

Erin's Green Shore

One evening of late as I rambled by the edge of a clear purling stream
I dreamt that I saw this fair maiden, and I quickly fell into a dream
I dreamt that I saw this fair maiden, her equal I ne'er saw before
She sighed for the wrongs of her country as she rambled 'round Erin's green
    shore.

Her eyes were like two sparkling diamonds, or like two suns on a clear frosty
    night
Her cheeks were like two blooming roses, her teeth were like ivory white
She resembled the goddess of freedom, and green was the mantle she wore
Embroidered with shamrocks and roses as she rambled along Erin's green
    shore.

I boldly addressed this fair maiden, might you, pray tell me your name
To this country I know you're a stranger, or I'd not have asked you the same
I'm a sister to Daniel O'Connell, to this country I've lately sailed o'er
To awaken my brothers' long slumber, I have sailed unto Erin's green shore.

A further verse that appears in some versions (Zimmerman 2002: 27) is as follows:

In transports of joy I awoke, but alas, I found 'twas all a dream
The beautiful damsel was fled, and I longed for to slumber again
May the powers above be her guardian, I'm afraid I will ne'er see her more
May the sunbeams of freedom illume her, dear brothers round Erin's green
    shore.

Daniel O'Connell, mentioned in the fourth verse, was an important political leader in the first part of the nineteenth century; he campaigned to repeal the Union and for the emancipation of Catholics. He was an advocate for non-violent resistance, and held meetings that drew upwards of 100,000 people at a time. This song is only one of many that mention O'Connell or celebrate his ideals; others include "The Shan Van Vocht" ("The Poor Old Woman"—a frequent metaphor for Ireland and her people), "The Grey Mare," and "The Kerry Eagle."

Songs that simultaneously reference several events in Irish history are common. "Skibbereen" is a dialogue song of the nineteenth century between a father and son. It appears in a songbook of 1880 attributed to Patrick Carpenter, a poet from Skibbereen. The American son asks his Irish father why he left Skibbereen (a town in County Cork in Ireland's southwestern region), and what follows is a litany of his bitter experiences

Figure 3.8 "Skibbereen"

at home. The father talks about the small harbor town of Skibbereen in County Cork and why he had to leave; the place was very hard hit during the Famine and is home to mass graves containing thousands of Famine victims. By the end of the song the son, now inspired to act, promises to return "home" to Ireland and wreak revenge on the English. The song references the 1798 Rebellion as well as the Famine (about fifty years apart). To this day, the final line of the song ("revenge for Skibbereen") can still be seen among other themes in Irish graffiti.

"Skibbereen" can be performed as a rowdy rebel song in 6/8 time, or as a much slower song with rich vocal ornamentation in the old style. The melody, in Aeolian mode, is in an ABBA style, in which the first and last lines of each verse are the same, and the second and third lines are the same (Figure 3.8).

Skibbereen

Oh, Father, dear, I often hear you speak of Erin's isle
Her lofty scenes, her valleys green, her mountains rude and wild
They say it is a gentle land, wherein a prince might dwell
Oh how could you abandon it, the reason to me tell.

My son, I loved my native land with energy and pride
Till the blight came over all my crops, my sheep and cattle died
My rent and taxes were so high, I could not them redeem
That's the cruel reason I left old Skibbereen.

It's well I do remember the year of '98
When I arose a Fenian to battle against our fate
I was hunted through the mountains as a traitor to the Queen
That's another reason I left old Skibbereen.

It's well I do remember the cold November day
When the landlord and the sheriff came to drive us all away
They set our roof ablaze in fire with their damning yellow spleen
That's another reason why I left old Skibbereen.

Your mother, too, God rest her soul, fell on the snowy ground
She fainted in her anguish, the desolation round
She never rose but passed away from life to mortal dream
She found a grave and place of rest in dear old Skibbereen.

You were only two months old, and feeble was your frame
I could not leave you with my friends, you bore your father's name
I wrapped you in my *cótamór*, at the dead of night unseen
We heaved a sigh and bid goodbye to dear old Skibbereen.

Oh father, dear, the day will come when on vengeance we will call
When Irishmen both stout and stern will rally one and all
I'll be the man to lead the van, beneath the flag of green
And loud and high we'll raise the cry, "Revenge for Skibbereen."

Cultural Revival and the "Celtic Twilight"

The aftermath of the Famine included several major legacies: the drop in population by more than half; the defeminization of the Irish countryside as many more women than men went abroad (and those women who remained often sought work in the cities or served as nuns); the English consolidation of Irish land into very large areas for grazing; families broken up and scattered, rather than thriving in the tightly-knit *clachan* communities; and the re-Catholicization of the people as much of the country shifted toward a more conservative approach to religion. Ireland after 1860 experienced significant growth in its urban areas, a depopulated countryside, and part of every family gone to North America and England. Excessive rents and evictions increased, and even as the Irish struggled to recover from the Famine, many of them became increasingly politicized.

Part of the task facing the Irish in their struggle of nation building was the celebration of Ireland's history, language, mythology, customs, and unique features in a post-Famine climate. By the end of the nineteenth century four significant political and cultural movements had gained currency. The Land League (founded 1879) had developed to secure the rights of tenants on English-owned land, and to advocate for Home Rule. The Gaelic Athletic Association (founded 1884) was formed to promote sports competitions that were entirely of Irish origin (hurling and Gaelic football, for example); it also had significant political undercurrents. The Gaelic League (founded 1893) was intended to foster all manner of traditional culture, from poetry, literature, and songs in Irish, to dance, instrumental music, and other artistic genres. The National Literary Society (founded 1892) was dedicated to the development of a native Irish literature, but written in English. It is the latter movement that caught the imagination of writers and artists outside of Ireland, and which brought renown to its primary creators.

This period in Irish history—the 40 years surrounding the turn of the twentieth century—is both the time in which Ireland experienced a significant cultural revival (often referred to as the "Celtic Twilight"), and the time in which the War of Independence occurred. The period is rich in music, poetry, and literature. Three Protestant writers founded the National Literary Society: William Butler Yeats (1865–1939), John Millington Synge (1871–1909), and Lady Augusta Gregory (1852–1932). These three co-founded the Abbey Theatre in Dublin in 1904, with the aim of producing Irish plays by Irish writers. Yeats wrote poetry and plays, Synge lived in the Irish-speaking Aran islands and wrote plays (in English) intended to reflect the speech patterns and the nature of the island people, and Lady Gregory published—in English—the Irish-language stories and folklore of the people who lived in a village near her estate. They were eager to develop in their Irish readers a sense of passion and commitment for all things Irish by reminding contemporary people of the great heroes of Irish mythology. Collectively, the literary movement was intended to instill pride in being Irish *while speaking English*, the language of modernity. Indeed, the movement was a legacy of Thomas Moore's *Irish Melodies*; taking Irish materials and recontextualizing them in a newly Anglicized culture. The National Literary Society, the Gaelic League, the Gaelic Athletic Association, and the Land League were often at odds with each other, yet all shared the goal of an Ireland for Irish people.

Of the many Yeats poems that include references to music, "The Host of the Air" describes a wedding and the piping as accompaniment to the celebration. The title refers to the fairy "host" (beings)—particularly those who inhabit the air—who were feared for their ability to steal the soul of the bride at a wedding. The famous lines "and never was piping so sad, and never was piping so gay" (*gay*, until about the mid-twentieth century, simply meant joyous or free of constraint) accurately describe the simultaneously major- and minor-sounding (or, more bluntly, "happy" and "sad") melodies of the dance tunes in Dorian and Mixolydian modes. Yeats himself is widely cited as having described someone this way: "Being Irish, he had an abiding sense of tragedy, which sustained him through temporary periods of joy." This following poem is an appropriate rendition of precisely that sentiment. Many of Yeats' early poems include references to fairies, life-cycle celebrations, and the (lost but worthy) Irish past:

"The Host of the Air," poem by William Butler Yeats

O'Driscoll drove with song
The wild duck and the drake
From the tall and the tufted reeds
Of the drear Hart Lake.

And he saw how the reeds grew dark
At the coming of night-tide
And dreamed of the long dim hair
Of Bridget his bride.

He heard while he sang and dreamed
A piper piping away
And never was piping so sad
And never was piping so gay.

And he saw young men and young girls
Who danced on a level place

And Bridget his bride among them
With a sad and a gay face.

The dancers crowded about him
And many a sweet thing said
And a young man brought him red wine
And a young girl white bread.

But Bridget drew him by the sleeve
Away from the merry bands
To old men playing at cards
With a twinkling of ancient hands.

The bread and the wine had a doom
For these were the host of the air
He sat and played in a dream
Of her long dim hair.

He played with the merry old men
And thought not of evil chance
Until one bore Bridget his bride
Away from the merry dance.

He bore her away in his arms
The handsomest young man there
And his neck and his breast and his arms
Were drowned in her long dim hair.

O'Driscoll scattered the cards
And out of his dream awoke:
Old men and young men and young girls
Were gone like a drifting smoke.

But he heard high up in the air
A piper piping away
And never was piping so sad
And never was piping so gay.

Musical activities of the period were supported by the Gaelic League. The membership held competitions in piping, poetic recitation, singing, dancing, and other activities, with prizes awarded to those who best represented the great traditions of the past. The Gaelic League was primarily a middle-class urban movement whose cultural conservatism was underpinned and encouraged by the Catholic Church. It is because of the efforts of the Gaelic League in the promotion of a "right way" of doing things that the American subculture of Irish step-dancing (see Chapter 9) is focused on the promulgation of a particular ideal through classes and competitions. In fact, foreign branches of the Gaelic League developed the culture of conservation and preservation to the point that musical changes taking place in Ireland have been resisted abroad.

The importation and availability of musical instruments in Ireland increased dramatically during this period, including melodeons, concertinas, and flutes (see Chapter 6). Men and women both played instruments as diverse as the bagpipes, concertinas, and fiddles, though more women tended to play the concertina and more men tended to play the fiddle. Singing changed as well, as influences from continental opera began to filter down into local popular tradition. The development of an urban parlor culture, particularly in Ireland's largest cities, led to the emergence of what has now become a cultural stereotype of both Ireland and Irish America: the Irish tenor.

Thomas Moore's *Irish Melodies* had come into print earlier in the nineteenth century while opera grew in popularity in Italy and Germany. The sound of vibrato (in which the singer rapidly oscillates his or her pitch above and below the center of the note to sound "sweeter") became a feature of Italian operatic style, known as *bel canto* ("beautiful song"). Operatic arias (the short songs that highlight the emotional content of an opera) were being performed in Europe and North America, particularly once the piano became more affordable. By the end of the nineteenth century, *bel canto* style was being applied to urban Irish song performances, including those perfoming the songs of Thomas Moore. It was believed that none were more suited to their performance than tenors, whose English-speaking, literate, urbane, and sophisticated manner (as initiated by Moore himself) represented to the people of the National Literary Movement the best of Irish parlor music. Both Yeats and James Joyce aspired to be singers, and Joyce actually won the bronze medal in the same competition that the great tenor John McCormack had won first prize in the year before.

Why "Danny Boy"?

The song "Danny Boy" has risen to the top of all the English-language songs associated with the Irish around the world. Thousands of people sing it every year, on St. Patrick's Day, without fail; the roster of those who have recorded it includes such well-known (and not always Irish) singers as Bing Crosby, Jackie Wilson, Carly Simon, Harry Belafonte, Elvis Presley, Johnny Cash, and Harry Connick Jr. It continues to be one of the top karaoke songs in Japan and elsewhere. The song has become part of a cluster of Irish symbols that populate Irish-American culture: funerals, alcohol, St. Patrick's Day, family, tears, and "Danny Boy."

Frederick Weatherly, an English barrister (attorney), wrote the lyrics of "Danny Boy" and published them in 1913. The earliest known recording of the song was in 1915, by the Prague-born, Bohemian-American operatic contralto singer Ernestine Schumann-Heink. The melody of "Danny Boy" had been published in 1855 by a music collector named Jane Ross under the name, "The Londonderry Air." Londonderry is the colonial name for the Northern Ireland town of Derry. The air (tune) has been used for countless other songs; such separation of lyrics from melody is common across the United Kingdom and North America. In the case of "Danny Boy," however, the melody we know today was not the melody that

Frederick Weatherly chose; it turns out that his Irish-born sister-in-law recommended the one we know to him.

By the time the song came from England to the United States in the 1920s, its use of Irish-sounding images (glen, meadow, grave, summer, valley, etc.) hit immigrants from Ireland (and elsewhere in Europe) to America in the heart. The United States Johnson-Reed Act of Immigration in 1924 established annual restrictive quotas for potential immigrants from various European countries; the annual quota for Irish people was over 28,000. By way of contrast, potential immigrants from Asia were excluded entirely. With the overwhelming challenge of leaving home and trying to establish oneself in America came the powerful draw of longing and nostalgia embodied in songs with classic images and themes.

> Oh Danny boy, the pipes, the pipes are calling
> From glen to glen, and down the mountain side
> The summer's gone, and all the roses falling
> It's you, it's you must go and I must bide.
> But come ye back when summer's in the meadow
> Or when the valley's hushed and white with snow
> It's I'll be here in sunshine or in shadow
> Oh Danny boy, oh Danny boy, I love you so.
>
> But when ye come, and all the flowers are dying
> If I am dead, as dead I well may be
> You'll come and find the place where I am lying
> And kneel and say an "Ave" there for me.
> And I shall hear, though soft you tread above me
> And all my grave will warmer, sweeter be
> For you will bend and tell me that you love me
> And I shall sleep in peace until you come to me.

The melody of this song has been sung and/or played at the funerals of thousands of people, including President John F. Kennedy in 1963 and, in 1998, Princess Diana. In the widely publicized 2018 funeral of American politician and World War II veteran John McCain, opera singer Renée Fleming sang it to great acclaim; it was widely reported as a "moving rendition of the Irish ballad." The soaring high note of the second stanza ("It's I'll be *heeeere*") is often the breaking point for people trying not to cry, and Fleming gave it her all with expected results. In contrast, episode 520 of the Muppets featured the characters of Beaker, the Swedish chef, and the Animal dressed in cream-colored sweaters and green tam o'shanters (a type of Scottish hat connected to an eighteenth-century poem by Robert Burns). In this video, the three muppets perform as The Leprechaun Brothers, introduced by Kermit the Frog with "Yay and begorrah!" along with a claim that all three had "kissed the Blarney Stone" (a tourist attraction near Shannon International Airport). While the Muppets do not sing the actual lyrics in order, the song is clearly "Danny Boy"; they all break down in tears at the high point of the song.

What do these two renditions have in common? First, they both rely on popular knowledge of the song, and secondly, everyone seems to know that the highest note of the melody is the moment to cry.

Frederick Weatherly wrote two verses only. There are several versions of a "third verse" (often touted as having been in the original Weatherly version); they generally refer to dying for Ireland and fighting to set her free… from the English, obviously. The likelihood of Englishman Weatherly having written that third verse is low.

Even if you do not read music, you can scan the transcription and see that the melody is quite plain. However, it is precisely the song's very plainness that offers so much freedom to singers. In addition, each phrase starts on a low pitch, walks up the scale to a high note, and comes back down. That pattern is repeated eight times in a single verse. Some have likened that rising and falling of the melody to (variously) breathing, getting your hopes up and having them dashed, and to the "sunshine and shadow" of the lyrics. In the musical accompaniment, the chords shift between major and minor throughout. The highest point of the song moves from dark, sad, minor chords to major chords with their happy, life-affirming, confident, restorative, and reassuring sensibility right at the moment that the lyrics confirm the steadfast love between the one who remains alive and the one who has died. Ireland's musical culture is famous for its rich combination of happiness and sadness; "Danny Boy" checks each box handily.

If you listen to different versions of it online, you will notice that the singers lengthen and shorten the notes, add melodic variations, and essentially make it much more expressive than the notation would indicate. Sinéad O'Connor's performance on *The Late Late Show* is whispered and intimate. Harry Belafonte's version is very much a *rubato* or flexible rhythm piece with plenty of open space between phrases. The Celtic Woman ensemble performs it *a cappella* with creative contemporary harmonies that would surprise Frederick Weatherly. Both Bing Crosby and Donegal crooner Daniel O'Donnell put small turns in the melody at specific places. Johnny Cash has a very spare style of singing it, accompanied in this case by the organ; the use of the organ immediately signifies its near-sacred quality to (some of) its listeners. Elvis Presley's "Danny Boy" includes his characteristic vocal breaks, slides, vocal fry, and his backup singers filling in with "oooh" and "aaaah." Countless instrumentalists appear on YouTube performing "Danny Boy" as well, including Eric Clapton, Bill Evans, George Benson, and others.

The song's popularity at funerals has been controversial; it is not part of the normal Catholic liturgy or pattern of worship. Acceptable readings and performances at Catholic funerals include selections from the Old or New Testament, as well as standard hymns and psalms that have been set to music. In Providence, Rhode Island, the church diocese banned "Danny Boy" in 2001 from funerals because it has nothing to do with the faith. Similarly, an Irish pub owner in New York City banned the song from his pub in 2008 because he deemed it "too depressing." It is also a near-constant request of bands playing at pubs on St. Patrick's Day.

But why the cluster of tears and funerals and St. Patrick's Day? Ireland has plenty of heart-wrenching songs; just read some of the lyrics in Chapters 7 and 8. So why "Danny Boy"? First, the link between English-language songs about Ireland and post-immigrant sadness was established by the songs of composer Thomas Moore (1770–1852). A slight man whose publishing contract required him to perform in Victorian English parlors, Moore himself was the one who established the ideal of the Irish tenor: a genteel, civilized, English-speaking, non-threatening, colonized man who could sing songs of the Irish past. Moore's *Irish Melodies* were the most popular songbooks in North America for decades, and they are rich in lyrics that evoke tears (see, for example, his song, "Erin, the Tear and the Smile in Thine Eye"). Second, St. Patrick's Day celebrations in the United States far outshine the holy day in Ireland, and some of the most popular songs associated with the Irish and St. Patrick's Day are rarely—if ever—performed in Ireland. "Danny Boy" is short-hand in North America for claiming Irishness, yet one would be (very) hard-pressed to find it performed in Ireland itself beyond the confines of a tourist pub.

The music sung by Irish tenors was in English, and—like the poetry and prose of the writers of the National Literary Movement—celebrated a heritage of loss. New compositions highlighted the stone cottage, the weeping mother, the sound of the bagpipes, the Irish flag, and variations on the homeland/motherland. Romantic nationalism was a strong undercurrent of these songs, including "Mother Machree" and "Danny Boy." "Mother Machree" ("machree" is from the Irish *mo chroí*—"of my heart") leans on a similar set of images, all concerned with the emphatically rural past. In many ways, the imagery of Ireland is the imagery of the rural "home." In this stanza, the singer assures his mother that nothing and no one will come between him and his love for his mother:

> Sure, I love the dear silver that shines in your hair
> And the brow that's all furrowed and wrinkled with care
> I kiss the dear fingers so toilworn for me
> Oh, God bless you and keep you, Mother Machree.

Figure 3.9 "Danny Boy"

Ireland Since Independence

The conflict that resulted in the division of one island into two nations is complicated and fraught with competing stories from all sides. Here, then, is one concise view of what happened. By the early twentieth century, the island's population included several million Catholics and about a million Protestants. The Protestants were, for the most part, descended from those who had come to the northern part of the island from the Scottish borderlands several hundred years earlier. Ireland and England had been united under the Acts of Union in 1800, and those who wished for Ireland to remain a part of the then-United Kingdom of Great Britain and Ireland (now just "and Northern Ireland") were, and are, called "Unionists." The idea of Home Rule for Ireland was an important priority of various political parties, and it became a definite possibility just before World War I broke out. Other political groups were advocating for an independent Ireland altogether, and were actively involved in resistance movements against English rule. As soon as the war began, Home Rule (let alone complete independence for Ireland) was effectively off the table for the time being.

The Easter Rebellion of 1916 (sometimes referred to as "the revolution of poets")—in which a small group of people took over Dublin's post office and declared Ireland's independence—might have passed almost without notice were it not for the dramatic overreaction of the English, who responded with enormous force and executed almost all of the rebels. The events surrounding the 1916 rebellion galvanized many into action, and over the next few years a precarious revolution, fraught with disagreement and internal conflict against the backdrop of World War I, resulted in the partition of the island in 1921 into the twenty-six counties of what is now the Republic of Ireland and the six counties of Northern Ireland. The twenty-six counties were mostly Catholic, and the six counties in the north were mostly Protestant. In a strange twist of geographic-religious fate, some of the counties belonging within the Republic ("in the south") are *further north* than some of the six counties "of the north." The name "Ulster," which generally meant the northern province of nine counties (compare with the other provinces: Connacht, Leinster, and Munster), came to refer—for some, but not all people— to just the six counties in Northern Ireland.

The Unionists, then, felt that they were in danger from the south, and only somewhat protected from strife by the British. The Northern (Catholic) Irish knew themselves to be a minority in the north, and believed themselves to be entirely unprotected from British hegemony. In Northern Ireland the system of voting through proportional representation was halted, leading to the Unionists seizing control over hitherto Catholic majority areas. The police and civil services became entirely Protestant-run, and unemployment disproportionately affected Catholics. These changes set the stage for the Troubles that occurred later in the twentieth century. The complicated events leading up to independence, and the ensuing Irish Civil War of 1921–22, are still heatedly discussed in pubs and kitchens all over Ireland. Which side one's family fought on during the Irish Civil War is enough to precipitate bitter divisions, arguments, and fights.

In the post-Civil War climate of Ireland in the 1930s, radio and recordings brought changes to music in Ireland. Jazz from the United States excited some and scandalized others, leading to the development of various kinds of dance bands in Ireland. American recordings of the great Irish fiddle players Michael Coleman, Paddy Killoran, and James Morrison (all from Sligo, all of whom had moved to the States) and other musicians proved to be a great inspiration to, and hugely influential on, players in Ireland. For the first time, musicians in Ireland had the chance to hear an abundance of tunes and songs from outside their immediate parish or county, and the stylistic differences between the regions became obvious immediately. In addition, the repertoire of tunes played nationally began to expand as radio penetrated the smallest villages.

The Public Dance Halls Act of 1935 was a reaction to the perceived lack of control over house and crossroads dancing (see further discussion in Chapter 9). At these dances, the sexes would mix freely late into the night, hosts would raise funds for political groups, and neither the clergy nor the police could control who might appear or what might happen behind the scenes. Both the Gaelic League and the Church advocated for licensing of dancing in a public space overseen by the clergy only. The Dance Halls Act resulted in an end to most crossroads dancing, the condemnation from the pulpit of private house dancing, and the development of the "céilí band" dominated by the accordion. "Dancers were thus separated from the process of music-making, standards of appreciation declined, musicians lost local importance, and became discouraged" (Vallely 2011: 201).

The 1940s and 1950s saw serious economic decline. The government's refusal to modernize its economy, coupled with the devastating cost of nonstop emigration from the country, kept it at a low ebb of development. At a time when families produced many children, Ireland's population held steady because of emigration; the lure of economic prosperity meant that the nineteenth-century custom of sending young people abroad to find work continued apace. Traditional musicians found almost no work at home, and even though the Gaelic League continued its competitions, lively house sessions at which musicians gathered became a thing of the past—or perhaps only a custom of Irish musicians transplanted abroad.

The Troubles

By the 1960s, the political scene in Northern Ireland had begun to heat up. The English government, the political parties of Northern Ireland, and thousands of average citizens of Northern Ireland became embroiled in a power struggle between those who wanted Northern Ireland reunited with the rest of Ireland, those who wanted Northern Ireland to remain connected to the United Kingdom, and those who wanted Northern Ireland to be independent. Clashing loyalties, high unemployment, the availability of powerful weapons to disenfranchised people on both sides, political decisions, and a profoundly difficult colonial history fueled the conflict. Now known as the Troubles, the era was an explosive period of unrest that resulted in several thousand deaths, spanning all sides of the conflict, and a collective sense of lingering trauma for the people of the region, made worse recently by discussions of Brexit (the UK's decision to leave the European Union). To outline the full scale and timeline of the Troubles would take longer than the available space here, but the interested reader is directed to *Making Sense of the Troubles: The Story of the Conflict in Northern Ireland* (McKittrick and McVea 2002). Instead, this section of the chapter focuses on two kinds of musical responses to both identity issues and political currents: the sectarian songs of the Catholics, and the marching bands of the Ulster Scots.

You have already encountered songs of political response and rebellion in this chapter; a large body of songs developed between the 1960s and 2000, by which time both economic and political conditions had improved. These songs were written by insiders and outsiders to the conflict, and have been sung thousands of times around the world, including by those who have no connection to the political situation at all. In summing up some of the expressive responses to the events, this section presents selected verses of a handful of songs. All of them are available to hear, in their entirety, performed by an array of performers on both iTunes and YouTube, and the complete lyrics are readily available online. The selection that follows ignores entirely the hundreds of songs written (and performed) about the immediacy of local events across both the Republic of Ireland, and Northern Ireland as well, focusing instead on some of the better-known songs that one still hears regularly in Ireland and abroad. This first selection represents some perspectives from the Catholic side of the conflict, represented by a large number of political parties, including the most visible one: the Irish Republican Army and its offshoots. Its political wing, Sinn Féin ("We Ourselves"), continues to play a role in current mainstream politics.

Dominic Behan, younger brother of playwright Brendan Behan, wrote the song "The Patriot Game" in response to a failed Irish Republican Army attack on a Royal Ulster Constabulary barracks in 1957. Sung from the perspective of a young IRA man killed during the attack, the song is one of the most popular of the Irish folksongs about the Troubles. A popular book (1987) and film (1992)—Tom Clancy's *Patriot Games*—were named after this very song. The first verse borrows from the standard "come all ye" opening of many traditional folksongs, and offers a cautionary note at the very beginning:

> Come all you young rebels and list' while I sing
> For the love of one's country is a terrible thing
> It banishes fear with the speed of a flame
> And it makes us all part of the patriot game.

The song continues with the story of the attack, and concludes with the protagonist dying and blaming those who sold him (and others) out. The voice of the dead is a powerful one in Ireland, frequently encountered in the English-language songs (see Chapter 8).

In the song "Four Green Fields," Ireland's four provinces are imagined as fields owned by a "poor old woman," the personification of Ireland (a concept that should be familiar to the reader by now). This first verse sums up several centuries of Irish history in metaphor, from the perspective of the late folksinger Tommy Makem, who wrote the song in 1967 after driving through a portion of Northern Ireland.

> What did I have, said the fine old woman
> What did I have, this proud old woman did say
> I had four green fields, each one was a jewel
> But strangers came, and tried to take them from me
> I had fine strong sons, they fought to save my jewels
> They fought and died, and that was my grief, said she.

The hunger strike is a method of protesting injustice that has deep roots in Ireland, even having a place in the early legal system (the Brehon laws). In 1981, a group of jailed men accused of being paramilitaries for the IRA protested a change in their status from "Special Category" (i.e., political prisoners) to that of "regular" criminals. A first hunger strike in 1980 was called off, but then reinstated in 1981—in serial fashion—when conflicting demands and agreements warranted its reinstatement by the prisoners. Francie Brolly's "The H-Block Song" of 1976 has as its chorus a protest against the political prisoners being required to dress like regular prisoners:

> So I'll wear no convict's uniform
> Nor meekly serve my time
> That Britain might brand Ireland's fight
> Eight hundred years of crime.

Seamus MacMathúna's "O'Hara, Hughes, McCreesh and Sands" refers to the first four hunger strikers who died: Bobby Sands (May 5), Francis Hughes (May 12), Raymond McCreesh and Patsy O'Hara (May 21), all in 1981. The hunger strike generated world headlines. The second verse of the song (after a first verse with a "come all ye" beginning) explores what happens when "poor men's sons" (the soldier-representatives of the English, many of whom came from working-class families) fight disenfranchised Irishmen. It also recites the names of the four hunger strikers (though ten ultimately died) at the end of each verse:

> Young Irishmen in Ulster born, deprived of freedom, work and home
> Oppressed by ruthless races, laws that drive men down beneath the yoke
> And when the bloodhound comes at night to terror strike across the land
> With their tanks and guns and poor men's sons, O'Hara, Hughes, McCreesh
>   and Sands.

Phil Coulter wrote "The Town I Loved So Well" about his hometown of Derry, which by the late 1970s had become a battleground. In his first few verses he celebrates the continuation of living even as Derry began to fall apart. He leaves home to find work and a wife, and then notes the changes upon his return:

> But when I returned how my eyes have burned
> To see how a town could be brought to its knees
> By the armoured cars and the bombed out bars
> And the gas that hangs on to every breeze.
> Now the army's installed by the old gasyard wall
> And the damned barbed wire gets higher and higher
> With their tanks and their guns, oh my God, what have they done
> To the town I loved so well.

"Peter Pan and Me" was released in 1992 by Mickey McConnell, a songwriter and *Irish Times* journalist from Fermanagh who also wrote the well-known song "Only Our Rivers Run Free." These two verses of "Peter Pan and Me"—about how the people of his generation attempted to fight against an organized, well-armed enemy—echo some elements of the other songs in this section in their discussion of their connection to place and home:

We knew we faced the power that comes from money
When we marched against the empire's mighty schemes
They were armed with special powers and legislation
While we were armed with youth and foolish dreams.

But we soon learned the truth of street rebellion
As our city crumbled round us stone by stone
Betrayed by those who promised they would help us
Against tanks, and troops, and guns we stood alone.

By the end of the eighteenth century a series of local fraternal organizations comprising working-class men had been formed to defend the faith on each side. The Ancient Order of Hibernians represented the Catholic defenders of the faith; initially called "Ribbonmen," the AOH has had a strong role in North American politics and parading since at least the nineteenth century. The Orange Order is a Protestant political group based at least in part on Ulster Scot identity politics. Named after William of Orange (Protestant William III of England), the Order established the famous parades during the summer "marching season." In these yearly parades, members of the Orange Order focus primarily on issues of heritage and identity, though political views vary within its membership. Carrying flags with historical figures (particularly the leaders of battles in which Protestants were triumphant over Catholics) and political symbols, the marchers use large bass and snare drums and flutes. The flute bands, called "blood and thunder" bands, have tended to play instrumental versions of Orange songs. Blood and thunder bands are emphatically *not* Irish bands. "Bands are at the heart of loyalist political culture in so far as they are an essential ingredient at the major public commemorations and celebrations" (Jarman 2000: 159).

One of the songs associated with the Orange Order is "The Sash My Father Wore," based on an earlier Irish tune called "Irish Molly-O." It references several major battles in the chorus: Derry (the 1689 siege of Derry), Aughrim (the 1691 battle of Aughrim), Enniskillen (the 1689 battle of Newtonbutler), and the Boyne (the 1690 battle of the Boyne). The use of symbolism is equally important on each side of the conflict. The reference to the "Twelfth" is July 12th, an important marching day that celebrates the Battle of the Boyne.

It is old but it is beautiful, and its colours they are fine
It was worn at Derry, Aughrim, Enniskillen and the Boyne.
My father wore it as a youth in bygone days of yore,
And on the Twelfth I love to wear the sash my father wore.

According to Zimmerman (2002: 300):

Most of the ballads and songs fall into one of these five categories: ballads commemorating past victories or persecutions of the Protestant cause – convivial songs – sentimental texts – descriptions of party fights – songs concerned with the ritual and mysteries of the Orange Institution and of other Orders.

Jigs, reels, hornpipes, and other forms of traditional music in Ireland were once simply a part of the whole island, and the repertoire drew from Scotland for musical materials as well. With partition, the Civil War, the economic desperation of the 1940s and 1950s, and finally the Troubles in the latter part of the twentieth century, the musicians of the North separated into Protestants playing one repertoire and Catholics playing a separate repertoire. Playing a jig or a reel, performing on an instrument like the harp or pipes, speaking Irish, and singing in Irish were all politicized as exclusively Catholic if one lived in the North. In some ways, that is still the case. In the Republic, jigs and reels were just the music that some people played, because "the people" were, for the most part, Catholic. As the situation in Northern Ireland intensified and the barriers went up, artists from each side expressed themselves through visual art, slogans, and murals, all of which are widely available for viewing on the Internet (look under "Belfast murals" or "Derry murals").

By the 1970s, the blood and thunder bands were mostly independent of the Orange Order, and focused on community participation and the celebration of Ulster Scots identity. Having been long exposed to hard rock and punk, the bands were "loud and proud"—fundraising for uniforms, establishing competitions, and parading outside the confines of Orange Order politics. In recent years, indoor performances after parading—complete with dancing, refreshments, trophies, and celebration—have established a new social and musical identity for the bands (and their fans) separate from that of the earlier traditions.

Reflecting a politically ambivalent and secularized society, the Ballykeel Loyal Sons of Ulster (a blood and thunder Ulster Scots flute band from Ballymena) has won awards and has developed an impressive following. Their niche in the flute band genre has been to perform a variety of traditional tunes from Scotland, Ireland, America, and Ulster, with only a few instrumental versions of Orange or Unionist songs: for example, the Scottish "Battle of Garvagh," the Orange jig "The Protestant Boys," the obviously Catholic "St. Patrick's Day," and the Ulster tune "Billy's March." Seeing loyalist audiences dancing to traditional tunes is now just another part of the contemporary fabric of Ulster identity (Ramsey 2011).

The Ulster Scots musical identity walks the fine line between Ireland and Scotland, because Scotland and Ireland are geographically so close together. While the days of the Troubles are essentially over, clashes of opinion, periodic outbreaks of violence, political maneuvering and economic issues continue to strain both sides in the wake of the Good Friday Agreement of 1998. In spite of the chaos of this era, and dire prophecies about the island's economic future, the 1990s and beyond—discussed in Chapter 9— were to usher in an era of startling new prosperity and new directions in traditional music and dance.

Discussion Questions

1. What would happen in your life if the contents of every known library, bank, and computer were destroyed in just a short time?
2. Why do you think the leader of a colonizing force would target the musicians, poets, and scholars of a nation it wants to colonize?

3. If you wanted to try to save something from dying out (a musical style, a language, an endangered species, or a culture), what steps would you take—not just to preserve it, but to help it thrive?

4. Do you believe that the National Literary Movement, the Gaelic Athletic Association, the Land League, and the Gaelic League were working at cross-purposes, or were they aiming toward a common goal? How did they achieve that goal, assuming they did?

5. How do you see music being used as a tool on both sides of the Troubles? Was it effective in achieving the aims of its performers and audience members?

6. What is the attraction, decade after decade, of "Danny Boy"?

PART II

Music Traditions Abroad and at Home

CHAPTER 4

Musics of the "Celtic" Nations

Is maith an scáthán súil charad ~ A friend's eye is a good mirror.

In this chapter, having covered aspects of Ireland's musical (and—more generally—cultural) history, we turn to a broader view of Ireland's context among related nations... Ireland's "musical friends," perhaps. In looking more broadly at Ireland's musical neighbors (both among the islands and on the mainland), our goal is to locate a set of shared histories, musical styles, and approaches to music while differentiating some key elements. You already know from reading earlier chapters that most Irish musicians tend to avoid using the word "Celtic" in describing the music they play, even if they sometimes bring into their playing a few tunes from Brittany or Scotland or the Shetland Islands. Its use in CD marketing has come to dominate all other intended meanings of the word. However, by understanding its use as a linguistic term, you should be able to both distinguish the Celtic from the non-Celtic, and to know why and how these related regions come together in this chapter.

Ireland was already sustaining a mixed population of Celts and non-Celts from the first millennium B.C.E., and its neighboring countries—including what would someday be called France and Spain—harbored a large proportion of Celts among their people. To call the *music* of these regions (Ireland, Scotland, Wales, Cornwall, Northumberland, the Isle of Man, Brittany, and Galicia in Spain) "Celtic" is, however, to stretch a point based on a historical distinction of linguistics. It is indeed more useful to think of anything "Celtic" as a linguistic definition first, rather than a musical or even a cultural one. Consider as well the idea that the Celtic languages are all minority languages (Kuter 2000: 319), no matter where they are spoken (Gaelic in Ireland and Scotland, Welsh in Wales, Cornish in Cornwall, Breton in France). Galego, spoken in the autonomous region of Galicia in northwestern Spain, is emphatically *not* a Celtic language. However, in the twenty-first century some people in the region have joined the Celtic musical bandwagon as if it were part of the Celtic linguistic—as opposed to musical—spectrum. In general, where minority languages are spoken, language activists tend to support local music, especially local songs in the minority language, in highlighting the importance of maintaining a local cultural identity.

One point to consider about how (and why) these regions might fit together into a single chapter of this book is that the archaeological record of the regions speaks quite strongly of similarities: all the regions, including northwestern Spain, feature pre-Celtic Neolithic standing stones, stone circles, dolmens and other burial tombs. Links between the regions are old. Considering their proximity to the ocean, particularly how easy it might be to cross from the islands to the mainland and back, one can envision at least a few links between some of the earliest pre-Celtic, stone-building, mariners.

In the early eighteenth century, the Welsh scholar Edward Lhuyd published *Archaeologia Britannica* (1707), in which he was the first to point out in print the linguistic differences between the languages spoken in Cornwall, Wales, and Brittany, on the one hand, and Ireland and Scotland, on the other, as well as the overall similarities joining them (Sykes 2006: 46). Hearkening back to the ancient Greeks, who first came up with the term *Keltoi* (an unflattering Greek term for "outsider"), Lhuyd began to examine the idea of "Celtic" languages in Ireland, Britain, and the western tip of France. And so the development of the concept of Celtic Otherness—linguistically, racially, and culturally separate from the English—began. It continued with the "Celtic Twilight" literary and artistic movement before the turn of the twentieth century, and is even now a part of the "Six Celtic Nations" promotion on the festival circuit, in which performers from Cornwall, the Isle of Man, Brittany, Ireland, Scotland, and Wales (not all quite "nations") are presented in a kind of musical (and sometimes athletic) Celtic roundtable. It is also useful to note that sometimes Northern Ireland counts as one of the "six nations," and sometimes Galicia and/or the Isle of Man do. It is a distinction based primarily on ideology. Lastly, we see this conflation in the marketing campaigns of New Age recordings, in which the word "Celtic" plus a natural feature ("mist," "stone," "valley," etc.) translates into CD sales for *all* the regions. "Celticism thrives, as pilgrimage, in the context of New Age spirituality, post-Cold War religious revivalism, and a mass-mediated 'postmodern' syncretic multiculturalism" (Stokes and Bohlman 2003: 10).

Ethnomusicologists have already pointed out how difficult it is to discuss an entity called "Celtic music" (see, for example, Porter 1998: 205–24) because it means so many different things to so many people. It also seems to mean so *little* to Irish and Scottish musicians in particular. Scott Reiss points out that the very term "Celtic" effectively "embraces those traditional musics whose proponents reject Celtic as a category" (Reiss 2003: 145). In the twenty-first century, "Celtic music" has become a modern construction emerging from a perceived shared identity in opposition to a dominant culture. This construction plays out in the pan-Celtic festivals, radio and concert programming, supergroup jam sessions that cross national boundaries, and the North American search for a unified "Celtic" past that encompasses the multiple nations (and emotional neediness sometimes engendered by being) of mixed heritage.

In terms of contemporary connections, one finds fiddles, bagpipes, accordions, flutes, frame drums, and other related instruments and dances across the region. Yet, before subscribing with too much enthusiasm to the claim that "therefore, they *must* be Celtic," note that *all* of these instruments are found *all over* northwestern Eurasia, and that bowed string instruments (including modern violins), transverse flutes, and bagpipes are played in India, too. Solo song traditions can be found in each area discussed in this chapter, but the entire continent happens to be peopled with solo singers from Ireland to farthest Siberia. For all the scholars, musicians, and marketers of CDs who struggle to define Celtic music, most succeed only in defining what it *isn't*, or pointing out that they know it when they hear it. So while there is no one type of "Celtic music," there are, in fact, types. James Porter argues that what one can now safely call Celtic music must reflect "the distinctive genres, styles and repertoires from those areas in which a Celtic language was historically, and is now, spoken" (Porter 1998: 215). That would rule out Galicia! Nonetheless, beginning here with Ireland's closest cousin, Scotland, and continuing to its most distant (and potentially non-Celtic) cousin, Galicia, this chapter focuses on musical and cultural connections between the regions, while noting the distinctions as they occur.

Scotland

Scotland's cultural geography includes differences between religious, linguistic, and musical traditions depending on the area within Scotland. Scottish regions include the northeast, where the Orkney and Shetland islands reflect considerable Scandinavian influence; the highlands, which are home to a number of families who still speak Gaelic at home; the lowlands and borderlands; the urban-industrial stretch across the midsection; and the western islands. The Scots are not just the closest musical cousins to the Irish; a shared history of early Catholicism and English colonialism under Oliver Cromwell and others have linked many of the Irish and Scots together. The two also share a history of Gaelic grammar and a large part of their vocabulary, though the spelling differs between the two languages in particular ways. Both Scotland and Ireland have instituted Gaelic immersion schools, which have produced fluent non-native speakers from English-only homes. Furthermore, Irish speakers often come from the western coasts of Ireland (whether they live there as adults or not), and Gaelic speakers of Scotland are largely highland and Outer Hebridean island dwellers. Yet Scotland has a third language, distinct from English and Gaelic: it is Scots, a language of the border region, known internationally as the dialect of the eighteenth-century poet Robert Burns. Between English, Gaelic, and Scots (Pictish is long extinct), each region of Scotland has something to offer in terms of song, and each region is rich in instrumental music.

Scottish singing in Gaelic occurs in both the highlands and southern islands, where the song genres run the gamut from labor songs to psalm singing to love songs and ballads. The Hebrides islands are known for waulking songs; these responsorial songs accompany the shrinking of woolen tweed. In the context of Hebridean life before the twentieth century, women would gather around a table with a length of wet tweed, lifting and slamming the tweed against the table while rotating its length from person to person. The lead singer would offer a verse (often a funny or entertaining one), and the other women would respond in chorus. Because shrinking the tweed is time-consuming, songs had to last a long time and be rich in verses. These songs are a source of rich documentation of the daily lives of Gaelic women. With the advent of mechanization in the twentieth century, the original context for the songs disappeared. However, women still sing these songs as part of the revival movement, both in Scotland and in maritime Canada (where men engage in the same activity, referred to as "milling"). Waulking songs were not the only labor songs; men and women alike used songs to accompany all kinds of island tasks, including milking, spinning, weaving, and rowing (Porter 2000: 361).

Ballads in Scotland, as elsewhere, develop a narrative over a series of verses. That narrative uses "stock" phrases (milk-white steed, for example, or gay gold ring), follows a relatively clear storyline, and may or may not include a chorus or refrain. Ballads are sung in English, Gaelic, and Scots, and do not shy away from some of the gory details of narrative. Lyric songs tend to reflect influences from Europe (particularly France) in that they focus more on emotional content rather than moving a story forward. Many of the singers in Scotland have been women, singing in the home; men sing as well, however, and have been more featured on stage and in recordings until recently. In the highlands, many of the songs include a chorus joined in by all present. The poet Robert Burns (1759–1796) collected songs, wrote poetry extensively, and wrote (or reworked) songs as well. His work, like that of many of his cohorts elsewhere, was at least partly a response to the current of Romantic nationalism that had taken hold of the European imagination so strongly. Some of his most popular songs, such as "My Love is Like a Red, Red Rose" or "Scots Wha Hae," are staples in the Scottish singing tradition.

Òran mór ("great song") is the Scottish equivalent to Irish *sean-nós* singing. It is sung in Gaelic, uses relatively free rhythm (depending primarily on the rhythm of the poetry rather than an external beat), is unaccompanied, and uses small vocal ornaments such as grace notes and turns. It appears in both the highlands and the islands, with significant variation between the two. Love laments, an important element in Irish song, are also found in Scottish song. "Tha Thìde agam Èirigh" ("It is Time for Me to Rise") of Lewis island is the story of a young man who has gone to see his sweetheart and discovers that she has died (compare this plot with the song "Úna Bhán" in Chapter 7). It has an interesting form: for each two-line verse, the second line forms the first line of the next verse. The lyrics are used for two different melodies (the melody of the first line and the melody of the second line), as in the two complete verses of Figure 4.1. Notice that the melody of the second line of the first verse is the same as the melody of the first line of the second verse. This configuration requires that the poetic rhythm of each line is equally applicable to either melody.

'S tha thìde agam èirigh ach a lèir dhomh mo bhrògan
'S gus a lèir dhomh mo bhata 's gun thoir e tacan a roid mi.

Figure 4.1 "Tha Thìde agam Èirigh"

I got myself up and put on my shoes
And I picked up my staff and was shortly rushing home

'S gus a lèir dhomh mo bhata 's gun thoir e tacan a roid mi
'S mi dol a shealltainn air a' ghruagaich a bha sa bhuaile na h-ònar.
And I picked up my staff and was shortly rushing home
And it's me going to see the honorable young woman.

'S mi dol a shealltainn air a' ghruagaich a bha sa bhuaile na h-ònar
Ach nuair ràinig mi am baile cha robh a thaigh marbu chòir dha.
And it's me going to see the honorable young woman.
But when I came home, things were not as they should be.

Ach nuair ràinig mi am baile cha robh a thaigh marbu chòir dha
Bha mo ghruagach dhonn mhìn-gheal 's i na sìneadh san t-seòmar.
But when I came home, things were not as they should be
My bright, brown-haired sweetheart lying down in the room.

Bha mo ghruagach dhonn mhìn-gheal 's i na sìneadh san t-seòmar
'S i na sìneadh fon uinneig far nach cluinninn-sa còmhradh.
My bright, brown-haired sweetheart lying down in the room.
She was lying under the window where I could not hear her speak.

'S i na sìneadh fon uinneig far nach cluinninn-sa còmhradh
'S i na sìneadh air dèile 's i na lèine fuar reòite.
She was lying under the window where I could not hear her speak
She was lying on a board in her shroud, cold.

'S i na sìneadh air dèile 's i na lèine fuar reòite
Thì a chruthaich na saoghail, glèidh mi gun dhol gòrach.
She was lying on a board in her shroud, cold
Thou who shaped the worlds, keep me from going mad.

Thì a chruthaich na saoghail, glèidh mi gun dhol gòrach
Glèidh rium-sa mo chiall 's na leig a dh'iarraidh an còrr mi.
Thou who shaped the worlds, keep me from going mad
Keep me from losing my reason, and let me endure no more.

Religious song performance includes Gaelic psalmody, a type of Presbyterian responsorial singing in the Church of Scotland, in which the leader (called a precenter) "lines out" the words and melody of the song, and the congregation joins in response. The religious currents of the mid-sixteenth century caused Presbyterianism to experience a great upswing in popularity; today, a number of Scottish Presbyterian institutions hold services in Gaelic.

Some Scottish singers perform *puirt-a-beul* or "mouth music": it uses percussive lyrics that are sung very rapidly (almost instrumentally). The poetic rhythm of the lyrics (which, in Gaelic, emphasize the first syllable) gave rise to what is called the "Scottish snap" in instrumental music, in which the first note of a measure is short (and often played staccato). This characteristic snap does not appear in most of Irish instrumental music. Mouth music is used specifically for dancing. It is rhythmic and percussive, and aspects of it imitate both the percussive sounds of the pipes and of fiddle bowing, giving "lift" to the feet of the dancer.

Scottish music is famous for supporting multiple distinct instrumental traditions. The harp (*clàrsach*) and pipes (*pìob*) of various kinds are among the oldest of the Scottish instruments, and the fiddle is the most common. Each of these instruments is generally played separately from the other, and each represents different aspects of Scottish social history. The accordion—both the melodeon and piano accordion—remains popular throughout the islands of Britain and Ireland, and its appearance in Scotland (particularly for dance accompaniment) is to be expected.

The harp or *clàrsach* was once considered the national instrument of Scotland (as it was in Ireland and Wales), but as the older context for harping began to disappear, the bagpipes took over that role. At its beginnings prior to the ninth century (represented by the Pictish carvings on stone found in northeastern Scotland), the harp was considered the most prestigious of the instruments. The twelfth-century Welsh traveler and historian Giraldus Cambrensis, who continually offers us insights on early performance practice, notes that the Scottish wire-strung harp was perhaps the strongest (and most pleasing, to his ears) of the harping traditions:

> In the opinion of many people, Scotland has not only equaled her mistress, Ireland, in music, but today excels and surpasses her by far. For that reason, people look upon her now as the fountain of the art.
>
> (cited in Ralls-MacLeod 2000: 44)

The Scottish harping tradition fell away with the encroachment of the English in the 1600s, but the instrument was revived by the end of the nineteenth century as a gut-string harp (Figure 4.2). Since the 1960s, the number of performances, festivals, and concerts on the Scottish harp has exceeded all expectations, and it is now one of the essential Scottish solo instruments once more, performed at home and abroad.

The basic materials of the bagpipes—a reed inserted into a "chanter" with holes on which to play a melody, a bag to maintain a steady flow of air, and one or more pipes for drones—can be found anyplace with sheep or goats in the local economy. Europeans use many types of bagpipes, and their use extends to India. The Scottish bagpipe itself occurs in several forms. The best-known Scottish bagpipe is the *pìob mhòr* ("great pipes"), familiar as the instrument played in large groups for parades, and solo for funereal events, particularly for firefighters and police officers. In Scotland, the pipes were banned during the 1746 Act of Proscription as weapons of war. Scottish pipe instruments also include lowland smallpipes and border pipes (which were largely replaced by the fiddle at the start of the nineteenth century).

The *pìob mhòr* or Great Highland Pipes include the basic elements of any bagpipe, with three drone pipes. The conical bore of the chanter produces a sound that can be heard from some distance away (Figure 4.3). They have been associated with hereditary piping families (the MacCrimmons, MacGregors, and others). Solo free-rhythm playing is called *piobaireachd* or *ceòl mòr* ("great music"); lighter dance tunes are called *ceòl*

Figure 4.2 A contemporary Scottish gut-string *clàrsach*, made by Jack Yule of Midlothian, Scotland. Photo courtesy of Seumas Gagne

beag ("little music"). *Piobaireachd* (pronounced "pibroch") is a type of theme and variations, in which the player performs a fairly basic melody (the *ùrlar* or "ground"), then varies that theme in increasingly complex ways. The term *canntaireachd* ("singing") refers to a way of transmitting and recalling the piping tune repertoire vocally.

The Scottish fiddle divides into roughly four styles, encompassing the regions of the northeast (strathspeys and airs), the border (airs and hornpipes), the northern islands (primarily polkas), and the highlands (reels and jigs). Note that across the border in Northumberland, hornpipes and airs are also quite popular. All tune types are played in each area, but some areas tend to favor certain types. Fiddle tunes are often named after people, regions, or events, but in practice, many players pay little attention to the tune titles, focusing instead on the tunes themselves. The fiddle has been common in Scotland since at least the sixteenth century, and it has been the primary traditional instrument used to accompany dancing.

The Northern Isles

The Northern Isles, to the north of Scotland, include both the Orkney Islands and the Shetland Islands; they are distinct from the Hebrides (which lie to the west of Scotland), and are directly on the route to (or, perhaps more accurately, *from*) Scandinavia. They present a fascinating case study in musical transmission and culture in diaspora. Each set of islands comprises an archipelago of dozens of small islands; they have developed

Figure 4.3 The Scottish *pìob mhòr*, played by John Dally

their own set of historical, linguistic, and cultural values, in part, from a history of Neolithic settlement, Pictish culture, invasions from Norway, and eventual annexation by Scotland. These layers of settlement are visible in the islands in particular because stone was the primary building material available. Ruins from every layer dot the wind-swept, nearly treeless islands, and the latest layers of modern Scottish and Scandinavian culture form a thriving part of island life across the north as well.

Evidence of Viking occupation still permeates the islands, but it is different here from what the Vikings left behind in Ireland. From many of the island names ending in "-ay" (from Old Norse *ey*, island), to the ubiquitous place name *holm* (Old Norse *holmr*, islet; cf. Stockholm), most place names are Viking in origin. Inhabitants of the Northern Isles do not necessarily think of themselves as being particularly Scottish. Norn—a Western Scandinavian language spoken in both the Orkney Islands and the Shetland Islands until the early nineteenth century—persists in a few nouns and adjectives. The Picts, who are believed to have inhabited part of the northern mainland and the islands until the arrival of the Vikings in the early ninth century, were skilled stoneworkers. Some of their earliest works include a (mainland) depiction of a harper, revealing harping to be part of early music of the region. The Vikings significantly intermarried with some of the Picts, particularly on the islands, and both sets of islands were dominated by Viking rule until the fifteenth century. At that point, the Orkneys and the Shetlands were ceded to Scotland. On both sets of islands, local traditional songs tend to focus on the sea and on one's livelihood—fishing in the Shetland Islands, and farming in the Orkney Islands. The rough water around the islands has reinforced for the islanders a sense of hardiness, rather than one of isolation.

The Orkney Islands—just ten miles to the north of Scotland—include fiddle and piping band traditions, as well as singer-songwriters. Accordions, guitars, tin whistles, mandolins, and contemporary instruments are common. The tunes performed locally are drawn from Scotland, Scandinavia, Ireland, and the Shetland Islands, and there is a distinctive local tune repertoire as well. One might well find a Swedish *ganglåt* (a march-like "walking" tune) such as "Gärdebylåtten" performed immediately after the locally-based "Dancing Waves." The islands' proximity to the mainland of Scotland enables considerable cross-fertilization, with both import and export of tunes, dances, and songs. Ceilidhs (dances) feature quadrilles, reels, jigs, and polkas, often in local versions, together with dances specific to the islands. Many family names of Orcadians are Scandinavian rather than Scottish, and there is a sense of local pride in independence—or at least a sense of autonomy—from the mainland of Scotland.

If the Orkney Islanders regard themselves to be a separate entity from Scotland, the citizens of the Shetland Islands consider themselves to be even more so. About seventy miles north of Scotland, the Shetland Islands (Old Norse: *Hjaltland*) are like the centerpiece of a three-pointed equidistant star including the Faroe Islands, Bergen (Norway), and Aberdeen (Scotland). The islanders have a much more explicitly Scandinavian set of influences in their forms of musical expression specifically, and cultural expression more generally. The Viking Fire Festival (called the Up-Helly-Aa, and worth locating images of online!) is held each January in Lerwick; a celebration of Viking culture with music, dance, alcohol, and costuming, it culminates in the ritual burning of a Viking galley after a torchlight parade.

Whereas on the Orkney Islands one can find Scottish pipe bands and even a few tartans, the Shetland Islanders tend to make their forms of expression specifically Shetland; neither entirely Scandinavian nor entirely Scottish. For example, fiddle playing is common from Scotland to Norway, including the islands in between. In southwestern Norway, however, a particular variant of the fiddle—the *hardingfele*—uses sympathetic strings underneath the normal strings of the fiddle. These sympathetic strings vibrate when the normal strings are bowed, producing a unique ringing that is absolutely characteristic of the *hardingfele* sound. In the Shetland Islands, some fiddlers brush one or more of the neighboring strings of the melody string they happen to be bowing, creating a soft ringing sound reminiscent of the *hardingfele* but not entirely like it. While mainland Scottish fiddlers can choose to employ drone strings to support the melody in their playing, the Shetlanders who use this technique are not droning so much as ringing.

Many islanders credit Tom Anderson (1910–1991) with reviving the Shetland fiddle tradition. In the 1950s, he was concerned that the fiddle tradition was dying out (as a result of a religious revival in the nineteenth century that had also severely impacted the fiddle traditions of Scandinavia), and gathered those Shetland players that he believed to be the best together in "Da Forty Fiddlers" to reaffirm and promote the Shetland tunes and fiddle styles. He was a member of the Shetland Folk Society, a committed collector of fiddle tunes, and a tune composer himself. He taught many young fiddlers to play Shetland-specific tunes, both within the schools and privately. His collection of Shetland tunes forms some of the core fiddle repertoire of the area.

Local dance versions of Scottish reels—accompanied by the fiddle—were already being described in the local literature by the early nineteenth century, just a century after the introduction of the fiddle to the islands (Cooke 1986: 7). By the twentieth century, the accordion, guitar, and other instruments had become a part of Shetland "traditional" music, and many of the same debates about traditional and modern carried on in the islands, just as on the mainland of Scotland and the other regions mentioned in this book. In addition, the twentieth century saw the beginning of Shetland women playing the fiddle, and the gradual shift toward the accordion being used more for dancing, along with the fiddle used more for listening. Contemporary music of both the Orkney and Shetland Islands runs the gamut from rock to music influenced by the Scottish and Irish supergroups.

Cape Breton

It would be a disservice to discuss Scotland without including Cape Breton in the maritime Atlantic region of eastern Canada. After the Highland Clearances of the late eighteenth and early nineteenth centuries, in which thousands of people were forced first to the coasts and then abroad so that the land could be used for grazing, Cape Breton in Nova Scotia became home to 25,000 displaced Scots. Even as the use of Gaelic plummeted in Scotland, it continued in Cape Breton, to the point that even now the region is home to a small but growing number of native speakers. In Cape Breton, the song repertoire includes both Scottish songs and those native to Nova Scotia. The waulking songs of Scottish women were in Cape Breton sung by both men and women, offering a unique male perspective in a similar context. Because the area supports a thriving cultural revival, genres such as *puirt-a-beul* or "mouth music" are becoming better known to the fiddlers (though mostly the Gaelic-speaking ones), who accompany dances.

One of the main characteristics of songs composed in Cape Breton has been spontaneity, with verses created on the spur of the moment about a neighbor's sheep caught in a snare, the immediacy of household and barnyard chores, roofing shingles falling on a flock of chickens, and occasional teasing verses about physical prowess or sexual potency (in metaphoric terms). *Puirt-a-beul* songs are used to accompany dancing; in particular, solo step dances of various kinds, or social dance involving small groups of dancers. The following *puirt-a-beul* verse (from a song—or a tune?—titled "U Goraidh Giridh Goraidh") references fiddlers.

> *Làn taighe dh'fhìdhleirean*
> *Làn taighe chaileagan*
> *Làn taighe luba dubha*
> *'S làn a' mhuidhe mharagan.*

> A house full of fiddlers
> A house full of girls
> A house full of black pudding
> And full of churned pudding.

Cape Breton has served as a repository, in some ways, for tunes (and some songs) that left Scotland with the Highland Clearances and fell out of the repertoire. Some Scottish fiddlers have actually come to Cape Breton to discover new/old tunes from the eighteenth century and revive them in the Scottish repertoire. The sight of a dozen or more

Cape Breton fiddlers seated near an upright piano "chording" out the accompaniment is a common one, particularly in the summers during the festival and tourist season. Furthermore, the Scottish tradition of step dancing, which came to Cape Breton and thrived, died in Scotland and is only now being revived through events such as the Ceòlas summer school, held yearly in the Hebridean island of South Uist. Lastly, the entire scene is enlivened by an impressive array of traditional festivals (*féisean*, pronounced "feshin") throughout Scotland and in North America as well.

Celtic Britain: Wales, Northumberland, Cornwall, and the Isle of Man

Within the boundaries of the island of Britain, several regions bear some musical evidence of a shared history with Ireland and Scotland. Wales, to the west of the island, is in the midst of a strong cultural revival, with harpers and singers touring internationally. Northumberland, in northeast England just below the border with Scotland, hosts a revived piping tradition. Cornwall, in the extreme southwestern peninsula of England, was and has been a home to the fiddle, harp, and bagpipe. The Isle of Man, to the west of Britain, is heavily influenced by both Scotland and Ireland. The geography of these regions is windswept and at least partially bounded by the sea. As is generally the case in the other regions of this chapter, the Welsh, Northumbrians, Cornish, and Manx people (particularly those involved with the revival/folklore movement in music and/or language) sometimes envision and define themselves in opposition, more or less, to the mainstream of England. All the areas are rich in Neolithic-era stone monuments.

Part of the cultural revival movement in Wales has to do with a resurgent interest in the Welsh language. Cornwall once had a distinct language related to both Welsh and Breton. However, the last native speaker passed away in the eighteenth century, and only recent efforts have seen results in terms of the potential for revival. Speakers of Cornish and Breton actually stand a good chance of understanding each other through their shared vocabulary. Many Northumbrians speak a local dialect called "Geordie" (and variations thereof), and a man from the area might be referred to as a "Geordie," just like "Jock" for Scots, "Paddy" for Irish, and "Taffy" for the Welsh. It is worth noting that outsiders tend to use these terms, accurate or not, and that many people from this part of the world refer to *all* North Americans as "Yanks." However, the dialects of the Northumberland region are not radically distinct from English the way Welsh and Cornish are as separate languages.

Wales

Wales is a part of the island of Britain, yet it continues to maintain its own cultural autonomy amidst a growing language revival. In contrast to the Irish, more than a quarter of the Welsh population is bilingual, and that number continues to grow; its Welsh name, Cymru, is pronounced "*kum*-ree." It has had a strong harping tradition that dates as far back as that of the Irish, and the Welsh are well known for their choral harmony singing. The fiddle is an essential Welsh instrument, and the ubiquitous guitar—nothing particularly Welsh about it—has a strong presence as well. Welsh musical traditions also include solo singing in both Welsh and English, from life-cycle/calendrical and work songs to ballads and love songs. Many of the songs reference the natural world and the place of humans in it, from dialogue songs with birds to songs about particular places (Kinney 2000: 344). Plenty of Welsh musicians are involved in the performance of contemporary musical genres. Indeed, part of the cultural revival in Wales includes a deep sense of pride and connection to home regardless of music genre. The Welsh language is deeply embedded in that sense of home.

The most famous of the early Welsh bards is Taliesin, believed to have lived in the sixth century and often linked with the Irish poet Amairgin (see Chapter 2). The word for song/tune (*cerdd*) is linked to the earliest bards (*pencerdd*), who performed for the royal and elite members of Welsh society, just as the Irish and Scottish bards did in their home countries. The bagpipe (*pybeu*) had been popular in Wales relatively early on; however, piping was not part of the bardic heritage, and therefore adhered to a lower status (ibid.: 348). The iconographic record reveals a region rich in multi-drone pipes and their pipers, particularly at weddings, from as early as the eleventh century (Mathews 1999: 424).

The earliest bardic instruments in Wales included a type of bowed lyre called the *crwth* (pronounced "crowd"). The *crwth* was constructed with a flat rectangular frame and included up to six strings played in a kind of repeating pattern (Rees 1999: 425). The repeating or *ostinato* pattern served as a backdrop to whatever needed to be sung, whether it was someone's family history, accounting of livestock, or explanation of a place name. It was part of a larger group of bowed lyres found not just in Wales, but on the Continent as well, where it was known by various names, including the *crotta* (Bevil 1973). Both the harp and fiddle superseded the *crwth*, and its entire repertoire has disappeared.

Giraldus Cambrensis was, in a sense, the first Welsh ethnomusicologist. He toured Wales in 1188 and—in addition to discussing Ireland and Irish music fairly extensively—gave us our first detailed written descriptions of Welsh music, including the fact that the main instruments were the harp, *crwth*, and pipes (Kinney 2000: 349). In his 1194 *Descriptio Cambriae*, he includes this controversial passage: "When they make music together, they sing their songs not in unison, as is done elsewhere, but in parts, with many modes and phrases, so that in a crowd of singers you would hear as many songs and differentiations of voices as you could see heads." Why is this passage important? Because it implies that polyphonic (multi-part) singing was common in Wales at about the same time as its appearance on the Continent. The development of polyphony (at Notre Dame in Paris) is believed to have been one of the most important developments of Western music in the medieval era. The Welsh have not historically been credited with the independent development of polyphony; if this passage were true, it might cause some music historians to spin in their graves!

The Welsh harp or *telyn* is the national instrument of Wales. Most distinctive (and radically different from Ireland and the other regions) is the "triple harp" or *telyn deires*, which came to Wales from Italy in the early seventeenth century (Fulton 1991: 3). Its three rows of strings allow the player to perform any note desired (unlike in classical harping, in which one must manipulate pedal tuners rapidly to reach various pitches). Comparing the three rows of strings, the inner strings include the "accidentals" (sharps and flats), while the outer strings are tuned in unison. The form of the triple harp was finalized in the eighteenth century, and although it is difficult to play, its unique nature among all the other harps of the region has led to an almost fierce celebration of it as a national instrument. Note, in the following verse from the Welsh national anthem (Bowen 1991: 9), the reference to both poet and harp:

Os treisiodd y Saeson fy ngwlad dan eu troed
Mae heniaith y Cymry mor fyw ag erioed.
Ni luddiwyd yr awen gan erchyll law brad,
Na thelyn berseiniol fy ngwlad.

Even if the English have trampled my country underfoot,
The old tongue of the Welsh is as alive as ever.
The poets have not been silenced by the ugly hand of treachery,
Nor has the sweet harp of my land.

Some of the harpers of medieval Wales traveled to Ireland for specialized training (Ralls-MacLeod 2000: 55). The harp tradition in Wales is proudly described as remaining unbroken "dating from prehistoric times to the present day" (Bowen 1991: 9), even as various attempts to still or suppress it occurred. The courtly context for harp playing diminished after the annexation of Wales to England, so the songs of the Welsh bards shifted toward lyrics having more to do with the natural world, love, and other less-courtly subjects. The Welsh noblemen had by that time taken over the system of patronage from the royals. It was common at that point for harpers to teach the children of noblemen to play and sing.

The *cerdd dant* is a type of song performed with the harp as a partner, not as accompanist. While North Americans are accustomed to using a plucked stringed instrument (guitar, harp, banjo) as accompaniment to the voice, the idea of the harp as an equal contributor to a performance is unusual. Knowledge of this tradition unique to the Welsh was required for advancement as a bard to the level of *pencerdd* (Rees 1999: 427). The Welsh language, while belonging within the Celtic language family, uses an accent pattern different from the Gaelic languages. Whereas the Irish accent the first syllable of their words, for the most part, the Welsh tend to accent the penultimate syllable, creating particular rhythmic stresses in the songs (Saer 1974: 11). Other Welsh song genres included laments about specific tragedies (such as the Bardsey Boat Lament, "Galarnad Cwch Enlli," lamenting the drowning of six people in 1822), carols (religious folksongs performed at various religious holidays, not just Christmas), macaronic (bilingual) songs, and worksongs.

A number of English laws were passed with the intention of suppressing Welsh culture. To that end, Elizabeth I set a decree against Welsh bards in 1568, intended to "rid Wales of numerous vagraunt and idle persons naming theim selfes mynstrelles Rithmers and Barthes" (Suggett 2003: 157), and a number of libraries and monasteries were destroyed in the mid-1600s. In *The Times* of London, an editorial in 1867 suggested the following:

An Eisteddfod [the annual Welsh literary and musical festival] is one of the most mischievous and selfish pieces of sentimentalism which could possibly be perpetrated. It is simply a foolish interference with the natural progress of civilisation and prosperity ... The sooner all Welsh specialists disappear from the face of the earth, the better.

(Sykes 2006: 41)

Religious songs, including psalms and hymns, had been performed as a part of Welsh religious services for some time. The development in Wales of both the Methodist and the Nonconformist Puritanical Protestant Churches in the eighteenth century, which condemned the performance of non-religious music, had a diminishing effect on secular music and dance. In fact, the dance tradition never fully recovered from its suppression in the name of religion (Kinney 2000: 353). Instruments were banned and burned, even as recently as 1905, in a series of Methodist revivals (Mathews 1999: 424). Some Welsh people still dance a semblance of the old dances, but what they dance is a reconstruction in a (somewhat) post-fundamentalist climate.

One of the common places to experience traditional Welsh music and dance is at the *noson lawen,* similar to the *noze looan* of Cornwall and the *fest noz* of Brittany; these are small music and dance parties celebrated by people in the immediate neighborhood. Another Welsh context for music is the two great competitive festivals or *eisteddfod.* The first *eisteddfod* took place in the 1600s; it was a gathering of singers, harpers, and poets. Festivals celebrating a variety of Welsh sacred and secular music continue today, and are attended by thousands of people. In addition, the performance of rock, pop, hip hop, and reggae using the Welsh language is a lively part of the popular music scene, and a healthy sign of Welsh youth taking ownership of their language as well as their culture.

Northumberland

Northumberland, in the far northwest of England, is as far away from London as one can travel and still be in England. Its location on the border of Scotland has enlivened the traditional music repertoire with tunes from the border counties of Scotland, the entire northern portion of England, Northern Wales, Ireland, and its own rich local tunes. The Gateshead/Newcastle urban area has seen considerable immigration for several hundred years as miners and others have sought work in the area, bringing tunes from their home areas. Attending a music session anywhere from Durham to the Scottish border will net a bountiful listening experience, as the tunes shift from Northumbrian to Scottish to Welsh to Irish—and even to a few American "Scots-Irish" tunes from the southern mountains.

The fiddle and pipes are among the most visible of the Northumbrian musical instruments, but melodeons (a smaller version of the accordion, commonly used in regional musics), guitars, flutes, concertinas, and other local instruments appear at music sessions along with the fiddle and pipes. Harps were once played in the region, but are no longer part of the local tradition. As in sessions from Ireland, a song might be called for once or twice in an evening, but generally singers tend to go to gatherings intended specifically for songs rather than wait their turn among the jigs, reels, and hornpipes.

The fiddle tradition of Northumberland has thrived since at least the seventeenth century. Several manuscripts survive that indicate a rich repertoire of regional dance tunes, particularly hornpipes (see Chapter 6). One of the features of Northumbrian playing, however, is the localization of tunes from outside the region. For example, a strathspey (characterized by Scottish melodies played in a short–long, short–long rhythm) might be turned into a hornpipe (long–short, long–short). Jigs, reels, and marches are also popular in the region. The fiddle overwhelmingly dominates music sessions (in terms of sheer numbers of instruments) simply for its ease of portability and playing, compared to the Northumbrian pipes (called smallpipes). The fiddle is often paired with the smallpipes.

The Northumbrian smallpipes are the region's most distinctive instrument. The smallpipes, related to the Irish *uilleann* pipes and the Scottish smallpipes and border pipes, are not mouth-blown; instead, they are operated with a bellows under the right arm, while the left arm supplies a steady stream of air to the chanter and three drones. Many Northumbrian tunes feature a shift between two different keys, "based on the alternation of tonic major and supertonic minor chords" (Gammon 2000: 331). The pipes are very quiet and often described as "sweet" because the chanter is cylindrical rather than the more brassy-sounding conical chanters of Scotland (Feintuch 1999: 5). In addition, all sound can stop, depending on the actions of the player, which enables the player to use silence as a musical element. Another important aspect of the small-pipes is the players' use of intricate variations. Unlike the Irish pipes, however, they can be played sitting or standing.

The Northumbrian piping tradition has been associated primarily with piping families, as in Scotland. The development of the Northumbrian Pipers' Society, with its attendant publications, competitions, and other events, has contributed significantly to the current strength of the instrument. Its revival, spurred at least partly by its inclusion in regional popular music, has attracted new players to the tradition. Kathryn Tickell, in particular, stands out as one of the most famous female players of the instrument *and* as someone who has combined the pipes with more standard rock'n'roll instruments.

The local singing tradition is quite rich. Singers such as Lou Killen (1934–2013) have done much to popularize both the songs and the style. In a region in which "language and music are two markers of identity" (Feintuch 1999: 5), a combination of societies (the Northumbrian Language Society, for example), language books, songbooks, and recordings combine to keep local interest in regional traditions strong. Folk clubs and festivals also serve to highlight both the instrumental and vocal traditions of the region, continually reinforcing its sense of difference from the rest of England.

Cornwall

The music and culture of Cornwall are historically connected with that of Brittany, not only for linguistic reasons but for geographic ones as well. Brittany is only about a hundred miles from Cornwall. Both belong to the Brythonic language branch (one of the two major branches of the Celtic language family—the other is Goidelic), both experienced combat with the Vikings, and both are home to a similar set of musical traditions. In medieval Cornwall, harpers and poets regularly performed at the homes of the aristocracy. A series of laws enacted by the English changed the legal and financial status of the harpers' patrons, and gradually the Cornish tradition of harping suffered the same fate as in some of the other areas: it diminished, fell out of favor, and eventually died out prior to its contemporary revival.

The performance of instrumental dance music was further hindered by social changes (spurred by religious reforms) that included growing disapproval of nonreligious music and dance performance. However, throughout the nineteenth century the influence of the Romantic nationalist movement was felt throughout the British Isles, and Cornish people continued to uphold their local traditions. For example, the *troyl*, a kind of music and dance party, continues to be performed in small towns. Local names for instruments found all over the region include the *crowd* (fiddle) and *crowdy crawn* (frame drum). The *crowd* is used to perform a variety of tunes, and has never been restricted to the Cornish repertoire. The accordion accompanies traditional dancing because of its ability to penetrate the noise of a group of dancers, as well as its ability to provide a percussive chordal accompaniment to the melody.

An ensemble once common in Cornwall was the Cornish *pyba* (a local variant of the bagpipe) combined with a *bombarde* (a kind of double-reed folk oboe) and accompanied by drums. This particular combination is also found in Brittany and Galicia; in Cornwall, it had died out completely, and was revived only in the last few decades. The ensemble also has a role in the revivalist movement, in which people interested in regaining a sense of regional identity perform Cornish traditional music exclusively. The older vocal music of Cornwall saw a decline with the diminished use of the Cornish language, so the region's more recent folk music is performed almost entirely in English. Some of the older songs are still performed as instrumental tunes. The bands Skwardya and Krena perform contemporary music (rock, punk, funk, etc.) using both Cornish and English.

The Cornish people have a celebration similar to the Irish *céilí* and the Breton *fest noz*; called the *noze looan*, this event is a chance for people to spend time together singing, dancing, and socializing. Dancing is particularly important at these events, and local dances and tunes predominate. The bagpipes of Cornwall have a double chanter, which makes them stand out in comparison to pipes of the neighboring regions. The double chanter allows for harmony or drone playing by one or the other chanters.

As with any revival music in its early days, particularly in Britain and Ireland, enthusiasm for the pipes, harp, and fiddle, and for the local repertoire, rests in the hands of just a few people. It is often a matter of developing high-profile festivals, influential recordings, and significant (televised) concerts that can make the difference between a revival movement grinding along with grim determination, or one that actually takes flight. In Cornwall, all of the elements are in place for traditional music to thrive: it hosts its own pan-Celtic festivals, it sends performers to other pan-Celtic festivals frequently, and the growing strength of the language and other forms of cultural expression are being cited as potential reasons for Cornwall to gain its own Assembly within the British Parliament, like those of Scotland, Wales, and Northern Ireland.

Cornish regional identity is multifaceted, and includes naming traditions (last names beginning with the letters "Tre-" are classic Cornish names, as in Tremain, Trelawny, Trevelyan, and others). The song "Trelawny" is often performed at rugby matches as a kind of regional anthem. Several of Cornwall's musicians and musical groups have begun to adapt non-Cornish instruments (the banjo, for example) to Cornish music. The Cornish people do not automatically claim or enjoy the music from their region; like all of the areas in this chapter, they pick and choose the music that they prefer. However, the development of a pan-Celtic identity seen elsewhere has had an impact in Cornwall too, particularly among the language revivalists.

The Isle of Man

While not quite sharing the same relationship to the British crown as, say, Cornwall, the Isle of Man is another territory of the region with a Celtic language and both instrumentation and songs that link it, profoundly, with the others in this chapter. Citizens of the Isle of Man have passports that identify them as "British citizens," but the island belongs neither to the United Kingdom nor the European Union. Manx, the (reviving) language of the island, belongs in the category of the Goidelic languages (with Irish-Gaelic and Scots-Gaelic), and the island itself is named after Manannan Mac Lir, the ancient god of the sea. The language—Manx—underwent a collapse after the island became a possession of the British Crown in 1765. Yes, Manx cats (the ones with no tails or stubby tails) are also from the Isle of Man.

The central position of the Isle of Man (between Ireland, Scotland, Wales, and England) has led to its reception of musical influences from each area (and Norway as well), and the development of its own syncretic traditions. The island hosts yearly festivals (both local and pan-Celtic), particularly Yn Chruinnaght ("The Gathering"). In addition, the recording industry has supported the continuing cultural revival by releasing new recordings of the island's musicians and singers. Island singers perform solo songs in both Manx and English, and draw from the repertoires of the neighboring regions as well. The local version of the carol (religious song), called the *carval*, derives from a much earlier mainland tradition (Bazin 1999: 226).

The fiddle, harp, guitar, tin whistle, and other instruments common to the region are all a part of the island's musical history. Though harps and pipes were absent by the seventeenth century, probably because of the absence of a healthy patronage system, the revival has reached Manx musical culture along with everywhere else in the region. As is the case with the other regions described in this book, contemporary enthusiasm for Manx music is tightly linked with enthusiasm for the language; the "revival," then, is one in which music and language are intertwined and infused with identity politics. Though the island is small, as one of the "Six Celtic Nations" it sends musical representatives to the pan-Celtic music festivals.

Celtic Western Europe: Brittany and Galicia

Two peninsulas jut into the Atlantic from Western Europe: Brittany (Bretagne) and Spain. Brittany's size dominates the much smaller peninsula of Normandy (to its immediate north), and its growing importance as one of the distinctive regions of France has led to increased politicization of the region. Galicia is an autonomous region of four provinces in northwestern Spain, directly north of Portugal. Asturias, to the right of Galicia, also lays claim to "Celticity," though it is not so famous in musical circles as Galicia. A map of Iberia (including Portugal) would reveal the northwestern region as a kind of cultural peninsula. Both Brittany and Galicia have experienced layers of influence from the Romans, the Celts, and the island of Britain. The coastal areas of both regions depend on the sea for their livelihood, while the inland areas are more agricultural. Tourism is important to the local economies. Finally, both regions divide into sub-regions, with differences of language and cultural expression highlighted in music and dance.

Brittany (Western France)

Approximately 20 percent of people over the age of 15 in Lower Brittany (French: *Basse-Bretagne*) speak Breton (Breizh) as their daily language, and many more speak it at least some of the time. Breton is related to the Welsh and Cornish language groups, and indeed the region and its many small islands saw settlement by Welsh and Cornish travelers as early as 100 C.E. The Celts had come through the area 600 years prior, and the Romans after them. But its pre-Celtic dolmens, megaliths and extraordinary 7,700-year-old stone formations at Carnac (more than 2,000 standing stones in alignment) attest to its significant history in relationship to the other regions in this chapter (and other areas with megaliths, including Belgium). Brittany comprises a large peninsula extending parallel to the British peninsula of Cornwall, and it held cultural ties to both Wales and Ireland in the first millennium. In fact, Brittany maintained its political independence until the early 1500s, at which point François I forcibly united Brittany with France. That Brittany has maintained a sense of cultural unity, at least in parts of the lower (peninsular) region, is impressive given its vulnerable position on the French Atlantic coast, as well as its political ties to France.

Lorient, the largest city on the southern coast, has been an essential port in France's military efforts; its large protected harbor (together with the three rivers) enables large ships to come and go safely. Lorient is now also the site of the famous Inter-Celtic Festival, held yearly in August and hosting musicians, dancers, and writers from Wales, Ireland, Scotland, Spain, Brittany, and Cornwall. Musical identity in Brittany itself is, generally, a strongly local practice. No one musical tradition or style or person dominates the musical scene; instead, what the people in one's own area are playing or singing is what is important. This tendency reflects a larger cultural focus on the local (Badone 1987: 16); the subculture, not the region, has been dominant until recently. Nonetheless, musicians across the region feel very strongly that they are Breton. Furthermore, musical performance is part of the regular lives of Bretons, not a construction for tourists (Wilkinson 1999: 41).

Bretons have a strong history of musical performance, both instrumental and vocal. As was the case with Ireland, Scotland, and Wales, there once was a thriving harp tradition in the region. Called the *telenn* (compare with the Welsh *telyn*), the Breton harp was played by bards during the medieval period, but declined at approximately the same time as the other harping traditions due to changes in patronage, the growing popularity of baroque music in the homes of the aristocracy, and other factors. Harp performance practice died out entirely until the efforts of luthier Jord Cochevelou led to the painstaking reconstruction of the local harping tradition in the 1950s. Cochevelou's famous son, Alan Stivell, has popularized the Breton harp in festivals and concerts, and the likelihood of its disappearance now is remote. Some of the international popularity of the Breton harp stems from its appearance on various New Age recordings, and some of it also has to do with its appearance as a "new voice" with an entirely different repertoire at a Celtic musical table generally dominated by the Irish.

In southwestern Brittany, the *biniou* (bagpipe) functions as a kind of musical symbol of the region. While bagpipes may be found in other parts of France, they do not possess such a symbolic cultural function as they do in Brittany. Two essential musical ensembles serve this purpose: the first and older ensemble is a pair of reed instruments that play in call-and-response style. The *biniou koz* (a single-drone, mouth-blown bagpipe) and the *bombarde* (a lower-pitched, oboe-type wind instrument, one octave below the *biniou*) are played together in a relatively circumscribed area within the region (Kuter 2000: 560), most commonly at weddings. The *bombarde* is played somewhat like a tin whistle, but requires considerably more pressure to produce the sound because of the reeds.

The second major ensemble, which dates from after World War II, is called the *bagad*, and comprises a bagpipe band of *biniou braz* ("big bagpipes") and multiple *bombardes* with drums. *Bagadou* are modeled roughly after Scottish bagpipe bands, which were introduced to Brittany at the end of the nineteenth century. Prior to the introduction of Scottish bagpipe bands, the *biniou* and *bombarde* were played exclusively in pairs. By the turn of the twenty-first century, *bagadou* had become more important than the original *biniou–bombarde* pair.

A single *bagad* includes equal parts *biniou* and *bombarde*, snare drums, a pair of parade drums, and a bass drum. Like the Scottish pipe-and-drum bands from which they derive, *bagadou* continually create new works, new arrangements, and work together with the dance and culture revivalists (known as the Cercle Celtique or "Celtic Circle") to continually inspire and support an already vigorous tradition of music and dance. Competitions spur further development of musical skills and enhance the visibility of local musicians, as do multiple regional festivals, though they draw musicians from all genres of Breton music, not just the *bagadou*. Their presence at the festivals also further cements the sound of the instruments in the minds of the listeners.

Early representations of the combination of *biniou* and *bombarde*, together with the drums, appear in religious writings of the 1600s, and seem to have been part of a larger effort to curtail their use by church authorities (Kuter 2000: 561). In these depictions, the musicians playing the instruments appear to be animals representative of the Devil: cloven-hoofed beasts and monkeys. The suppression of local musical traditions has much to do with strictures against dancing. However, economic conditions in Europe generally favored migration to the cities in the post-World War II era. The overwhelming influence of popular culture from Paris, London, and the United States also had a hand in twentieth-century suppression of Breton culture. Since World War II, dancing has been a thriving activity in the region, and many of the younger people in the region now know more dances than the older people, thanks to the efforts of revivalists and language activists (Wilkinson 1999: 41).

Another reed instrument is the *treujenn-gaol* ("cabbage stalk"), a type of local clarinet (single reed, as opposed to the double-reed *bombarde*). The *treujenn-gaol* was once different from the modern clarinet in that it had from 4 to 13 keys instead of the 24 of the kind you would see in a Western orchestra. In its contemporary form, the *treujenn-gaol* is a normal clarinet, played in the normal way. Its role would be to play in pairs for wedding processions, somewhat like the *biniou–bombarde*, but it has been played in areas where the *biniou–bombarde* pair did not exist.

The hurdy-gurdy, a special type of keyed lute bowed with a wheel, is more closely associated with northeastern Brittany (and other parts of France) than with the heart of Breton traditional music. The concert flute has recently grown popular since the 1980s, and Irish groups of the 1980s had a strong influence on local choices for back-up instrumentation, including the guitar and bouzouki (see Chapter 6). Other Breton instruments include the accordion and fiddle, both of which are found all over Europe. The fiddle, which has had a prominent role in wedding bands across Europe and North America, gradually has given way to the accordion because of the latter instrument's louder sound and stronger percussive capability. When many people are dancing, it is difficult to hear a fiddle in the background.

Dancing is one of the main contexts for Breton instrumental music. The dance names often refer to the immediate region in which they are danced (Wilkinson 2003: 222), and occur in both round and line dances as opposed to sets (of eight people, for example). Dances occur at weddings, festivals, contests, and in hundreds of classes taught all over the region by Cercle Celtique and other organizations. One type of festival unique to Brittany (compared to the rest of France) is the *fest noz* or night festival. These are local music and dance parties originally intended to celebrate the end of a workday, and they have now grown somewhat beyond the intimacy of their original context. At the *fest noz*, certain choices about which tunes and dances are performed reinforce a kind of pan-Breton identity (ibid.: 223).

In addition to instrumental music for dancing, any *fest noz* will feature Breton singing, which has always been at least as important as its instrumental traditions, if not more so. The vocal genre for which Brittany is best known, and which sets it apart from that of Ireland, Scotland, Wales, and elsewhere, is a type of two-person responsorial singing called *kan ha diskan*. While the Scots also have responsorial singing in the form of psalm singing and waulking songs, only the Bretons perform this particular genre. *Kan ha diskan* songs can accompany dancing, but they are known especially for the way in which they are performed. Two singers perform successive phrases that overlap, with one singer (the *kaner*) beginning a phrase that concludes with the second singer (the *diskaner*) joining in with the same phrase. The first singer then joins the second singer at the end of the next phrase. Other song genres include religious hymns (*kantig*), narrative ballads (*gwerz*), and lyric songs (*son*—songs of light-hearted content). Note, however, that all these regions include hymns, ballads, and lyric songs as well.

Regardless of whether Breton music belongs strictly or academically within the category of Celtic, musicians and audience members seem to agree that it does. Desi Wilkinson points out that, "People travel to Brittany from many parts of the country [France] to experience the *ambiance celtique*, a synonym for many for the simple notion of having a good time" (ibid.: 228). Ironically, as Breton music continues to grow in popularity, its performance has become increasingly urbanized. This urbanization is both a positive and a negative influence as the original contexts for musical performance diminish while new opportunities arise.

Galicia (Northwest Spain)

The lush green northwest tip of Spain, often referred to as "Celtic Spain," is one of Spain's seventeen autonomous regions. Galicia is unlike anywhere else in Spain. Its language, Galego, closely resembles Portuguese but has been a distinct (though politically contested) language since the medieval period. Precisely like the other languages that fall under the linguistic category of Celtic, Galego was outlawed for a time (under the law of Franco, Spain's military dictator, rather than because of English colonial policy or French nationalism). It has virtually no linguistic ties to the northern countries, save for a few place names (Lugo, for example, refers to the Celtic sky god known in Ireland as Lúgh). Galicia enjoys frequent rainfall, and the good weather supports a thriving wine industry. Like the other regions discussed in this chapter, Galicia's coastal regions are known for their seafood and easy access to the sea. Note that much of what appears in this section also applies in some respects to Asturias, the neighboring autonomous region, but Galicia is better known for its music outside of Spain.

Richard Sykes points out in his book *Saxons, Vikings and Celts* that the Y-chromosome predominant in the Irish is found also "among the Basques of north-eastern Spain and among the people of Galicia in the north-west of Spain" (Sykes 2006: 162). He argues for the male lineage in Ireland having come from northern Spain, not from Central

Europe. "In Ireland, the maternal lineages are diverse and very old," he adds, "while the Y-chromosomes are unexpectedly homogeneous, and at first glance look comparatively young" (ibid.: 163). What this means for our purposes is that at least some of what we know of Ireland, we know also of Galicia, not the least of which is a long-term passion for music (Trend 1924: 16) in spite of shifting political and religious currents.

In Chapter 2 you read about some of the first settlers to Ireland originating from the Iberian Peninsula. Crossing the Bay of Biscay to come north to Ireland in good weather is neither difficult nor time-consuming; that there should be cultural ties between the two regions should not surprise anyone, based on what you know now. The Galicians are known for traveling, having exported hundreds of thousands of their people to South America, particularly to Argentina and Brazil (where the surname "Gallego" or "Gallegos" is common). Anyone in South America speaking with a Spanish accent is referred to as a "Gallego," no matter where in Spain they came from. As Galicians have traveled, so have they absorbed; yet Galicia has developed its own expressive culture that is *not* an import from Ireland or the other regions.

Santiago de Compostela, the provincial capital, has been a major pilgrimage site for Christians since the ninth century. Pilgrims still travel to Santiago from all over the world, crossing northern Spain on foot until they reach the great cathedral of Santiago ("Saint James"). Santiago is the alleged location of the relics of Saint James, and an entire economy has for hundreds of years been based on the influx of international pilgrims to the site. Early travelers noted the bagpipes of the region, the songs bearing "distinctive traces of Irish" (or Scottish, or Breton, or perhaps even local) sounds, and the similarity of local modes to those used on the far northern island coasts.

The bagpipes of Galicia reflect a larger distribution of pipes across the Eurasian continent. Known as the *gaita galega*, the Galician bagpipe (Figure 4.4) was first mentioned in the medieval manuscripts of the poet/musician Martín Codax, and continues today as a highly symbolic instrument of the region. However, the characteristic sound of *multiple* Galician pipes playing in close harmony is unlike any other sound. Its use declined during the next several hundred years, but the instrument (and local music in general) saw a resurgence in the 1970s as part of a larger folk revival movement. The *gaita* includes a bag, a conical chanter (*punteiro*), and one or more drones, and it is mouth-blown rather than using the elbow (as in Irish piping).

In addition to the *gaita galega*, Galicians play the *pitu* (an eight-holed oboe), the *requinta* (a six-holed transverse flute), and other wind instruments. The region also has many imported instruments found all over Western Europe, including the fiddle, the hurdy-gurdy, and the accordion. Both the *bombo* (a large bass drum) and the *tamboril* (a snare drum played with two sticks) are used to accompany the *gaita galega*. Most of the instrumentalists are male, and most of the well-known singers are female.

Songs are another point of symbolism for the region. The *alalá*, a type of short religious chant sung between *gaita* interludes, is just one form of the musical expression of identity for local people. The *muiñeira* is very closely related in feel to the jig of Ireland or Scotland; it is performed in 6/8 time and is used for dancing. It also appears in the repertoire of some of the contemporary Irish supergroups such as Lúnasa. 6/8 time also characterizes the rhythm of a number of other Galician dances, including the *redonda*, the *chouteira*, and the *carballesa*. The steps of the dances, however, differ for each dance, and other dances such as the *ruada* (a marching song), for example, use entirely different rhythms. Melodically, the four musical modes characteristic of Irish and Scottish

Figure 4.4   Galician bagpiper in Santiago de Compostela

music (major/Ionian, minor/Aeolian, Dorian, and Mixolydian) are also characteristic of the music of Galicia.

Like the other regions of this book, Galicia's music revival gained momentum in the 1970s. By the 1990s, the *gaita* player Carlos Nuñez was collaborating in performance with The Chieftains, appearing on international television programs, performing at Celtic music festivals to represent Galicia, and selling thousands of recordings. The members of the Spanish supergroup Milladoiro, who sometimes include Irish and Breton tunes on their many recordings, have quite effectively internationalized the music of Galicia. As Nuñez and Milladoiro have paved a musical path out of Galicia, a greater number of recordings, festival invitations, and concert appearances have engaged the music of other local groups. As was the case with Breton music, a devoted international fanbase of "Celtitude" continues to be hungry for new Galician musical materials that offer simultaneously a sense of authentic Old Celticism and new connections to other people on the perceived margins. Knowing that Galego is not a Celtic language does not seem to faze the fans of Galicia's music, nor does the knowledge that several other autonomous regions in Spain are equally adept at Celtic identity politics.

In this chapter the subject has been the music of regions related to Ireland either through proximity, language, shared history, or musical style. In each case, the region boasts a unique arrangement of musical instruments and vocal traditions, with corresponding dances that reflect local ideals. Between the Atlantic weather characteristic of all these areas, the tendency for the regions (as opposed to the mainstream societies to which they belong) to ascribe special importance to music-making with related instruments and dance styles, and the original linguistic connections for most of the areas under discussion, these regions do, in fact, belong together. Ireland is no different from the others in that it, too, has unique musical instruments and vocal traditions, local dance styles, and a particular musical aesthetic that occupies the minds and directs the conversations of musicians and listeners well into the early hours of the morning. Keep in mind that this book could have been written entirely about any one of the regions mentioned in this chapter. That it was not is a result of historical, social, and musical forces detailed in the book's concluding chapter.

Discussion Questions

1. Why might "Celtic" be somewhat inappropriate to use as a term describing music? Do you understand its use as a CD marketing term? How do its two uses differ?
2. What are the elements that distinguish Scottish music from Irish music? They share similarities in instruments, song types, and language. How can you tell if you're listening to Scottish music?
3. Why have a pan-Celtic music festival? Who gets invited, and why?
4. How does the section on Galicia enhance your understanding of Spain? What was your understanding prior to reading this chapter? Were you relying on popular media images of Spain (guitars, bullfights, sherry, flamenco dancing, "Olé!," the Alhambra Palace, etc.)?
5. Could this book, in fact, have been written about any one of the regions mentioned in the chapter? How would it be different, and why?

CHAPTER 5

The Green Fields of America

Bíonn siúlach scéalach ~ Travelers have tales to tell.

The 1990s marked the first time in over a century that the Irish population saw steady increases, together with an influx of Irish people *returning*, rather than leaving (Dezell 2000: 208). The tide of emigration turned when the Irish economy awakened from its long dormancy; it coincided with several other sociohistorical factors that began to bring Irish people home. Prior to the current period, the Irish were having enough children to triple the population, yet with such large families in economic difficulty, most of the children would emigrate to England, Scotland, or North America rather than staying home. The typical Irish family of the late nineteenth and most of the twentieth centuries, therefore, was stretched across the globe; this phenomenon extended Irishness, and the reach of Irish musical culture, across the globe as well. As part of the process of exploring traditional music in Ireland and related musics in nearby countries, this chapter examines Irish musical culture abroad, particularly in North America. The enduring ties of Ireland and Irish North America were initiated as family ties, and have continued as economic, cultural, and musical ties up to the present.

Scholar-monks began leaving Ireland as early as the sixth century. From the earliest days of the monks establishing monasteries across Europe (St. Gallen in Switzerland, among others), the Irish have traveled abroad. Perhaps the most legendary expedition of an Irish person is the Voyage of St. Brendan (*Navigatio Sancti Brendani Abbatis*), in which the saint was alleged to have sailed across the Atlantic, encountering a "crystal column" (perhaps an iceberg?), a "flaming mountain" (volcano?), and other (Icelandic-sounding) wonders. Written and distributed in the ninth century, this text was popular in Europe and has led to speculation—however far-fetched—that St. Brendan made it all the way to North America. Much later, two major migrations brought the Irish to

North America *en masse*. The first, sometimes called "The Great Migration," brought approximately 200,000 of the Protestant "Scots-Irish" in the eighteenth century. The second, occurring in the several decades before, during and after the Famine of 1845–1850, brought several million Catholic Irish. Irish people also came before and after these more prominent migrations.

North America has generally been called simply "America" by the Irish. While current politics in North America require that we all think exclusively of Canada, the United States, and Mexico in terms of national boundaries, it is still, in many ways, all America to the Irish. Furthermore, North Americans are all "Yanks" (short for Yankee, a term with very specific historical and geographic parameters). Even the native Irish who return to Ireland after only a few years in North America can be called Yanks. While it can be frustrating to be called a Yank in Ireland when one is from the American south, or west, or anywhere in Canada, it is even more surprising and annoying for the Irish to hear North Americans describe themselves (or indeed, anyone with red hair, freckles, or a temper) as "Irish."

Though national borders separate the United States from Canada, the northeastern region of North America on both sides of the border has been rich with fiddle music, dancing performed to fiddles (and accordions), and the mixing of musics from different root sources. Ontario's Ottawa valley is a major center of Canadian Irish fiddle music. The region of maritime Atlantic Canada continues to support a rich array of musicians playing Scottish, Irish, Welsh, Acadian, and Mi'kmaq fiddle tunes; it depends on where you live (or visit). In fact, it is remarkably easy for a fiddler in the region to point to any number of locations (New Brunswick, Newfoundland and Labrador, Nova Scotia [home to Cape Breton Island], Prince Edward Island) as "homes" of Irish and Scottish fiddle music. Throughout the region, a sort of hybridized Irish identity has developed in which, for example, distinctions between Catholic and Protestant musical genres and venues are blurred. The lack of significant recent immigrants has softened the edges of Irishness, leading to such surprises as Irish traditional music sessions—largely associated with Catholics—taking place in a lodge founded by the (emphatically Protestant) Orange Order (Peter Toner, personal communication).

During the Famine, thousands of Irish people came to Grosse Île on the Saint Lawrence River (approximately 100,000 in 1847 alone) near Quebec City and waited for their quarantine period to end; at least six thousand of them ended their journey there, and are buried in mass graves. Passage fares to Quebec were one-third the price of passage to the United States, so many Irish came to Canada and either settled there or traveled south after their arrival. With several hundred thousand Irish settlers in the region, it is easy to see why the Irish have had such a strong Canadian presence (see multiple articles in O'Driscoll and Reynolds 1988), even though their overall percentage of the population has diminished over the past century. Patterns of settlement included gatherings of people from Munster in Ottawa, Connemara people in Montreal, and Ulster/Donegal people in Toronto. Newfoundland is the only North American region to have its own Irish name: *Talamh an Éisc* ("land of the fish"). Irish was spoken throughout the maritime region, and there was even a movement in 1890 to establish it as the third national language of Canada!

The intermarriage of North Americans from different ethnic backgrounds has resulted in many citizens being only somewhat Irish, with the further result that Americans have the ability to opt into (or out of) an endlessly attractive (and fluid) array of ethnic identities. The choice to emphasize one's Irish roots is a result of a complicated set of stereotypes that have shifted according to the decade in which they were formed, or to whatever political and social advantages have accrued to the Irish over time (Waters 1990: 83). In fact, claiming Irishness, with its rich history, beautiful music, and long story of hardships at home and in America, brings a kind of "value-added" complex whiteness to one's identity, which Diane Negra refers to as "enriched whiteness" (Negra 2006: 1). Since just before the turn of the twenty-first century, the mania for all things Irish has burned at a feverish pitch, and is no longer limited to the week of St. Patrick's Day celebrations in March each year.

After the earliest days of St. Patrick's Day in America, when military parade units of Irishmen marched in British uniform (Glazier 1999: 821), the parades were reconceived as a way to show off the Irish of New York City as calm, stable, and safe for "modern" America. Quebec City's first celebration (in 1765) served a similar purpose. So much of what North Americans took—and, frankly, still take—for Irishness was neither limited to Irish people nor any indication of Irish character; rather, it was a product of multiple circumstances including dislocation, poverty, a fragmented community, and the ready tendency of the mainstream to paint anyone different in caricature (Stivers 2000: 180). But in order to turn around some of the ideas about the Catholic Irish that had already formed in America prior to the Famine, the need to make the Irish seem respectable was taken up by men who held power in the growing community of Irish-Americans.

> The Ancient Order of Hibernians [a powerful fraternal society that runs the New York City parade to this day] seized control of New York's St. Patrick's Day celebration in the late 1850s and turned it into a prototype public relations campaign to send a favorable message about the Irish at their best to the rest of the city. Each year, they assembled thousands of impeccably dressed Irish to march in a solemn display of probity and patriotism through Manhattan's wealthiest neighborhoods.
>
> (Dezell 2000: 19)

This holy saint's day in Ireland has, in North America, become a moment to engage in the selling of many of the stock images that now characterize the Irish for Americans (Casey 2006: 84–109), and many of those images (largely of Irish people as drunks and hooligans) were established in the nineteenth century as part of the early Tin Pan Alley and music hall song compositions (see below). Another particularly North American custom has been the eating of corned beef and cabbage and some kind of green dessert, a meal that most Irish people neither serve nor like (Waters 1990: 123). St. Patrick's Day is celebrated with small parades in Kyoto, Munich, Sydney, and Singapore, among other diverse places (Williams 2006a: 101). The one constant to these events, however, is music, because enacting Irishness everywhere outside of Ireland requires music.

Irish music in North America divides into multiple strands. One of the first strands comprises the music of the descendants of some of the first Protestant migrants from Ulster who settled in the northeast, then moved to the southern mountains of the United States. Their music shows up most clearly today in the old-time genre of fiddle and banjo instrumental music, together with the ballad traditions of the southern mountains. Another strand belongs to the Catholic Irish, who established important centers in the major cities of the east coast and Midwest of the United States and Canada, and saw several American traditions evolve from nineteenth-century Irish music. Among these traditions are minstrelsy, variety, and vaudeville shows, some of which became a home for the parlor songs of Thomas Moore, exhortations to "free Ireland," and popular Tin Pan Alley compositions about Ireland and the Irish. Another development was the twentieth-century transference and standardization of the Irish music session into the North American urban pub culture scene. The most recent development has been the upswing in popularity of Irish and Irish-American punk (see Chapter 9). Each of these strands has built the Irish-American musical fabric, and yet each one has tended to stand on its own, responsive only to an exclusive constituency of Americans (including those who bear no Irish heritage).

The "Great Migration" of the Scots-Irish

The Plantation of Ulster, with its established settlements after 1610, brought displaced and marginalized people from the borderlands region of northern England/southern Scotland to what is now Northern Ireland. English policies that turned Catholics into second-class citizens also worked against Presbyterians; those who did not join the Church of Ireland (a branch of the Anglican Church of England) were discriminated against over a long period of time, as you read in Chapter 3. The Ulster Scots settlements form the core of northern Protestantism today, but they also form the root source of those who are now referred to in America as the Scots-Irish (or "Scotch-Irish"). Initially simply called "the Irish" by other Americans, thousands of migrants came to the United States, particularly Pennsylvania at first, to settle, find land, or work their way into freedom and land-owning capability through indentured servitude. Not all of them were Presbyterians; instead, the people who have come to be called the Scots-Irish in the United States represented a plurality of beliefs, intentions, and backgrounds (Doyle 1999: 842). Over time, some (though not all) of these people migrated further southward, joining those who had come through Delaware, and they eventually formed the Scots-Irish population of the southern mountains. From their customs to their architecture, from their speech patterns to the tunes they played on their front porches, the early Scots-Irish were culturally not so far removed from their Ulster cousins (McDonald 1998: xxi; Moloney 2002: 8).

When the Catholic Irish began immigrating to the United States and Canada by the hundreds of thousands, the earlier Irish immigrants began referring to themselves as the "Scots-Irish" to distinguish themselves from those whom they felt shared none of their values. They also wished to escape Yankee discrimination against the Catholic Irish, particularly in the northeastern cities. By claiming Scots-Irish ancestry, the earlier immigrants from Ulster separated themselves not only from the Catholic Irish, but also from the Yankees, whose identity by the end of the eighteenth century had shifted toward the celebration of their status as (mostly) English-descended New Englanders.

The Scots-Irish who migrated southward established homes in the Virginias, the Carolinas, eastern Kentucky, Tennessee, and the frontier territories west of the Alleghenies (Leyburn 1962: 185). Musical instruments included fiddles, more than any other instrument, but others—generally homemade instruments—contributed to the overall sound. The banjo in particular, which originated in West Africa and was brought to the United States with the slave ships (both through the technical knowledge of its builders and in the form of actual musical instruments), became established in the southern mountains as well. The combination of fiddle and clawhammer-style banjo (and later, the guitar) is now called "old-time" or "old-timey" music (and has been since early in the twentieth century). It features not only some instrumental dance tunes from the Scots-Irish, but some rhythmic elements from African-American music. A characteristic of old-time music is its relatively unadorned sound, compared to the ornamentation in Irish instrumental music.

> [T]ypically, the song and fiddle styles of West Virginia generally have less melodic ornamentation than related Celtic traditions. In old-time fiddling, complex rhythmic patterns created with the bow arm often replace the intricate, melodic embellishments Celtic fiddlers add through "noting" with the left hand. The emphasis on rhythm in old-time music is often believed to be derived from African-American musical influences.
>
> (Marshall 2006: 149)

The Appalachian Banjo

The Appalachian banjo has become a symbol, in many ways, of outsiders' negative beliefs and stereotypes of the Scots-Irish in the southern mountains. The instrument became firmly established in American popular consciousness through a pivotal scene in the 1972 film *Deliverance* as the sonic representation of everything urban white men were supposed to fear. The iconic tune from the film's soundtrack, "Dueling Banjos," became a #1 American hit in 1973 and led to every American banjo player, including the author of this book, being asked to play it right up until the present. The connection between stereotypes about old-time banjos within their social context and stereotypes connected with Irish fiddlers playing jigs ("Play 'The Irish Washerwoman'!") is revealing. The Scots-Irish and the Catholic Irish continue to have to fight negative beliefs about class, respectability, intelligence, and suitability for employment over and over again.

In its texture, American old-time music is heterophonic (see Chapter 1), just like Irish traditional instrumental music. The fiddle and banjo play essentially the same melodic material within the given limitations of their instruments. Fiddlers may use drone strings (in imitation of pipes), alternate tunings (besides the standard G–D–A–E tuning), occasional plucking of fiddle strings, a thin sound with no vibrato, and a variety of positions to hold the instrument (under the chin, against the chest, against the shoulder, etc.). The clawhammer-style banjo player brushes down across the strings with the nails and plucks on the fifth string with the thumb in an upbeat "down, down–up, down, down–up" rhythm (a quarter note followed by two eighth notes), as in Figure 5.1. The player can also use the nail of the index finger to strike down on the melody notes, and the thumb to pluck the melody notes on strings other than the fifth string, a technique called "double-thumbing." Most of the banjo player's left-hand work occurs close to the far end of the neck, away from the body of the instrument (what classical string players would call "first position"). The banjo player can also use creative rhythmic syncopation to play with the rhythms in the melody.

It is precisely the use of rhythmic syncopation that separates old-time music from Irish music. The clawhammer banjo—which appears in a variety of tunings, just like the fiddle—draws heavily from its West African polyrhythmic roots in old-time music. In Figure 5.2 the old-time tune "Benton's Dream" (which appears on the online soundtrack

TRACK 3

Figure 5.1 Clawhammer playing on a fretless gourd banjo

Figure 5.2 "Benton's Dream"

for this book) reveals a complicated melodic rhythm featuring dotted quarter notes in what is sometimes referred to as the "Bo Diddley" pattern: **1**–2–3 **1**–2–3 **1**–2. This polyrhythmic pattern, popularized by the rock'n'roll guitarist Bo Diddley, derives its roots from West Africa and offers considerable musical interest in many old-time tunes. As you listen to the recording, notice the ways in which the *uilleann* pipes, fiddle, and clawhammer banjo layer the rhythms of three beats against two. Be aware as you listen, of course, that pipes do *not* normally appear in old-time music!

The inclusion of African and African-American elements in old-time music is just part of a larger synthesis and exchange taking place all across the American South in the early part of the nineteenth century, as amply documented by the painter William Sidney Mount (Smith 2009). Irish and African-Americans worked in many of the same quarters at some of the same jobs, to the point that reels, hornpipes, dance steps, and musical instruments were a part of *both* traditions of the time. Although the appropriation and staging of the banjo as a white person's instrument in the twentieth century had in many ways led to its shunning by African-American players, its reclamation in African-American tradition has grown significantly since the turn of the twenty-first century. See, for example, the exceptional clawhammer-style banjo playing of Rhiannon Giddens, whose "Follow the North Star" connects with the unbroken musical traditions of her own African-American family and community.

In addition to the layers of rhythms, a number of other features—the high-pitched fifth string of the banjo, for example, and the occasional use of a drone by the fiddler— serve to fill out and add depth, heterophonic interest, and color to the old-time musical experience. Guitars, mandolins, and other instruments now provide a more filled-out sound to the genre, but the core of the old-time sound is the fiddle and banjo. While just a few of the tunes are directly Irish in origin, enough of them sound vaguely Irish or Scottish in style that it is deceptively easy to ascribe Irishness to them, regardless of the reality of tune importation.

Many of the fiddle tunes played for dancing in the southern mountains of the United States are tied to songs. In Ireland, it is primarily the slow instrumental airs that are tied to song lyrics, and when an instrumentalist plays a song air, he or she generally performs it in a way that reflects the poetic rhythm of the lyrics (see Chapter 6). In Scotland and in Cape Breton, Nova Scotia, tunes of the *puirt-a-beul* ("mouth music") genre have lyrics, and are performed for dancing. In a remarkable statement that indicates the links between practices in the States and in Ireland and Scotland, a West Virginia fiddler named Lester McCumbers was quoted as saying "You have to play accordin' to *whatever rhythm is on that type of song*, is what you have to do. If you don't, it don't sound the same, you see" (Marshall 2006: 124, emphasis added).

The song "Cluck Old Hen" is a standard of the old-time repertoire. It is both sung and played, and it works equally well as an instrumental tune and as a song. While the musical transcription (Figure 5.3) includes the lyrics, it would be played essentially the same way as an instrumental tune. Sometimes, in a long session of old-time music, the tune might be on its sixteenth repetition before someone sings a verse; it may go into

Figure 5.3 "Cluck Old Hen"

many more repetitions before another verse emerges, and that verse might be sung by a different singer. Another possibility is that no one sings at all.

One of the forms of Irish music that did not survive the transition to the southern mountains was the jig. Its dance rhythm is ill-suited to playing on the clawhammer-style banjo, though it can be done. In Ireland and Atlantic Canada, however, the jig is still played frequently. The irony is that the Irish and Atlantic Canadians have lived and worked in as equally challenging conditions as the people in the southern mountains, and the jig was never "abandoned" there the way it was in the south. The likeliest explanation is that jigs simply were not brought to the south in large numbers, and did not catch on the way they did in the north.

Perhaps the most surprising element of old-time music, as far as Irish musicians are concerned, is the seemingly endless repetition of the tune. A single old-time tune, particularly when played by a crowd, can go through as many as fifty or sixty repetitions, rather than the short suite of two tunes repeated three times each (for example) that characterizes contemporary Irish performance practice. The multiple repetitions of the tune—as well as the phenomenon of a large crowd of old-time players—parallels the development of the pub session in Ireland, and is a direct product of the old-time revival.

An addition to the southern repertoire of old-time tunes is the tag, a single-measure melodic line (Figure 5.4) that alerts other musicians, dancers, and listeners that the tune is about to end. Notice, by the way, that the third measure is a variant on the same "Bo Diddley" rhythm you heard and saw in "Benton's Dream." Sometimes the pattern in measures three and four is called "shave and a haircut—two bits."

Old-time music is now performed all over North America, and incorporates many more tunes (including hundreds of original and local tunes) than the Scots-Irish ever brought to, or created in, America. It can even be heard on "world music" shows on Irish radio stations! The roots of the tradition lie, however, in the confluence of Scots-Irish and African-American instrumentation, melody, and rhythm.

The Southern Ballad Tradition

The other major contribution of the Scotch-Irish to American music is the many ballads originating in both the Scottish borderlands and Ulster in the northern part of Ireland. The English ballad collector Francis James Child (1825–1896) published his famous collection of ballads, referred to now as "Child ballads" because he cataloged and numbered them toward the end of the nineteenth century. This urge to collect and catalog was quite widespread in the British Isles and Ireland at the time, so *The English and Scottish Popular Ballads* were a masterful result of that urge. In this collection, Child noted multiple versions and variants of each ballad (a "different version" might be a small change in a detail, while a "variant" would require a different storyline within the same ballad). The English folklorist Cecil Sharpe performed a similar task in the American southern mountains during World War I. He based some of his work on the

Figure 5.4 A standard old-time "tag" for the fiddle

guidance of his collaborator Olive Dame Campbell, a folklorist who researched Scots-Irish and English ballads being sung in Kentucky and Tennessee (and on whom the film *Songcatcher* was rather loosely based).

Ballads are among the most important forms of sung narrative in the English-speaking world. They come in several different forms, and are characterized by singing in short stanzas, stock characters ("milk-white steed," for example), and "leaping and lingering"—moving through significant action, then pausing the narrative for a conversation. They have traditionally been passed down orally, though much of that has changed (or gone into secondary orality in that contemporary singers often learn from recordings).

A typical ballad documented by Francis James Child is "Lord Thomas and Fair Ellinor" (Child ballad No. 73). In this story of a love triangle, Lord Thomas is in love with Fair Ellinor. His mother, however, counsels that he should marry another woman (the "brown girl") who is richer. Being the obedient (but perhaps foolish) son that he is, Lord Thomas rides off to invite Ellinor to his wedding to the "brown girl." Ellinor's mother (wisely) suggests that she stay home, but she dresses up and is treated well at the wedding. The bride, not to be outdone, stabs Ellinor and kills her. In retaliation, Lord Thomas kills the bride and then kills himself. That was quite a wedding!

Let us look at two versions of this ballad: first, a Scottish borderlands version collected by Francis James Child, and then an Appalachian version sung by Jean Ritchie of Viper, Kentucky. Remember that the borderlands were where the Ulster Irish (later known as the Scots-Irish) came from. Some versions of this song—a broadside ballad from the mid-seventeenth century—have thirty or more verses. Notice, in particular, how closely related these two versions are; the first two lines of the borderlands version do not appear in the Kentucky version, and the last two lines of the Kentucky version do not appear in the borderlands version.

Lord Thomas he was a bold forrester, and a chaser of the king's deer;
Fair Ellinor was a fair woman, and Lord Thomas he loved her dear.

Come riddle my riddle, dear mother, he said, and riddle us both as one
Whether I shall marry Fair Ellinor, and let the brown girl alone.
The brown girl she has got houses and lands, and Fair Ellinor she has got
    none
Therefore I charge you on my blessing to bring me the brown girl home.

And as it befell on a high holidaye, as many did more beside
Lord Thomas he went to Fair Ellinor, that should have been his bride.
But when he came to Fair Ellinor's bower, he knocked there at the ring;
But who was so ready as Fair Ellinor for to let Lord Thomas in.

What news, what news, Lord Thomas, she said, what news hast thou brought
    unto me?
I am come to bid thee to my wedding, and that is bad news to thee.
Oh God forbid, Lord Thomas, she said, that such a thing should be done

I thought to have been thy bride my own self, and you to have been the
  bridegroom.

Come riddle my riddle, dear mother, she sayd, and riddle it all in one
Whether I shall go to Lord Thomas's wedding, or whether I shall tarry at
  home.
There's many that are your friends, daughter, and many that are your foe
Therefore I charge you on my blessing, to Lord Thomas's wedding don't go.

There's many that are my friends, mother, if a thousand more were my foe,
Betide my life, betide my death, to Lord Thomas's wedding I'le go.
She cloathed herself in gallant attire, and her merry men all in green
And as they rid thorough everye towne, they took her to have been a queene.

But when she came to Lord Thomas's gate, she knocked there at the ring;
But who was so ready as Lord Thomas, to lett Fair Ellinor in.
Is this your bride? Fair Ellin she sayd, methinks she looks wondrous browne;
Thou mightest have had as fair a woman as ever trod on the ground.

Despise her not, Fair Ellin, he sayd, despise her not now unto mee;
For better I love thy little finger, than all her whole body.
This browne bride had a little penknife, that was both long and sharp
And betwixt the short ribs and the long, prick'd Fair Ellinor to the heart.

Oh Christ now save thee, Lord Thomas he said, methinks thou lookst won-
  drous wan;
Thou wast usd for to look with as fresh a colour as ever the sun shin'd on.
Oh art thou blind, Lord Thomas? She sayd, or canst thou not very well see?
Oh dost thou not see my own heart's blood, runs trickling down my knee?

Lord Thomas he had a sword by his side, as he walked about the hall;
He cut off his bride's head from her shoulders, and he threw it against the
  wall.
He set the hilte against the ground, and the point against his heart;
There was never three lovers that ever met more sooner they did depart.
                                        (Sargent and Kittredge 1904: 155)

In the following version, from the singing of Jean Ritchie, the details of the song are
remarkably similar: the story line holds true, the brown girl is still rich, fair Ellender
is still ready to let Lord Thomas come in, the mother still advises against attending the
wedding, and the brown girl still has a pen knife and knows how to use it. The melody
as sung by Jean Ritchie is quite spare (Figure 5.5).

Mother, oh mother come riddle it down, come riddle two hearts as one
Say, must I marry fair Ellender, or bring the brown girl home.
The brown girl she has houses and lands, fair Ellender she has none

Mo-ther oh mo-ther come rid-dle it down, come rid-dle two hearts as one. Say must I mar-ry fair

El - len- der, or bring the brown girl home? Oh the brown girl she has hous-es and lands; fair

El-len-der she has none. So the best ad-vice I can give you my son, is to bring me the brown girl home.

Figure 5.5 Jean Ritchie's version of "Lord Thomas and Fair Ellender"

Oh the best advice I can give you my son, is go bring me the brown girl home.

He rode till he come to fair Ellender's gate, he tingled the bell with his cane
No one so ready as fair Ellender herself, to arise and bid him come in.
Oh what's the news, Lord Thomas, she cried, what's the news you brung to me
I've come to ask you to my wedding, now what do you think of me?

Oh mother, oh mother, come riddle it down, come riddle two hearts as one
Oh must I go to Lord Thomas's wedding, or stay at home and mourn.
Oh the brown girl she's got business there, you know you have got none;
Oh the best advice I can give you my daughter, is to stay at home and mourn.

She dressed herself in a snow-white dress, her maids they dressed in green
And every town that they rode through, they took her to be some queen.
She rode till she come to Lord Thomas's gate, she pulled all in her rein;
No one so ready as Lord Thomas himself, to arise and bid her come in.

He took her by the lily-white hand, he led her through the hall
He seated her down in a rockin' chair, amongst those ladies all.
Is this your bride, Lord Thomas, she cried, she looks so wonderful brown
You once could-a married a maiden as fair as ever the sun shone on.

Dispraise her not, fair Ellender, he cried, dispraise her not to me
For I think more of your little finger, than of her whole body.
The brown girl had a little pen knife, it being both keen and sharp
Betwixt the long ribs and the short, pierced fair Ellender to the heart.

Oh what's the matter, Lord Thomas he cried, you look so pale and wan
You used to have as rosy a color as ever the sun shone on.
Oh are you blind, Lord Thomas, she cried, or is it you cannot see?
And can't you see my own heart's blood, come a trickling down to my knee.

Lord Thomas he drew his sword from his side, as he run through the hall
He cut off the head of his bonny brown bride, and kicked it against the wall.

Then placin' the handle against the wall, and the blade a-towards his heart
Said, did you ever see three true-lovers meet, that had so soon to part.
(sung to the second half of the tune)
Oh mother, oh mother, go dig my grave, and dig it both wide and deep
And bury fair Ellender in my arms, and the brown girl at my feet.

(Ritchie 1965: 66–7)

Both versions of this song are violent, passionate, and incorporate issues of class, race, and money. Both result in multiple deaths. As part of the legacy of the Scots-Irish in America, the rich ballad and other song traditions of the American southern mountains of Appalachia have been widely celebrated, and are a root source of the storytelling tradition in country music. While some Catholic Irish also migrated to the South, their presence formed just one of the later layers in the area. Instead of having quite as strong an impact on the southern mountains as the Scots-Irish, the Catholic Irish made their mark in the northern cities first, then in places such as Butte and San Francisco, building railroads, working mines, and working cattle out west. The rest of this chapter is their story.

Searching for Home

A defining feature of Irish-American song and instrumental music has been the profound link to home that it envisions, no matter how distant, bittersweet, or unattainable it might be in real life. Song lyric images of Ireland-as-homeland—which appeared not only in parlors but onstage in music halls—are highly evocative; they include the stone cottage, the saintly mother, the sweet girl, the shamrock, the flag, the harp, the west, the patriotic father who "fought for Ireland," and other tropes designed to elicit solidarity, patriotism, and longing for the homeland. William H. Williams points out that "these symbols and the sentiments they called forth had already reached the stage of being acceptable and endlessly repeatable elements in the common currency of American popular culture," marketed not just to the non-Irish, but to the newly arrived Irish and their descendants as well (Williams 1996: 108).

James L. Russell's 1905 song, "Where the River Shannon Flows," contains some of the customary imagery that is intended to trigger longing for home. The lyrics are thick with references to land, fairies, blarney (congenial talk among friends), a shillelagh (a stout stick used as a weapon), a girl (the "colleen," from the Irish *cailín*, "girl"), the Shannon river (in the west), a shamrock, the Irish rose (girl), and lyrics that indicate the singer wishes he were at home, not abroad in a strange land. As cringe-worthy as these lyrics might appear in current parlance, in the context of first-generation Irish thinking about home, they're a first-rate combination of all the essential elements.

Where the River Shannon Flows

There's a pretty spot in Ireland I always claim for my land
Where the fairies and the blarney will never never die
It's the land of the shillelagh, my heart goes back there daily
To the girl I left behind me when we kissed and said goodbye.

Where dear old Shannon's flowing, where the three-leaf shamrock grows
Where my heart is, I am going to my little Irish rose
And the moment that I meet her, with a hug and kiss I'll greet her
For there's not a colleen sweeter where the river Shannon flows.

More daughters than sons emigrated to North America; one of the most important reasons for this trend was that—in a large family of children—Irish girls had few chances to make it on their own without a dowry or without marrying an elder son. By emigrating, a daughter could dramatically increase her chances of marrying, finding respectable work, or supporting her family. She might even be able to bring one or more of her sisters and brothers across as well. This sibling-to-sibling support system was called "chain migration," and resulted, in some cases, in all the children living in a single city in the United States or Canada while the parents remained at home (with, perhaps, the eldest son—the only one to inherit the land). Songs such as "The Irish Mother's Lament" spoke to the loss of family members through emigration (Moloney 2002: 13). The separation of mothers from children—fathers were less frequently mentioned—was a topic that tugged at the heartstrings of the nineteenth-century American Irish, and it continues to appear in songs.

The power of mothers in Irish culture was also celebrated in American song compositions, with songs such as "Mother Machree" (mother *mo chroi*—"mother of my heart") acknowledging in particular the power of the mother over any potentially threatening daughter-in-law. This 1910 song, with lyrics by Rida Johnson Young and melody by the songwriting team of Chauncey Olcott and Ernest R. Ball, is still well known.

Mother Machree

There's a spot in my heart which no colleen may own
There's a depth in my soul never sounded unknown
There's a place in my memory, my life that you fill
No other can take it, no one ever will.

Chorus:
Sure, I love the dear silver that shines in your hair
And the brow that's all furrowed and wrinkled with care
I kiss the dear fingers so toil-worn for me
Oh God bless you and keep you, Mother Machree.

Every sorrow or care in the dear days gone by
Was made bright by the light of the smile in your eyes
Like a candle that's set in a window at night
Your fond love has cheered me and guided me right.

The explicit declaration that *no colleen may own* the son's heart because it already belongs to his mother is another stereotype ascribed to Irish-American males; the song was such a hit that multiple spin-offs ensued, some of which celebrated other powerful women of the family, such as the sister ("She's the Daughter of Mother Machree," by Jeff Nenarb and Ernest Ball, Figure 5.6), all at the emotional expense of the wife. In fact,

Figure 5.6 Cover image from "She's the Daughter of Mother Machree" by Jeff Nenarb and Ernest Ball

following its success there was a surge in popularity of Irish mother songs for the next two decades (Williams 1996: 216).

As the Irish at home heard more about the opportunities to be had across the Atlantic, some songs dwelt not on the pain of being away from home, but on the chance to establish a *new* home. The song "The Green Fields of America" (sometimes called "The Green Fields of Canada"), resurrected by Paddy Tunney, continues to be popular for a number of reasons: it has a beautiful air (Figure 5.7), it begins with the pathos of departure, and it ends with a great sense of hope and triumph. In some ways, its message of leaping into the new land and succeeding in creating a home is more American than Irish. Its final passages are brimming with American optimism, and the earlier verses paint the bleakest (Irish) picture imaginable. Why would anyone want to stay in Ireland when one could "grow weary of pleasure and plenty" in America? Note also the conflation of Canada and the United States into "America" in this song.

> Farewell to the groves of shillelagh and shamrock
> Farewell to the girls of old Ireland all round
> May their hearts be as merry as ever I would wish them
> When far away across the ocean I'm bound.
> Oh, my father is old and my mother's right feeble;
> To leave their own country it grieves their heart sore,
> Oh the tears in great drops down their cheeks they are rolling
> To think they must die upon some foreign shore.

Figure 5.7 "The Green Fields of America"

But what matter to me where my bones they be buried
If in peace and contentment I can spend my life
Oh the green fields of Canada they daily are blooming
It's there I'll put an end to my miseries and strife.
Then it's pack up your sea stores and tarry no longer
Ten dollars a week isn't very bad pay
With no taxes or tithes to devour up your wages
When you're on the green fields of Amerikay.

The sheep run unsheared and the land's gone to rushes
The handyman's gone and the winders of creels,
Away across the ocean, good journeyman tailors
And fiddlers that play out the old mountain reels
Ah but I mind the time when old Ireland was flourishing,
When lots of her tradesmen could work for good pay
But since our manufactures have crossed the Atlantic
It's now we must follow to Amerikay.

Farewell to the dances in homes now deserted
When tips struck the lightning in planks from the floor
The paving and crigging of hobnails on flagstones
The tears of the old folk and shouts of encore.
For the landlords and bailiffs in vile combination
Have forced us from hearthstone and homestead away
May the crowbar brigade all be doomed to damnation
When we're on the fields of Americay.

The timber grows thick on the slopes of Columbia
With Douglas in grandeur two hundred feet tall
The salmon and sturgeon dam streamlet and river
And the high Rocky Mountains look down over all.
Over prairie and plain sure the wheat waves all golden
The maple gives sugar to sweeten your tay
You won't want for corn cob way out in Saskatchewan
When you're on the green fields of Amerikay.

And if you grow weary of pleasure and plenty
Of fruit from the orchard and fish from the foam
There's health and good hunting way back in the forests
Where herds of great moose and wild buffalo roam.
And it's now to conclude and to finish my ditty
If ever friendless Irishman chances my way
With the best in the house I will treat him, and welcome
At home on the green fields of Americay.

(Tunney 1991)

Once the Catholic Irish had begun to come to North America in great numbers, new songs were created about the Irish and about the conditions that they faced upon arrival. These included poignant songs, angry protest songs, and politically-charged songs. Many of the urban Irish of the northeast coast in the United States lived in tenement buildings and faced extremely low wages when they could find work. The song "No Irish Need Apply" refers to the discrimination that the Irish faced when applying for jobs: the abbreviation N.I.N.A. ("no Irish need apply") or even the words "No Irish" would appear at the end of an advertisement for work. This song, written by John Poole of New York, was popular in the 1860s (Moloney 2002: 16).

TRACK 12

The melody of "No Irish Need Apply" is relentlessly cheery (Figure 5.8); it is also easy to sing, and includes a sing-along chorus that encourages Irish pride. On the online soundtrack accompanying this textbook, the singer Mick Moloney accompanies himself on the guitar with easy-to-play chords.

I'm a decent boy just landed from the town of Ballyfad
Oh I want a situation and I want it mighty bad
A position I saw advertised, 'tis the thing for me, say I
But the dirty *spáilpín* ended with "No Irish Need Apply."

Oh says I, "But that's an insult, but to get this place I'll try"
So I went to see that blackguard with No Irish Need Apply
Well some may think it a misfortune to be christened Pat or Dan
But to me it is an honor to be born an Irishman.

I started out to find the house and found it mighty soon
He was seated in the corner, he was reading the Tribune

Figure 5.8 "No Irish Need Apply"

When I told him what I came for he in a rage did fly
And he says, "you are a Paddy and no Irish need apply"

Then I gets my dander rising and I'd like to black his eye
To tell an Irish gentleman "No Irish Need Apply"
Well some may think it a misfortune to be christened Pat or Dan
But to me it is an honor to be born an Irishman.

Well I couldn't stand his nonsense so ahold of him I took
And I gave him such a beatin' as he'd get in Donnybrook
And he hollered "Milia murther!" and to get away did try
And swore he'd never write again "No Irish Need Apply."

He made a big apology and I bid him then goodbye
Saying when next you want a beatin' write "No Irish Need Apply"
Well some may think it a misfortune to be christened Pat or Dan
But to me it is an honor to be born an Irishman.

Sure I've heard that in America it always is the plan
That an Irishman is just as good as any other man
Now home and hospitality they never will deny
To strangers here, or ever say "No Irish Need Apply."

Ah, but some black sheep are in the flock, a dirty lot, says I
A decent man will never write "No Irish Need Apply"
Well some may think it a misfortune to be christened Pat or Dan
But to me it is an honor to be born an Irishman.

Now old Ireland on the battlefield a lasting fame was made
To all who heard of Meagher's Men and Corcoran's Brigade
Though fools may flout and bigots rage, "Fanatics!" they may cry
But when they want good fightin' men, the Irish may apply.

And when for freedom and for rights they raise the battle cry
Those rebel ranks will surely think "No Irish Need Apply"
Well some may think it a misfortune to be christened Pat or Dan
But to me it is an honor to be born an Irishman.

The population of the southern mountains kept itself separate from the urban lowland Catholic Irish, who moved into the coastal South in increasing numbers by the middle of the nineteenth century. Important coastal cities included, for example, Charleston, Savannah, and New Orleans; these and many others had Irish Catholic populations. The French culture of New Orleans, which was also Catholic, had already interwoven populations from Africa, local Native Americans, and French-speaking Acadians from maritime Canada (which later gave the blended population of Southern Louisiana the name "Cajun"). The Irish were employed as canal-workers, sailors, and longshoremen; in fact, the word *loingseoir* (pronounced "longshore") refers to a person who works on or around boats.

Ethnic stereotypes about Irish fighting and drinking had (mostly) begun to move on to other ethnic groups by the twentieth century (Williams 1996: 197). However, those images of the Irish have resisted the homogenizing effects of American popular culture, appearing primarily in the few days surrounding St. Patrick's Day in March of every year, and in the "fighting Irish" slogan of Notre Dame University.

> It isn't Irish music, literature, or accomplishment that are celebrated most often on American St. Patrick's Day. It isn't even Irish conviviality emblematized by a glass. It is weakness for drink and what drunkenness engenders: the fightin' Irish; the tears near beer; the lachrymose renditions of 'Danny Boy' sung in Irish theme bars.
>
> (Dezell 2000: 118)

Alcohol abuse has for a long time been more common in older Irish-American populations than in Ireland, and the American understanding of what it means to be Irish is changing as a much younger demographic of Irish immigrant has begun showing up in academic, technological, and medical fields. Stereotypical expressions such as "get your Irish up" (to become angry) or referring to a fistfight as an "Irish wedding" are diminishing in use, particularly as younger generations of multicultural North Americans fail to see much cultural specificity about being Irish (or much humor in ethnicity-based caricature).

In the one-hundred-year period between 1850 and 1950, the Irish made a deliberate shift in their public image in North America: from "shanty Irish" to "lace curtain" Irish (Dezell 2000: 103). "Shanty Irish" refers to the very poor living conditions faced by some—though not all—of the Famine-era Irish immigrants in the first few years after they arrived in their new home. A shanty (often assumed to come from *sean teach*, the Irish for "old house") was a shack built from salvaged wood, and was often located in the poorest districts of the cities. The term "Shanty Irish" was widely used by both Irish and non-Irish people alike as an epithet to describe the "wrong kind" of Irish: those who had not yet assimilated into mainstream society (O'Brien 2004: 43). Lace curtains—a strong symbol of middle-class, mostly assimilated Irishness in North America—separated the upwardly mobile from the rest, and are still used in some Irish-American homes today. The term itself is also broadly used to describe the "right kind" of Irish.

> The adjective ['lace curtain' Irish] has always signified a mind-set more than a window treatment—a hybrid of Victorian primness, Catholic Puritanism, and social insecurity that would characterize much in Irish American life long after many families packed away the diaphanous fabric that hung in the windows of brownstones, triple-deckers, and two-flats, and moved to the suburbs.
> (Dezell 2000: 103)

The shift in the public image of the Irish toward assimilated respectability continued beyond the Kennedy years, and was cemented by the breakdown of the parish system in the 1970s. In particular, it was important for some Irish-Americans to maintain the surface-level American trappings of Irish heritage without the very real prospect of traveling back to Ireland and facing its grim economic and cultural realities.

Minstrels, Music Halls, and Movies

Many moviegoers are familiar with the Sondheim/Bernstein musical *West Side Story*, a 1950s adaptation of Shakespeare's *Romeo and Juliet*. But did you know that—rather than focusing on the lives, worries, and passions of disenfranchised Puerto Rican and white teens—it was originally intended to focus on the lives, worries and passions of disenfranchised Irish and Jewish teens? A Jewish boy and a Catholic girl were supposed to come together on one romantic (and violent) Easter/Passover weekend for *East Side Story* (the musical's original title). It was rejected when the producer felt that the play *Abie's Irish Rose*, based on a similar theme, was too close in content. Considering the richness of Irish and Jewish musical traditions in the United States, the original idea might have been just as extraordinary (and rich in musical material) as the final version. And it would have been just one in a long line of depictions of the Irish—positive and negative—on the American stage as well as on movie and television screens.

Blackface minstrelsy, a branch of American musical theater that began early in the nineteenth century, was an ancestor of today's late-night talk shows, hosted by Irish-Americans Jimmy Fallon, Conan O'Brien, and Stephen Colbert. A combination of music, dance, jokes, recitation, and other elements, blackface minstrelsy featured actors (mostly white but also black) who covered their faces with burnt cork to perform grotesque characterizations of black people. The characters they portrayed were stock figures, such as the slave, the nattily dressed dandy, and others. Many of the white performers were Irish immigrants or Irish-Americans (Ignatiev 1995: 42), including the composer and actor Dan Emmet, one of the founders of the genre. The close connection of the Irish who had moved to the coastal South with the locals of African descent was part of the melting pot of performance practices that led to minstrelsy, but some of the first formal performances were held in the North, in New York City. Several writers have indicated that by putting on blackface to perform, Irish performers of the mid-nineteenth century were effectively able to remove their "ethnic color" at the end of the performance (Roediger 1991: 104), and reinforce their whiteness.

By the middle of the nineteenth century dozens of minstrel shows were touring the United States and abroad. Dan Emmet and the Virginia Minstrels toured England and Ireland in 1843, 1844, and 1845, and were the first to bring the banjo to Ireland (Moloney 2002: 29). While there is debate about who brought the (shorter) fifth string of the banjo into use (the Irish-American minstrel Joel Walker Sweeney is often credited), banjo-like instruments of West Africa also include a shorter string fixed halfway up the neck. The use of both the banjo and the "bones" (wooden or bone percussion sticks) in minstrelsy was as common as the stock characters portrayed by the actors, and when the banjo and bones came to Ireland, they were as easily absorbed there as the other "foreign" instruments such as the fiddle and accordion were before them.

Concomitant with the rise of minstrelsy in popularity was the development of the variety show. Variety was a mainstay non-narrative show of the English and American stages. It also featured a multiplicity of acts (juggling, acrobatic acts, comic songs, etc.), but these were not performed in blackface, nor were the performers acting exclusively as African Americans. Instead, many ethnic groups were represented, including Jews, Germans, Irish, Italians, and others. According to Gillian Rodger, as a non-narrative genre, the elements of variety—unlike any other theatrical form of the nineteenth century—could be interchanged depending on the context. Furthermore, many of the tunes used in variety were derived from Irish tunes, such as "The Irish Washerwoman" (Gillian Rodger, personal communication).

> The stereotypical Stage Irishman was a hugely popular comic figure in American variety theater. As blacks had been before them, the Irish were portrayed on the popular stage as apelike, ignorant, illiterate, credulous, and superstitious; servile, debased, and degraded.
>
> (Moloney 2002: 29)

Because variety theater covered topical material and performance genres more broadly than minstrelsy did, variety reached a broader audience. Its interchangeable sections meant that variety theater in, for example, Milwaukee could emphasize particular elements relevant to local interests and popular tastes that could be quite different from variety theater in Savannah. Its inherently flexible structure increased its viability, and its use of a great range of acts (including animal acts) kept it fresh for audiences. Variety was often performed in places that served alcohol, effectively limiting its audience.

Vaudeville, from the French *vaux-de-ville* ("voice of the city") was another theater performance genre that both employed and caricatured Irish people. It comprised a combination of elements in terms of its origins (both European and American), but its features included an array of performance genres for mixed-gender audiences and a (relatively) "cleaned up" sensibility. Chains of vaudeville halls of various sizes engaged touring performers: vocalists, comedians, animal acts, acrobats, dancers, etc. Though the vaudeville halls were considered a step up in terms of their respectability, portrayals of the Irish (including by the Irish themselves) featured the stock Irish characters of the clumsy maids, boorish politician, weeping mother, and brawling drunks at weddings, wakes, political meetings, and other Irish-themed stage sets. Vaudeville was also an important venue for the American establishment of the Irish tenor, with songs rich in

Italian *bel canto*-influenced vibrato calling for Irish independence and celebrating the days of noble Ireland as presented in the *Irish Melodies* of Thomas Moore.

The vaudeville song "Muldoon, the Solid Man" represents the Irish-American politician at his most gregarious, charismatic, and powerful. Some of the Irish found great success in American politics toward the end of the nineteenth century, particularly in the big cities of the east coast and the midwest. Folklorist and performer Mick Moloney notes that the Irish-American politician has been stereotyped as "a glib, politically astute Tammany Hall boss with ties to a variety of shady business interests" (Moloney 2002: 25). This song about Muldoon (written by Ed Harrigan and David Braham) includes a verse in which the title character proudly outlines the areas under his control.

> I control the Tombs, I control the island
> My constituents they all go there
> To enjoy their summer's recreation
> And take the enchanting East River air
> I'm known in Harlem, I'm known in Jersey
> I'm welcomed hearty at every hand
> And come what may on Saint Patrick's Day
> I march away like a solid man.

Minstrelsy, variety, and vaudeville were not the only theatrical genres of the nineteenth century. Many Irish immigrants wrote and acted in plays, composed songs for performance in parlors and onstage, or found other ways to be involved in performance to make a living. The playwright Dion Boucicault wrote and staged full-length plays depicting Irish as *normal* people other than as the stock characters of their previous portrayal. Playwrights Ed Harrigan and Tony Hart wrote dozens of musicals about the lives and concerns of the lower classes; not just about the Irish but the Italian, German, Chinese, and African Americans as well (Moloney 2002: 33). These musicals used elements of Stage Irishness to sell tickets, but often had an underpinning of social justice themes. Irish-American playwright Eugene O'Neill was the best-known of the 20th-century playwrights. The lively interest in local community theater that has been so strong in Ireland has also been a feature of Irish-American life, and the shift from stage to film was a logical one for many Irish and Irish-Americans in the twentieth century.

Cinematic Portrayals of the Irish (and Irish-Americans)

The Irish have been well represented in American film. From the early part of the twentieth century to the present, films from *Yankee Doodle Dandy, Going My Way*, and *Long Day's Journey into Night* to *Darby O'Gill and the Little People, The Brothers McMullen* and *In America* have represented the Irish, veering wildly from stock figures to gritty realists, from caricatures to everyman. While older Americans immediately recognize Pat O'Brien or Bing Crosby as types, the characteristic behaviors they and others similar to them exhibit do not necessarily translate into contemporary American multiculturalism. Instead, American viewers have been offered an array of Irish (or Irish-themed) films that are intended to appeal to two particular demographics: Americans of Irish descent, and Irish who sometimes see themselves through an Irish-American lens. Note that the latter (particularly the older generation) also have heard themselves represented through songs such as "Mother Machree" and "Did Your Mother Come from Ireland?"

Many white Americans of the South consistently point to the 1939 film *Gone with the Wind* as "their" story; the movie was not screened in Ireland at the time of its release because the producer had to withdraw it when too many cuts were requested (Pramaggiore 2006: 120). The themes of deep connection to the land, survival in the face of great hardship, regional pride, standing up for what's right, fighting for one's honor … all of these characterize both Southern popular culture and Irish popular culture. Irish names permeate the film: O'Hara, Kennedy, Butler, Slattery, Hamilton; Ashley Wilkes, the only primary character with an English name, is weak and indifferent. In the case of both the book and the film, the Catholicism of the characters has been secularized, and the setting thoroughly adopted as an "everyperson's history" so that the comparative rarity of actual plantations in the South—then or now—ceases to be important. What matters in this film is that Southern (white) values can be (and sometimes are) conflated with Irish values.

Singing in the Rain (1952), which examines Hollywood's transition into talking films, stars two Irish-American actors (Gene Kelly and Donald O'Connor). In a memorable early scene, Kelly's character publicly discusses his genteel—lace curtain—upbringing in the finest schools, with training at the conservatory and ballet, and happy engagement in the finer things in life. In the gritty visual flashbacks accompanying his uplifting monologue, we see his hardscrabble—shanty—childhood dancing for coins in pool halls, fiddle and dance performance on the vaudeville stage, and other, more typically Irish-American, misadventures. It is the entertaining contrast between word and action that captures in a nutshell the reframing of one's Irish or Irish-American past through oral narrative. The film also shows the two men taking elocution lessons from an English speech coach; not only do they speak more cleverly than he does, without having to read from a book, but they (literally) beat him at his own game. Yet again, the (Irish) boys win out against all (English) odds; it is a classic narrative of American history, and it is essential that they succeed.

Many Irish immigrants established themselves in the northern cities when they first arrived, and the new sense of place that developed in their North American urban homes was based on three institutions: the church, the political ward, and the union. The women of the Irish-American urban communities were central to the life of the church, significantly contributed to the financial health of the church, and were the driving force of the community. The priests were responsible for the spiritual life of the community, and the nuns generally ran (and taught in) the schools, which were Catholic-specific. In the unions, where the Irish were extremely well represented, membership was an essential aspect of the life of the Irish-American male. Political bonding through voting and canvassing was a near-occupational effort for many men after work. The cohesiveness of the community—as well as political territorialism—was part of being Irish in America.

In the 1960s and 1970s many of the urban lace curtain families moved out to the suburbs as their finances permitted, leaving the life of the parish, sending their children to public schools instead of Catholic schools, and altering their own cultural landscape. The Irish-American community no longer resembled those driven by the union, church, and political ward as represented in films such as *Going My Way* (1944, starring Bing Crosby) and *The Last Hurrah* (1958, starring Spencer Tracy). "Buying a single-family home in the suburbs during this period was practically a patriotic act, a way of celebrating individualism and capitalism and denouncing Communism" (O'Brien 2004: 93).

By the 1980s and 1990s the film industry had begun to present (both in Ireland and in the United States and Canada) an array of heritage films that depicted a kind of perpetual Irish past toward which Americans could look with nostalgic ownership. While this trend had been started in earlier films such as *The Quiet Man* (1952), the pace accelerated with films such as *My Left Foot* (1989), *The Field* (1990), *The Playboys* (1992), *The Secret of Roan Inish* (1994), and many others. Animated films include *The Secret of Kells* (2009) and *Song of the Sea* (2014) as full-length features, and numerous short films.

> The Irish heritage film is nostalgically uncritical about the past; it displays a longing for a 'pastoral innocence' (often featuring narratives focused on childhood); it tends to have rural settings or eschew modernity; it offers conservative portrayals of gender and sexuality; it endorses the value of family and small community; and it avoids contemporary political violence.
>
> (Pettit 2000: 115)

In the 1990s, the economic situation in Ireland had changed visibly enough that news of its prosperity was appearing in American newspapers. In 1994, Ireland elected a female attorney, Mary Robinson, to the presidency, and a new show called *Riverdance* was making its way across the Atlantic. Musicians who called their sound "Celtic" had been making waves in American popular and New Age music: Afro-Celt Sound System, Enya, Loreena McKennit, and others (see Chapter 9). Suddenly, it became hip to be Irish in America *beyond* St. Patrick's Day. By the late 1990s, with the rise in popularity of tattoos in Americans in their twenties and thirties, Irish-themed designs also grew rapidly in popularity. Professors of Irish Studies found themselves responding to urgent messages and phone calls to supply translations *into* Irish of English tattoo-able words such as "strength" and "unity." Irish-themed weddings became another popular trend, featuring Irish music, corned beef and cabbage, shamrocks, and other American symbols of pride in being of Irish descent (Dezell 2000: 77).

A series of memorial events following the tragedy of September 11, 2001 were shaped into a kind of celebration of Irish-American heroism through the use of Scottish bagpipes at the funerals of firefighters and police officers. Historically, Irish-American men have had a significant presence in the firefighting and police forces of all the east coast American cities. Because so much of the popularity of Irish-themed weddings and funerals has hinged on a generic rendering of Irishness into an Americanized Celtic pastiche, however, the "Irish" music of funerals is often played by Scottish bagpipes, and one of the most popular of the tunes played on Scottish pipes at these Irish (and generally Catholic) funerals in America is a Southern Protestant song associated with slavery, "Amazing Grace." Until the American recession at the start of the twenty-first century, tourism to Ireland was booming, as many American and Canadian tourists on heritage tours visited the land that few (or no one) in their families had gone "home" to since the ancestors had left in the 1850s. The metamorphosis of the image of the Irish abroad into one of success was nearly complete.

Irishness and Magical Whiteness In Twenty-First Century America

In the twenty-first century, American popular attention has focused on issues of heritage and race in a specific way as a result of the availability of DNA testing. For a fee, one can send a saliva sample to a company to receive a rough estimate of where one's ancestors came from. Television commercials tout the tantalizing possibility of finding long-lost relations (in Ireland!). As DNA technology changes over time, some of those initial results have been reformulated—often to the great surprise of those who were celebrating (or mourning) their initial results. As someone whose DNA test results revealed mostly Welsh heritage (reflected by our father's Williams surname) in dramatic contrast to her brother's DNA results pointing to our German Swiss heritage (reflected by our mother's Gonzenbach surname), I can attest to its attraction. However—privacy invasion concerns aside—the DNA kit boom has led to many conversations about what heritage means.

If you, as someone born and raised in North America, have been brought up to believe that your family is "Irish," including having corned beef and cabbage for St. Patrick's Day, singing Irish-American hits, and celebrating your family's conviction that you were all descended from Irish royalty, the news that your DNA places you in what is now Russia or Sierra Leone might be a tough pill to swallow. As mentioned earlier in this chapter, for some, claiming Irishness equals the assertion of a "home," with all its beauty and history. For others, Irishness refers to an unassailable sense of being *white*, among all the available ethnicities and races of North America.

As the Irish came to North America and experienced elements of marginalization and discrimination, they quickly learned the value and importance of fitting in with other "ethnic whites." Blackface minstrelsy, which included performances by many Irish immigrants, was just one of many ways to affirm whiteness in a society not well-disposed to accept difference. Across the twentieth century, the initial mainstream objections to the Irish (and their Catholicism) were mostly buried under the fear and resentment of newer immigrants—Slavs, Chinese, and others—and what they represented. Irish laborers who had started at the lowest rungs of society in the nineteenth century began to move up the socioeconomic ladder, becoming supervisors and politicians. North American popular culture needed to reflect that shift. From the heritage films mentioned earlier to musicals such as *Finian's Rainbow* and Lucky Charms breakfast cereal, the more Irish you were, the more (white) American you were, too.

Irish heritage pride and the "value-added" sense of white ethnicity held by some North Americans has led to the assertion that being white can be achieved *only* through the magic of proving one's Irishness again and again. Even as Ireland has undergone a stunning sea change since 1990, becoming significantly more willing to confront its past and take radical steps toward greater equity and inclusion, Irish America has experienced elements of fragmentation. Part of that fragmentation has resulted in the use of Irish symbols, such as "Celtic" crosses, the Irish language, the Irish flag, and Irish music in connection with white supremacist ideology.

Ethnomusicologist Benjamin Teitelbaum describes three types of nationalists in the Nordic countries: "race revolutionaries, cultural nationalists, and 'identitarians'" (2017: 4). The first connects white nationalism to historical Nazi ideology; the second celebrates specific cultural practices regardless of one's heritage; the third group leans on race and identity as the determining factors of nationalism. These three Nordic types of nationalists connect to those in North America who would utilize Irish music and Irish symbols to celebrate their white identity through a sense of "implicit whiteness" through participation in Irish music events (2017: 107). While those who overtly connect (Irish-American) white nationalism to historical Nazi ideology are the exception, cultural nationalists and those who celebrate the idea that being Irish means being white are within the larger group of enthusiasts of Irish culture in the United States. Irish expressive culture and, by extension, Scottish and other "Celtic" expressive cultures, then serve as a low-key but available signifier of whiteness.

While white supremacy has always had some kind of foothold in North American popular culture, its existence became increasingly public with the rise of social media. Suddenly, the popularization of this ideology went from sharing on slow-loading email listservs to exploding into full prominence with all the visual and ideological manipulation necessary to appeal to those ready to believe. With that proliferation came requests not just for "Celtic"-themed tattoos and translations, but for access to the perceived whiteness of ancient Ireland. The specificity of that need belies the reality of white homogenization, in which Ireland's diverse areas, histories, languages, and musics are lumped together with all kinds of perceived white American cultural materials, so that to be Irish American is to be a white American, regardless of the actual place from which one originated.

The Anti-Defamation League highlights the "rounded cross" or "Celtic" cross as one of the primary symbols of various white supremacist groups. Medieval-era stone monuments on which the image is based—standing high crosses with a ring encircling the center of the cross—are common across Ireland (see Chapter 2). In themselves, they have nothing to do with white supremacy; they predate it by centuries. Just as the original followers of the indigenous Nordic Ásatrú belief system might be startled to find their beliefs and runic writing associated with elements of violent racism in twenty-first-century North America, so might the nuns and monks of Ireland's twelfth-century Catholicism be appalled. Irish medieval art—with its lovely intertwined knotwork and fanciful depictions of humans and animals—represents a medieval understanding of the world rather than a contemporary white nationalist one.

The symbol of the shamrock blankets Irish-American businesses and business cards. A plant allegedly used by Saint Patrick to demonstrate the presence of the Holy Trinity within a monotheistic Christian belief system, it is a simple, attractive shorthand for indicating Irish heritage (or being welcoming to Irish people, or Catholics, or Irish culture). At least one hate group has adopted it for their logo, which has it in combination with a swastika and letters that indicate its name. Some websites have included images of the Irish, United States, and German Third Reich flags together.

How does all of this symbolism connect to Irish music? First, sounds can function as symbols of belief systems and identities too. Second, depending on how those sounds are deployed, they can indicate the full range of emotional content, and evoke political, religious, patriotic, nostalgic, extremely negative, and extremely positive reactions in the members of an audience. Try to imagine one of your favorite Irish heritage films *without* the sounds of the *uilleann* pipes or fiddles; it just might leave you cold. People dealing in symbols understand their power.

Songs such as those used in the 1798 or 1916 rebellions, in commemoration of the Famine of 1845–50 or, more recently, the Troubles of Northern Ireland, can be a convenient tool for the expression of rebellion against a perceived enemy bent on changing one's way of life. Irish-language slogans used by members of the Irish Republican Army (such as "Tiocfaidh ár lá"—our day will come) sometimes serve as stand-ins for American white nationalist sentiments in the guise of asserting one's Irishness.

A popular but absolutely incorrect meme in recent years has been the "white Irish slavery" claim (that the Irish were enslaved for centuries, and had it worse than African and African-American slaves), usually followed by a claim that the descendants of African slaves shouldn't complain. This claim first began in 1998, and surfaces on white nationalist websites, also appearing periodically on social media. Research librarian Liam Hogan has thoroughly debunked this idea in a five-part series on Medium.com; most of the memes use photographs or artwork depicting people who are not Irish, for example, and "historical" quotations that either never occurred or refer to other people or events. Instead, the "white Irish slavery" meme should be seen as a way to exaggerate a historical truth: that Irish Catholics were discriminated against and placed on the periphery when they arrived in North America. Slavery and indentured servitude, however, are radically different systems, and should never be equated.

It should be quite clear that there is no single monolithic "Celtic culture," and that beliefs and symbols and behaviors run the spectrum across time and space. In their writing about white ("Celtic") identity in connection to white geography, McCarthy and Hague note that:

> As with all racial discourses, that surrounding Celtic identity both collapses and creates differences; it erases them among those included with the constructed racial or ethnic group and reinforces them between members of this group and those excluded from it. [...] Those claiming Celtic identity simultaneously maintain a white identity and assert distance from a privileged, dominant position in society
>
> *(2004: 389).*

Furthermore, the assumption that there is just one monolithic type of Celt (or Irish person)—and that the image of the heroic, emotional, solo warrior stands the test of time—is a regrettably simple stamp on a complex set of histories. We know better.

Your takeaway information is this: the use of Irish music, language, "Celtic" crosses, tattoos, and shamrocks do *not* a white supremacist make. Nor does getting a DNA test mean that you are, somehow, in search of magical whiteness. The symbols are sometimes misused to represent a badly misplaced understanding of race and heritage, but since "white identity" was not a part of pre-Christian or early Christian Ireland, all of these symbols are simply examples of appropriation by those who wish to use them for something other than their original intent.

Discussion question: Would you get—or have you gotten—a DNA test? What was the impulse that led you to it? When you received the results, what was your reaction?

Irish Music Around the World

While it is relatively easy today to find Irish traditional music—especially its instrumental music—performed in every major city of North America (and plenty of minor cities and towns), that was not always the case. Irish instrumental music in North America has waxed and waned in popularity according to the vagaries of status accorded to Irish immigrants. Many waves of musicians arrived from Ireland in each decade of the twentieth century, and those waves affected performance practice in various areas of North America. Those Irish-American musicians who live in an area such as greater New York City, Boston, or Chicago have had an almost continual renewal of influences from Ireland due to the constant influx of new players from "home," keeping change to a minimum, whereas the places with sparse immigration tend to stick less with tradition (Moloney 1999: 416).

In New York's outer boroughs, in Chicago, in Boston, and in many other American cities, the social and professional life of the musician was for decades tied up in the dance hall. Susan Gedutis writes eloquently in *See You at the Hall: Boston's Golden Era of Irish Music and Dance* that Irish instrumental music in America had its heyday in the large dance halls (particularly of Boston), so much so that the dance hall was *the* place to see and be seen, to get business done, to meet friends, and to find a date.

> Over the click-clack of high heels on pavement, the careful listener could pick out accents from all over Ireland—the singsong rhythm of Cork, the flat tones of Tipperary, the country inflections of Galway and Kerry, the Donegal people who always sounded as though they were asking a question even if they were telling you a tale. Above it all, the lively lilt of an accordion would spring out of a third-floor window. A saxophone, fiddle, guitar, and drums played an Irish jig or reel amid laughter and the shuffle of hundreds of dancing feet.
>
> (Gedutis 2004: 2–3)

For the young descendants of the Irish (and immigrants such as Saoirse Ronan's character Eilis in the film *Brooklyn*), going to a dance hall in the early-to-mid-twentieth century was the primary social outlet. Many of the people dancing at the halls were non-musicians, but the background context of Irish dance music created a welcoming environment in which people of Irish descent could dress up, find others like themselves, and reinforce their cultural solidarity (Patrick Hill, personal communication). Bands played jigs and reels as well as instrumental versions of popular music hall songs from vaudeville, such as "When Irish Eyes Are Smiling" and "My Wild Irish Rose" (Gedutis 2004: 71). The popularity of the dance hall was at its height well before the Americans appeared to codify which instruments were sufficiently "traditional" to Irish music (pipes, fiddles, button accordions, etc.), and it is appropriate to underscore the frequent appearance of the saxophone, piano, drumset, trombone, trumpet, and other instruments at the time that would surely raise an eyebrow at a pub session today.

One of the more comical aspects of North American instrumental music is that the American session scene can be quite rigid, with despotic session leaders, instrumental (and personnel) hierarchies, a limited number of tunes, tune lists, and other elements with the potential to get in the way of great *craic* (fun times). Ireland itself is not immune to these problems, because the pub session was an artificial construct in the first place. First-rate sessions are themselves a moving target as players come and go. These problems have to do with the apparent need for an idealized authenticity and the creation of community, the comparative rarity of house or kitchen sessions in which solo playing or singing is the norm, and the pervasive worry that somehow, somewhere, someone is not doing it correctly. The scene, however, is quite different in Canada, where the rigidity is replaced by a distinctly local interpretation of Irish music. Waltzes are common, solo airs are rare, and a single tune set can draw easily from American, Irish, Scottish, French, and Canadian sources (Trew 1999: 50).

In terms of songs, the majority of singing in North America is in English, and many of the songs performed in recent years have been gleaned from recordings of Irish singers. North America has plenty of song circles, particularly at summer folk festivals, and many of the song circles feature Irish or Scottish songs. Outside of *Irish* festivals, competitions, and camps in North America, however (at which songs are taught at workshops or in classes and performed in the evenings), an average song circle features just one or two Irish songs mixed in with original singer-songwriter compositions and ballads. Coming to an instrumental session in the hope that someone will call for a song once during an evening is an exercise in futility. It is also useful, however, to keep in mind that certain areas of North America have a greater or lesser connection to Ireland. Many Irish-American people who had "made it" in the northeast appeared to want very little to do with Irish traditional music during the height of lace curtain respectability, because of its connection to a past that some wished to forget. On the other hand, places such as Chicago, San Francisco, and Butte were lively with traditional musicians and dancers by the early twentieth century.

If you were to travel to Japan, you would find images and sounds of Ireland all over the country, if you knew where to look. Sold-out performances of *Riverdance*, Irish music festivals, touring musicians from Ireland, intimate pub sessions, dance workshops, singing classes, and academic poetry readings all reflect an abiding interest in Ireland by a small number of dedicated Japanese enthusiasts. Ireland's musical culture engages with the important Japanese value of nostalgia, to the point that Japanese people recognize Irish music as belonging, in part, to themselves.

When Japan entered its international period at the start of the Meiji Restoration (1868–1912), a series of schools were set up all over the country, and an American music teacher—Luther Whiting Mason—worked together with Japanese scholar Isawa Shuji to import, translate, and disseminate an array of Irish, British, and American songs to schoolchildren all over Japan. These songs then became so familiar to Japanese schoolchildren over the next fifty years that the sound of an Irish melody elicits fond remembrances of one's (rural or semi-rural, or merely idealized) Japanese childhood (Williams 2006: 101–19). In particular, it is a sense of unrequited longing for a fictive Irish homeland that appeals so deeply to some of the Irish music enthusiasts in Japan. The marketing of Irishness has spread extensively across the globe, to the point that a shamrock on the door of a pub or restaurant is enough to signify fidelity to the expected experience of familiarity (Figure 5.9). Traveling in St John (in the Caribbean), one just might encounter the "Quiet Mon" pub ("We are 4,000 miles from County Mayo, but you'll still feel like an Irishman with us!")!

The musician and scholar Fintan Vallely eloquently describes the Irish-themed "Pub in a Box" that inhabits many a street corner location in Osaka, St Petersburg, and every large city in North America.

> Critical to the 'Irish pub' is décor—hard benches, stressed pine furniture, caustic-dipped and worm-perforated, package-ornaments that include obsolete and valueless indifferent book-club editions, household and farmyard utensils—bricolage hoarded in anticipation of the boom by a thousand junk-shops nationwide.
>
> (Vallely 2011: 363)

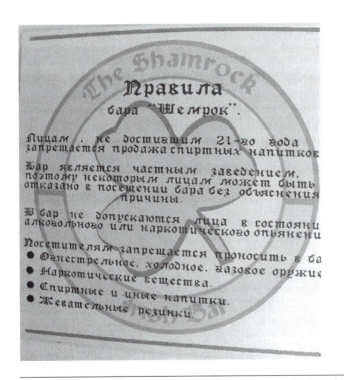

Figure 5.9 From the door of "The Shamrock" Irish pub in St Petersburg, Russia

The nineteenth-century division of the immigrants into "Catholic Irish" and "Scots-Irish" still fuels suspicion and separation of the two subcultures, but the sheer numbers of people with some kind of Irish heritage (10 percent of the United States) is overwhelming the segmentation, particularly since the 1990s economic boom and the concomitant diminishment of sectarianism in Ireland. Given both the high rate of Irish heritage in North America, and the Irish-American tendency to marry people of non-Irish descent, it should come as no surprise that *all four* of the candidates for American president and vice president in the 2008 election were of Irish descent. Barack Obama, Joe Biden, and Sarah Palin all are at least partly of Irish Catholic, Famine-era ancestry (Kearney, Finnegan, and Sheeran, respectively); John McCain's ancestry was Scots-Irish (McKean).

The Irish in North America have had a lasting impact on politics, regional Catholicism, cultural celebrations, and widespread assumptions about Irishness and Irish heritage. The American popular media of film and television—but earlier, too, the minstrel shows and vaudeville stages—were fundamental to the establishment of that impact. Musically, the combination of Irish instrumental music in American Irish-themed pubs and the enormous body of Irish-American song continues to have an impact on the music scene in Ireland, where the performance of the American-composed 1912 song "When Irish Eyes Are Smiling" for American tour groups still elicits a profound nostalgia for the Ireland of nineteenth-century American dreams. Irish-American punk music beats (hard) in the chests of many young Americans, from Boston (Dropkick Murphys) to Los Angeles (Flogging Molly), and strongly engages American soldiers stationed abroad (see Chapter 9). The ancient Irish symbol of the serpent with the tail in its mouth is even now reflected in the cyclic North American search for a heritage of authenticity through the experience of listening, singing, playing, and dancing to Irish music at home and abroad.

Discussion Questions

1. What are the essential features of ballads? Could you write one today? What subject would you write about?
2. Does it matter whether you have Scots-Irish or Catholic Irish heritage? Would it matter if you were Irish instead of North American? Why and/or why not?
3. What role does nostalgia play in Irish-American identity?
4. What do you assume about an Irish character in film or on television? Why?
5. What do you think draws people from all over the world to play Irish music?

CHAPTER 6

Irish Instrumental Music

Nuair a stadann an ceol, stadann an rince ~ When the music stops, the dancing stops.

Now that we have covered both a historical introduction to Ireland and Irish America and their music, together with a brief survey of related musics in Scotland, Wales, and elsewhere in Western Europe, it is time to turn our attention fully to contemporary performance practice in Ireland itself. This chapter focuses entirely on Ireland's instrumental traditions; first, on the instruments themselves, then on the multiple forms in which Irish instrumental music occurs, concluding with matters of style in playing Irish music. For many Irish instrumentalists, and also those who play Irish music at home and abroad, the *instrumental* music is the heart and soul of Irish culture; yet for those who sing, the songs are what it's all about. For those who play the instruments, know the forms, and have the repertoire firmly in hand, it serves as a link to a network of players, regardless of one's language capability, finances, or proximity to Ireland. Generally speaking, music is *not* an international language. However, Irish instrumental music spans multiple languages and contexts (note its presence in Japan, Russia, Brazil, and elsewhere, none of which use English or Irish as a *lingua franca*), and at the very least connects human beings for an evening session or a round of tunes in a kitchen, pub, or festival.

The titles of Irish tunes cover a variety of topics. Some tunes include the name of the form (reel, jig, hornpipe, etc.): "The Concertina Reel," "Morrison's Jig," "Sean Ryan's Polka." Other tune titles refer to a person or place ("Julia Delaney," "The Musical Priest," "The Road to Lisdoonvarna"). Animals figure prominently ("The Gander at the Pratie Hole," "Langstrom's Pony," "Pigeon on the Gate"), and some indicate an action ("Sailing into Walpole's Marsh," "Smash the Windows," "Tripping Up the Stairs"). Many tunes are someone's "favourite," as in "Charlie Mulvihill's Favourite," or were composed by someone specific ("Father Kelly's," "Cooley's," "Dennis Murphy's"). The well-known

East Galway fiddler Paddy Fahey wrote dozens of tunes, *all* of which are called "Paddy Fahey's"! Irish-language tune titles are rare. Incidentally, many Irish players do not bother with tune titles; they simply play the tunes without naming them. Furthermore, if they do need to refer to a tune by name, it might simply be "the one that comes after that one." Most players know more tunes than they know tune titles, and once a musician has been playing for years, it is nearly impossible to estimate the number of tunes in his or her repertoire.

This chapter includes a special feature in its second half. *Join the Session* is a series of musical transcriptions located in the section on the instrumental forms, and it is intended to encourage musicians unfamiliar with Irish instrumental music to try to play each one of the forms. For each form (say, a march, or a reel), a transcription allows you to play one of the tunes on the online soundtrack, or one that you can find on iTunes or YouTube or another online source. Be forewarned, however: sometimes the transcribed tune is the second or third tune in a set of tunes! The explanations of the tunes in that section are also intended primarily for those who can read music already; keep in mind also that many Irish musicians do not read music at all, so if you cannot read music, you are in great company. The website connected with this textbook features a number of recordings for close listening.

Musical Instruments

Traditional Irish musical instruments fall into several categories: the ones for which Ireland is best known (harp, *uilleann* pipes, fiddle), the free reeds (various accordions and concertinas), the mouth-blown instruments (flutes and whistles), the plucked instruments (banjo, guitar, and others), and the percussion instruments (frame drum and bones). This section takes into account that instruments have different histories and purposes, and that each one adheres to a particular set of practices. The following subsections explore some of the history, repertoire, limitations, and capabilities of each instrument or group of instruments. While none of these sections offer a complete picture, they serve as an introduction to the wealth of possible manifestations of Irish instrumental music.

Harps

You have already encountered the harp or *cláirseach* as both a national symbol and a musical instrument in Chapters 2 and 3, and learned not only of its association with the elite families, but also of its eventual decline due to sociohistorical factors. Chapter 3 included a brief discussion of the composer and harpist Turlough O'Carolan. In this chapter we consider the harp as a contemporary instrument. As the medieval harping style had died out at the end of the eighteenth century, the members of the cultural revival in late nineteenth- and early twentieth-century Ireland had to recreate the harping tradition. New harps, modeled roughly after seventeenth-century German harps, were built so that harpers could quickly adjust the tuning through short levers along the top of the harp, where the strings join the upper body (Rimmer 1977: 70). This efficient method of tuning, which allowed the harper to perform a tune that incorporated notes a half step apart as well as performing in multiple keys, is still used today.

The strings of a harp are perpendicular to its soundboard. If the strings were parallel, as in a piano, the instrument would be called a zither, rather than a harp. Most contemporary harpers play on nylon or gut strings, rather than the older style of metal strings. Many harpers use the same playing technique as the classical harpists who use pedals, in that they use the pads of the fingers rather than fingernails (Figure 6.1). The right hand is responsible for the upper melody line, and the left hand not only joins in performing the melody, but also picks out the bass notes. Since the cultural revival in the late twentieth century, a large amount of harp music (not just from the Bunting collections, but also from O'Carolan and others) has been published and is widely accessible. Unlike the harp music publications of the late nineteenth century, which were written to conform to pianistic styles and arrangements, contemporary harp arrangements are much truer to what players believe are the old ways (eighteenth century and before) of playing. For example, nineteenth-century harp arrangements tended to build in more functional (classical) harmony, rather than focusing on the primacy of the melody. In contemporary arrangements, the bass line may play in alternation with the melody, or simply play a single interval of a perfect fifth—as a type of drone—for each measure of the melody.

While all Irish harpers know about the three historic categories of harping (*geantraighe*, music for laughter; *suantraighe*, music for sleeping; and *goltraighe*, music for lamenting), each harper tends to select what she (or he) believes to be the most appropriate tunes for each occasion. The ratio of female to male harpers—not just in Ireland, but abroad—has been, perhaps, twenty to one, but the number of male harpers is rising.

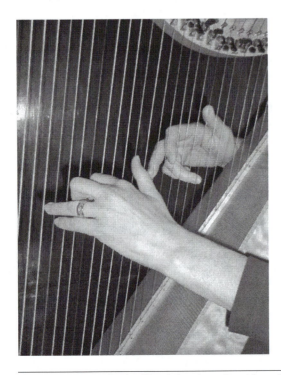

Figure 6.1 Harper Patrice Haan's hands on the strings. Photo courtesy of Tony Marcus

The earliest harpers depicted on stone crosses and elsewhere in Ireland were men, but the shift toward female harpers has occurred primarily in conjunction with the cultural revival, when harping became seen as an activity for women. After all, Ireland has for centuries been symbolized by both a harp and a female figure in need of "rescuing" by Irish heroes. The conflation of the two symbols and their manifestation in real-life performance practice is quite current.

Uilleann Pipes

In Chapter 4 you read a description of the Great Highland pipes or *pìob mhòr*. A similar instrument (the Irish "warpipe") has been a part of Irish musical history since as early as the eleventh century (Breathnach 1971: 69), and it can still be heard in large groups during parades of various kinds. However, the Irish *uilleann* pipes (pronounced *ill*-un) are now firmly associated with traditional dance music (as opposed to marching music) in the minds of their listeners. One of the earliest references to the *uilleann* pipes is from the late eighteenth century (McNamara 1999: 413), which marks them as a recent development. The term *uilleann* ("elbow") refers to the bellows pumped by the elbow of the right arm; unlike the mouth-blown Scottish highland pipes, the air supply of the *uilleann* pipes is refreshed by this bellows-pumping action alone.

Uilleann pipes include the normal cloth-covered leather bag, a double-reed chanter with a two-octave range (most bagpipes have a range of just one octave and one note), and drones in three octaves in addition to the bellows. However, the pipes also include a special feature that has a strong impact on its overall sound. This feature is the regulators. Regulators are rows of stopped, keyed pipes played with the heel and wrist of the right hand, set up to play sustained or rhythmic harmonic accompaniment. Regulators have double reeds inside, and their sound can be stopped and started quickly, which allows them to be used almost in the manner of percussive chordal accompaniment. The amount and style of regulator usage in performance vary among pipers. The first regulator was added by the late eighteenth century; the full complement of three regulators, however, was added in the nineteenth century. Regulators are now an integral part of the instrument, and they definitely set the *uilleann* pipes apart from other bagpipes. In addition to the unique sound and function of the regulators, the piper may use an array of techniques to vary the sound produced by the chanter, including sliding it off the knee to accent a note, and adding various ornaments and grace notes to the melody (McNamara 1999: 413). By lifting the bottom of the chanter off the knee the piper can facilitate different tone colors and make adjustments to the volume, as well as play the same pitch as the drones on the lowest note of the chanter (D).

The drones and regulators lie sprawled across the right knee of the piper. Between the harness that connects the bellows and bag to the player's body, the drones and regulators, and the chanter resting on the piper's knee, the instrument might look a little cumbersome at first (Figure 6.2); however, every aspect of this instrument serves a musical purpose. To create the sound, the piper inflates the bag with the bellows, turns on the drones (if desired), and lifts one or more fingers from the holes of the chanter. On most varieties of bagpipe, once the chanter's holes are unblocked, sound can proceed continuously. In order to play two identical notes in succession, the piper must play a very brief intervening note to differentiate the two notes from each other, or stop the airflow completely by closing all the holes. The *uilleann* pipes, however, have a special quality in

Figure 6.2 Eliot Grasso playing *uilleann* pipes pitched in B, built by Andreas Rogge. Photo courtesy of Ivor Vong

that when all the fingerholes are covered, and the end of the chanter is stopped on the knee, *no* sound is produced, and this facility is used to great effect to introduce silences into the tune, enabling a whole gamut of staccato techniques alongside the more familiar legato ornaments and grace notes. The piper can also lift or depress the fingers slowly to slide between notes.

As with the harp, so with the pipes: the tradition of *uilleann* piping had nearly died out by the beginning of the twentieth century, but revival efforts have more than brought it back from the brink. Associations such as Na Píobairí Uilleann ("the *uilleann* pipers"), various pipers' clubs and schools, and online resources have, since the 1960s, been essential in the continuation and promotion of the tradition through festivals, competitions, collections, and publications. Ciaran Carson has pointed out that there are probably more *uilleann* pipers right now than at any other time in the history of the instrument (1986: 17). Bagpipers—solo or in conjunction with other instrumentalists—perform dance music of various kinds, and solo slow airs (free-meter tunes that may or may not derive from songs). In a near exact opposite correlation of gender ratios for the harp, the ratio of male to female pipers in Ireland and abroad is about twenty to one, and represents a shift from the early twentieth century when lady pipers were at least somewhat in evidence. As was the case with the harp, the skewed gender ratio of the last hundred years has begun to reflect the greater participation of the opposite sex (particularly in recent years). A look at a series of pipers' biographies (O'Neill 1987: 222–348), however, reveals that a male-dominated piping scene persisted over at least two hundred years.

Fiddles

The fiddle is found all over Ireland, and indeed anywhere that people play Irish music in the world. It is an essential instrument at music sessions, dances, and performances because of its easy portability and the fact that many dance tunes are easy to play on it (and were created by fiddlers). There is no standard way to learn the Irish fiddle, though many simply pick it up and work out the tunes on their own; others watch their family members or friends play, and learn directly from them. The instrument is a standard classical violin (always called a fiddle in Ireland when played for traditional music), but its sound, repertoire, and performance practice make it characteristically Irish to those who listen closely. In other words, an Irish fiddler never plays "just" the notes and rhythms of a tune as they might appear on a page. The fiddle has four strings, tuned (from lowest to highest) to G, D, A, and E. Its neck is held in the left hand, and its body rests against the player's shoulder, neck, or chest. The right hand holds a bow, which—when drawn across the strings—provides a continuous sound. Most left-hand playing occurs without the hand ever having to move from the first position up the neck (Figure 6.3), which gives it the range of two octaves (just right for most tunes).

Irish fiddling often relies on the rich resonance of the instrument ringing during a pitch, rather than on a left-hand vibrato, to sweeten the tone of a tune. The use of the vibrato is usually restricted to the performance of airs, at least partly because many tunes fly past so quickly that there simply isn't enough time to vibrate any of the pitches. Vibrato is more of a classical convention than a traditional one, though it's quite likely

Figure 6.3 Fiddler Randal Bays. By permission Wil Macaulay, wil.macaulay@gmail.com

that it was more pronounced, as in the United States folk music scene, *before* the cultural revival. In terms of where the technical artistry of fiddling takes place, the bowing of the fiddler's right hand is crucial (just as the right hand on plucked stringed instruments plays a large role in determining the quality of sound). The direction of the bow (up or down), whether one crosses several notes or a bar line in a single bow stroke, the grip, the pressure on the strings, where the bow rests on the strings, the place along the length of the bow where the hairs grip the strings, and other features all matter very much to fiddlers. The bow can be held in any number of ways, including along the bow stick itself rather than at the frog (the end of the bow), as in classical playing. Many of these elements are transmitted purely by osmosis, rather than being explicitly taught to perpetuate a particular sound.

When Irish instrumentalists discuss regional variation in music, such differences are often most pronounced in the fiddle playing (Ó Canainn 1978: 102). Because Irish musicians now have instant access to recordings and radio performances of fiddlers from all over Ireland (and the rest of the world), those distinctions have become much more a matter of personal preference and style than one strictly defined by area. Furthermore, some "styles" seem to be defined more by the forms of the tunes rather than a particular bowing style. Nonetheless, several regional styles persist in Irish fiddle traditions. Among these are the Sliabh Luachra style of the southwest (with its danceable backbeat used in local polkas, and the slide, a regionally favored form); the East Clare style (with its many reels, its long bow strokes slurring over many notes, and its slightly flatted thirds and sevenths); the Sligo style of the middle northwest (with its "bouncy" rhythms and many melodic ornaments); and the Donegal style of the far northwest (with its single bow strokes, bowed triplets, and drones). And yet these are rank generalizations about only *some* of the regional styles! Within the regions, fiddlers are well aware of the other styles, and do not necessarily restrict themselves to a particular set of playing conventions.

Accordions and Concertinas

Free reed instruments—such as accordions or harmonicas—are wind instruments in which a reed is attached to a frame by both ends of the reed; air blows freely across the main section of the reed. Oboes and clarinets are also reed instruments, but in the case of (double reed) oboes, the reeds vibrate against each other; in the case of the (single reed) clarinet, the reed vibrates against wood. A free reed designation, therefore, means that the reed vibrates against air alone (like a harmonica, which also makes an appearance in Ireland). If you have ever produced a squawking sound by blowing across a flat blade of grass pinned between your thumbs, you have played a free reed instrument; the principle is (roughly) the same, though the blade of grass has nothing on the musical instruments in either tone or melody! In Irish music, four primary types of free reed instruments are prevalent: the piano accordion (using piano keys), the melodeon (a single row of ten buttons), the button accordion or "box" (a double row of 21 buttons in alternation), and the concertina (a hexagonal box with a bellows in the center and buttons on both ends). All are operated with a bellows arrangement by the hands, all arrived in Ireland during the late nineteenth century, and all generate a somewhat similar "reedy" sound.

Almost all of the instruments in this category include melody notes played by the right hand and bass notes by the left. The number of reeds used per note varies according to the instrument and model; melodeons, for example, can have up to four reeds per note (resulting in the ability to project across a noisy dance floor), while concertinas use just one reed per note (resulting in a much quieter sound). While context and preference determine the choice of free reed instrument, some of the instruments are more closely associated with certain musical forms; the concertina, for example, is traditionally associated with hornpipes.

The accordion was developed in Vienna in the early 1800s, and arrived in Ireland within a few short years. In the years prior to the late twentieth-century cultural revival, use of the piano accordion was quite strong in both the northern counties of Ireland and in North America. The instrument has a range of two or three octaves (depending on the model), and the notes sound the same regardless of the direction in which the bellows are pulled or pushed. The piano accordion was once much more prevalent in Irish music because its loud sound enabled the melody to penetrate the noise of many dancers at a *céilí*. It has fallen out of favor in recent years, however (S. Quinn 1999: 5), having been replaced primarily by the button accordion. In Figure 6.4 you see John Whelan posed with his button ("box") accordion.

The melodeon is a one-row, ten-button accordion first popularized in the United States, then brought to Ireland in the latter part of the nineteenth century. It produces a different sound for pushing than for pulling, which enables the player to create a diatonic (seven-note) scale. It also comes in different keys; regional preferences indicate stylistic conventions and general tone, whether smooth or choppy (Vallely 2011: 4). Its use has fallen out of favor recently, also having been replaced by the

Figure 6.4 The button accordion, played by John Whelan. Photo courtesy of Doug Plummer

button accordion. Also called the "box," the button accordion has seen considerable growth since the 1990s. The tuning of the button accordion is set so that the "voices" of the individual sets of reeds are deliberately tuned slightly differently from one another to create a particular sound. It allows for chromatic playing through the button set-up of two rows of buttons a half-step apart. Both the melodeon and button accordion are considerably lighter in weight than the piano accordion, though they are still worn around the body of the player with a harness so that they may be played standing up.

Concertinas are the gentle cousins of the free reed family. Played with both hands in a melodic capacity (unlike the others, which divide left and right hands into bass and melody, for example), the Anglo concertina—mass-produced in England based on German models—is the most common concertina used in Ireland (Figure 6.5). The Anglo differs from other concertinas in that each button produces two different notes, depending on whether the player is "pressing" or "drawing" the air (ibid.: 83). Concertinas that play the same note whether one presses or draws are also played in Ireland, but are less common. The concertina was, for a time, popular as a parlor instrument; its quiet sound enabled it to be played in a small room and heard by just a few guests rather than filling an entire dance hall. Similarly, some of the homes in rural County Clare—the region with which the instrument is most closely associated—used to have a small concertina niche in the wall by the fireside, allowing a busy mother to take down the concertina for a minute or two of quiet playing for herself or for her children to dance or play to (Mick Moloney, personal communication). Keeping the instrument by the fire kept the reeds and bellows dry as well. All these free reed instruments, including the concertina, are able to use the bass notes for a lightly percussive element to accompany Irish dancing.

Flutes and Whistles

The Irish transverse ("sideways") flute differs from the silver flute of classical music in two major respects: it is made of wood, which gives it a softer (yes, "woodier") sound

Figure 6.5 The Anglo concertina, played by Burt Meyer

than the purity of the silver flute, and it generally has six holes with up to eight keys to supply multiple semitones. Besides the sonic difference, the two types of flutes also differ in their key system, though some wooden flutes use the silver flute (Boehm) key system. The Irish wooden flute came into traditional music from Continental baroque and classical music in the late eighteenth century and grew in popularity, particularly by the time silver flutes became mass-produced in the nineteenth century. In the 1970s, Irish flute makers began to produce instruments to meet the increasing demand for good quality local flutes; designs were closer to the highly favored nineteenth-century models (Hast and Scott 2004: 80), and the standard set during the 1970s has continued to the present. In fact, the wooden flute has become so much more common than the silver flute at sessions that a silver flute might well be greeted as a decidedly "foreign" instrument (which, of course, they both are). The fact that the wooden flute (Figure 6.6) is also foreign is not as important as its symbolism as a traditional instrument (one now being used in traditional music, at least), distinguishing it from the *more* foreign-seeming silver flute.

The flute is associated with particular regions of Ireland, particularly the western and northwestern counties such as Sligo and Leitrim. Yet in each area its players have developed individualized styles; while there is still an emphasis on a generally local sound, a growing number of recordings has led to the emergence of important individual players who have influenced countless others. As the cultural revival continues to expand, the status of the flute has grown with it. It is now normal practice to find one or two flutes along with other instruments in a session; however, it is unlikely that one will encounter a "wall of flutes" the way one finds a "wall of fiddles" in some sessions. The flute's woody tone and louder volume make it stand out more audibly than the fiddle.

Figure 6.6 Chris Norman and Catherine McEvoy at the Boxwood Festival and Workshop. Photo courtesy of Paul F. Wells

The tin whistle or *feadóg* (sometimes called a pennywhistle, though it has been many years since it cost a penny) is simple, inexpensive, and easy to find both within and outside of Ireland. The *feadóg* in its original form was made of willow, and it was often given to children as a first instrument. In its current form, it is a plain metal tube with holes and a head—like that on a recorder, but with only six holes—that enables the player to easily create a sound (Figure 6.7). What is *not* so simple is becoming skilled on the whistle, playing gracefully and with taste, and adding the ornaments and variations that characterize so much of Irish music.

Because the fingering arrangement is almost the same as that for the flute, and close to that of the *uilleann* pipes (though the whistle is an octave higher), flute players and pipers often bring along a tin whistle to gigs or sessions for instrumental variety. The whistle is often taught in Irish schools, too. Shops in Ireland (and the ubiquitous Irish-themed shops found in every large North American city) readily stock tin whistles for under twenty dollars, complete with little booklets that guarantee one's ability to play "Danny Boy." Yet because the whistle is so easy at its most basic level, many people start (and sometimes end) their entire Irish music journey with the whistle rather than with one of the "harder" (or more expensive) instruments.

Both flute and tin whistle players favor certain tunes, particularly those that do not cross below the bottom note of the instrument. As was briefly mentioned in the "Musical Textures" section of Chapter 1, an Irish flute or whistle player is limited to the bottom pitch of the instrument (a D whistle cannot go below D; a C whistle cannot go below C). If the flute or whistle player wishes to play a melody that explores the lower

Figure 6.7 The tin whistle, played by Morgan Black

range, he or she must leap up an octave. A tune such as "Garrat Barry," which never once reaches below the pitch of D, suits a D whistle or flute player much more than "The Silver Spire," which spends at least some of the tune well below the bottom note of the instrument. For certain tunes, this leaping up an octave when the tune goes *down* can result in awkward melodic lines. It is a sign of skill and good musicianship when a fine player can make the transitions between octaves—due to the limitations of the instrument—appear effortless.

Guitars, Banjos, and Other Plucked Instruments

The plucked stringed instrument family has often been a kind of first stage for outsiders to Irish music. Guitarists, tenor banjo players, bouzouki players, mandolin players, and those who play hybrid stringed instruments can move easily from one genre of music to another, including Irish music as part of their musical exploration without being limited to it. Ethnomusicologist Christopher Smith points out that inherently Irish instruments such as the *uilleann* pipes do not afford their players that kind of luxury. A piper cannot easily shift genres, while plucked stringed instrument players have access to a much broader musical spectrum.

The guitar first appeared in Ireland as a parlor instrument, where its use in the nineteenth-century classical repertoire paralleled its appearance on the mainland. It did not enter the vernacular realm until the twentieth century, when guitars and pianos were brought in to the early recording studios to accompany melody instruments. As has been pointed out in print on several occasions (see, for example, Smith 2003: 34) and widely discussed among musicians, the early accompanists had little to no understanding of the melodies, modes, or overall feel of the tunes. Instead, they simply pounded away on their chordal instruments in the background, driving future generations of players to distraction in their attempts to access the original recordings of some of the great fiddlers of the early twentieth century. The guitar and tenor banjo were also a feature of *céilí* bands in the dance halls, but they did not carry a central role.

Since the 1950s, the easy availability of the guitar in Ireland and elsewhere has brought it into use as a kind of workhorse accompanimental instrument. In the hands of a folksinger, it accompanies the voice (usually tuned to the normal E–A–D–G–B–E). While many traditional singers prefer to perform unaccompanied, an equal number accompany themselves on guitar. The popular D–A–D–G–A–D tuning has been in use since the 1960s, when guitarists Davey Graham and Martin Carthy first popularized it. Referring to the tuning of the strings from lowest (pitched) to highest, this tuning enables players to use open chords, drones, and alternatives to major and minor in accompanying songs and instrumental tunes.

The problem with standard tuning is that it tends to drive accompaniment into either a "major" or a "minor" feel. By locking in tunes to either major or minor, the lovely ambiguity, tonal shifts, and modal shifts in Irish music can be overwhelmed or lost altogether. The D–A–D–G–A–D tuning removes the third degree of the scale, and in doing so, allows the pitches within tunes to shift from sharp to natural and back without forcing a particular mode.

In addition to being used to accompany singer-songwriters, the guitar can be an important supportive instrument for fiddles, flutes, and other instruments. At sessions, the guitarist—and there should generally be just one guitarist—uses a guitar pick and plays on just a few of the strings in a lightly percussive chordal style (without the alternating bass of American folk music). The best Irish guitar playing supports and lifts the melody without driving the tempo.

The current usage of the four-string tenor banjo in Ireland is as a melody, not a chordal, instrument. Tuned G–D–A–E, one octave below the fiddle, it is played with a pick and has a rich, characteristic blend of the banjo's "plunky" sound and the fiddle's "lift." Though both the four- and five-string banjo have a history in Irish music (including in the United States, with the playing of tenor banjoist Mike Flanagan in the 1920s era of 78 rpm recordings), it was not until the 1970s and the cultural revival that the folk music boom in North America brought the banjo to stay. Tommy Makem played the five-string banjo in his performances with the Clancy Brothers, though it was not as a melody instrument; he played it in a style closer to fingerpicking guitar to accompany singing (closest to the style of the American banjo player and folksinger Pete Seeger). Any Irish musician playing the five-string banjo is either playing American bluegrass or old-time music, or is playing in this fingerpicking guitar style *à la* Tommy Makem and Pete Seeger.

Barney McKenna of the Dubliners (in the 1960s and 1970s) established the tuning of the tenor banjo as one octave below the fiddle. When one hears the four-string banjo today, it is always played as a melodic instrument. Good four-string banjos are prized for their workmanship and clear, robust sound (Figure 6.8), even though the early twentieth-century American banjos were designed for higher-pitched tuning for jazz and other genres. Tenor banjos, like guitars, sometimes appeared at *céilí* dances,

Figure 6.8 Pauline Conneely and her tenor banjo. Photo courtesy of Maryann Mangan

but the main instrumental combination at those dances was the more characteristically "Irish" instruments in front (pipes, fiddles, accordions) and dance band instruments in back (Smith 2003: 35). When performed as a melody instrument, the sound of the tenor banjo can cut through the noise of a crowded dance floor almost as easily as an accordion. Tenor banjo players tend *not* to crowd their melodies by playing every single note of a tune because of the way the sound can dominate a session; instead, they add a rich sense of color and deep grounding to the fiddles and other higher-pitched instruments, and their lively use of triplets and slides (from a C# to D, for example) give the instrument its characteristic sound.

Another stringed instrument used in sessions and on recordings is the bouzouki, a flat-backed adaptation of the Greek instrument that entered Irish traditional music circles in the 1970s. Like the mandolin, the bouzouki (Figure 6.8) has four paired "courses" of strings, but the bouzouki is usually tuned G–D–A–D, whereas the mandolin is tuned like a fiddle. While the bouzouki has been used as a melodic instrument, its rich percussive and chordal capability is used to accompany melody instruments as well. The bouzouki is much rarer in casual moments of playing music than, for example, the fiddle, but its sound has become a normal part of traditional music (especially in recordings). Furthermore, because it is not generally the kind of instrument that one might have around the house (like the fiddle that belonged to an uncle or cousin), it takes a specialist interested specifically in the "zouk" to seek it out, purchase it, and learn to play it.

The bouzouki (Figure 6.9), with its "open" tuning that enabled it to accompany modal tunes easily, was essential in some of the recordings of the Irish supergroups of the 1970s

Figure 6.9 Roger Landes playing the bouzouki. Photo courtesy of Wil Macaulay

(see Chapter 9). Specifically, its sound (and, for that matter, the sound of the guitar in D–A–D–G–A–D tuning) imitated the droning sound of the pipes, bringing a more specifically Irish sensibility to the recordings. This was in contrast to the triadic chords (including the tonic, third, and fifth degree of each chord) that were in use to accompany American folk and folk-rock, and served, along with the absence of a drum kit, to set the sound of the supergroups apart from standard-issue rock'n'roll in the States.

Percussion Instruments

Because so much of Irish instrumental music was originally intended to accompany dance, percussion has often been supplied by the dancers' feet. However, two percussive instruments find their way into Irish performance practice: the *bodhrán* and the bones. The *bodhrán* (pronounced "*bow*-rawn") is an old style of frame drum, but its use in Irish traditional music is neither historically popular nor particularly traditional. Until its extraordinary revival in the latter half of the twentieth century, the *bodhrán* was used mainly for Wren Boy celebrations the day after Christmas, when young boys would kill a wren and take it from house to house, singing songs and asking for money to "bury the wren." It was popularly used in community music-making *only* after it appeared in revivalist recordings of the 1970s. Its current popularity both as a musical instrument and as a beloved tourist souvenir to hang on the wall—complete with painted Celtic knotwork designs and phrases in Irish—is both remarkable and recent.

Made of goatskin stretched over a round wooden frame of approximately 18 inches in diameter, the *bodhrán* is held against the body with the left hand, and struck by the right hand with a single two-headed stick called a tipper; any perusal of YouTube clips of bodhrán playing will reveal not just what the instrument looks like, but how it is played. Other instrumentalists tend to disparage the *bodhrán*, perhaps because so many beginners play it so poorly (and so loudly, or at least with a bit too much enthusiasm) at music sessions (Schiller 2001: 28). Jokes about the instrument abound—perhaps as the Irish equivalent of viola jokes in classical music or banjo jokes in folk music—and more than one of these drums at a session is too many drums. Most of the best players play quietly, listen responsively, and allow the melody instruments to determine both the tempo and feel of the tune before entering. They also tend to know the tunes well, and can be responsive to both the rhythmic and melodic shapes of the melody.

Bodhrán players normally outline the form of the tune—as in the jig, reel, hornpipe, or other form—through a series of down and up strokes on the head of the drum. The most basic playing pattern for a reel might be "down, down–up, down, down–up" in a four-beat pattern. A double jig pattern (in 6/8) would—again, at its most basic—be played "down, up, down, down, up, down." A hornpipe, in contrast, could include the triplets (sometimes called "rolls") characteristic of hornpipes, and would use both ends of the tipper (in rapid succession) to do so. Some players lightly strike the rim of the *bodhrán* to include variation in the pattern, or use the left hand to apply pressure to the skin head (and therefore to vary the pitch). The style of individual players depends on how they hold the tipper (or whether they use one at all), how the drum is held, the pressure of the left hand on the skin, and other technical issues (Cunningham 1999: 31).

The bones are a pair of flat percussive sticks, initially made from cow ribs but now constructed of wood, approximately six inches long and often slightly curved. They are held in one hand and strike against each other to create an interesting rhythmic backdrop that is radically different in timbre from that of the *bodhrán*. Because bones playing is so individualized, and is not notated, any number of rhythmic and tonal possibilities are available to players. Historically, the bones were brought to Ireland through traveling minstrel shows from the United States and were used primarily to accompany dancing until they appeared onstage and in recordings with the Chieftains in the 1960s (Mercier 1999: 34). Their use in a full arrangement of traditional materials—an important feature of the Chieftains' performances—led to more groups incorporating the use of the bones. Today, bones are available for sale at music shops specializing in Irish instruments, and their use appears primarily onstage (as opposed to in sessions, where they almost never appear).

The Forms of Irish Instrumental Music

Irish instrumental music was originally used primarily as accompaniment to dances; these dances were almost all in common practice by the end of the eighteenth century (McCullough 1977: 85). The forms discussed in this section are all dance forms, with the exception of the airs. Most forms last 32 measures, taking up just eight measures for each of two repeated sections (the "A" section or the "tune," and the "B" section or the "turn"). Some tunes have more than two sections, but two sections is the norm. It is also normal to combine two or three tunes in succession without pausing, as long as they are related in some way (being in the same or a related key, for example, and the same form, or even with related titles such as "The Sporting Pitchfork" and "The Rambling Pitchfork"). Many players follow the set choices of a musician on a particularly iconic recording, and refer to the "set" by the name of the musician on the recording, as in "the Michael Coleman set." In addition to the dance forms described below, Irish musicians frequently borrow from other genres (contradance tunes, for example, or tunes from Scotland or Brittany), depending on the context in which they are playing. Remember that each instrument has its own way of encountering a tune, and each player has his or her own relationship to each tune. By joining the session, you too can find your own way on the instrument you play.

Join the Session: Reels

One can find reels almost anywhere in Ireland. They are an extremely popular staple of the repertoire, and are often played publicly at high speed in 4/4 time (though they do not have to be played fast to be reels). Players cover eight eighth notes in two groups of four within a single measure. Outside of parts of Donegal, many players slur across several notes at a time when playing reels and other tunes; an important measure of taste lies in balancing the slurs with the singly-bowed notes. Reels are the most common form of tunes in Ireland as well as abroad in the Irish diaspora; one can sometimes attend a session in which reels are the *only* form played all evening.

For many of the notes that last more than the length of an eighth note, a competent Irish musician might insert a roll (on measure 1, below, the first note would sound like a slurred F–G–F–E–F). "Charlie Mulvihill's" is a reel in the key of B flat major

TRACK 6

(Figure 6.10). Listen to Joanie Madden playing this reel on the accompanying online soundtrack; it is transcribed here in B flat major because that is the type of tin whistle that she is playing. Other tin whistle players might play it in D.

Join the Session: Jigs

Jigs come in three types: single, double, and slip. Single jigs are also called slides (see slides, below). Double jigs are the most common form of the jigs, and are played in a rapid 6/8 time: six eighth notes per measure. Players usually perform a string of several double jigs (generally just called "jigs" rather than differentiating double jigs from the others) in a single favorite key, like D. Or, instead of a string of tunes, fiddlers might choose a "mighty tune"—a multipart double jig with four or five sections, such as "The Humours of Ballyloughlin" or "The Gold Ring."

"The Hag's Purse" is a lovely tune with a cringe-worthy title, and it is a fine introduction to playing jigs. It is in the key of D Mixolydian, which means it is like a D major scale with a flatted seventh degree (Figure 6.11). Never let the title of a tune deter you from playing it! Just remember that Irish musicians remember tunes, but they do not

TRACK 5

Figure 6.10 "Charlie Mulvihill's" (reel)

Figure 6.11 "The Hag's Purse" (double jig)

always remember (or care about) the titles of the tunes they play. Listen to the jigs on the accompanying online soundtrack to hear what this one sounds like. If you are trying to play this one, try following the slurs (and listening to the recording) and see how the overall feel of the tune changes with or without them. You may also wish to experiment with your own slurs, but try not to have them be predictably the same in each measure. Part of the reason you have the notation here as well as the recording to listen to online is so that you can try to actually play what you hear. You will know the tunes so much better if you do.

Slip jigs are in a moderate 9/8 time: nine eighth notes per measure, fixed into three groups of three. "Elizabeth Kelly's Favourite" (Figure 6.12) showcases a tune arrangement that—missing the F (or F#), the sixth degree of the scale—could be either in A Aeolian or A Dorian. This makes the tune *hexatonic*—six pitches—rather than *heptatonic*—seven pitches. Who could tell which mode it is in, when the only difference between the two modes is a single note? This first slip jig, which occurs on the online soundtrack accompanying this book, is played at a moderate tempo. Notice the symbols to indicate an ornament: right on the very first note of the tune. Instead of playing a dotted quarter note on A, try playing a grace note: A–B–A, with the B occurring on the second half of the second beat in the dotted note.

TRACK 10

Join the Session: Hornpipes

Imported from England, a 4/4 hornpipe can be performed quite slowly (to accompany a step dancer, for example) or nearly as fast as a reel, depending on the context. The hallmark of a hornpipe is its slightly dotted rhythm, and therefore its implication of a triplet feel. In a medium tempo, hornpipes tend to include actual triplets as speed and taste dictate. If you were to play a hornpipe as if it were *all* in triplets—rather than in eighth notes, the way it is normally notated—you would come much closer to the overall correct feel and "swing" of regular performance practice.

Try playing the following hornpipe, "Moran's Fancy" (Figure 6.13) with evenly-spaced eighth notes. Then swing it as if it were all in triplets (rather than two eighth notes, play a lengthened first eighth note and a shortened second eighth note); as long as you understand the intention of the hornpipe, you will have no trouble swinging it. "Moran's Fancy" appears on the accompanying online soundtrack; listen to Tim Collins playing it on his concertina (the classic hornpipe instrument!) and find your own balance between swinging the tune and straight-ahead playing. Can you find the wandering tone?

TRACK 2

Figure 6.12 "Elizabeth Kelly's Favourite" (slip jig)

Figure 6.13 "Moran's Fancy" (hornpipe)

Join the Session: Marches

A march can be used for dancing, for marching, and for listening. In tune books, marches can be listed as jigs (if they have a dotted feel), as reels, as polkas, and as barndances! For some players, especially those who care only about the tunes and not about the finer points of distinguishing one dance style from another, it's a march if the title says it's a march, as in "March of the Kings of Laois." However, marches are those tunes either specifically written to march to—based on a military past—or written in the style of other marching tunes. The march, unlike reels or jigs, is *not* determined so much by its time signature as by its intention.

TRACK 13

If you examine the following march, you will note that it has a "dotted feel" (as in the "Humpty Dumpty" rhythm), can be played relatively slowly without losing its internal coherence, and would, in fact, be quite easy to march to. This tune is in D Mixolydian, which means it is like a regular D major scale, but with a flatted seventh degree. In addition to trying it out here as written, you can listen to the recording of this march on the accompanying online soundtrack. While it is frustrating to work with a form that can be in several different time signatures, think about the characteristics of marching: you need strong beats at the beginning and middle of each measure. "March of the Kings of Laois" fulfills that requirement (Figure 6.14). (Note: "Laois" is the name of one of the Irish counties, and is pronounced "leesh.")

Join the Session: Slides

The slide is an uptempo dance tune in 12/8 (sometimes called a single jig, but based on a different dance historically), and is most commonly associated with the Sliabh Luachra area in the southwestern Cork/Kerry region. While it might seem the same as a double jig—note that a double jig is in 6/8, while a slide is in 12/8—the dance is different (Cowdery 1990: 18) and the overall feel of slides is different. Notice, for example, that some of the figures are one quarter note plus an eighth note. A single jig also has groupings of one quarter note plus an eighth note (again, as in the rhythm of "Humpty

Figure 6.14 "March of the Kings of Laois" (march)

Figure 6.15 "The Rathawaun" (slide)

Dumpty"). In a double jig, most of the groupings are in sets of three eighth notes. Slides and polkas are often associated with set dancing (see Chapter 9).

"The Rathawaun" is in D major with plenty of stepwise motion and few intervals larger than a third (Figure 6.15). When you listen to the accompanying online soundtrack, notice that this tune has more of a flowing feel to it rather than a bouncy, divided feel (which it might have if it had bigger intervals). Compare its stepwise motion (particularly in the B section) to some of the other tunes, which might feature intervals of a fifth or an octave.

TRACK 11

Join the Session: Polkas

The polka is a dance tune in 2/4 time, and in Ireland is generally associated (together with slides) with the Sliabh Luachra area of the southwest. However, musicians all over Ireland play polkas, as doing a set of polkas offers a nice change from the jigs and reels; they are also considered fairly easy to play. They are often among the first tunes that beginners learn to play, but very experienced players enjoy them as well because a good tune is not defined by its ease of performance. While originally from the Czech area of Europe (created by the Czechs in imitation of Polish dances), the polka has a history in Ireland of over a hundred years, and the polkas played in Irish traditional music are local creations. All the Irish polkas are notated in two quarter notes per measure with an AABB form of eight bars per section. While the dance that goes with the polka has some regional variations, the way polkas are played in sessions is too fast for most dancers.

TRACK 14

The difference between Sliabh Luachra polka playing on the fiddle and polkas from elsewhere is that in a long bow stroke for a polka, the Sliabh Luachra fiddler emphasizes the second of every two eighth notes by speeding up the bow for a fraction of a second, creating a louder, pulse-like sound akin to a backbeat. Whatever instrument you try to play these polkas on, consider slightly emphasizing the second beat. In "Dan O'Connell's Favourite" (featured on the accompanying online soundtrack for this book), notice the lively tempo of the accordion player. Start out slowly on this one first (Figure 6.16), then gradually increase your speed.

Join the Session: Mazurkas

Mazurkas are dance tunes in a moderate 3/4 time, originally imported from Poland but now composed locally. The dance itself came to Ireland in the decade before the Famine, and spread across the north in particular. Generally, mazurkas emphasize the second or third beat of the measure, rather than the first, and that emphasis appears in the dance as well. It is popular in Donegal (in the Northwest of the Republic), where the second of the three beats is often emphasized in a variety of forms. Ireland has few mazurkas (fewer than two dozen), but they are important in the northern dances. One of the most ubiquitous is titled "Shoe the Donkey," and it is a lively (and very easy) two-hand dance moving clockwise around a circle… gradually increasing in tempo until all the dancers are laughing and out of breath.

This next mazurka—like many Irish tunes—goes by an array of titles. While its primary title is "Proinsias Ó Maonaigh's" (Figure 6.17), it is also known as "Frankie

Figure 6.16 "Dan O'Connell's Favourite" (polka)

Figure 6.17 "Proinsias Ó Maonaigh's" (mazurka)

Mooney's"—the English version of the name Proinsias Ó Maonaigh (who was himself the father of fiddler and singer Máiréad Ní Mhaonaigh of the supergroup Altan). Another name for it is "The Glenties," which refers to the Donegal town of Glenties. Mr. Ó Maonaigh (1922–2006) was a highly respected Donegal fiddler; pronounce his name (and that of this tune) as "*pron*-shas oh *mwee*-ney." Mazurkas are played at a moderate tempo, slightly emphasizing the second beat of each measure.

Join the Session: Barndances

A barndance is a medium-speed dance tune—like a slightly accelerated hornpipe—in 4/4 time but without the emphasis on triplets. Sometimes these tunes are called *germans*, particularly in Donegal, even though they are locally composed. Barndances—often described as "Scottish sounding"—are performed most commonly in Donegal and Northern Ireland, in close proximity to Scotland; they are also performed in the area of Clare. Note that a tune performed like a slightly accelerated hornpipe has a "swing" or a dotted feel to it.

Playing a barndance at a session might happen just once in an evening, or not at all. Because they—together with highlands—are so characteristically associated with the northern part of the island, starting one up elsewhere in the country may result in blank looks. It might also result in everyone jumping in with enthusiasm or set off several sets of barndances; you never know until you try. Notice, in "Kitty Sheain's" (named after Kitty Sheain of Teelin, Co. Donegal), that a quarter note often begins a measure (Figure 6.18). Unlike a hornpipe, a barndance uses quarter notes much more frequently.

Join the Session: Highlands

These dances were imported from Scotland, and—like barndances and mazurkas—tend to be most favored in the north, which after all saw plenty of commerce with Scotland. A highland is performed as a rapid 4/4 dance tune with two rhythmic patterns: a dotted eighth note followed by a sixteenth note, and a sixteenth note followed by a dotted eighth. The latter pattern is sometimes called a "snap." The difference between highlands

Figure 6.18 "Kitty Sheain's" (barndance)

and barndances—both are in 4/4 time with a bouncy feel—is that highlands do not usually begin each measure with a quarter note or two quarter notes. The term "highland" is sometimes interchanged in Ireland with the terms "strathspey" and "fling," which are Scottish dance forms.

TRACK 16

The accompanying online soundtrack for this book includes a recording by a brother and sister—Róisín (Harrigan) McGrory and Damien Harrigan—performing a pair of highlands: "Casey's Pig" and "Dúlamán na Binne Buídhe." Notice several large intervals in the melody of the second highland ("Dúlamán na Binne Buídhe"), particularly between measures six and seven below; this is characteristic of some highlands (Figure 6.19). "Dúlamán na Binne Buídhe" ("Seaweed of the Yellow Cliffs") is pronounced "*doo*-la-mon nuh *bin*-ya bwee." Irish-language titles of tunes are uncommon, but they do appear in Gaeltacht (Irish-speaking) regions. Try playing it while listening to the online soundtrack; notice how important the dotted notes are in providing a sense of "lift" to the feel of the tune. What is "lift"? Compare the idea of "lift" to what this tune might sound like with straight eighth notes; perhaps the approximate feel of *that* sound might be "plodding"!

Join the Session: Waltzes

One might hear a waltz performed at the *end* of an evening of dances; usually not before. The dance is a nineteenth-century European creation, performed in a gentle 3/4 time, and many of O'Carolan's tunes in that time signature are played (and danced) as waltzes, even though they were not intended as such. In terms of their contemporary use, many waltzes are derived from popular *céilí* band tunes, and can be instrumental versions of Irish-American songs. Other Irish tunes in 3/4 time qualify as waltzes; "The South Wind" is one example of such a locally composed (i.e., non-European mainland) tune. The fact that "The South Wind" has become popular is a testament to the fact that Irish traditional music is a living tradition, and that waltz tunes can just as easily fit into the repertoire as jigs and reels. Many musicians (including, for example, Tommy Peoples, Liz Carroll, and others) create tunes and play them in sessions (and classes, and music camps, and on recordings), where they shift into the public repertoire.

Figure 6.19 "Dúlamán na Binne Buídhe" (highland)

Figure 6.20 "The South Wind" (waltz)

"The South Wind" was written in the 1700s by a man named Freckled Donal Macnamara, apparently in homesickness for his home in County Mayo (Figure 6.20). Its characteristic pattern, which is not specific to every waltz, is a dotted quarter note followed by an eighth note, followed by another quarter note. Dancing to this one would require taking even steps against the dotted rhythms of the tune; it adds rhythmic interest to the dance. It is in an uncomplicated D major: no "wandering notes," no special challenges. Part of what makes it such a pleasing melody is its stepwise motion; notice in the B section especially that it begins on the high pitch D and walks all the way down an octave. Stepwise motion is a frequent technique in songwriting, so when we hear it in a tune, it sounds that much more "singable."

Don't Join the Session: Airs

An air is a slow tune, often (but not always) in free meter. Some airs are based on Irish-language *sean-nós* songs or piping airs, some are original compositions for a specific instrument, and still others might be drawn straight from the harp compositions of Turlough O'Carolan. Many musicians use a light vibrato as a kind of gentle ornament when playing airs, even though vibrato is sometimes frowned upon in both song and air performance. Anyone performing an air that has its origins in an Irish-language song is expected to know the song, so as to understand the proper placement of melodic ornamentation (see Chapter 7). On the other hand, playing an air that did not come from a song—called a *port*—offers much more freedom (at least from linguistic constraints) to the player, as well as (often) a fixed meter tune. In an entire evening of instrumental music, you might expect to hear just one person play an air. Depending on the nature of the session, however, one could go for several weeks without hearing one.

Instrumental airs can, depending on the instrument, include notes or entire passages that are impossible to render on the voice. Because the singer is constrained by the lyrics, variations in the melody are often connected to the way the singer's family or community has performed the song. Instrumentalists feel fewer constraints that way.

On the one hand, playing an air with other people is inappropriate, so suggesting that you "join the session" by playing this with others doesn't make sense. So don't. On the other hand, you should still try to play it. Fiddler James Kelly performs the air "Cath Chéim an Fhia" on the accompanying online soundtrack, so it might be useful to listen closely to the way he plays it, over and over, and then try it yourself. Notice that he uses an almost breathing rhythm in his playing, and that unlike some of the dance tunes in this chapter, he infuses the air with rich ornamentation that renders it profoundly difficult to notate.

COMPANION @ WEBSITE
TRACK 8

Chapter 3 included mention of the song "Johnny Seoighe" (Figure 6.21) as an example of a Famine song in Irish whose lyrics have been, until recently, still a little raw for Ireland's contemporary sensibilities. Being a Famine song, the content of the song is sad. It deals with the betrayal of the hopes of a poor person by a wealthy person, and the content of the lyrics makes people uncomfortable because it is *not* generic; it refers to a specific area within Connemara. The transcription is duplicated here to illustrate an air derived from a song.

Matters of Style

Irish tunes tend to work more effectively with one instrument type rather than another. For example, fiddle tunes fit very well under the players' hands in first position on the neck of the fiddle, or are particularly well suited to effective bowing patterns. Keys, also, are chosen because they are suited to particular instruments. Many Irish tunes are in sharp keys (G, D, A, etc.), because these keys suit the pipes, fiddle, and flutes, better than flat keys (F, B flat, E flat, etc.). Concertina players tend to prefer tunes in the keys of G and C, depending on the instrument. Related keys (A minor, B minor, E minor, etc.) are popular because they draw from the same tonal material as C major, D major, and G major, respectively. It is rare to find players (outside of the West Galway area) ready to join in on a tune in a key with more than two or three flats, for example.

Many musicians in Ireland learn the tunes off by heart from repeated listening and long familiarity with them. Most musicians never see the tunes printed out in notated form. This method of learning is called oral transmission, and is an especially important way of understanding the overall style and feel of Irish music. If you were to take an instrument and play straight from the notation, without having heard Irish music live or in recording, you would completely miss the point. The regimented format of

Figure 6.21 "Johnny Seoighe" (air)

notation does not allow the music to "swing"; that is, to vary the length of the notes within a measure while keeping a steady tempo.

All the notes in a tune might look the same—they are identical eighth notes, aren't they?—but in practice a double jig has an almost "dotted note" feel—with the first note of the triplet given slight emphasis, and the second and/or third notes somewhat deemphasized. Classical violinists who turn to Irish music for variation or fun often find themselves confounded by the fact that the *prescriptive* notation of Irish music does not *describe* how it is actually played. Bowing, which plays such a crucial role in fiddling style, is rarely if ever notated. Anyone sightreading a tune without the notated bowing will sound terribly stilted; a fiddle player accustomed to a particular Irish style, however, will easily and automatically bow the tune according to regional stylistic conventions, placing the ornaments where they feel and sound right (notated or not). This is why, as a musician learning about Irish music, you should listen, listen, and listen some more.

An ornament is a decoration or addition to a melody for aesthetic and rhythmic purposes. Typical ornaments include, among others, rolls, turns, and cuts. A roll is a set of five notes (for example, B–C–B–A–B), generally bowed in one stroke or blown with a single breath. A turn is a set of several notes intended to decorate a transition from one note to another (for example, B–C–B–A). A cut is a single non-melodic note rapidly interspersed between two others. Ornaments are more important in some parts of Ireland than in others, but most players use them as a matter of taste and to give the tune life and beauty.

Cranning began as an ornament specific to the pipes, in which a series of repeated notes are played with short upper notes interspersed. With the short notes, then, as with cuts, the actual pitch is less important than that the bottom note is interrupted. Fiddlers, for example, simply touch a finger to an upper note without actually pressing it down onto the neck; it interrupts the vibration and adds rhythmic interest. The point of cranning is to sound somewhat like an *uilleann* piper. Grace notes are a way to lead into a held note; for example, they can be used to great effect in the playing of airs.

Another aspect of style has to do with articulation and phrasing (McCullough 1977: 89); in other words, whether a musician performs with a more staccato (choppy) sound, or a more legato (smooth) sound. Various instrumentalists approach this issue according to their capabilities as musicians, the limitations of their instruments, and the conventions of their home district. When one joins multiple notes together with a single bowstroke, for example, the notes are gathered in a phrase. Fiddlers sometimes bow across the measures of a tune (where one might think that a player would change bow direction) to add rhythmic interest and musicality to the phrase. Phrasing, then, has to do with how one groups the notes of the melody, and good phrasing refers to how musically appropriate the results are. Too much legato playing results in an unintelligible mush of notes with no discernible beginning or ending of phrases, while playing that is too staccato is choppy and sounds as if it has no phrases at all. How a player phrases his or her tunes is one of the essential aesthetic elements of Irish traditional music, and separates the great players from the hacks.

Style in Ireland is also very much associated with individuals, particularly those who have become well known from their travels abroad or through their recordings and concerts. Long before the contemporary fiddler Martin Hayes (or the Irish-American fiddler Eileen Ivers) began pushing out the boundaries of traditional Irish music, three

Sligo fiddlers moved to the States between 1915 and 1925: Michael Coleman, James Morrison, and Paddy Killoran. Each one made dozens of highly influential recordings that were marketed in Ireland and served to spread the Sligo sound (with its rich ornamentation and tune variation) to other areas in the country. Since that time, the influence of the mass media on traditional music has been all-encompassing in Ireland. Rather than pointing to regional sounds and styles as a musical "home," new players are absorbing the widely divergent sounds, techniques, and local repertoires of scores of individual musicians—not all of them Irish—that they hear on the radio, on recordings, and in concerts or sessions.

In Ireland, public performances tend to focus on instrumental music, not vocal. Yet pubs, festivals, competitions, and concert halls are not the only location of musical performance, and instrumental music is not the exclusive sound of Irish music. Vocal music holds some of Ireland's most powerful poetic voices and forms of expression; as we turn our focus to the vocal traditions in Irish and English, we now come to the heart of this book.

Discussion Questions

1. What are the elements of an "international language" of music? Why doesn't that concept work most of the time? Why might it work in Irish music?
2. Based on listening to the different instruments on the online soundtrack for this book, and your understanding of those instruments from this chapter, which one might you be willing to try to play? Why that particular one?
3. Why do you suppose there are so many more jigs and reels than any other kind of tune? What is it about them that causes people to play them all over Ireland?
4. "But I thought polkas came exclusively from Poland!" (They don't, and they didn't originate there either.) When Irish people play a polka created in Ireland, is it still a polka? What about a mazurka? Or a waltz?
5. Why can't musical notation capture a sense of the style—the lift, the swing, the nuance—of Irish music? How are you supposed to learn to play if the notation isn't precisely accurate?

PART III

Focusing In
Vocal Music in Irish-Gaelic and English

CHAPTER 7

Vocal Music in Irish-Gaelic

Ná bíodh do theanga faoi do chrios ~ Don't keep your tongue under your belt.

Part I offered a historical account of Irish music, as well as an introduction to the basics of contemporary performance practice. Part II took a broader view of "Celtic" music, explored Irish music in the diasporic settings of North America and elsewhere, and began to narrow the field of inquiry by examining Irish instrumental music, its forms, and some of its stylistic issues. Part III—Focusing In—takes us deep into the vocal practices of Irish music in both Irish and English, and brings us to the present and future of what is now called Irish traditional music in a climate of modernization and globalization. The current chapter examines the Irish language song traditions, particularly *sean-nós*, the solo, unaccompanied song style, together with other Irish language (and macaronic or bilingual) song types.

The Irish vocal tradition called *sean-nós* ("old style," pronounced "shan-nōs" with a long "o" and a hard "s") forms an essential core of the tradition, yet several factors seem to make it an unlikely core. Consider the fact that most *sean-nós* singing is done in Irish, yet most Irish people have at best a passing familiarity with the basics of the language. Consider also that more than a few session instrumentalists dislike the sound of the singing, which is often characterized as nasal or stark. In Ireland and its many diasporic locations, with their many public Irish instrumental music sessions and folk-song clubs, listeners' eyes tend to glaze over before the singer has completed even the first verse (of perhaps 12 or 16, but maybe only 3) of a *sean-nós* song. More than one person singing in Irish has heard the exhortation to "sing an *Irish* song" by audience members (including in Ireland); the audience preference for English-language songs is quite clear in that context!

Yet *sean-nós* is frequently lauded as a central locus of traditional identity, as the main expressive element of the Irish-speaking districts (the Gaeltacht), and as one of Ireland's great contributions to European classical music. It is profoundly connected to poetic expression, which is one of the main reasons why instrumentalists are supposed to know the lyrics of the songs that they perform as instrumental airs. The term itself is also applied to an increasingly popular solo dance form, particularly in the Connemara region (see Chapter 9). We will begin this chapter with some basics of the Irish language, and continue by sorting out why *sean-nós* should present such a paradox of importance coupled with apparent unpopularity.

An Introduction to the Language

The English language is rich with words derived from Irish; though few people pay attention to etymology—the study of word origins—the connections are clear. Have you ever used the word "galore" in a sentence? Notice that native English speakers always say (for example), "There was chocolate galore." No one says "galore chocolate." If you substituted delicious for galore, though, you would place delicious *in front* of the chocolate (delicious chocolate), not after it (chocolate delicious). Why do we do that? The Irish word *go leor*, which means enough but implies abundancy, comes *after* the noun in an Irish sentence, as do nearly all adjectives: *Bhí sé seacláid go leor*; there was chocolate galore. In this case, we adopted not only the word—galore—but its position in the sentence directly from the Irish language. English is full of such adoptions, and not just from Irish. In Chapter 1 you read about the roots of the language as part of the Gaelic branch of the Celtic language family. Together with Scots-Gaelic and Manx, Irish-Gaelic (referred to here mainly as "Irish") is not just a rich source for English-language expressions, but lies at the heart of what makes *sean-nós* singing uniquely Irish.

At the beginning of Chapter 3 you might have noticed a proverb in Irish: *ní tír gan teanga* or "[There is] no country without [its own] language." Another popular expression is *tír gan teanga, tír gan anam* ("land without language, land without soul"). The language movement in Ireland waxes and wanes, depending on the latest political winds, funding from the European Union, and with which side various charismatic personalities have cast their lot. What is clear, however, is that the language is currently in a stronger position than it has been in years, and that the whole idea of revival (resuscitating something that has already died) is being replaced by the idea of strengthening a living tradition instead. Even as members of the Gaeltacht (Irish-speaking minority) have become almost entirely bilingual, some members of the Galltacht (English-speaking majority) in Ireland are discovering new and interesting ways to engage the language. The "new and interesting" part has much to do with the fact that pedagogical methods have improved dramatically, bilingualism has started to become an asset rather than a liability, and the Internet has revolutionized many aspects of communication. This introduction to the language is intended to reveal what it is about *sean-nós* singing that separates it from "traditional Irish singing" in English.

The customary word order of Irish is verb–subject–object; in English it is subject–verb–object. The Irish sentence *tá* (verb "there is") *sé* (subject "he") *liom* (object "with me") shows up in English as "he is with me" (subject, verb, object). By emphasizing action words—verbs—rather than subjects—people, for example—Irish sentence construction has more to do with *being* than, say, with *having* (Collins 1990: 22–6). In fact, the verb "to have" does not exist in Irish, though there are ways of indicating some aspects of its meaning. Are you accustomed to answering questions with a plain "yes" or "no"? The Irish usually answer with the positive or negative form of the verb, because "yes" and "no" are not used in Irish. The closest the Irish come to yes and no is "*is ea*" (it is it) and "*ní hea*" (it is not it); yet both are still forms of the verb "to be." Furthermore, whereas in English we might say, "I am sick (or angry, or joyful)," in Irish we would say that "sickness (or anger, or joy) is *on* me." How different this concept is from English! Imagine speaking a language in which a particular condition is "on" you, but does not define who you are. These are just a few of the important conceptual differences between Irish and English, but there are many more.

In general, Irish words emphasize the first syllable. Thus the rhythm of sentences and songs in Irish is trochaic—a term from poetry—meaning strong/weak, strong/weak. English words in the trochaic rhythm include "*mou*ntain," "*ta*ble," and "*co*ffee." The opposite rhythm of trochaic—iambic—is represented by the rhythm of weak/strong, weak/strong, as in "e*clipse*," "to*day*," and "be*gin*." Few Irish words use iambic rhythm, but many English words do. An English sentence—with its borrowings from so many different languages—can be an awkward jumble of stresses and rhythms. Irish is far more predictable in its rhythmic organization. In English, those syllables representing the weaker portion of the word are often collapsed into mere shadows of sounds. In Irish, it is those very unstressed syllables that host the majority of vocal ornaments in Irish language singing, *sean-nós* or not. Read those last two sentences again.

The use of Irish declined dramatically during Ireland's colonial period, due to a combination of factors including the scattered prohibition of its use, the fact that it placed people at an economic disadvantage, and a colonial-driven sense that it was backward—representing the "bad old days" of the Famine, poverty, and the past. Poor teaching methods and ineffective official language policies after Ireland gained its independence did not help its continuation, and multiple generations of English-speaking Irish schoolchildren were raised to simply detest the language and all that it was connected to during their twelve years of compulsory Irish-language studies in school. It was only after the emergence of the now-famous "Celtic Tiger"—Ireland's economic boom of the 1990s—that speaking the language became associated with a newly hip bilingualism, separate from entrenchment in the past. The emergence of a new kind of private school (*gaelscoileanna*) in which instruction is offered exclusively in Irish (primarily for the children of English-speaking parents) has gradually begun to increase—by the thousands—the number of children speaking Irish, developing their own slang, and engaging the language in a twenty-first-century context. Some children of immigrants attend these *gaelscoileanna* too, resulting in first-generation children of Chinese, Nigerian, Brazilian, and Iraqi parents becoming fluent in Irish.

The Gaeltacht or Irish-speaking regions, of which there are fewer than a dozen (primarily clustered along the west coast), were set aside in the 1930s by the first Irish head of state, Éamon de Valera, as havens of traditional culture. In these regions, Irish was expected to be the language of the home, of school, and of business. The expectations that de Valera placed on a kind of entrenched traditionalism as the savior of Irish culture were disastrous in their implication for Ireland's economic future during the next forty years, led to a near continuous stream of emigrants leaving the young nation, and were among the factors that led to a sneering disregard for the language among people born outside the Gaeltacht.

In some places the language has continued to thrive, while in other places English has replaced Irish entirely as the public language spoken in the region. In particular, the influx of tourists anxious for an authentic Irish experience, coupled with the large number of newly wealthy Irish (speaking exclusively English) who have built holiday homes in the Gaeltacht, have contributed to the bifurcation of society in some Gaeltachts into a public, English-speaking scene and a private, Irish-speaking family life. The new Irish-language schools are all outside the Gaeltacht, and there is current controversy over whether the financial support should go to the English speakers or the few native Irish speakers. It is in this context of language decline, renewal, and transformation that Irish-language singing appears today.

Sean-nós Singing

Even though the words *sean-nós* denote an older style, calling a song *sean-nós* might have come as a surprise to the people singing new songs in the sixteenth and seventeenth centuries. In fact, the term *sean-nós* is a twentieth-century invention to describe the "old way" of doing things. The collapse of the old Gaelic Order and the dissolution of the patronage system for bards combined with the prohibitions by Henry VIII and Elizabeth I against certain harpers and musicians resulted in the loss of many of the old poetic meters (specific patterns of vowels and rhythms), together with the actual poetry that the bards had performed. During this time of cultural implosion, the most prominent and highly trained bards gave way to contemporary composers of *sráid-éigse*—street poetry. These new verse-makers were often itinerant singers, writing in much more simple poetic meters than what had been composed before. After a time, the street poetry evolved into *sean-nós*—the now-venerable "old style" as it is known today. "It was only after the complete break-up of the Gaelic polity, after the wars of Cromwell and of William, that the verse-maker merges in the musician, and the harper and the bard become fused in one" (Hyde 1910: 497).

Combined with this emergence of a more contemporary kind of poetic song was the strong connection to European love songs that developed in the seventeenth and eighteenth centuries. The *amour courtois* or courtly love song tradition came to Ireland with the Normans between the thirteenth and fifteenth centuries, and evolved into the significant love song tradition that characterizes much of *sean-nós* singing today. Love songs, generally, are less about narrating a particular sequence of events than about expressing profound emotions and connecting with the community as each listener recalls his or her own experiences of grief, loss, love, and relationship joys and woes.

All of the attention is placed on the song through the singer, who can pour his or her utmost expressiveness into the song. Yet that expressiveness rarely includes a dramatic increase in dynamics, for example, or the use of broad hand gestures or overt body movements beyond the occasional clasping of the hand of one's neighbor. Instead, expressiveness in *sean-nós* performance is subtle; melodic variations arise between verses, ornaments appear here and there, and the overall feel of the meaning of the song is conveyed through the melodic recitation of the song's poetry. The poetry, of course, offers the literary context for the emotional content celebrated through the song.

In Ireland, the important relationship between story and song cannot be overstated. Many songs, in fact, tell a story by expressing the emotional depth of an existing story known to the audience. The expression *abair amhrán, inis scéal* ("say a song, tell a story") links the two ideas and gives a sense of performance practice as well. No less an authority than Breandán Breathnach (one of the most respected of the traditional music scholars of Ireland) regards the expression as a mistranslation of the Irish, and insists that *abair*—say—ought to be "sing" (Breathnach 1971: 102). However, perhaps we might look at it as both. To "say" a song, one takes the emphasis off oneself. Singers generally refrain from engaging the audience in eye contact; they usually withdraw behind the curtain of anonymity provided by the song. At an Irish-language song performance, the audience may disengage from the personality of the singer to allow the meaning of the song to speak more directly and emphatically to them. In past times, a male singer might even pull his cap down to partially obscure his face, or even turn away slightly from other participants. This disengagement is not the rule, however; unspoken rules tend to be much more rigid than living performance practice will tolerate. While an American audience might feel slighted by the apparent lack of relationship, the traditional Irish audience might actually feel *more* engaged. Only the song and its meaning hold the moment together, almost like suspending time and place, yet the song connects singer and audience more powerfully than broad gestures, personal charisma, or other visible physical elements (Figure 7.1). At that moment, the singer *does* in fact "sing" (as well as "say") the song.

Telling a story, on the other hand, can rely quite readily on the storyteller's engagement with the audience. The storyteller, male or female, leans forward, draws the

Figure 7.1 The late *sean-nós* singer Dara Bán Mac Donnchadh, right, with poet and singer Mícheál Ó Cuaig next to him

listeners in, gestures, sometimes changes voices to reflect the story's speakers, and asks rhetorical questions like "and then didn't the poor man get down on his two knees and beg forgiveness?" The audience, for its part, can laugh out loud, groan, gasp, and otherwise respond eagerly to the storyteller and the story both. *Sean-nós* singers also sometimes tell a story prior to starting the actual song. The *údar an amhrán* or "story of the song" brings the audience into the scene, because some *sean-nós* songs begin after the action (or narrative) concerning the song has already been taking place. Yet in *sean-nós* singing, the story within the song is often a metaphor for a larger issue—religious expression, or veiled rebellion, or lost love. That larger issue can then be appreciated at multiple levels of meaning, from its most literal sense to the expression of larger societal concerns about, for example, hope and loss. Lyrics are articulated quite clearly in this style; it is a mark of the heightened respect held by the community for the poetry and the story of the song that emphasizes this clarity.

The point at which saying a song and telling a story come together can rest between the verses of songs and at the ends of songs. When the singer executes a particularly lovely turn of phrase, or comes to a meaningful section of the song, the audience might chime in with "Good man!" or "Dia leat!" ("God with you!") or any number of encouraging shouts in Irish or English. Audience members react clearly and visibly to fine, effective singing, but less effusively than they might to storytelling. Though less common in the twenty-first century, one can sometimes see an older person (usually male) grasp the hand of the singer and gently guide it in a circle, pausing at the ends of phrases with a strong, almost vibrating grip. The experience feels like an electric current and is powerfully supportive.

In a traditional setting in the Gaeltacht—but also in urban singers' clubs such as Dublin's An Góilín, that try to replicate a more rural experience—the host or the most recent singer calls out the next singer. The *fear a' tí* or *bean a' tí* ("man of the house," "woman of the house") makes the choice when no one offers to sing next. Joe Heaney, the great twentieth-century *sean-nós* singer, also described the practice of going counterclockwise around the room as "turning back the clock," and said that choosing the next singer is "the Golden Call." It is an honor to be asked to contribute to an evening's entertainment, even if one doesn't have more than a few songs; it is also polite to defer (at first) an invitation to sing. A story, a joke, or a memory will do; as there is no stage, the performance is informal. The important contribution each person makes, in whatever form, allows for the development of a climate of friendship and reciprocation. Such a climate is essential in a rural setting, where neighbors have long depended on each other to bring in the hay or to cut turf for their fireplaces.

Characteristic features of sean-nós songs

Contemporary hallmarks of *sean-nós* singing include performance in Irish, but that is not the only criterion. Plenty of songs are sung in Irish that do not necessarily belong to the genre of *sean-nós*. However, *sean-nós* songs are performed in a relatively free meter, so that one can breathe, complete a musical phrase in the time necessary rather than being beholden to an accompanist, and use vocal ornaments (rolls, turns, and melismas) according to stylistic appropriateness, individual choice, or not at all. The great freedom accorded *sean-nós* singers has much to do with the fact that *sean-nós* is usually sung unaccompanied. Without a guitar or other instruments providing a tempo and divisible measures, the temptation to tap one's foot is minimized. Watch a singer closely, however, and you just might see him or her tapping a foot according only to the poetic rhythm of the song. If that song were the Connemara favorite "Anach Cuain," featured in this chapter, the poetic rhythm would focus on the stressed syllables, as in the first phrase *má aimse sláinte is fada bheas tráchta*, "if my health is spared I'll be long relating."

The *sean-nós* singer with a store of hundreds of songs is rare. Instead, most singers develop a smaller repertoire in the dozens, and those songs are chosen—with care—for particular occasions. In a small village where all the singers know each other, it is considered polite for singers to avoid performing the favorite songs of their friends and neighbors, to give them the opportunity instead. As a result, most singers are known for their particular renditions of individual songs, even if the entire community knows the songs too from having heard them so many times. In addition, it is normal for a singer to consider in advance what song he or she might perform at a gathering, and to run through it in his or her mind (occasionally with printed lyrics, if it is a "mighty" song with many long verses) first. No one wants to be caught unprepared! Should the worst come to pass, and the singer forgets the lyrics, neighbors and/or family members will readily supply the start of a phrase to encourage the singer to continue. Such an event is momentarily embarrassing, but holds no lasting consequences, because it is all about the experience of singing as a member of a community with shared experiences.

Most *sean-nós* song sections occur in stanzas of four or eight lines each; the four-line stanza is a classic form common in Western Europe as well as North America, and the eight-line verse is important in some parts of Ireland (particularly the south). Furthermore, each Irish language song has a particular poetic rhythm that determines the relationship between the notes of the melody and the melodic ornaments that occur in many of the songs. Ireland's regionalism has led to the development of varying and competing ideas regarding song treatment; in some areas the *sean-nós* songs may follow a very subtle underlying beat, as in Donegal in the north. In other areas the song almost seems to come to a halt because particular passages include so many ornamented syllables, as in Connemara in the west.

Many of the Gaeltacht areas have some type of *sean-nós* singing (and all of them feature singing in Irish), but what constitutes *sean-nós* is inherently regional. Beyond regionalism, of course, is individual performance practice, in which a singer represents not so much a regional style but his or her own interpretation of, and intimate relationship to, a song.

Connemara sean-nós *songs*

In order to musically illustrate a melody and its potential for ornamentation in *sean-nós* singing, the following examples come from Connemara, famous for its melismatic ornamentation (as well as for its great singing tradition in general). By way of a reminder, a melisma is a short melodic phrase sung with a single syllable. In Chapter 3 you first encountered an Irish-language lament, "Caoineadh na dTrí Muire" or "The Lament of the Three Marys." That song focused attention on the lyrics through its relatively simple melody, its repetitive lament of *óchón*, and its use of variation from verse to verse. Listeners (and singers) consider their own losses in connection with the grieving of the women surrounding Jesus at his death. A more modern (nineteenth-century) lament, "Anach Cuain," focuses attention again on loss. Composed by Anthony O'Raftery in the 1800s, this lament chronicles the true story of a wedding-day tragedy that befell a number of couples who drowned while crossing a small bay near Galway. In this first verse the stage is set so that we can *see* just as easily as we can *hear* the establishment of the plot: the fine day, the heavily loaded boat, and the weeping of the families. The song is longer than the three sample verses included here, but what happened is clear.

Má fhaighimse sláinte is fada bheas tráchtadh ar an méid a báthadh ó Anach
    Cuain
's mo thruaigh amáireach gach athair is máthair, bean is páiste atá ag sileadh
    súl;
A Rí na nGrásta, a cheap neamh is párthas, a Dhia cer chas dúinn beirt nó
    triúir
Ach lá chomh breá leis gan gaoth ná báisteach, lán an bháid a scuabadh ar súil.

Nár mhór an t-ionach os comhair na ndaoine, iad a fheiceáil sínte ar chúl a gcinn
Screadach is caoineadh a scanródh daoine, bhí gruaig dá cíoradh is an chreach
    dá roinnt;
Bhí buachaillí óga ann ag tigheacht don fhómhar, dhá síneadh ar chróchair 's
    dhá dtabhairt go cill
Ba é gléas a bpósta a bhí dhá dtórramh, ach a Rí na Glóire, nár mhór an feall.

Baile Cláir a bhí in aice láime, níor lig an t-ádh dhóibh a dhul aníos
Bhí an bás chomh láidir níor thug sé cairde, d'aon mhac máthair dár rugadh
    riamh;
Bhris an bád is báthadh na daoine scaip na caoirigh anonn sa snámh
A Dhia, nach ansin a bhí an feall mór déanta ar aon fhear déag agus ochtar
    mná.

If my health is spared I'll be long relating of those that sailed out of Anach
    Cuain
My pity tomorrow for the fathers and mothers, women and children who are
    weeping;
King of Graces who created heaven and paradise, two or three would have
    been bad enough
But such a fine day, without wind or rain, a full boat to be swept away.

Wasn't it a wonder for the people to see them stretched out there
Screeching and wailing that would terrify people, tearing of hair and grief
    being shared;
Young boys there for the coming harvest were laid out on biers and taken to
    the graveyard
Their wedding clothes were those they were waked in, oh King of Glory, what
    a great pity.

Claregalway was near at hand but fate wouldn't let them come up
Death was so strong that it gave no credit to any mother's son who was ever
    born;

The boat broke apart and the people were drowned, the sheep scattered in the
  water
Oh God, wasn't that the great tragedy for eleven men and eight women.

Note that *sean-nós* songs do not have to dwell on the gory details to get the point across.
Later verses of this song speak instead of a lace cap with white ribbons worn by one of
the young ladies, and of a strong man having his strength broken by women holding
onto him when he tried to swim for shore.

    Melismatic style—the application of multiple notes to a single syllable—differs from
syllabic style, in which each syllable is performed with a single note. The song "Úna Bhán"
("Fair Úna") is one of the most famous of the classic eighteenth-century love songs of the
sean-nós style. The singer berates his deceased beloved for having abandoned him, but he
nonetheless sings her praises with great eloquence ("you were a harp playing music before
me on the road," "your mouth is as sugar, as the new milk and the wine on the table").
Some versions of this song have as many as 45 verses! The *údar* or "story of the song," as
related by the *sean-nós* singer Joe Heaney (Figure 7.2), is as follows:

> Well, Úna Bhán, her real name is Úna Mac Diarmada, or Úna MacDermott.
> She was a well-to-do, rich man's daughter, and she fell in love with a man called
> Thomas Costello. And he was otherwise known as "Strong Thomas Costello."
> And she lived in Mayo, and he lived about eight miles away from her. Well, this

TRACK 17

Figure 7.2 The late *sean-nós* singer Joe Heaney. Photo courtesy of the University of Washington
Ethnomusicology Archives

time she fell sick, for the love of Thomas Costello, and her father would have nothing to do with him. But she was so ill that they sent for him to come to her bedside. And while he was there, she got better, and better. And as she got better her father saw no more reason to keep him in the house, so he sent him away, still refusing to let him marry her. And he swore if he crossed a certain river called the Donoghue River, that he would never come back to the house no matter how ill or anything she got after he left. Well, he left the house, and he went into the river. And he put the horse he was riding back and forth in the river for a couple of hours, and still there was no call from the house for him to come back. So eventually he crossed over to the other bank. And the minute he was on the other bank, the father ran after him calling him back. But he had given his oath that he wouldn't come after he crossed the river, so he went on his way home. And two days after, she died, and he came to the graveyard where she was buried, and he sang the lament over her grave, every night for a week. Eventually they found him dead on top of the grave.

The song follows a basic four-line stanzaic format, with the melody conforming to an ABBA pattern in which the melody of lines 1 and 4 are roughly the same, and lines 2 and 3 are roughly the same. The melody, as sung by Joe Heaney (Figure 7.2), is rich in ornamentation (Figure 7.3). To hear this song in performance, listen to the online soundtrack for one version of the song as performed by Joe Heaney. Because Heaney was from the Connemara region, where many singers tend to use long melismatic ornamentation, the degree of ornamentation in this song should be considered typical of the region. Even if you do not read music, you should notice that this transcription includes many dense clusters of notes; they represent the way that Heaney and many others decorate their songs with extra notes that—while conforming to the melody, more of less—carry their own decorative weight, musically speaking.

Is a Úna Bhán nach gránna an luí sin ort
I do leaba chaol chláir imeasc na ndáinte corp

Figure 7.3 "Úna Bhán" ("Fair Úna"—pronounced "oo-na wawn")

Mar dtige tú le fóir orm a ghrá a bhí ariamh gan locht
Ní thiocfaidh mé chun t-áras go brách ach an oíche anocht.

Is a Úna Bhán ba rós i ngairdín thú
Ba cláirseach a'cheoil romham sa mbóthar thú
Ba chéiliúr is ba cheolmhar ag dul an bhealaigh seo romham thú
Seo mo chreach mhaidhne bhrónach nár pósadh le do ghrá geal thú.

Tá an sneachta seo ar a' lár is é dearg le fuil
Ach samhail mo ghrá ní fhaca mé in áit ar bith
Féachaíse a mhná cé b'fhearr ná an t-óchón sin
Aon ghlaoch amháin a' ghabháil Áth na Donóige.

Dá mbeadh píopa fada cailce agam is tobac a bheith ann
Tharrangóinn amach é is chaithfinn de mo sháith
Is maith a d'insioinnse dhíbhse cé gcónaíonn Úna Bhán
I gCill Bhríde is gCrích Mha Chill 'mo chreach is mo chrá.

'S mo scrúdadh thú Úna Mhic Diarmada óig
An chéad scoth do na mná buartha agus Brianach óg
Do bhéal mar a bhfuil siúcra mar an leamhnacht 's an fíon ar bord
Do chois lúfar a shiúlfadh go fíor i mbróig.

Fair Úna, ugly do you lie there
In your bed of planks among a host of corpses
If you don't come and succour me, oh love that was ever without fault
I'll not come to your place again, save tonight

Oh Fair Úna, you were a rose in the garden
You were a harp playing music before me in the road
Melodious and musical you were going on the road before me
It is my utter ruin that you were not married to me.

The snow is on the ground and it is red with blood
But the likeness of my love I never saw anyplace at all
Is it a better choice to hear the women keening
Or to let out just one call toward the Ford of Donoghue?

If I had a long clay pipe at me and tobacco being in it
I'd draw it out and smoke my fill
It's good to hear from you where Fair Úna lived
In Cill Bhríde and Crich Mha Chill is my ruin and my sorrow.

You try me severely, Young Úna Mac Dermott
All the best to the sorrowful women and young Brianach
Your mouth is as sugar, as the new milk and the wine on the table
Your agile feet walking well in shoes.

The love song "Eileanóir a Rún" is rooted in a story by and about Cearbhaill Ó Dálaigh, an eighteenth-century poet. In the story, Cearbhaill is sent to watch an enchanted cow about to give birth. Because of a twist of fate, he himself receives the first drop of milk intended for the calf (compare with Fionn MacCumhaill and the salmon of knowledge), and he receives the gift of fine speech. With his newfound gift, he woos Eileanóir, and they elope, the telling of which makes a long story. Although the song has a refrain, it is not intended for others to sing. Notice the way in which the second verse of this song highlights a series of liminal ("in-between") elements. The appearance of a kiss, dawn, the cuckoo, and revival from death, are all important aspects of an earlier mythology that celebrated liminal places (crossroads, the shore, wetlands), creatures (shapeshifters, seals), and acts or events (kissing, sexuality, death, birth, etc.).

> Mo ghrá thú, den chéad fhéachaint, Eileanóir a Rúin
> Is ort a bhím ag smaoineadh, tráth a mbím i mo shuan
> A ghrá den tsaol, is a chéad searc, is tú is deise ná ban Éireann.

> Chorus:
> A bhruinnilín deas óg, is tú is deise milse póig
> Chuns a mhairfead beo beidh gean agam ort
> Mar is deas mar a sheolfainn gamhna leat, Eileanóir a Rúin.

> Bhí bua aici go dtóigfeadh sí an corp fuar ón mbás
> Ba milse blas a póigín ná an chuachín roimh an lá
> Bhí bua eile aici nach ndéarfad, 'sí grá mo chroí, mo chéad searc.

> From the moment I saw you I loved you, Eileanóir my love
> It is of you I think when I'm resting
> O love of life and my first love, you are fairer than all the women of Ireland.

> Chorus:
> O young fair maiden you have the nicest and sweetest kiss
> As long as I live my affection will be for you
> For I'd gladly drive the calves with you, Eileanóir my love.

> She had a gift that she could revive the cold corpse from death
> The taste of her little kiss was sweeter than the cuckoo at dawn
> She had another gift I'll not mention, she is the love of my heart, my first love.

Donegal sean-nós songs

TRACK 4

Ireland has many powerful love songs in Irish. The image of unattainable (or unrequited) love has a long history in Europe, and is readily found in Ireland as well (often with a bitter tinge to it). "Ag an Phobal Dé Domhnaigh" ("At the Congregation on Sunday") from Donegal is transcribed from the singing of Donegal sean-nós singer Lillis Ó Laoire, and reflects the particular approach to sean-nós singing that is more common in the north of Ireland: a gentle, slow, triple-meter pulse underlying the melody, and the addition of subtle—as opposed to explicit and lengthy—ornamentation (Figure 7.4). The contrast

Figure 7.4 "Ag an Phobal Dé Domhnaigh" ("At the Congregation on Sunday"—pronounced "egg unn fubbel jey dow-nee")

in style between the Connemara style of "Úna Bhán" and the Donegal style of "Ag an Phobal Dé Domhnaigh" is strong, yet the two styles of *sean-nós* are equally profound in both lyric and musical content. Note the difference between the melodic patterns of "Úna Bhán" and those of "Ag an Phobal Dé Domhnaigh." In the former, the melody is decorated with melismas (multiple notes on one syllable). In the latter, the poetic rhythm gives the song considerable interest, while the melodic decoration is minimal. Listen to the version of "Ag an Phobal Dé Domhnaigh" performed by Lillis Ó Laoire on the online soundtrack for this textbook, and note the difference in style: Lillis sings with a much more open sound than Joe Heaney. That open sound is much more characteristic of Donegal singers, whereas Connemara singers often sound slightly more nasal. Remember, though, that individual style generally subverts regional style.

Ag an phobal Dé Domhnaigh thug mé mórchion don chailín
Sí ba deise is ba bhreácha dar tógadh riamh i mbaile
Bhí a béilín mar bheadh an rós ann is bhí a caoinchom mar bheadh an
  sneachta
'S a Rí nach bhfuil mo lóistín san áit a gcoirionn sí a leabaidh.

Tá an rógaire 'o mo mhealladh is tá'n peacadh a dhéanamh
Tharraing sé mo chroí istigh agus bhí sé arís a shéanadh
Ach má tá do bhean sa bhaile agat nó do leanbán le bréagadh
Pill arís uirthi a shladaí 's cha bhíonn roinnt agam féin leat.

Dá mbíodh a fhios ag mo dheartháir mo leatrom ba trua leis
Dá mbíodh a fhios go dearfa bheadh air imní agus buaireamh
Fá mo chéad searc bheith mo thréigean is an créatúr bocht a lua liom
'S tú m'ansacht ar fhearaibh Éireann a's in do dhiaidh atá
  mé buartha.

Dá mbíodh péire glan sciathán as mo chliatháin féin anuas liom
Dá mbíodh fhios go dearfa go rachainn ón buachaill
D'éireochainn féin in airde mar bheadh an éanlaith fá na cuanta
Nó go n-insínn mo ghearán do mo leannán ar an uaigneas.

Bliain agus daichead dá mairfeá thusa a bhuachaill
Do ghrása cha dtabharfainn do éinneach ar an domhan
Ach nuair nach bhfuil na buaibh agam ná na buaraigh lena gceangal
Seo mo chúig bheannacht déag duit is beimid araon ag goil 'na bhaile.

At the congregation on Sunday I gave great affection to the girl
She was the prettiest and the finest that was ever reared in any townland
Her little mouth was like roses and her gentle waist like snow
And God I wish my lodging was where she dresses her bed.

The rogue is seducing me and the sin is being committed
He drew my heart inside and denied it thereafter
But if you have your wife at home and your little child to coax
Return again to them, you wrecker, and I'll have nothing to do with you.

If my brother knew my oppression he would pity me
Indeed if he knew he would be worried and upset
Because my first love was deserting me and the poor creature being engaged
    to me
You are my beloved of the men of Ireland and after you I am sorrowful.

If I had a smooth pair of wings down by my sides
Indeed if I had I would go from the boy
I would rise up like the birds by the sea bays
To tell my story in solitude to my lover.

A year and forty if you lived my boy
Your love I'd never give to anyone in the world
But since we haven't cattle or the spancels to tie them with
My blessings upon you and let us each of us go home.

In the first verse of "Ag an Phobal Dé Domhnaigh," the man speaks longingly of his lover, but the remaining verses belong to the woman, who reveals to us that he is married with a child. In spite of his married state and the fact that she is clearly angry with him, she bitterly acknowledges that her heart is broken without him ("he drew my heart inside and denied it thereafter"). She blesses him in the final verse as they part forever.

The song "Tá Mé 'mo Shuí" ("I am Awake") is a well-known Donegal-area song in the *sean-nós* style. It features a man sitting up all night in the presence of his sleeping family members, longing for the beloved. This song appears in other versions in other regions of Ireland, including in Connemara where it is known as "Amhrán Rinn Mhaoile," and further south where it is called "Táimse i mo Shuí." Here, however, it follows the (mainly) stepwise motion of a Donegal song and focuses attention on the beauty of the beloved, along with the sadness of being separated. Although this song does not appear on the online soundtrack, it is easily located on the Internet.

Figure 7.5 Singer Lillis Ó Laoire. Photo courtesy of Garrett Hurley

Tá mé 'mo shuí ó d'éirigh'n ghealach aréir
Ag cur teine síos gan scíth is á fadó go géar
Tá bunadh a tí 'na luí is tá mise liom féin
Tá na coiligh ag glaoch 'san saol 'na gcodladh ach mé.

'Sheacht mh'anam déag do bhéal do mhalaí is do ghrua
Do shúil ghorm ghlé-gheal fár thréig mé aiteas is suairc
Le cumha do dhiaidh ní léir dom an bealach a shiúil
Is a charaid mo chléibh tá na sléibhte gabhail idir mé 's tú.

Deireann lucht léinn gur claoite an galar an grá
Char admhaigh mé é no go raibh sé 'ndiaidh mo chroí istigh a chrá
Ó aicid ró-ghéar, faraor nár sheachain mé í
Chuir sí arraing is céad go géar trí cheart-lár mo chroí.

Casadh bean-tsí dom thíos ag Lios Bhéal an Átha
Is d'fhiafraigh mé díthe an scaoilfeadh glas ar bith grá
Is é dúirt sí os íseal i mbriathra soineannta sáimh
"Nuair a théann sé fán chroí cha scaoiltear as é go bráth."

I am up since the moon arose last night
Putting down a fire again and again and keeping it lit

The family is in bed and here am I by myself
The cocks are crowing and the country is asleep but me.

I love your mouth, your eyebrows and your cheeks
Your bright blue eyes for whose sake I gave up contentment
In longing for you I cannot see to walk the road
Friend of my bosom, the mountains lie between me and you.

Learned men say that love is a fatal sickness
I never admitted it until now that my heart is broken
It's a very painful illness, alas, I have not avoided it
And it sends a hundred arrows through the core of my heart.

I met a fairy woman in the hollow of Béal an Átha
I asked her would any key unlock the love in my heart
And she said in soft, simple language
"When love enters the heart it will never be driven from it."

"Críocha an Oileáin Úir," an emigration song, praises the beloved far away in America. The song translates as "The Ends of the New World," from its first line, and is quite poignant. A young man laments his sweetheart's decision to travel to the New World and imagines how happy they would be if she were to return. The high rate of emigration for young women from Irish-speaking districts did not, perhaps surprisingly, result in a large number of love laments about the departed female. Instead, songs in which the young woman laments her young *man's* departure seem to be far more common. The song was composed by Seán Bán Mac Grianna of the well-known Mac Gríanna family of poets and singers in Rann na Feirste, Donegal.

I bhfad ó bhaile a thriall mo stór go críocha 'n Oileáin Úir
Is d'fhág sí mise anseo faoi bhrón, 's gan triomú ar mo shúil
Luaigheadh mé léithe i dtús mo lae 's nach trua leat féin mo scéal
Ó 'grá mo chroí mo chailín deas, 's í thógfadh domhsa cian.

Is mór mo chumhaidh 'do dhiaidh a rún, ó d'éalaigh tú thar toinn
Tá 'n saol faoi ghruaim tá 'n aimsir fuar, tá mé cráite buartha tinn
Beo ní bhead le cumhaidh 'do dhiaidh, 's a stór táim cloíte i bpéin
Ó 'grá mo chroí mo chailín deas, 's í thógfadh domhsa cian.

A rún mo chléibh 'nois pill arís, go bpóstar mé 'gus tú
Beidh só 'gus aoibhneas inár saol, 's beidh buaireamh 'n tsaoil ar shiúl
Beidh saol a' phósta séanmhar sóúilu, suáilceach sona súairc
'S ní bhead aríst faoi bhrón mar bhí, 's ní baol domh choíche gruaim.

Far from home, a journey my love, to the ends of the New World
And she left me here in sorrow without drying my eyes

I was promised with her from the beginning, isn't it a sad story of my own
Oh love of my heart, my pretty girl, she would lift my spirits.

It's great my homesickness after you, treasure, since you crossed over the
waves
Life is under sadness and the weather is cold, I am broken up with sickness
I won't live after you, and treasure, I am devastated
Oh love of my heart, my pretty girl, she would lift my spirits.

Oh dear, my treasure, return again, that we might be married
It will be great in our life, we won't have a care in the world
Our married life will be joyous, luxurious, lucky, happy, content
It would never be sad like I was, surely I'd never be sad again.

Munster sean-nós *songs*

The third major *sean-nós* region of Ireland is in the southwest, in the region of Counties
Cork and Kerry. Munster songs are often called *amhráin mhóra*—big songs—because
so many songs use an eight-line form and include a section that soars in range. Compare
the two songs below ("Cois Abhánn na Séad" and "Cath Chéim an Fhia") with those of
Connemara and Donegal, and the sheer length of the verses is the first thing that one
notices. The richness of imagery that characterizes many *sean-nós* songs is also present,
much more so in Irish than in the songs' English translation.

The song "Cath Chéim an Fhia" ("The Battle of Deer's Leap") refers to a battle that
took place in 1822 between the "Whiteboys" (a secret society of tenant farmers—in
Irish "Na Buachaillí Bána") and a coalition of landlords. Composed by Máire Buí Ní
Laoghaire (1774–1849)—one of the southwest's finest women poets in the nineteenth
century, who could neither read nor write—the song describes eloquently the reactions of the local people to the battle. The online soundtrack includes "Cath Chéim
an Fhia" recorded as an instrumental air by James Keane, and the lyrics are provided here with many thanks to Eilís Ní Shúilleabháin for both the lyrics and their
translation.

Cois abhann Ghleanna an Chéama in Uíbh Laoghaire 'sea bhímse
Mar a dtéann an fia san oíche, chun síor-chodladh sóghail
A' machnamh séal liom féinig 's a déanamh mo smaointe
Ag éisteacht i gcoillte le binn-ghuth na n-eon
Nuair a chuala an chath a' teacht aniar, is glór na neach a' teacht le sians'
Le fuaim a n-airm do chrith an Sliabh 's níor bhéinn liom a nglór
Thángadar go námhadmhar mar a thiocfadh gárda de chonaibh nímhe
Agus cumha mo chroí, na sár-fhir, d'fhagadar gan treoir.

Níor fhan fear, bean ná páiste im mbun áitribh ná tí ann
Na gártha goil do bhí 'ca is na mílte ologon
Ag féachaint ar an ngárda bhí go láidir 'na dtimpeall
Ag lámhach is ag líonadh 's ag scaoileadh 'na dtreo

An liú gur leath i bhfad i gcian, 'sé dúirt gach flaith gur mhaith leis triall
Gluaisíg go mear, tá 'n cath dá riar is téimís 'na chomhair
Thángadar na sár-fhir, guim áthas ar chlanna Gael
Is chomaineadar na páinthig le fánaig ar seol.

Níorbh fhada dhúinn go dtáinig lámh-láidir 'nár dtimpeall
Agus scaipeadar ár ndaoine ar gach maoilinn faoin gceo
Bhí an Barrach 'na bhumbáille 'ca Barnet agus Beecher
Hedges agus Sweet, is na mílte eile leo
A Rí na bhFeart go leagaigh iad, gan chlú, gan mheas, gan rath, gan séan
Go teintibh meara imeasc na bpian, gan faoiseamh go deo
Ach céad moladh mór le h-Íosa nár dhíolamar as an gcóir
Ach bheith a' déanamh grin de 's á insint ar sógh.

By the river of the glen of the high road in Uíbh Laoghaire they were
Where the deer goes at night to seek quiet refreshing sleep
I was meditating to myself
Listening in the woods to the sweet voices of the birds.
When I heard the battle coming from the west and the sound of the horses coming
The mountain shook to the sound of their weapons and I didn't find their sounds sweet
They came with enmity like a guard of poisonous hounds coming
And sadness of my heart, the great men lay scattered.

Neither man, woman nor child stayed in their houses there
The crying shouts that were at them, and the lamenting
Looking at this army that was around them in strength
Shooting and reloading and shooting in their direction
The shout went up, spread far and wide, all the noblemen wanted to go with them
March quickly, the battle is on, let us go toward it.
The great men came, I wish joy to the Irish clan
And they drove the big-bellied people away.

It wasn't long before violence came around us
And they scattered our people on every hill under the fog
Mr. Barry the leader of them, Barnett and Beecher
Hedges and Sweet and thousands more
King of Deeds, may you knock them down without reputation, respect, luck, or happiness
To quick great fires among the pains, without relief ever
But a hundred praises to Jesus that we didn't fall for it
But we made fun of it while sitting around the fire.

TRACK 18

The song "Cois Abhann na Séad" ("By the River of Jewels") is from the Cúil Aodha (pronounced "koo-lay") district of the Múscraí (Muskerry) Gaeltacht, in the southwest

Figure 7.6 "Cois Abhann na Séad" ("By the River of Jewels"—pronounced "kush *aw* vin nuh *sheyd*")

of Ireland. The melody, like many of the area, follows a basic AABA form, with the high notes in the third line (Figure 7.6). The song is an evening *aisling* ("ash-ling") or vision song, in which a young man encounters a woman by a stream and speaks to her (compare with "Erin's Green Shore" in Chapter 3). "Cois Abhann na Séad" is not a political song. If it were, the young woman would be the embodiment of the nation, or the people, of Ireland. Instead, the man praises the woman (her beauty, her singing) and complains that without her signifying her affection, he may be forced to emigrate. What might seem like an idle threat between lovers was all too real in the eighteenth and nineteenth centuries in Ireland, when emigration provided one not only with significant possibilities for financial gain, but also with many more potential candidates for a relationship.

Noting down *sean-nós* songs in free rhythm is an inexact science. If you were to follow the online recording of Eilís Ní Shúilleabháin singing "Cois Abhann na Séad" exactly as transcribed, the two would not match. Instead, the transcription in Figure 7.6 is an approximation of the song, highlighting structural tones and offering in free meter a sense of the song's contours of AA'BA'. The song is in a major key and has as its signature the leap upward (to pitch B in this transcription) in measures 3, 11, and 27. In the third line (beginning halfway through measure 16), the rapid upward climb of the melody is the other, soaring, signature part that is one of the hallmarks of many of the "big songs" from the Irish southwest.

TRACK 15

> *Cois abhann na séad ar uair bhig a' lae, 's mé ag imeacht fé dhéin mo shláinte*
> *Mar a mbídís caora 's cnó buí ar ghéaga 's mil bheach 'na shlaod ar bhánta*

Do labhradar na h-éin, do lasadar na spéartha, bhí an fharraige 'na caor-
  luisne lán suas
Do nhúscail an ghrian a bhí le sealad mór fé chiach agus d'érigh an t-iasc 'na
  lán rith

Ansúd ar dtúis ar imeallaibh ciúise coille cumhra do tharla
An fhinne-bhean fhionn gur bhinne liom a tiúin ná an fidil, an fliúit ná 'n
  cláirseach
Ba bhreá deas a súil, a mala caol cumtha, a leaca bhí mar chumhar na trá
Ba ghile í ar a píb ná an eala ar a' linn is do lion mo chroí le grá dhí.

Nuair a dhearcas í ansúd mar a bhí—an ainnir ba chaoine 's ba bhreátha
Bhí scáil na gcaor 'na leacain réidh agus fátha bhí 'na gáire
Dob é an chom slim do lagaigh mé im chroí le taithneamh dá cló 's dá gáire
Ó bhaitheas go bonn bhí a ciabh leí go trom is a cúl buí go casta fáinneach.

By the river of jewels at the small hour of day; I progressing for the sake of my
  health
Where berries and yellow nuts were on branches and honey flowing on the
  meadows
The birds sang, the skies lit up, the sea was full with a blinding red light
The sun, which had been occluded for so long, awoke and the fish rose up in a
  full run.

There at first at the edge of the fragrant forest I encountered
The fairest of fair women whose music I found sweeter than fiddle, than flute,
  than harp
Her fine pretty eye, her slender well-formed brow, her cheeks like foam on the
  shore
Her neck was whiter than the swan on the lake and my heart filled with love
  for her.

When I saw her there as she was—the maiden most gentle and fine
The sheen of berries lit up her smooth cheeks and a smile played on her laugh
It was the slim waist that weakened my heart with pleasure at her shape and
  her laughter
From her forehead to her soles her tresses fell heavily and her luxuriant twist-
  ing ringlets.

Some *sean-nós* songs are performed all over Ireland because of their enduring popularity. "Dónal Óg" ("Young Dónal") is one such song. From a woman's perspective,
the bitterness of lost love in the song "Dónal Óg" reflects the unfulfilled promises of
the lover. This song is performed in many of Ireland's *Gaeltachtaí*, in different melodic
versions depending on where it is sung (and who is singing). Like the other songs in
this section, the four-line stanza of "Dónal Óg" divides the story into segments. What
makes this song so effectively Irish is that—even in a European love song context in

which young women commonly sing laments for their fickle lovers—in the Irish case, it is generally made clear that the loss is permanent and profound (Shields 1993: 79). The young woman's love lament is believed to be "the oldest type of love-song extant in the romance languages" (Quinn 1999: 342). Three verses are translated here.

'Gus fheall tú dhom agus rinne tú bréag liom
Go mbeitheá romham ag cró na gcaorach
Lig mé fead ort is míle béice
Ach ní bhfuair mé romham ann ach na huain a' méileach.

You promised me, and it was a lie you told me
That you would be before me at the sheep pen
I let out a whistle and called a thousand times
But I got only the bleating of the lone lamb in reply.

The narrator accuses her lover of offering her promises that would be impossible to fulfill, even if he had actually planned to stay with her:

Do gheallais domh-sa ní nár bhféidir
Go dtabharfá lámhainne de chroiceann éisc dom
Go dtabharfá bróga de chroiceann éan dom
Is culaith den tsíoda ba dhaoire in Éirinn.

You promised to me what could never be possible
That you would give me gloves of fish skin
That you would give me shoes of bird skin
And a suit of the most expensive silk in Ireland.

In the devastating final verse, she accuses him of leaving her with nothing; the main character of the song bares her soul:

Do bhainis soir dhíom, is do bhainis siar dhíom
Do bhainis romham is do bhainis im'dhiaidh dhíom
Do bhainis gealach is do bhainis grian díom
's is ró-mhór m'eagla gur bhainis Dia dhíom.

You have taken east from me, you have taken west from me
You have taken what is before and what is behind from me
You have taken moon and sun from me
And it is my great fear that you have taken God from me.

The stark lyrics of this woman's love-lament point to an aspect of Irish-language *sean-nós* songs: Irish songs in English generally do not express these particular sensibilities. As an earlier version of the French *amour courtois* sentiment that "without woman's love God is unattainable, and only through woman's love can God be fully experienced" (Ó Tuama 1960, cited in Vallely 1999: 341), "Dónal Óg" has a particularly female, Irish take. At the time that Ireland was becoming more engaged with English-language sing-ing, many of the songs had already been through the editorial eye of eighteenth- and nineteenth-century salon culture. While the English-language songs in Chapter 8 have a unique and rich narrative voice, they speak to a different side of Irish culture.

The Paradox

At the beginning of this chapter, *sean-nós* was described as something of a paradox, as the heart of the tradition, for its apparent remoteness to the lively and famous instru-mental tradition. How can it still function as the core of Irish traditional music if it is so hard to learn and perform? Consider this statement:

> It is the author's belief that no aspect of Irish music can be fully understood without a deep appreciation of sean-nós (old style) singing. It is the key which opens every lock. Without a sound knowledge of the sean-nós and a feeling for it a performer has no hope of knowing what is authentic and what is not in playing and decorating an air.
>
> (Ó Canainn 1978: 49)

The view of *sean-nós* as a tradition locked behind the door of a difficult language has led to the unfortunate sense that it is impossibly difficult and inaccessible. In an increasingly international Ireland, in which a musician from outside can, through careful listening and excellence of skill, play jigs and reels appropriately within the tradition, it is possible that *sean-nós* is one secret that is not so easily revealed. But does it really pertain to *every* aspect of Irish music? Perhaps it does not, and perhaps Ó Canainn (above) protests too much. However, the correct performance of an instru-mental air based on a *sean-nós* song does require an intimate knowledge of the song, because the poetic rhythm of the song determines the placement of the ornamenta-tion. Some singers and players would likely agree with the statement, but not every air is based on a *sean-nós* song. Some players avoid *sean-nós*-based airs altogether if their own grasp of Irish is poor or if they are sufficiently intimidated by the songs. Others pick up the correct ornamentation from respected players or recordings, trusting their own experiences and instincts to guide them in musically appropriate ways. But if the *sean-nós* songs are the heart of the tradition and determine, in large part, the correct performance of most airs, it is appropriate for Irish instrumentalists to take a second look at the songs!

Other Irish-Language Songs

Sean-nós is held up as representative of all Irish-language singing. However, all regions include hundreds of other songs, from children's songs to lilting songs; from tongue twisters to lively semi-improvised dialogue singing in duets (called *lúibíní*). Even rock music, country, and hip hop have found a uniquely Irish-language place (see Chapter 9). Many songs outside the realm of *sean-nós* have a fixed rhythm, and often that rhythm is 6/8—the same as that used for double jigs. The following song, a lively (and funny) Connemara song called "Bean Pháidín," speaks from the perspective of a woman curs-ing the fact that she is not married to "Paddy," and that Paddy's wife is still alive.

Figure 7.7 "Bean Pháidín" ("Páidín's Wife"—pronounced "ban faw-jeen")

Chorus:
'Sé an trua ghéar nach mise, nach mise
'Sé an trua ghéar nach mise bean Pháidín
'Sé an trua ghéar nach mise, nach mise
Is an bhean atá aige a bheith caillte.

Rachfainn go Gaillimh, go Gaillimh
Is rachfainn go Gaillimh le Páidín
Rachfainn go Gaillimh, go Gaillimh
Is thiocfainn abhaile go mbád leis.

Rachfainn go haonach an Chlocháin
'S isteach go Béal Átha na Báighe
Bhreathnóinn isteach trína bhfuinneogaí
Ag shúil is go bhfeicfinn Bean Pháidín.

Go mbristear do chosa, do chosa
Go mbristear do chosa, a Bhean Pháidín
Go mbristear do chosa, do chosa
Go mbristear do chosa is do chnámha.

Chaith mé mo bhróga, mo bhróga
Chaith mé mo bhróga i ndiaidh Pháidín
Chaith mé mo bhróga, mo bhróga
Chaith mé na boinn is na sála.

Chorus:
It is a bitter pity that I am not, that I am not
It is a bitter pity that I am not the wife of Paddy
It is a bitter pity that I am not, that I am not
And the wife he has is not dead.

I would go to Galway, to Galway
I would go to Galway with Páidín

I would go to Galway, to Galway
And I would come home in the boat with him.

I would go to the fair of Clifden
And into Ballinaboy
I would look through the windows
Hoping to see Páidín's wife.

May your legs, your legs, be broken
May your legs be broken, Páidín's wife
May your legs, your legs, be broken
May your legs and your bones be broken.

I wore out my shoes, my shoes
I wore out my shoes, after Páidín
I wore out my shoes, my shoes
I wore out the soles and the heels.

People who know this song often sing along with the chorus. After explaining the situation, the narrator continues in a later verse to curse Páidín's wife: *go mbristear do chosa, do chosa* ("may your legs, your legs be broken"). Men and women both sing this song with great enthusiasm, and it appears in contemporary song sessions, concerts, and recordings as a light-hearted respite from the intensity of *sean-nós*. The melody (Figure 7.6) responds to the potentially dark nature of the lyrics by bouncing along in a major key. It is the juxtaposition of a major key with serious-seeming lyrics that make the song so entertaining, together with the sentiment expressed by the lyrics.

Another song, "An Cailín Deas Donn" ("The Pretty Brown [Haired] Maid"), is also performed in 6/8 time and includes a chorus. In many versions of this song, a young man sees a girl pulling rushes (a useful type of reed plant that grows in wetlands) and seduces her before they discover that he is her long-lost brother. Most versions of "An Cailín Deas Donn" today allude only vaguely to a seduction, but nineteenth-century versions made it quite clear in that the couple openly discusses what should be done with the baby, should one result from their liaison ("my mother will care for it"). Liam Mac Con Iomaire points out correctly that "The songs in Irish reflect an outlook on life and a view of the world that is quite different to the songs in English" (Mac Con Iomaire 1999: 336). While he was speaking specifically about *sean-nós* singing, his observation rings true with almost all of the songs in Irish compared to those in English. The English-language songs of Ireland are certainly sung by the Irish, but the influences they carry from England and its worldview are simply different.

> "Ó is cailín ag baint luachra an cailín deas donn!"
> "Ó, is ea 'gus í in uaigneas!" a dúirt sí liom.
>
> Chorus:
> Sláinte agat mo chailín deas donn, a' céad míle fáilte romhat a dúirt sí liom.

"Cá gceanglód mé mo ghearrán a chailín deas donn?"
"Ní raibh claí riamh gan stocán," a dúirt sí liom.

"An raibh deartháir agatsa, a chailín deas donn?"
"Ó bhí deartháir agam," a dúirt sí liom.
"Cá ndeachaigh do dheartháir, a chailín deas donn?"
"Ó chuaigh sé 'na hoileáin," a dúirt sí liom.

"An n-aithneofá do dheartháir a chailín deas donn?"
"Ó d'aithneoinn ach é a fheiceáil," a dúirt sí liom.

"Cén comhartha bhí ar do dheartháir, a chailín deas donn?"
"Bhí ball odhar ar a chliathán," a dúirt sí liom.

"Ó, mise do dheartháir, a chailín deas donn"
"Ó tabhair le mo 'bhaile!" a dúirt sí liom.

"That maid pulling rushes there is a pretty brown maid!"
"Oh yes, and she's lonely!" said she to me.

Chorus:
A health to you my pretty brown maid, and a welcome to you, she said to me.

"Where can I tie up my mare, O pretty brown maid?"
"There's no ditch [stone wall] without a stake," she said to me.

"Had you ever a brother, O pretty brown maid?"
"Oh, I had a brother," said she to me.

"Where did he go, O pretty brown maid?"
"He went off to the islands," said she to me.

"Do you think you would know him, O pretty brown maid?"
"I'd know if I saw him," said she to me.

"What marks had your brother, O pretty brown maid?"
"On his side a brown birthmark," said she to me.

"I am your brother, O pretty brown maid"
"I'm going home!" said she to me.

Are we supposed to enjoy their courtship, or to become alarmed with this exchange: *"An raibh deartháir agatsa, a chailín deas donn?"* ("Did you ever have a brother, pretty brown maid?"), and her response: *"Ó bhí deartháir agam," a dúirt sí liom* ("oh yes, I had a brother," said she to me)? Neither: we are supposed to laugh at their potentially incestuous predicament.

Neither "Bean Pháidín" nor "An Cailín Deas Donn" belongs necessarily in the category of *sean-nós*, but they are popular among Irish speakers, easy to sing, use a dance rhythm (6/8), include a chorus, and could easily appear in an evening's song session in the Gaeltacht. Why is *sean-nós* believed to be more important than these two upbeat, somewhat salacious, Irish-language songs? It is about the relative weight of the songs' meaning. These songs, along with many other repetitive songs performed in a fixed meter, and often with a refrain or chorus, deal with sex and love readily granted, in the context of humor. It is the life cut short, the love unrequited and/or unexpressed in the first place, and the starkness of life's experiences that engage Irish-speaking audiences in a performance of *sean-nós*.

Macaronic Songs

Ireland was bilingual for several hundred years, and parts are still bilingual. Because of shifts in colonial language policies over time, it gradually became more advantageous to speak English. The first macaronic songs in Western Europe included verses in Latin interspersed with verses in the local vernacular, as part of a larger post-medieval shift toward a more secular society. Over time, Irish macaronic songs came to shift between Irish and English rather than Latin and a vernacular language, and while the intent might sometimes be to humorously obscure the meaning of the portions sung in Irish, they generally follow the storyline rather than obscure it.

> In those places where the people were comfortable in both Irish and their new English, a certain pride was shown both by the makers of the bilingual songs and those who sang them, the same sort of pride that led to the clever linguistic mixes heard in medieval taverns from the lips of the wandering scholars.
>
> (Ó Muirithe 1999: 356)

In this example of a macaronic song, the Irish portions are translated—but not sung—in brackets. The English title comes from the first line of the song. The melody (Figure 7.8) is in a fixed-rhythm, 3/4 time, and the poetic rhythm is predictable throughout.

Slán is Beannacht le Buaireamh an tSaoil ("One Morning in June")

One morning in June, *agus mé ag dul ag spaisteoireacht* [and me going rambling]
Casadh liom cailín, ba ródheas a gnaoi [I met a girl, very fine in appearance]
She was so handsome, *gur thit mé i ngrá léi* [that I fell in love with her]
D'fhága sí arraing i gceartlár mo chroí [she left an arrow in the center of my heart]
I asked her her name, *nó cad é an ruaig bheannaithe* [or what blessed chance]
A chas insan áit thú, a ghrá gheal mo chroí? [brought you here, bright love of my heart?]

One mor-ning in June, a-gus mé dhul ag spáis-teoir-eacht, ca-sadh liom cai-lín ba ró dheas a gnaoí;

she was so hand-some gur thit mé i ngrá léh, d'fhá ga sí ar-raing i cheart-lár mo chroí. I asked her her name, no cad

é an ruaig bean-nai-the, chas in-san áit thu a grá geal mo chroí; that

I'm a young man who is to-t'lly in love with you. Sure-ly my heart is from ro-guer-y free.

Figure 7.8 "Slán is Beannacht le Buaireamh an tSaoil" ("Farewell and Blessings to the Worries of Life"—pronounced "slawn iss *ban-nakht* leh *boo-ryoo* unn teel")

My heart it will break if you don't come along with me
Slán is beannacht le buaireamh an tsaoil [farewell to the worries of life].

Cailín beag óg mé ó cheanntar na farraige [I'm a little young girl from the coast]
A tógadh go cneasta mé i dtosach mo shaoil [reared decently in the start of my life]
I being so airy [carefree] *ó 'sé siúd ba chleachtadh liom* [since that was what I was used to]
That made my own parents and me disagree.
A chuisle 's a stór, dá n-éisteofá liom tamall [darling, if you'd listen to me awhile]
I'll tell you a story *a b'áit le do chroí* [that your heart will like]
That I'm a young man, who is totally in love with you
Surely my heart is from roguery free.

Muise, go you bold rogue, sure you're wanting to flatter me
B'fhearr éan ar an láimh, ná dhá éan ar an gcraoibh [better a bird in the hand than two birds on the branch]
I've neither wheat, potatoes or anything
Ná fiú an phluid leaba bheadh tharrainn san oíche [nor bedspread to cover us at night]
Ceannóidh mé tae agus gléasfad in aice seo [I'll buy tea and I'll dress nearby here]
Gúna English cotton *den fhaisiún atá daor* [a dress of expensive English cotton]
So powder your hair, love, and come away along with me
Slán is beannacht le buaireamh an tsaoil [farewell to the worries of life].

There's an alehouse nearby, *'s beidh muid go maidin ann* [we'll be there till
   morning]
If you're satisfied, *a ghrá gheal mo chroí* [bright love of my heart]
Early next morning we'll send for a clergyman
Beidh muidne ceangailte i ngan fhios don tsaol [we'll be united unknown to
   the world]
Beidh muid ag ól a fhad 's a mhairfeas an t-airgead [we'll drink while the
   money lasts]
Then we will take the road home with all speed
When the reckoning is paid, who cares for the landlady
Slán is beannacht le buaireamh an tsaoil [farewell to the worries of life].

A macaronic song can shift quickly into an intelligible song with unintelligible portions when the second language is unknown to the singer (or audience). The popular song "Siúil Arúin" has an Irish-language chorus, translated below, and an English-language set of verses about a girl who wants to follow her lover around the world:

Siúil, siúil, siúil arúin
Siúil go siocair agus siúil go ciúin
Siúil go dhin doras agus éilig liom
Is go deo thú mo mhuirnín slán.

Walk, walk, walk, darling
Walk safely and walk calmly
Walk through the door and fly with me
And you will be safe, darling, forever.

In an American, non-Irish-speaking folksong context, singers (who didn't know the original Irish lyrics) turned these words into nonsense syllables in the song "Buttermilk Hill"—which is how the author of this book sang it as a child:

Surely, surely, surely mana roo
Saddle mana rattle back, saddle babble coo
Then I'd sigh for saddle babble-een
Come a dibble all a do sal dory.

While it is easy to note the loss of meaning in a macaronic song when only one of the two languages is known to the singer or audience members, it is harder to bring a lost song back into the macaronic fold without the melody. Fortunately, "Siúil Arúin" (Figure 7.9) and "Buttermilk Hill" (Figure 7.10) share a nearly identical descending melody in some versions.

"Slán is Beannacht le Buaireamh an tSaoil" and "Siúil Arúin" are just two of many dozens of macaronic songs and their use reflects two different eras: first, the long period of bilingualism during which time English gradually came to supplant Irish in everyday speech over most of Ireland, culminating in the nineteenth-century period of the

Figure 7.9 Chorus of "Siúil Arúin"

Figure 7.10 Chorus of "Buttermilk Hill"

Famine (when hundreds of thousands of Irish speakers died or emigrated); second, Ireland's current status as one of the richest nations in Europe, together with its slowly increasing acceptance of contemporary Irish use in a European (not just an exclusively Irish) context, reveals the performance of a macaronic song to be a sign of the growing health of the language in the current era.

The Irish-language song tradition is clearly rich in variety, limited neither by subject matter nor by rhythm, relative antiquity, or melody. It has not been revived because it never died. While *sean-nós* is at the heart of the Irish music tradition, it is not the only type of Irish-language song being sung daily in Irish homes, pubs, singing clubs, recording studios, and stages. Instead, it happens to lie at the core of a much larger dual-language singing tradition that has itself had an impact on instrumental airs, which some might argue are a central aspect of the instrumental tradition. As one half of that dual-language tradition, Irish song is in some ways presented in opposition to English traditional song in Ireland. Yet the two traditions each seem to require the presence of the other, as complementary reflections of a set of values, needs, and relationships that underlie many aspects of Irish traditional culture.

Discussion Questions

1. How can a "folk music" (e.g., *sean-nós* singing) be considered a nation's contribution to classical music? What do those terms mean to you?
2. What is the paradox of *sean-nós* as described in this chapter?
3. What makes songs such as "Bean Pháidín" (Paddy's Wife) and "An Cailín Deas Donn" (The Pretty Brown-haired Maid) so funny? Why would people sing songs about breaking the legs of one's rival, for example, or about incest?

4. Can you think of any macaronic songs from your childhood? Or songs you feel that you know well, but don't know all the lyrics to? What do you do when you're singing a song and don't get all the lyrics?
5. What are your best options if you want to learn to play an instrumental air, but you don't speak any Irish?

CHAPTER 8

Vocal Music in English

Bocht an duine bhíos gan cheol ~ Poor is the person without music.

Sean-nós singing usually refers to songs performed in Irish, rather than those sung in English. However, some people use the term fairly casually to refer to all songs performed unaccompanied, regardless of their language or whether their meter is fixed or flexible. For the purposes of this book, Irish songs *in English* generally fall under the rubric of Irish traditional song, and Irish people who sing in English are often called Irish traditional singers. This distinction is offered in spite of the fact that many Irish singers are comfortable performing in Irish *and* English! In examining Irish song, regardless of the language in which it is sung, it would be impossible to cover all varieties. Instead, the aim of Chapters 7 and 8 is to examine the bigger picture of Irish song—from laments and love songs to more lighthearted songs—by using a few specific examples to illustrate particular points. Our initial encounter with the ballad was in Chapter 5, when you read about the Scots-Irish migration to North America. In this chapter, we consider a selection of the English language songs of Ireland—narrative ballads, lyric love songs, and lilting.

The English language has thrived in Ireland for hundreds of years, and songs in English (both originally from England and those composed in Ireland) have been present since the language's first use on the island. While the ruling classes and the military were primarily the provenance of the English language in the early days, a number of events in Irish history led to its increasing use and to the decline of the Irish language. English songs now constitute the majority of vocal musical expression in Ireland (and certainly in the Irish diaspora that includes England, Scotland, North America, Australia, and New Zealand). Even in the extremely rich musical territory of Ireland's *Gaeltachtaí* (Irish-speaking districts), English-language songs abound in the repertoires of people who speak Irish as their daily language. In spite of their separation into two chapters here, the reader is urged to recognize the friendly interdependence of the traditions in actual performance practice.

Having made that statement, it is also true that to sing in a language that differs from what one's neighbors and family members speak can be construed as something of a political act. The Donegal singer Lillis Ó Laoire speaks eloquently of growing up bilingual, and of the pressure not to succumb to speaking in English as a child (Ó Laoire 2004: 54). Angela Bourke describes a singing session in which several Irish-speaking women sang songs in English for her tape recorder, at which point "Cólaí Bán sang a highly ornamented 'Úna Bhán' [see Chapter 7] immediately after, as though in reproof, to remind the company to sing their own songs" (Bourke 2007: 47–8). Bourke further notes the appeal of the poetry, music, and variety in singing English-language songs in an Irish-speaking community, and suggests the possibility that some Irish-speaking women might be more comfortable singing English-language songs among themselves.

Similarly, singing an Irish-language song in an English-speaking song session brings its own risk of another kind of politicization. In Northern Ireland, to sing in Irish (or, for that matter, to play Irish traditional instrumental music) was practically—for a time—to declare one's affiliation with the nationalist cause and, by extension, to risk association with the IRA (Irish Republican Army). Until recently in the Republic, to sing in Irish outside of the Gaeltacht was to risk censure or scorn because of the language's association with the "bad old days" of poverty, the Famine, and pre-modern Ireland. Since the 1990s, however, the increasing acceptance of the language and the growing popularity of the Irish-language schools called *gaelscoileanna* mean that singing in Irish is becoming less of a political act than perhaps an attempt to add musical variation to an English-language session. Among devoted English-language singers, however, well-sung Irish-language songs are often welcome for their musical beauty and for the virtuosity of those who sing them.

The English-Language Ballad in Ireland

Ballads in English have had a history of several hundred years in Ireland, and their continuing popularity in sung performance indicates their ability to outlast significant changes in society. Scholars who study balladry note several characteristics about the songs. Among these characteristics is a narrative technique called "leaping and lingering," in which the plot moves rapidly forward, then halts for a verse or two of emotional content, dialogue, or some other element before leaping forward again. The stories are generally fictional (except for the broadsides, which are discussed below), and that feature sets them apart from most of the Irish-language songs referring to historical events from folk memory. Stock figures and objects ("her rosy red lips," the "nut-brown maid," the "milk-white steed," etc.) populate these songs, as do stock phrases ("come saddle me the berry brown horse," etc.). In their melodies, ballads tend to be performed in stepwise motion, with few large intervals. In the following examples of ballads, transcriptions reveal the stepwise movement of the melodies, together with melodic ornamentation that is similar in some ways to that which is used in *sean-nós*.

The publication of the groundbreaking work *The English and Scottish Popular Ballads* (Francis James Child, 1882–89) was a great boon to ballad collectors and singers alike. The development of a compendium of ballad texts meant that collectors could refer to an assigned number and set of characteristics for virtually any English-language ballad in Ireland, particularly the ones derived from England and/or Scotland. In general, most of the ballads that came to Ireland from England and Scotland arrived through printed means (on broadsheets and chapbooks), though many songs still came with migrants. Those that came from Scotland arrived via the north of Ireland and were transmitted orally (Shields 1993: 48). Many people from the north of Ireland traveled yearly to Scotland for work, and in the process learned Scottish ballads in English. The Irish who settled in Scotland did so in a pattern of chain migration, so as family members traveled to and from Scotland, they learned local songs while visiting family. The Irish who sought employment in England found a similar situation: small Irish communities brought people together, songs were transmitted, and some songs came home to Ireland.

Three examples of common English-language ballads in Ireland are "The Lass of Aughrim (Lord Gregory)," "The Night Visiting Song," and "Captain Wedderburn's Courtship." Each has long since been catalogued by Child as numbering among his popular English and Scottish ballads, and each can be found in many different versions and variants in Ireland as well as in Scotland, England, Australia, New Zealand, and North America.

"The Lass of Aughrim," also called "Lord Gregory" (Child Ballad No. 76), tells the story of an unfortunate young woman who has borne a child by a lord; she brings the baby to his home and is sent away (by the lord's mother) to drown herself and the baby in the ocean. In Scotland and parts of Ireland, the ballad is called "The Lass of Roch [sometimes "Loch"] Royal." The Irish lyrics often focus on the tension between the potential mother-in-law and the younger woman, placing the blame for the unhappy ending firmly on the older woman and exonerating Lord Gregory, who (apparently) loved the young woman after all and might have married her if his mother hadn't intervened. Notice in this ballad in particular the use of stock images and actions ("yellow locks," "saddle me the brown horse, the black or the grey," "who will shoe my babe's little feet"). These stock images appear in many different songs, and are a standard feature of English-language ballad singing.

Musically, "The Lass of Aughrim" starts and ends on the fifth degree of the scale (Figure 8.1), though the beginning of each verse functions as a lead-in to the tonic. This version of the song, transcribed from the singing of Joe Heaney, reaches a climactic

Figure 8.1 "The Lass of Aughrim" as sung by Joe Heaney

point in the third line with the introduction of the natural seventh degree of the scale in the upper register. Highlighting the seventh degree of the scale (particularly the natural seventh) is unusual in Irish songs, and makes this particular song stand out among other ballads.

> I am a king's daughter who strayed from Cappaquin
> In search of Lord Gregory, pray God I find him
> The rain beats at my yellow locks, the dew wets my skin
> My babe is cold in my arms, Lord Gregory, let me in.
>
> Lord Gregory is not home my dear, henceforth he can't be seen
> He's gone to bonnie Scotland to bring home a new queen
> So leave you these windows and likewise this hall
> For it's deep in the ocean you must hide your downfall.
>
> Who'll shoe my babe's little feet? Who'll put gloves on her hand?
> Who'll tie my babe's middle with a long and green band?
> Who'll comb my babe's yellow locks with an ivory comb?
> Who'll be my babe's father till Lord Gregory comes home?
>
> I'll shoe your babe's little feet, I'll put gloves on her hand
> I'll tie your babe's middle with a long and green band
> I'll comb your babe's yellow locks with an ivory comb
> I'll be your babe's father till Lord Gregory comes home.
>
> But leave you these windows and likewise this hall
> For it's deep in the ocean you must hide your downfall.
>
> Do you remember Lord Gregory that night in Cappaquin?
> We exchanged silken handkerchiefs, and all against my will
> Yours were fine linen, love, and mine was old cloth
> Yours cost one guinea, love, and mine none at all.
>
> Do you remember Lord Gregory, that night in my father's hall?
> We exchanged rings on our fingers, and that was worse than all
> Yours were fine silver, love, and mine was old tin
> Yours cost one guinea, love, and mine just one cent.
>
> But leave you these windows and likewise this hall
> For it's deep in the ocean you must hide your downfall.
>
> My curse on you mother, and sister also
> Tonight the lass of Aughrim came knocking at my door
> Lie down my little son, lie down and sleep
> Tonight the lass of Aughrim lies sleeping in the deep.

Saddle me the brown horse, the black or the grey
But saddle me the best horse in my stable this day
And I'll roam over the valley, and mountains so wide
Till I find the lass of Aughrim and lie by her side.

But leave you these windows and likewise this hall
For it's deep in the ocean you must hide your downfall.

Note that the recording on the online soundtrack that comes with this textbook not only has a very abbreviated version of the story, but also a melody different from the one transcribed in Figure 8.1. The melody (Figure 8.2) is the same as that sung at the pivotal moment in the film *The Dead*, based on the short story by James Joyce; it was, in fact, inspired by the song's performance in the film.

TRACK 9

Mythology and folklore play a large role in Irish singing and storytelling. The story of the person who makes love with his or her sweetheart, only to discover that the sweetheart has already died and is a ghost lover, is a common theme. The *revenant* (returned-from-the-dead) ballad "The Night Visiting Song" (Child Ballad No. 248) is one such song. As in "The Lass of Aughrim," "The Night Visiting Song" also uses stock images and phrases: the "lily-white pillow," "whispered softly through her window," etc. In this version, we are told only obliquely that the lover has died; in the first and last verses, he indicates that he must obey "the tempest's rages" and return "to the arms of the deep." Having drowned already, this night is his one chance to return for a final visit. In some versions, she remarks on the fact that he is "cold as the clay."

The melody of "The Night Visiting Song," like that of many other English-language ballads, is quite simple (Figure 8.3). Like "The Lass of Aughrim," "The Night Visiting Song" begins on the fifth degree of the scale as a way to highlight the tonic. Lines 1, 2, and 4 are nearly identical, with the only difference between them appearing at the end of line 2. The third line—as is often the case—is the high point of the song, beginning at

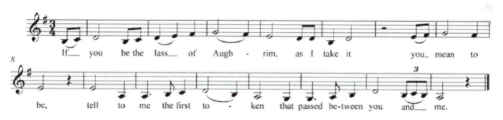

Figure 8.2 "The Lass of Aughrim" as sung by Susan McKeown

Figure 8.3 "The Night Visiting Song"

the tonic in the upper register and descending all the way to the lowest note (pitch five) before concluding with line 4.

> The night has passed, love, I can no longer tarry
> The tempest's rages I must obey
> I must away, love, without a slumber
> Into the arms of the deep.
>
> When he came to his true love's dwelling
> He sat down upon a stone
> He whispered softly through her window
> "Does my true love lie alone?"
>
> She lifted her head from her lily-white pillow
> She lifted the sheets from off her breast
> She whispered softly through her window
> "Who is disturbing my night's rest?"
>
> "It's I, it's I, your own true lover
> Open the door and let me in
> For I am tired, love, likewise I'm weary
> I am wet unto the skin."
>
> She got up with the greatest of pleasure
> She opened the door and let him in
> They lay all night in each other's arms
> Till the long night was passed and gone.
>
> When the long night was passed and over
> When the cocks began to crow
> He hugged and kissed her, and then he left her
> He mounted his horse, and away did go.
>
> The night has passed, love, I can no longer tarry
> The tempest's rages I must obey
> I must away, love, without a slumber
> Into the arms of the deep.

In a variant of this song, "The Yellow Silk Handkerchief," the young man ("of low degree") returns from the grave to spend the night in his lover's arms. She gives him a yellow silk handkerchief as a token of their love, which is later discovered tied around his neck when his body is exhumed. Angela Bourke mentions this song as well, using the title "The Holland Silk Handkerchief" (Bourke 2007: 54). The following verses of the song cover some of the same territory as "The Night Visiting Song," with a more explicit understanding of the lover's death.

> It's of a farmer lived in this town
> He was loved by all the neighbors round

He had a daughter, a beauty bright
The name they called her was Young Heart's Delight.

And many a young man came to court this maid
But none of them could her favor gain
Until a young man of a low degree
Came courting her, and she fancied he.

When her father knew she was thus engaged
He sent her away to a distant place
Forty miles or more he sent her away
For to deprive her of her wedding day.

One night she lay in her room alone
She heard a voice in the distant road
Rise up, my darling, come along with me
I own I love your own company.

She got up and put on her clothes
She ran away to the distant road
He pulled her up on his milk-white steed
Oh my dearest darling, do you remember me?

He put her arms around his waist
She stroked his neck and she stroked his hair
She kissed his lips and those words did say
Oh my dear, you're colder than the clay.

A yellow silk handkerchief she then pulled out
She put it around his neck and brow
He drew her arms around his waist
Oh my dearest darling, we cannot wait.

And when he came to her father's gate
He put her down and those words did say
Go home, my darling, go home and sleep
For I'm away now, no more to see.

And then she ran to her father's door
She loudly knocked and she loudly roared
O father, father, did you send for me?
By such a messenger, naming he.

Her father, knowing this young man was dead
He tore the grey hairs from his head
And when her father grieved heartful sore
This young man's darling cried more and more.

Then they went and they dug his grave
They opened his coffin and laid him bare
For although her true love was nine months dead
The yellow silk handkerchief was around his neck.

A drinking version of "The Night Visiting Song"—titled "I'm a Rover, Seldom Sober"—replaces the all-important first and final stanza with the following stanza:

I'm a rover, seldom sober
I'm a rover of high degree
And when I'm drinking, I'm always thinking
How to gain my love's company.

This stanza is also sung in the middle of the song, between when he knocks on the young lady's door and when she lets him in. The melody of "I'm a Rover" is bouncy and repetitive, and is quite easy to sing in solo or chorus (Figure 8.4); the melody is the same for both the replacement stanza (which functions as a refrain) and the rest of the song. In addition, the absence of the stanza that reveals the lover to have already died shifts the meaning of the entire song. In "I'm a Rover," the (normally dead) fellow simply shows up, gains his entry, spends the night, has sex, mounts his horse and rides away! In the new context and content of the song, the "spirit" of the dead lover is replaced by the "spirit" of the strong drink. As you look at the melody of "I'm a Rover, Seldom Sober," you can simply sing the verses of "The Yellow Silk Handkerchief" to that melody and change the meaning utterly!

TRACK 7

Ballads in which a couple fall in love and the young woman offers to come to sea with the young man are common in Ireland as well as in Scotland and England: "Adieu, Lovely Nancy," "Caroline and Her Young Sailor Bold," and others focus on the ways in which the young couple is parted by the sea, in spite of their best efforts to stay together. In most cases, the sea proves the death of one or both of them (though usually of the young woman, for straying out of her given role whether by joining him at sea or by having offered to do so in the first place). In "Adieu, Lovely Nancy," she stays at home after offering to cut off her curly yellow ringlets and dies of a broken heart. Versions of this song type usually end with an exhortation to avoid sailors. "Adieu, Lovely Nancy" appears on the online soundtrack for this book. The transcription (Figure 8.5) shows the many places in which the singer can (and does) place rapid vocal ornaments to decorate the melody.

Figure 8.4 "I'm a Rover, Seldom Sober"

Figure 8.5 "Adieu, Lovely Nancy"

"Adieu, lovely Nancy, for now I must leave you
For the far-off West Indies, I'm bound for to sail
But let my long journey be of no trouble to you
For my love, I'll return in the course of the year."

"Talk not of leaving me here, lovely Jimmy
Talk not of leaving me here on the shore
You know very well your long absence will grieve me
As you sail the wild ocean where the wild billows roar.

"I'll cut off my ringlets all curly and yellow
I'll dress in the coats of a young cabin boy
And when we are out on that dark, rolling ocean
I will always be near you, my pride and my joy."

"Your lily-white hands, they could not handle the cables
Your lily-white feet to the topmast could not go
And the cold winter storms, well, you could not endure them
Stay at home, lovely Nancy, where the wild winds won't blow."

As Jimmy set a-sailing, lovely Nancy stood a-wailing
The tears from her eyes in great torrents did a-flow
As she stood on the beach, oh, her hands she was wringing
Crying, "Oh and alas, will I e'er see you more?"

As Jimmy was a-walking on the quays of Philadelphia
The thoughts of his true love, they filled him with pride
He said "Nancy, lovely Nancy, if I had you here, love
How happy I'd be for to make you my bride."

So Jimmy wrote a letter to his own lovely Nancy
Saying "If you have proved constant, well, I will prove true"
Oh but Nancy was dying, for her poor heart was broken

Oh the day that he left her, forever he'd rue.

Come all of you maidens, I pray, take a warning
And don't trust a sailor boy or any of his kind
For first they will court you and then they'll deceive you
For their love, it is tempestuous as the wavering wind.

The ballad technique of interrogation between lovers—in which one asks the other a series of questions to test him or her—is an old one, and appears here in the ballad "Captain Wedderburn's Courtship" (Child Ballad No. 46). Any reader familiar with the song "Scarborough Fair" or "I Gave My Love a Cherry" will notice that "Captain Wedderburn's Courtship" also uses the technique of impossible-to-fulfill requests: the cherry without a stone, fruit in winter, etc. In this case, the reward for correctly and cleverly responding to the impossible requests is to spend the night with the one making the requests.

The melody is in ABBA form; lines 1 and 4 of each stanza are the same, and lines 2 and 3 are the same (see Figure 8.6). Because of the importance of the lyrics in "Captain Wedderburn's Courtship," though, neither the simple melodic material nor any particular array of vocal ornamentation plays a significant role in the song. Ornaments are limited to simple turns.

As a gentleman's fair daughter walked down a narrow lane
She met with Captain Wedderburn, he was keeper of the game
He said unto his servant, "If only for the law
I'd have that girl in bed with me, and she'd lie next the wall."

"Go your way, young man," she said, "and do not bother me
Before you and I in one bed lie, you must answer me questions three
Three questions you must answer me, and I'll set forth them all
Till you and I on the one bed lie, and I lie next the wall.

For my breakfast you must get for me a cherry without a stone
For my dinner you must find for me a chicken without a bone
For my supper you must find for me a bird without a gall
Then you and I on the one bed lie, and I'll lie next the wall."

Figure 8.6 "Captain Wedderburn's Courtship"

"A cherry when in blossom, surely has no stone
A chicken when it's in the egg, surely has no bone
The dove it is a gentle bird, it flies without a gall
Then you and I on the one bed lie, and you'll like next the wall."

"Go your way, young man," she said, "and do not me perplex
Before you and I in one bed lie, you must answer me questions six
Six questions you must answer me, and I'll set forth them all
Till you and I on the one bed lie, and I lie next the wall.

What is rounder than a ring, what's higher than a tree
What is worse than a woman's wrath, what's deeper than the sea
What bird sings best, what flower buds first, and on it the dew first falls
Then you and I on the one bed lie and I'll lie next the wall.

The world is rounder than a ring, heaven's higher than a tree
The devil is worse than a woman's wrath, hell's deeper than the sea
The lark sings best, the heath' buds first, and on it the dew first falls
So you and I on the one bed lie, and you'll lie next the wall.

You must get for me some winter fruit that in December grew
You must get for me a silk mantle that weft ne'er went through
A sparrow's horn, a priest unborn, who'll wed us two in twa
Then you and I on the one bed lie and I'll lie next the wall.

My father has some winter fruit that in December grew
My mother has a silk mantle that weft ne'er went through
A sparrow's horn is easily found, there's one on every claw
And Micheldeus was a priest unborn, so you'll lie next the wall.

This couple they got married, as you may plainly see
They live happily together, and children they have three
She set forth the questions, he answered one and all
He rolled her in his arms, but she lay next the wall.

Broadside Ballads

The broadside ballad is a subset of balladry—not just in Ireland, but all over Europe, and in England, Scotland, and the United States. The term broadside refers to a long narrow sheet of paper with an illustrative woodcut at the top, and the printed lyrics of a topical song (usually in English) on one side of the sheet. Often the sheet would include the instructions, "sung to the tune of…" followed by the title of a popular song of the era. What distinguishes a broadside from a regular ballad is its naming of names, places, and dates. Broadsides were the "scandal sheets" or tabloid newspapers of the day, selling millions of copies by focusing on the details of political scandal, sexual intrigues, and comic or impossible deeds. The publisher would sell them to street hawkers, who would carry an armload of broadsheets to street corners, singing the lyrics of the song to attract buyers. It was common to post broadsheets on the walls of a house for easy learning of the song.

The broadside ballad used here as an example is "Morrissey and the Russian Sailor." Johnny Morrissey was a real person in the nineteenth century who worked as both a professional fighter and an Irish-American politician. A quick glance at even one of the verses reveals almost immediate hyperbole: Morrissey fights round after round with a Russian sailor in Tierra del Fuego until he, the (Irish/American) hero must vanquish the (Russian) enemy. Thirty-eight rounds might seem excessive in real life, but this is emphatically *not* real life. No record exists, beyond the existence of the broadside itself, of the boxing match ever having actually taken place, but whether it occurred in history is less important than the fact that it was *alleged* to have occurred. In Irish song tradition, the word can be as important as the deed.

> Come all you gallant Irishmen, wherever you may be
> I hope you'll pay attention and listen unto me
> I'll sing about a battle that took place the other day
> Between a Russian sailor and gallant Morrissey.
>
> It was in Tierra del Fuego, in South Amerikay
> The Russian challenged Morrissey and these words to him did say
> I hear you are a fighting man and wear a belt I see
> Indeed I wish you would consent to have a round with me.
>
> Then out spoke Morrissey with heart both brave and true
> I am a valiant Irishman that never was subdued
> For I can whale the Yankee, the Saxon, Bull and Bear
> In honor of Ol' Paddy's Land I'll still the laurels wear.
>
> They shook hands and walked around the ring, commencing then to fight
> It filled each Irish heart with pride for to behold the sight
> The Russian, he floored Morrissey up to the 11th round
> With Yankee, Russian, Saxon cheers, the valley did resound.
>
> The Irish offered four to one that day upon the grass
> No sooner said than taken up and down they brought the cash
> They parried away without delay until the 22nd round
> When Morrissey received a blow that brought him to the ground.
>
> Up to the 37th round 'twas fall and fall about
> Which made the foreign tyrants to keep a sharp lookout
> The Russian called his seconds for to have a glass of wine
> Our Irish hero smiled and said, "This battle will be mine."
>
> The 38th decided on, the Russian felt the smart
> And Morrissey with a dreadful blow, struck the Russian on the heart
> The doctor, he was called in to open up a vein
> He said, "It is quite useless, he'll never fight again."

Our hero conquered Thompson and the Yankee Clipper too
The Buffalo Boy and Sheppard, he nobly did subdue
So let us fill a flowing glass, here is health *go leor*
To noble Johnny Morrissey that came from Templemore.

The "come-all-ye" is related to the broadside ballad in that many (though not all) broadsides begin with "come all ye" as a way to gather bystanders. Other come-all-ye's include narrative songs that do not specifically name names or places, but are composed in Ireland about Irish topics. The song "Molly Bawn" begins with the exhortation to any and all hunters of fowl to beware of shooting one's lover at sunset. In this popular song, the hunter mistakes his sweetheart for a swan (or sometimes a fawn or a heron) because of her clothing, and shoots her. In the subsequent trial, her ghost appears and begs forgiveness for him on account of her having worn clothing that would allow him to mistake her.

Singers use an array of melodies to produce this song. The fact that it is so common means that it thrives in multiple versions in Ireland and in the diaspora; Jennifer O'Connor noted at least 88 oral and printed variants of the song, collected in the Irish diaspora (O'Connor 1986). In North America it is sometimes known as "Polly Von" or "Polly Vawn." Missing from this version, for example, is the pair of verses that describe the delight of the local young women over the death of Molly Bawn, since she was seen as strong competition for the affections of the local young men!

Come all you young fowlers who carries a gun
Don't ever go a-shooting by the setting of the sun
I was once a brave young fowler, as you may understand
And I shot my own true love, I took her for a swan.

She was going to her uncle when the rain it came on
She went under a tree for to let the rain pass
With her apron all around her, I took her for a swan
Oh, I never would have shot my own Molly Bawn.

And when he came to her, and found it was she
His limbs, they were shaking, his eyes could not see
His heart it was broken with sorrow and with grief
And he implored up to heaven to give him relief.

Young Jimmy went home with his gun in his hand
Saying, "Father, dearest Father, I have done what's wrong
With her apron all around her, I took her for a swan
Oh, alas, and alas, I shot my Molly Bawn."

I wrapped her fair temples, and found she was dead
A torrent of tears for my true love I shed
And now I'll be forced by the laws of the land
For the killing of my darling, my trial for to stand.

> And the day of her funeral, her spirit it appeared
> Saying, "Uncle, dearest Uncle, do not hang my dear
> With my apron all around me, he took me for a swan
> Oh, he never would have shot his own Molly Bawn."

The late Irish scholar Hugh Shields argued that "Molly Bawn" is based on a true story that goes even deeper than the song lyrics reveal. Because some versions name specific names ("Molly Bán Lavery" and "James Reynolds"), and those names are Catholic (Lavery) and Protestant (Reynolds), the possibilities for sectarian intrigue make it even more interesting (Shields 1993: 61). Some versions of the song even include a place and dates where the event might have occurred, which Jennifer O'Connor believes may have been in the early to middle of the seventeenth century (O'Connor 1986). While broadside ballads may stray into hyperbole, as in "Morrissey and the Russian Sailor," others take specific events and build on them. Yet the process of folk transmission, in which names, dates, and places are lost over time, can render even the most specific of songs into a much more generic oral narrative.

Broadside ballads had entered Ireland by the sixteenth century. Already at that point, the "seditious ballad sheet" was considered troublesome by the English government as a prop of Irish Catholicism (Shields 1993: 43); these early English-language ballad texts were suspected of causing unrest in Ireland, and those who were caught with them in the early days were subject to fine or imprisonment. The broadside ballads reached the height of their popularity in the seventeenth and eighteenth centuries; they were a source of both information and entertainment, particularly in urban areas. They became an important tool of rebellion for the United Irishmen in the late eighteenth century (Vallely 2011: 41), and were also important in the "hedge schools," systems of informal education (in spite of the name, usually taught in homes) led by schoolmasters. Catholic education had been forbidden, but—prior to the establishment of the national schools in the 1830s—teaching children to read and write, understand math, and know something of history, Latin, and English was allowed. Broadsides or "broadsheets" were sometimes a part of that education. Broadside ballads faded in popularity and importance by the middle of the nineteenth century when newspapers became more common. Entertainment was to be had by other means, including pubs and the music hall scene.

Lyric Love Songs

The *amour courtois* tradition of love poetry (see Chapter 7) did not have an impact just on Irish-language songs. English-language songs are rich in lyrics that celebrate, lament, or otherwise describe the lover without actually telling a story or engaging anyone in dialogue. The further away from the beloved one became, it seemed, the more poignant the love song. The song "She Moved Through the Fair" does not tell a story so much as set up a context for expressing longing and describing the beauty of the beloved (who, it is revealed during the song, has already died but returns to speak with the protagonist). It is another type of *revenant* (re-awakened dead lover) song. Hugh Shields points out that the "emphatic denial of the natural order" (through the presence of the spirit of a dead lover, for example, or an image such as the sun setting in the east) serves to set up and maintain a sense of the timeless present: these are not events that happened exclusively in the past, but rather could happen in the past, present, or future (Shields 1993: 5).

One of the elements that makes the *revenant* song "She Moved Through the Fair" belong to the courtly love tradition is the remoteness of the lover. Although she speaks to the protagonist directly, touches him, visits him at night, and promises marriage to him, the fact that she is dead effectively dooms their relationship! Instead, the singer is left to admire the way she moves ("as the swan in the evening moves over the lake").

The modal (Dorian) melody of "She Moved Through the Fair" is one of its primary attractions for both singers and listeners, and is one of the main reasons that it continues its popularity as one of the most-favored songs of the English-language repertoire. Unlike some of the narrative ballads featured above, "She Moved Through the Fair" leaves considerable room for its singer to bring rich vocal ornamentation to bear in performance (Figure 8.7). The melodic form is the familiar ABBA. In the course of four verses, however, the singer can employ variation of ornaments and of the melody itself to keep the song interesting.

My young love said to me, my mother won't mind
And my father won't slight you, for your lack of kine
Then she stepped away from me, and this she did say
"It will not be long, love, 'til our wedding day."

She stepped away from me, and moved through the fair
And fondly I watched her move here and move there
She then turned homeward with one star awake
As the swan in the evening moves over the lake.

And the people were saying us two'd never wed
For one has a sorrow that I mustn't tell
She sighed as she passed with her goods and her gear
And that was the last I saw of my dear.

Last night she came to me, my dead love came in
So softly she came, her feet made no din
She laid her hand o'er me, and this she did say
"It will not be long, love, 'til our wedding day."

Figure 8.7 "She Moved Through the Fair"

As in Irish-language songs, alcohol can appear as a substitute for the beloved. In the song "Peggy Gordon," the (male) singer offers up the praises for the lover, and is frustrated by her unwillingness to spend time with him. He seeks his consolation in alcohol, which in turn makes him miss the beloved even more (see "I'm a Rover, Seldom Sober," above). "Peggy Gordon"—like most ballads—includes stock images and lines ("I wish I was away in some lonesome valley"), but without the narrative characteristic of balladry.

> Oh Peggy Gordon you are my darling
> Come sit you down upon my knee
> And tell to me the very reason
> Why I'm slighted so by thee.
>
> I'm so deep in love, I can't deny it
> My heart lies smoldered in my breast
> But it's not for you to let the whole world know it
> A troubled mind can find no rest.
>
> I leaned myself on a cask of brandy
> It was my fancy I do declare
> For when I'm drinking I'm always thinking
> Wishing Peggy Gordon was there.
>
> I wish I was in some lonesome valley
> Where womankind cannot be found
> And the pretty little birds do change their voices
> And every moment a different sound
>
> I wish I was away in Indie
> Far across the briny sea
> Sailing o'er the deepest ocean
> Where love or care never trouble me.

Songs such as "Peggy Gordon," with its expressed wish that the singer could live "where womankind cannot be found," represent an ideal vision of the separation of the sexes and the sublimation of sexual desire into alcohol. By the end of the nineteenth century, a loosely-based system of "men's groups" began to coalesce, in which men would gather in pubs as a way to be separated from the influence of women. The conservative Catholic movement that overtook Irish culture in the 1850s—the Devotional Revolution—persisted until the twentieth century; it celebrated the separation of the sexes, late marriage, and the establishment of a pub drinking culture with the view that drinking, compared to sexual activity (even within the confines of marriage), was the lesser of two evils (Stivers 2000: 103). Its effects are still being felt today, in various ways. It is in these pubs that ballad and lyric love song singing—separate from printed broadsheets—thrived as an expression of masculinity. By singing to other men about manly deeds and sporting exploits, men could affirm their collective strength and identity in a culture that was still under the dominion of the English. The separation of men's and women's spheres into the pub and the kitchen, respectively, provided new contexts for singing, listening, and learning.

English-language laments do not always focus on the lover (alive or dead). The frequency of childbirth, poor nutrition, and lack of access to health care meant that the Irish experienced a high rate of child mortality. Of great comfort to a bereaved mother was the idea that one's child had not actually died, but had been stolen—healthy—by the fairies and replaced by a "changeling"—a sickly fairy child. The song "Please Restore My Baby Boy" is the lament of a mother who has lost her child to the fairies. Notice that many of these lyrics are in the present tense (like "Peggy Gordon"), rather than relating a series of events that transpire over time.

> A mother came when stars were *paling*
> *Wailing* around the fairy **spring**
> Thus her tears were softly *falling*
> *Calling* on the fairy **king.**
>
> Why would spoil a mother's treasure?
> Courting him with a fairy joy
> Why would spoil a mother's pleasure?
> Please restore my baby boy.
>
> O'er the mountains, through the wild woods
> Where in childhood he loved to play
> Where the flowers are freshly springing
> There I wander day by day.
>
> There I wander, growing fonder
> Of the child that made my joy
> And the echoes while recalling
> Please restore my baby boy.
>
> But in vain my plaintive *calling*
> Tears are *falling* all in **vain**
> He now sports with fairy *treasure*
> He's the *pleasure* of their **train.**
>
> So fare thee well, my child, forever
> In this world I've lost my joy
> In the next we ne'er shall sever
> There I'll find my baby boy.

The rhyming words of the first verse echo a much older Irish poetic technique called *conachlonn*, in which the last word of the first line of a couplet rhymes with the first word of the next line (*italicized*): paling/wailing; falling/calling. Notice also that the final words of the second and fourth line (in **bold**) rhyme: spring/king. In the fifth verse, the rhyme scheme shifts to a technique called *amus*: the final word of the first and third lines (*italicized*) rhymes with a word in the *middle* of the following line: calling/

falling; treasure/pleasure. As in the first verse, the final words of the second and fourth lines (in **bold**) rhyme: vain/train. More simple rhyming characterizes the other verses of "Please Restore My Baby Boy."

In unaccompanied songs such as "Please Restore My Baby Boy," some words lend themselves to traditional modes of melodic ornamentation as might be found in Irish-language *sean-nós* singing. Words that emphasize the first syllable (referred to as "trochaic"), as many Irish-language words do, simply sound more Irish through their poetic rhythm, and are easier to decorate with grace notes, turns, and melismas. Taking a quick look at the song above, the many trochaic words leap to the fore (and repeat throughout): paling, wailing, fairy, softly, falling, calling, treasure, courting, pleasure, baby, mountains, childhood, freshly, springing, wander, fonder, echoes, plaintive, calling, falling, sever. Again and again throughout the song, the very lyrics pave the way for appropriate melodic treatment with Irish-sounding ornamentation.

In "The Nobleman's Wedding," the narrator relates his tale of being present at a wedding at which the jilted former lover sings at the wedding of his sweetheart to a wealthy man. She reacts badly and leaves the celebration; by the time her new husband embraces her, she has already died. The version comes from Connemara, but a version of this song from southwest Donegal has a very similar story and an entirely different melody.

> I once was invited to a nobleman's wedding
> All that were there were to sing just one song
> The first one to sing was the bride's former lover
> The song that he sang was "Of Days That Were Gone."
>
> "How can you sit at another man's table
> How can you drink of another man's wine
> How can you go to the arms of another
> You being so long a sweetheart of mine?"
>
> This maiden was sitting at the head of the table
> Hearing those words she remembered them well
> Hearing those words she no longer could stand it
> It's down at the head of the table she fell.
>
> Sighing and sobbing she arose from the table
> Sighing and sobbing she went up to bed
> And early next morning when her husband awakened
> He went to embrace her and found she was dead.
>
> "Oh Molly, lovely Molly, oh cruel-hearted Molly
> Your love and my love could never agree
> When first I separated yourself and your Johnny
> It was then I separated the bark from the tree."

One of the strongest lines of the song is the final line; separating the bark from the tree not only links the song to many other poems using nature as a metaphor for love, but also presents a powerful image to the audience. Separating the bark from the tree is bad for the bark and worse for the tree. The presence of a dialogue between lovers is in this song as well, but in modified form. The dialogue appears as an accusation from the jilted lover, a weeping response from the bride, and a remorseful statement of acceptance by the husband.

Praise Songs

Praise songs are an old aspect of Irish tradition; they appear in both Irish and English as honoring humans, honoring a place or time, or honoring tangible objects. With roots in the bardic tradition of (at least) the first millennium, the *planxty* of the harpers was part of a larger tradition of singing (and playing) the praises of someone or something. "An Crúiscín Lán" ("The Full Little Jug") was so well known at the turn of the century that popular newspaper columnist Flann O'Brien (using the *nom de plume* of Myles na gCopaleen) called his column "The Crushkeen Lawn." The translation of the Irish-language chorus from Irish to English is as follows:

> Love of my heart, my little jug, bright health my darling
> Love of my heart, my little jug, full, full, full
> Love of my heart, my little jug, bright health my darling
> It's all the same to me [if] your head [of hair] is black or white.

It is worth noting that the song's focus appears repeatedly on elemental aspects of life: farming, hunting, shepherding, drinking, love, and death. In addition, rather than exploring grim realities of sin, guilt, and the consequences of one's actions (including when Death appears), the singer is delighted with everything: his full little jug, his pretty girl, and his blessings from Bacchus, the god of wine. He even has the gumption to order Death to leave the scene! In no sense does alcohol replace his sweetheart, nor does he pine for anyone. Life is, simply, great.

The melody—in a minor key—belies the fact that the song is quite cheery in performance; it does this by relying more heavily on the fifth and seventh degrees of the scale than on the minor third (Figure 8.8). The fixed meter allows for little in the way of melodic decoration.

Figure 8.8 Chorus of "An Crúiscín Lán"

Let the farmer praise his ground and the huntsman praise his hound
The shepherd his sweet shady grove
I'm more blessed than they, spend each happy night and day
With my smiling little *crúiscín lán, lán, lán* (repeat).

Grá mo chroí mo chrúiscín, sláinte geal mo mhuirnín
Grá mo chroí mo chrúiscín, lán, lán, lán
Grá mo chroí mo chrúiscín, sláinte geal mo mhuirnín
Is cuma liom do chúilín, dubh nó bán.

Immortal and divine, sweet Bacchus, god of wine
Create me by adoption of your son
In hopes that you'll comply that my glass will ne'er run dry
Nor my smiling little *crúiscín lán, lán, lán* (repeat)

There's my *cailín deas*, she's a kind, true-hearted lass ["pretty girl"]
She's as modest, she's as gentle as a swan
Her smile is so divine, I could quaff it up with wine
Her sweet lips should be my *crúiscín lán, lán, lán* (repeat)

And when grim death appears in a few unpleasant years
And says that my glass it has drawn
I'll say, Begone, you knave, for great Bacchus gave me leave
To fill another *crúiscín lán, lán, lán* (repeat)

Then fill your glasses high, let them part with lips not dry
For the lark now proclaims it is dawn
And since we can't remain, may we shortly meet again
To fill another *crúiscín lán, lán, lán* (repeat)

Contemporary Songwriting

Given the popularity and ubiquity of the guitar, the easy first-hand relationship that many Irish people have with poetry, and the creativity inherent in those who sing and play guitar, it should be no surprise that Irish songwriters have developed a wealth of new songs in English. Songwriters in Ireland are not in the least constrained by academic definitions of country, folk, blues, rock, or Irish traditional music, the way many professional songwriters are in the United States. Like most Irish people, most Irish songwriters listen to all kinds of recordings and radio stations, attend concerts, travel, memorize the lyrics of their favorite songs by people they admire, and have highly individualized relationships with Irish traditional music. In other words, they are every bit as diverse as songwriters in Britain, North America, and Australia.

Contemporary songwriters in Ireland number in the hundreds. Many, however, have drawn their initial inspiration from some of the originals in folk and rock from abroad: Woody Guthrie, Bob Dylan, Jimi Hendrix, Muddy Waters, and many others. Songwriters that became household names (including those who went into rock and blues) include Rory Gallagher, Van Morrison, Philip Lynott (of Thin Lizzy), and Bono (of U2). A few singer-songwriters who started out as solo artists ended up in the Irish supergroups such as Planxty, the Bothy Band, Sweeney's Men and others, discussed in Chapter 9.

Many Irish songwriters, including the very prolific and political Christy Moore, Bob Geldof (of the Boomtown Rats and "Live Aid" fame), and Sinéad O'Connor, infuse their songs with irony, sarcasm, and forthright discussions of social justice issues from abortion to the Troubles to human rights in El Salvador, Somalia, and elsewhere. While the initial numbers of Irish songwriters were born in the 1940s and 1950s, each new generation since then has produced hundreds more. The current generation includes singer-songwriters such as Glen Hansard, whose work was recently featured in the film *Once*, and whose work is much more reflective of Ireland's cosmopolitanism than of its insularity. Contemporary Irish songwriters tend to be male by an overwhelming majority.

Many of the ballad singers and singer-songwriters without an international profile have performed at local folk clubs, which are periodic gatherings of singers and their friends at a public venue—often in the back room of a pub. In the days before home recording was made easy and accessible, performance at a folk club was a way to get one's songs out in the public ear, to make important social and professional connections, and to try out new songs for constructive criticism. The difference between a folk club and a pub session is that a folk club assumes that singing will be an important part of the evening, and that close listening is appropriate rather than continuous chatter punctuated by applause. Furthermore, while some of the songs lend themselves exclusively to electric guitar accompaniment, many can just as easily be accompanied by either acoustic or electric. Guitar tunings are usually standard (EADGBE), rather than the more Irish-specific DADGAD tuning, and many Irish songwriters are comfortable performing covers of other writers' songs as well as their own.

In turning to acoustic music by individual musicians, let us consider an example of a somewhat more contemporary song. Tommy Sands is a Northern singer-songwriter who draws from real-life issues to create songs concerned with social justice. He has written many first-rate songs, and one stands out and continues to endure because of its universality in regard to sectarian conflict. His best-known song, "There Were Roses," combines his own experiences of the Troubles with his lifelong hope for lasting peace in the region. The song follows the true story of two men—one Catholic, one Protestant—whose inadvertent encounters with sectarian violence in 1974 belied their own friendships and personal histories across religious lines, leading to an untimely death for each. It follows the pattern of dense, narrative-laden verses with a spare and singable chorus. The melody of the verse (Figure 8.9), which follows the pattern of ABCB, is entirely in a major key, uses just three chords, and is in a fairly consistent rhythm throughout the song. Its form of two verses, chorus, two verses, chorus, is also reflective of a more general folksong form that finds its way into rock'n'roll as well.

My song for you this evening is not to make you sad
Nor for adding to the sorrows of this troubled Northern land
But lately I've been thinking and it just won't leave my mind
To tell you about two friends one time who were both good friends of mine.

Alan Bell from Benagh, he lived just across the fields
A great man for the music and the dancing and the reels

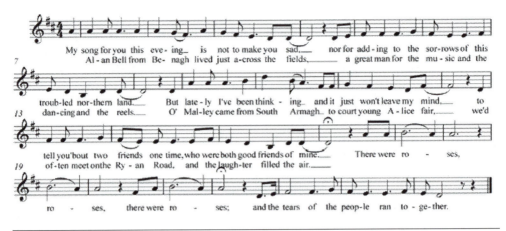

Figure 8.9 "There Were Roses," by Tommy Sands

O'Malley came from South Armagh to court young Alice fair
And we'd often meet on the Ryan Road and the laughter filled the air.

Chorus:
There were roses, roses, there were roses
And the tears of the people ran together.

Though Alan he was Protestant, and Seán was Catholic born
It never made a difference for the friendship it was strong
And sometimes in the evenings when we heard the sound of drums
We said, "It won't divide us, we will always be the one."

For the ground our fathers plowed on, the soil it is the same
And the places where we say our prayers have just got different names
We talked about the friends who died and we hoped there'd be no more
It's little then we realized the tragedy in store.

Chorus
It was on a Sunday morning when the awful news came round
Another killing has been done just outside Newry town
We knew that Alan danced up there, we knew he liked the band
But when we heard that he was dead, we just could not understand.

We gathered at the graveside on that cold and rainy day
And the minister he closed his eyes and he prayed for no revenge
And all the ones who knew him from along the Ryan Road
They bowed their heads and said a prayer for the resting of his soul.

Chorus
Well, fear it filled the countryside, there was fear in every home
When the car of death came prowling round the lonely Ryan Road

A Catholic would be killed tonight to even up the score
Oh Christ, it's young O'Malley that they've taken from the door.

"Alan was my friend!" he cried, he begged them with his fears
But centuries of hatred have ears that cannot hear
An eye for an eye, was all that filled their mind
And another eye for another eye, till everyone is blind.

Chorus
Now my song for you this evening is not to make you sad
Nor for adding to the sorrows of this troubled Northern land
But lately I've been thinking and it just won't leave my mind
To tell you about two friends one time who were both good friends of mine.

I don't know where the moral is, or where the song should end
But I wonder just how many wars are fought between good friends
And those who give the orders are not the ones to die
It's Bell, and O'Malley, and the likes of you and I.
Chorus

The poignancy of "There Were Roses" feels very different, and very contemporary, compared to the sectarian songs that you encountered in Chapter 3. This is one of the characteristics of contemporary songwriting: many (though not all) of the songs tend to focus less on historical issues and more on people's feelings, concerns, and interests of right now. More contemporary singer-songwriters include Paul Brady, Luka Bloom, Foy Vance, Luke Kelly, Damien Rice, Lisa Hannigan, James Vincent McMorrow, Hozier, and many others. None of these writers feels limited to writing about aspects of Ireland in their work; they are international artists. In addition, numerous non-Irish singer-songwriters perform contemporary Irish songs because of their appeal across national boundaries; "There Were Roses" has been covered by American country and bluegrass singer Kathy Mattea, for example. New instrumental tune compositions are also a continuing aspect of the contemporary scene (see Chapter 9).

How Do They *Do* That?

Listening to an Irish singer performing unaccompanied in either Irish or English can be a revelation for someone accustomed only to American hip hop or rock'n'roll. Irish people have a reputation internationally for their beautiful singing voices; this reputation comes from popular films, certainly, but also from the fame of the classic Irish tenor, an Irish archetype that first developed in the early nineteenth century in the person of Thomas Moore (see Chapter 3). The Irish tenor archetype continued during the nineteenth century and well into the twentieth century (with the many performances of John McCormack), and continues today with the music of the popular stars of North American public television, the "Three Irish Tenors" (Ronan Tynan, Anthony Kearns, Finbar Wright). With the exception of these tenors and, of course, the many classically trained singers who also happen to be Irish, most singers in Ireland use their normal speaking voices to sing. In other words, listening to someone speak is not very different from hearing that same person sing, in terms of overall vocal timbre. It sounds natural because it *is* natural.

The many high-speed twists and turns of Irish vocal ornaments can seem bewildering at first, and it can be difficult to figure out the underlying patterns that guide those ornaments. However, two main elements serve to guide the creation of vocal ornamentation: the melodic contours of the song, and the poetic rhythm of the lyrics. In following the melodic contours of a song, the singer has a variety of melodic ornaments at his or her disposal. Functionally speaking, an ornament can serve to connect two different pitches, to decorate a single pitch, and to highlight an important word in a song. In shifting from, say, the upper-register tonic down to the fifth, a singer might put in a turn prior to the descent, as in Figure 8.10. Notice that the ornament starts on the tonic, moves up one note, back to the tonic, down to the seventh, then down to the fifth, all on the second syllable of the word "nobleman." Furthermore, on the third syllable ("-man's"), the singer produces another turn on the fifth degree of the scale in order to move from the fifth to the third degree and down to the lower-register tonic. The two turns on one word allow the singer to drop a full octave gracefully and musically.

One of the great mysteries of Irish vocal ornaments is where to put them. In Chapter 6 you learned that it is important to know the actual songs upon which many instrumental airs are based, to "get" the proper ornamentation. In Chapter 7 you saw musical transcriptions of the complicated ornamentation in *sean-nós* songs. And in this chapter, above, you read about the importance of trochaic words in "sounding Irish." One key to the *placement* of ornaments in Irish songs has to do with the poetic rhythm: many of the most significant melodic ornaments occur on the *un*stressed syllables in the songs. When the language is primarily trochaic (emphasizing the first syllable of a two-syllable "foot" or metrical unit), whether it is in Irish or English, a melodic ornament is much more likely to occur on the second syllable. In the following example of a song fragment, notice that only one note occurs on the (stressed) first syllable, while a series of ornaments occurs on the (unstressed) second syllable. In Figure 8.11 (from the Irish-language song "An Tighearna Randal"), the trochaic word "leigí" includes an ornament on the second, unstressed syllable.

This principle of ornamentation does not determine the placement of every single ornament; however, it is one small window into part of a larger process. For one thing, not all words are trochaic, particularly when it comes to English-language songs. In

Figure 8.10 Fragment of "The Nobleman's Wedding"

Figure 8.11 Fourth line of "An Tighearna Randal"

the case of English-language songs with iambic stress patterns (emphasizing the second, rather than the first, syllable), the ornaments serve more of a connective purpose between main melody notes. Furthermore, in songs of either language with multisyllabic words, ornamentation reverts to following the pattern of appearing on unstressed syllables.

Many song verses in both languages feature a last line (or a first and last line) with very little melodic material, particularly at the end of the last line. Because the melody of the final line of each verse tends to focus on just one or two notes, even as the words continue to the end, it is common for the singer to speak the final words of the final verse. As a way of supporting the singer, other participants in the song session join in singing or speaking the final words. Doing so connects the singer to the rest of the group, shows respect to the singer and the song, and allows others the deep satisfaction that arises from participation. Anyone listening to either of these final lines knows that singing along quietly, or at least humming the last line, is appropriate.

Lilting

Irish people—not just singers and dancers, but many others as well—sometimes use "vocables" (words with no lexical meaning) to imitate the sound of instrumental music. This technique is called lilting, or diddling, or "mouth music." The fact that Irish lilting has no lexical meaning (in other words, there are no actual understandable words) is a major point of separation from the mouth music of Scotland (and Cape Breton). Lilting is handy when there are no instruments close by, when one musician is trying to remind another of how a tune proceeds, when one is trying to entertain children who would like to dance around, and for entertainment. The letters d, r, b, and l are most commonly used, as in "diddly-dye, dary do." The word "diddly" is often used to represent a triplet; in fact, Green Linnet Records produced a T-shirt with the words "diddly diddly" on it because the word was—and is—such a stereotypically Irish sound (and rhythm).

How does one lilt? Just for fun, listen to any one of the dance tunes on the accompanying CD and try to produce it just with your mouth. It's like singing along with a song, except that you're in charge of making up the sounds. Unlike in scat singing (in jazz), which also imitates the sound of a musical instrument, the amount of improvisation you are expected to develop is limited to minor variation, just as if you were playing a fiddle. Try "Moran's Fancy" or "The Hag's Purse," both of which are played at a moderate tempo. Try this phrase for the first phrase of "Moran's Fancy": "da-ry diddly do-dee ah-dul-eye-dul" and *keep going*. And for the first phrase of "The Hag's Purse," start out with "*dye*-dee-iddle-dum," and *keep going*. Use the same kinds of sounds. There are many right ways to do this sort of thing, and it is never formally taught; if you aren't having fun, though, you're not doing it right.

If lilting is never taught, and traditional singing in either language is supposed to be picked up through oral tradition, it can be more challenging when one grows up outside of the Gaeltacht. The *sean-nós* singer Joe Heaney used to announce to his American audiences that "you have two ears and one mouth, so that you can listen twice as much as you speak." While he probably said this to get his American audiences to listen more closely and fidget (or talk) less, he offered at least one way to learn the songs: listen! Prior to the nineteenth century, most singers picked up song lyrics and melodies from their family members, friends, and neighbors. The long nights of song repetition made transmission relatively easy from one person to the next. If the neighbors sang in Irish, one learned Irish-language songs; if one's family sang in English, then those songs would predominate. Songs that came home with family members who had traveled abroad were shared as well. Broadsheets spread up-to-date lyrics across the island as well, and the sheet music of Thomas Moore (see Chapter 3) brought standardized (and cleaned up) versions of many Irish songs into middle-class homes in both Ireland and Irish America. The radio, which was established in Ireland in the newly post-Independent days of the 1920s, brought music from all over Ireland (and abroad) into the homes of anyone with a "wireless" (radio). Early recordings—both domestic and American— had a similar effect; tunes and songs both were listened to with great interest.

Given the long history of the Irish and literacy (starting with the scholar-monks of the first millennium C.E.), it should come as no surprise that many of the songs passed on in both Irish and English should bear some influence from written lyrics. Many families participated in the efforts of the Irish Folklore Commission by collecting and writing down song lyrics from family members (and from themselves) in the nineteenth and early twentieth centuries. In addition, the marketing and distribution of broadside ballads contributed to the easy relationship between orality and literacy. By the end of the twentieth century, though, plenty of children in Ireland were being taught to sing local tunes by committed schoolteachers who were determined to keep the traditions going in whatever ways they could manage.

In contemporary terms, the fact that many singers can pull lyrics off the Internet and tunes from recordings by other singers has led to a type of secondary orality: one might not be learning from the original source, but one can still learn something from those who have passed away by accessing their recordings. What this learning method lacks is the human interaction between master and pupil, as well as the opportunity to hear fifty versions of the same song (and in so doing, to develop one's own relationship to the song). The precise duplication of "the master"—right down to the vocal ornaments or special turns of phrase from one verse to the next—through imitation of recordings is less of a fortuitous way to learn than listening to live music. It is still one way to work with the songs of some of the greatest singers, but it is no substitute for the original singer and his or her many and varied performances of the same songs. On the other hand, some of the greatest singers in history lived and sang in the twentieth century (and into the present), long past the advent of recording technology, and no one questions their integrity or their grasp of the authenticity of tradition. It is a testament to the flexibility and vitality of Irish song that multiple modes of learning can still produce magnificent singers in either language.

Discussion Questions

1. Why would it be a political statement to sing in one language or another?
2. Can you think of any contemporary songs (in hip hop, rock, pop, or country) that use the technique of "leaping and lingering"—zipping through the plot in order to focus on emotional content or dialogue?
3. If you were to write a broadside ballad today, what scandalous or currently newsworthy (but in the long run, perhaps not so relevant) topic would you choose?

4. Compare the lyrics of "The Lass of Aughrim" in Chapter 8 with the lyrics as sung on the accompanying CD. How do they differ, and what does each version tell you about the heart of the story?
5. Think about examples of melismatic singing—many notes being sung on one syllable—in American popular music. When do you hear it, who does it, and what impact does it have on the audience?

CHAPTER 9

New Contexts for Music and Dance

Ní ghabhann dorn dúnta seabhac ~ A closed fist won't catch a hawk.

In the Republic of Ireland, which had experienced considerable economic difficulties up to and including the early 1960s, the practice and performance of traditional music began to pick up in the late 1960s and 1970s. Prior to that time, the steady march of emigrants *out* of the island reflected the fact that economic opportunities were scarce whether one was a bricklayer or a musician, or both. The American folk music revival had, by then, spread to England and Ireland, leading to the cross-Atlantic popularity of the Clancy Brothers and Tommy Makem (guitar- and banjo-playing ballad singers who performed in rich harmony with robust voices). Some of the first factories opened in Ireland, employing young people and offering economic independence (and the ability to spend money on music). The Chieftains were formed; they performed careful arrangements of Irish instrumental dance tunes using traditional (and occasionally classical) instruments. The composer, musician, and academic Seán Ó Riada wrote influential film scores using Irish materials, and made a powerful impact through radio and journalism. Comhaltas Ceoltóirí Éireann ("organization of Irish musicians"), an organization that promotes Irish traditional music and dance, had been formed during the period in which Irish traditional music was at its most moribund, but it gained significant momentum during the 1960s and 1970s, hosting festivals and making recordings (see "The Revival(s)" below). Comhaltas Ceoltóirí Éireann is still thriving today.

Ireland joined what was to become the European Union in 1973, and gradually became the beneficiary of considerable money, planning expertise, and infrastructure over the next several decades. By the mid-1990s, Europe's once-poor cousin—the Republic of Ireland—had become popularly known as the home of the "Celtic Tiger" (named after the economic growth of the "Asian Tigers" of Singapore, South Korea, and others) for its extraordinary economic boom. Beyond the support coming from the

European Union, however, Ireland shifted very rapidly from a struggling young nation to one of the most economically solvent nations in Europe. Its musicians achieved international recognition, and the stage production *Riverdance* was playing to large audiences at home and abroad (see "Riverdance Dancing," below). The power of the Catholic Church had declined for multiple reasons, and Irish exiles began returning to take advantage of the economic opportunities that were appearing all over the country. Ireland was never so popular a place to visit, nor so economically successful, as it was at that moment in the late 1990s; for the first time in recorded history, more people entered it than left it.

By the end of the 1990s, the popularity of *Riverdance* and the economic boom in both Ireland and America made Americans aware that—at the time—Ireland was easy to visit, largely English-speaking, and relatively inexpensive. "Heritage tours" that had been quietly taking place for decades suddenly took on a new urgency, as North Americans decided to connect with their roots. Courses in Irish Studies became increasingly popular, and the North American ranks of step dancing classes swelled. The festivals and summer schools (mentioned in Chapter 1) drew, collectively, thousands of participants, all of whom returned home each year with stories, new tunes, and an enhanced understanding of the Irish traditional music scene and their role in it. Leaders in both the arts and academia in the United States conceived and developed multiple Irish music and culture events (Gaelic Roots at Boston College, Irish Arts Week in New York's Catskills, Milwaukee's Irish Fest, and both the Cascadia Irish Music Week and Sean-nós Northwest in Olympia, the capital of Washington state). That popularity persists today.

In terms of the recording industry, performers such as Enya, Loreena McKennit, and Iarla Ó Lionaird (*sean-nós* singer, also of Afro-Celt Sound System fame) saw strong sales of their recordings and concert tickets, and Europe's pan-Celtic music festivals took off in popularity. The word "Celtic" was *in*, and became a catch-all marketing term. Various Celtic-themed groups have included the current touring groups "Celtic Thunder" and "Celtic Woman," cashing in on the essentialist nature of the term and its marketability, particularly in the United States. Irish and Irish-American hard rock and punk acts are just as essential to the current scene as any of the others, and express yet another aspect of contemporary life.

What this cluster of timing, market forces, music, and a pervasive need for authenticity has created is an "everything and nothing" sensibility that aspires to be all things to all people, but may simply create more need. The contemporary reality of Irish music around the world is one in which cell phone ringtones can play a clip from one of the current Irish punk, or traditional, or pop hits; no area or style is truly undiscovered; and *sean-nós* songs are not limited to the Gaeltacht but are sung in San Francisco, Tokyo, *and* Dublin. Online discussions featuring enthusiasts from all over the world urgently debate the final measure of a particular reel, or argue whether something could rightly be called a highland; think of it as a kind of online pub discussion among amateur musicians, except that the participants will not be helping each other to bring in the hay the next afternoon. The island is increasingly wired for Internet use, and many people are politically active. The global interconnectedness of the Irish is old, but it seems much more explicit, and certainly faster, now.

By the end of the first decade of the twenty-first century, the headiness of the "Celtic Tiger" days had disappeared into cautionary tales about a recession, and jokes about how "we killed the Tiger." The people for whom Irishness was just a temporary infatuation had moved on to other things. By that time, Irish traditional music in its current form had become well established as a viable, unapologetically popular art form in many places. Many more people now take advantage of the ease of travel, the all-access aspects of the Internet for tune learning, and the wealth of local sources to play, sing, and listen to Irish music in numbers that have not been seen previously. The Irish music scene is, in fact, blossoming into a kind of new Golden Age at the start of the third decade of the twenty-first century, at least partly through the new media, the competitions, the festivals (see below), and to an even greater extent through the passion and dedication of thousands of players and enthusiasts.

Competitions and Festivals

Irish musicians and dancers have participated in competitions since the earliest days of oral tradition. Chapter 2, for example, discussed bardic competitions that reflected, for better or worse, on their patrons. It was partly because of these early competitions and festivals that the Belfast Harp Festival of 1792—which yielded such rich material for future generations—was held. It was also Ireland's history of competition that led the Gaelic League to make competitions and festivals a part of their list of priorities. Also known as Conradh na Gaeilge, the Gaelic League was and is a pro-Irish group established in 1893. It was originally conceived as an apolitical organization, but it attracted language enthusiasts (including its founder, Douglas Hyde), musicians, dancers, Church authorities, many members of various Irish Independence movements, and members of the openly political Gaelic Athletic Association. Part of the impetus behind the founding of the Gaelic League was to preserve and promote all things that were believed to be most traditionally Irish, including harp music, *uilleann* piping, the Irish language (spoken and sung), and dance. Note that in promoting what were believed to be the nobler aspects of traditional Irish culture, the Gaelic League was working hard against the stereotyped images of the stage Irishman (Whelan 2000: 17) being promoted in England and North America at the time.

The contemporary scene in music (for dance, see below) includes instrument-specific competitions, such as pipers' gatherings; competitions primarily for singers and reciters in Irish (in particular, the annual Oireachtas na Gaeilge); and weekend- and weeklong celebrations that also include competitive segments. A modern *fleadh cheoil* or music festival is intended to engage local attention and interest in traditional music. All summer long the *fleadhanna* and competitions thrive on the tourists who attend, but they are also popular among the many musicians and dancers who come "just for the *craic*," together with the local players and citizens. A well-known *fleadh* can attract thousands of people; the national (All-Ireland) *fleadh* can attract over 100,000 people (Vallely 2011: 269).

Perhaps the most important aspect of any festival or competition is the spontaneous musical activity occurring off stage. At almost any Irish festival, most of the nearby pubs are packed with bystanders who watch musicians performing at finger-blistering speeds, all of which are fueled by a combination of enthusiasm, alcohol, and competition. Halls or large tents are set aside for evening set dancing (sometimes preceded by a brief set of young children doing step dancing), and impromptu sessions can start up anywhere. The social scene at all of these events is quite lively; restaurants stay open late, people throng the shops in the town, and most of the local young people find a reason to be present at the goings-on. Some festivals feature a nightly "singers' club," in which a host acts as the MC by acknowledging singers of status, welcoming newcomers, telling jokes, encouraging the shy singers to participate, and ensuring that the evening passes congenially. As normal as it may seem, this sort of music festival, culminating in crowds of all-ages musicians sitting outside, playing jigs and reels (or polkas and slides) everywhere, has been taking place only since the 1950s.

A small town in County Clare maintains the appearance of hosting a lively *fleadh* on a daily basis, summer after summer. You first encountered Doolin (population 600) in Chapter 1; it is home to just a few pubs featuring traditional music, yet it caters to thousands of foreign tourists each year. It was one of the "source villages" of Ireland's revival of traditional music in the latter decades of the twentieth century (Kaul 2004: 22). In a strange combination of financial serendipity, planning, and the willingness of tour operators to bring their charges in full busloads, each of the pubs creates a seemingly authentic Irish musical experience for those who have a limited amount of time between visiting the Cliffs of Moher and the Lakes of Killarney. In a fairly typical scenario, a tour bus pulls up to one of the pubs, parking next to a handful of other tour buses. The people tumble out of the bus, run for the restroom, order their pints and a snack or a meal, and take photographs (and videos) of actual live musicians playing traditional Irish music. Some of the musicians, however, could easily be South African, or Polish, or German; one does not, after all, have to be Irish to play Irish music. After a suitable interval, the tourists climb back on the bus, and another bus rolls in just having visited the Cliffs of Moher. Rather than drifting in at some point after dinner for a pint and a few tunes, these are paid musicians who work shifts during the summer. Doolin is only one of a set of villages scattered across the west coast of Ireland whose inhabitants try to provide an authentic Irish musical experience.

Does this description fit in with your image of an authentically Irish experience? If not, how would you describe one? If you allow for the facts that a great instrumentalist of Irish music does not have to be genetically Irish, that Ireland is increasingly international, that the tunes being played are genuinely Irish for the most part, and that many tourists are present in tourist pubs to *see* rather than to *hear*, then a need has been met. Perhaps Ireland and its people have many ways, not just one way, to engage musically with outsiders, from playing side-by-side at a *fleadh* to inviting a conversation and a song from a foreigner in a pub. Authentic-seeming pubs, staged "Irish shows" in Dublin and other large cities, and the international phenomenon of *Riverdance* are just part of the musical texture that attempts to offer something for everyone. It is certainly worth asking how much a genre (or a culture, or a society) can change before it loses its integrity. By the same token, it is also worth considering whether demanding that a musical style remain frozen in time (and image) is either possible or desirable. Most musicians would say that it cannot and should not be.

Musical Notation

Ever since the time of Edward Bunting and his notations at the Belfast Harp Festival of 1792, musicians, composers, and scholars of Irish music have worked with notation as an archival resource and as a tool for learning and teaching. During the late nineteenth and early twentieth centuries when collecting local tunes (and stories, and aspects of

Irish folklore) was considered not just important, but functioned as part of the national-ist effort, there was a sense that some of the older tunes might be lost if people stopped playing them. This was also part of the motivation of RTÉ (Raidió Telefís Éireann) in sending out a mobile recording machine and technician during the 1950s and 1960s. Tunes that were recorded in this manner were then played on the radio; through nota-tion and dissemination via recordings and radio, many tunes that might have been lost were preserved and revived.

The notation of Irish music can take several forms. The most common notation is Western staff notation, such as is used in this book (see Chapter 6, for example). Because Irish music can be notated effectively in this manner (and can be therefore made acces-sible to anyone who can read staff notation), it is often a first choice for notation. Do not lose sight, however, of the fact that plenty of Irish musicians *themselves* can read music notation, but generally do not use, or need it. One's ready access to local play-ers through family and social networks generally negates the need for a contemporary written record of one's own local tunes.

Another type of notation is called abc, and was originally developed in North America as a method for computerized notation of Western dance music (not specifi-cally Irish); it is used for single-line melodies that would normally use one staff. In a typical example of abc notation, a double jig such as "The Cook in the Kitchen" would appear as follows, with the capital letters in the left column representing certain fea-tures explained here by the bracketed comments. Once the tune starts, each measure is represented by two groups of three notes; capitalized letters indicate the central octave on the staff; small letters indicate an octave above, while letters followed by a comma indicate the octave below. Sharps are indicated by a circumflex (^) before the affected note. A note held for two beats is represented by a letter and the number 2. First and second endings begin the measure with 1 or 2. Colons indicate repeat signs. This tune is divided into four lines: the first two lines are the tune, and the second two lines are the turn.

X:1 [number of tunes with this title]
T: The Cook in the Kitchen [title]
M: 6/8 [meter]
L: 1/8 [default note value]
R: jig (or double jig) [form or rhythm]
K: Gmix [key—in this case, G mixolydian; like a major scale with a flatted seventh]
:DGG GAG	FDE FEF	DGG G^FG	A2d cAG
DGG GAG	FDE F2d	cAG ^FGA	1BG^F G2E:	2BG^F G2A
:B3 BAG	A3 AGE	DGG G^FG	A2d cAG
B3 BAG |A3 A2d |cAG ^FGA |1BG^F G2A: |2BG^F G:	

Now compare this version of notation to the staff notation in Figure 9.1. If you can-not read music, but could find notes by name on an instrument (a piano, for example), would you be able to read abc notation? Some people find abc notation extremely help-ful and clear in the transmission of tunes, particularly because so few people have music notation software on their computers.

In addition to staff notation and abc notation, a number of musicians have developed their own systems of notation, including another version of abc! Some fiddle players

Figure 9.1 "The Cook in the Kitchen"

use a graph representing the strings and positions of the fingers on those strings. These systems are traded freely among musicians; however, keep in mind that notation itself is *not* the primary form of transmission of tunes or songs, and it is not even particularly common. No experienced musician uses notation to play in public, and few use it in private unless they are learning a new tune or recalling a forgotten one when no other musicians are around to ask. It is simply one of many ways—including making a recording—that some but not all people can use.

Many collections of Irish tunes are widely available. For some areas within the United States and Canada, a large city might have its own tune book, including the tunes that local players enjoy at sessions as well as those popular regionally or nationally. Other tune books simply try to cover as many tunes as the collector can find, or the favorite tunes of the collector. Many fiddle instruction books include a variety of common tunes, and are good resources for those who are first learning to play each of the forms.

Breandán Breathnach's four-volume *Ceol Rince na hÉireann* ("Dance Music of Ireland") has been one of several "bibles" of traditional dance music. Breathnach was a piper, writer, and collector who was crucial to the continuation of Irish traditional music in the twentieth century. In 1968, he founded Na Píobairí Uilleann, the major Irish piping society which thrives today in multiple branches both at home and abroad. Captain Francis O'Neill was a Chicago city chief superintendent of police; born in Ireland and having spent considerable time at sea, he was passionate about Irish music. He and his colleague James O'Neill (no relation) developed several resources for Irish musicians after realizing that not everyone knew the same tunes that he did. Their publications, *The Music of Ireland* (1903, containing 1,850 tunes) and *The Dance Music of Ireland—1001 Gems* (1907) have served as outstanding resources for enthusiasts of Irish music. *Irish Minstrels and Musicians* is another resource of biographical scholarship.

The ubiquitous nature of cell phones wherever Irish music is played assumes that people will record sessions, for better or worse. It is always right to ask before making a recording, and to promise not to post anything online without permission. Few people object to the person recording one round of a tune for the purpose of learning it before the next session. Several phone apps—TunePal is one—can make a short recording of a tune (live or on a recording) and offer suggestions as to which tune it might be.

Dancing Feet, On and Offstage

The image of the modern Irish female step dancer is quite a compelling one: the black shoes, white socks and bare legs, stiff body, heavy appliquéd costume, and bouncy wig of tight little curls appears as a classic image in the tourist literature, yet it is a fairly recent one. In North America, it is one of the most common images associated with the Irish. Yet in Ireland, this image is commonly associated with Irish *America*! One could be born and raised in Ireland and never see a step dancer, except perhaps on television or in a local parade. Even then, the dancers would likely be young girls, dancing together rather than solo. It is worth considering what it means to dance Irish dances from multiple perspectives, particularly Irish ones. Irish dance includes a handful of different styles: step dancing (both old style and modern), *sean-nós* dancing, set dancing (in a group), *céilí* dancing (also in a group), and, possibly, "Riverdance" dancing. The American *sean-nós* dancer and teacher Maldon Meehan breaks these down into categories of solo and social dancing, with Riverdance one step, as it were, beyond social dancing because it is staged, facing one direction, for a non-participatory audience. In addition to these categories, many local dances thrive in specific regions. This discussion is limited to what one is most likely to experience as a visitor. Note, also, that it is customary in Irish dance to refer to the male half of a dancing couple as the "gent," and the female half as the "lady," regardless of who is dancing. Because women often outnumber men at dances, partners new to each other will ask: Are you the gent or the lady? Understanding one's dancing role facilitates the ability of the two dancers to participate in a group. Furthermore, some of the holds described in the section on set dancing are also used in *céilí* dancing.

In the earliest days of the Gaelic League, both *céilí* and step dancing were being taught to the League's growing membership, with lively debates about the rules (and about pedagogy) filling the pages of the League's newspaper. Dances perceived as non-native—even if they were regularly danced and enjoyed by the Irish—were treated as worthy of banning by competing personalities both within and outside the League; it was "a cultural civil war with dance as the arena of combat" (Brennan 1999: 31). The early twentieth-century Commission for Irish Dance was another attempt to exercise control over Irish dance, weeding out undesirable elements (Ó hAllmhuráin 1998: 111), and promoting a certain comportment, set of steps, and—in essence—a particularly Catholic morality.

> When [the parish priest] came upon a house dance he would storm in the door and proceed to scatter the dancers with his blackthorn stick, beating the musician and often putting his instrument into the fire. The boys would also get a good belt of the stick, and the girls would be marched home to their fathers who were encouraged to put the fear of God into them with a few lashes of the belt. The priest, having performed his so-called godly duty, would then use his most powerful weapon of intimidation and fear—the denouncing of the dancers and musician to all the parish from the altar at Sunday Mass.
>
> (Whelan 2000: 16)

In such a climate of apparent repression, one might be tempted to think that dancing and music would cease, yet they did not. Even after the passing of the Public Dance Halls

Act in 1935, which decreed that all dancing, anywhere in Ireland, must be licensed (with priests holding the licenses), and many of the "house dances" that had been so popular across the country going into immediate decline, Irish dancing continued unabated. Because the United States did not have an equivalent of such a law, Irish dancing *grew* in popularity as a means of connection to the "old country." And now, after all these years, the Public Dance Halls Act is still on the books in Ireland, and one must still acquire a license for dancing. Even popular nightclubs and lapdancing clubs are subject to its effects. After the 1950s, the power of the Church began (slowly) to wane, and the cultural revival that had started as a literary trend at the turn of the century moved to music, and caught up with dance as well. By the 1990s, set dancing had become the most popular form of group dance in the southern part of the Republic, and *céilí* dancing drew large numbers of people further north. Both styles, however, are performed all over the island, and all over the world where Irish people gather for the *craic*—good times, laughter, and spending time with friends.

Step Dancing

Irish step dancers carry their bodies upright and keep their arms straight for specific reasons, but the folklore of *why* they do what they do is rich. Stories about the reason for the rigid body abound; some of the most common reasons that one hears are: (1) it was so that priests couldn't see if someone was dancing when they passed by the window; (2) it was because the English forbade dancing; (3) dancing on a half door meant one couldn't easily swing one's arms without hitting something or someone; and (4) keeping the arms still led to more attention being paid to the feet. Yet the strongest historical evidence for the straight body comes from the Gaelic League itself, which—in awarding prizes at competitions—held evolving standards of dance (and generations of dancers) to a specific set of rules that rewarded a more obedient, uplifted, and innocent look. Keeping one's back and arms straight is also very difficult; swinging one's hips or relaxing one's arms is much easier. For competitions, therefore, making everything more challenging enables the judges to hold everyone to a consistent standard. Dancers wear both hard shoes and soft shoes, and use them for different aspects of the dance: hard shoes are for some reels, solo set dances, hornpipes, and some jigs. Soft shoes are for slip jigs, other reels, and single jigs.

Step dancing began in Ireland with the development of the custom of traveling dance masters in the eighteenth century. A dance master would move from county to county every few weeks, teaching people particular steps, and they would carry that on after the dance master left. He might also teach deportment and genteel behavior to his charges (Whelan 2000: 12), and use a local barn for lessons. "Generally, a dancing master had no home of his own and lodged with a local family during his stay, when the family concerned would have the benefit of extra (and free) tuition" (Brennan 1999: 49). All of these lessons and development of local customs took place well before the Gaelic League attempted to regulate the steps or licensed any dancing masters. It was common for adults to step dance (both for fun and for informal competitions), and its relative degree of exhibitionism and celebration of the individual instead of the group was fluid as attention shifted from one dancer to the next.

The solo step dancer specializes in several of the forms described in Chapter 6, including the reel, the hornpipe, and jig; solo set dances are also a part of the repertoire.

While the hornpipe is English in origin, it is very popular among step dancers because, when the music is played slowly enough, the form allows the dancer to fill in a dazzling array of steps, including triplets. A solo set dance (not to be confused with "set danc-ing," below) is "set" in hard shoes to a specific tune, such as "The Blackbird" or "The Hunt" (Whelan 2000: 26). While for some Irish people step dancing is something best left to those under the age of 13, for others it is a joyous expression of youthful individu-ality that they still love to perform in adulthood. Step dancing can bring back happy memories; it can also express feelings of national pride (Figure 9.2).

Modern step dances are done in eight-bar sequences that allow the dancers to match the eight-bar structure of the music. In Chapter 6 you read about the different forms of tunes, and noted, perhaps, the consistency of the AABB structure in many of the tunes discussed. The "mighty tunes" with multiple parts (an AABBCCDDEE structure, for example) are more useful to someone doing a set dance, whereas a simpler tune with AABB structure is better for a hornpipe. In doing a particular step choreography, the dancer needs to be symmetrical in moving to the right, then duplicating the step by moving to the left. This symmetry in movement (to the right, to the left) is a hallmark of step dancing, both modern and "old-style" (see below).

Modern step dancing in particular can be intensely popular and competitive, par-ticularly in the United States, but also in Australia, England, and other diasporic areas. Frank Whelan estimates that about 50,000 Americans take classes in Irish step danc-ing (Whelan 2000: 22), and spend their weekends traveling to and from competitions. Dresses alone can easily cost upwards of several thousand dollars, and the frequency of competitions means that wins and losses are important topics of conversation. The

Figure 9.2 American step dancers at a competition. Photo courtesy of Caryn M. Ice

curly wigs, tiaras, spray-tanned legs, and heavy face makeup are all an aspect of post-1980s step dance competitions in the United States, and are making inroads in Ireland as well. Much of contemporary step dancing is done to recorded music except in competitions, and much of the recorded music is performed on an electronic keyboard. The supportive industry for outfitting the step dancers is significant; between the wigs, the jewelry, the costumes, and other accoutrements, there is plenty of money to be made.

While it might appear easy to dismiss the *idea* of step dancing in costume as something frivolous, other perspectives may add some clarity here. Competitive dancing is athletic; it takes a dozen hours a week or more of intensive practicing—no wig, no dress, no makeup—to maintain one's strength and form. The weekend meetings, competitions, and other events are an opportunity to see one's friends, enjoy dancing with like-minded people, and push oneself to do one's best. As for the makeup, the strong lighting onstage tends to wash out one's appearance just as in any performance, and the wigs turn out to be a handy substitute for forcing one's hair into ringlets by sleeping on curlers. While the United States has many more step dancers than Ireland has, the popularity of step dancing abroad—including in Japan and Australia—feeds back to Ireland in a continuous cycle.

"Old-style" Step Dancing

A related but distinct genre, old-style step dance, originated in the Munster (southwestern) region, and a variant of it is danced in County Clare. As the root form of contemporary step dance, old-style step dance derives from the tradition of the Munster dancing masters who—unlike those further north—were more settled in a particular area. Each dance master would have an acknowledged territory of a certain number of square miles; within that territory he (and it was a male teacher) would be responsible for teaching specific step dances and social dances. Breandán Breathnach notes that friendly rivalries would spring up between local dancing masters, and the competitions that ensued were danced publicly at such venues as fairs and sporting events (Breathnach 1971: 50). These very localized competitions eventually led to the entire custom of international competitions (*feiseanna*) for which modern step dance is so famous today.

> From references to step dance we find that the performance practice was one which was earthy in style, confined to personal space, and dominated by men. References to performances on half doors, flag stones, and tops of barrels is evident of this confinement of space. Indeed it was an aesthetic value that step dancers have the ability to perform within a confined space, thus requiring a neat performance directly under the dancer's centre of weight.
>
> (Foley 1999: 380)

In comparing old-style step dance with modern step dance, both physical and musical differences are clear. Modern step dancers perform many of the same steps in eight-bar patterns, but with more syncopation and flair. Like modern step dance, old-style dance includes symmetrical traveling patterns to both the left and the right. In old-style step dance the arms are more relaxed than in modern step dance, but not as loose as in *sean-nós* dance (see below). In further comparison, old-style step dance focuses energy and movement on the toes, whereas *sean-nós* dance relies primarily on the heels as the center of gravity. Old-style step dance is much more closely linked with the music than modern step dance, with fewer beats and somewhat slower music accompanying the individual steps to allow the open spaces to have their own musical function. Old-style dance *and* modern step dance each feature set dances, in which individuals dance to specific multi-part tunes, including "The Blackbird" (Munster) and "The Priest and his Boots" (Clare).

The contemporary context for old-style step dance is limited for two reasons. First, modern step dance dominates the world competitive scene entirely, and the written rules for it (set up by *An Coimisiún le Rincí Gaelacha*—The Irish Dancing Commission) are rigidly unalterable. Second, the only other established traditional solo style—*sean-nós* dance, below—has its own dominant scene in Connemara and at the Oireachtas competition for *sean-nós* singing. The more old-style step dancers that attend *sean-nós* dance events and join in the competitions, the greater the possibility of blending of the two distinct styles.

Sean-nós Dancing

What is now called *sean-nós* ("old style") dance comes primarily from the southern region of Connemara in the western Gaeltacht (West Galway), though other areas have local solo dance traditions as well. The term was first applied to the older style of step dance in the 1970s at an Oireachtas competition for *sean-nós* singing; prior to that point it was called *an bhatráil* (the battering), and it has experienced a resurgence in popularity that continues today (Brennan 1999: 383). *Sean-nós* dance features two highlights in particular: the relaxed upper body and arms, and the short distance between the soles of the feet and the ground (Figure 9.3). One idea behind its name is that it predates twentieth-century Gaelic League regulations; it is also markedly different from step dancing in its richness of individual style. Like *sean-nós* singing, it is what the individual brings to it that matters. Furthermore, *sean-nós* dance is generally performed to live music, allowing for and encouraging a high degree of artistic engagement between the dancer and the musician.

Each dancer has his or her basic step, and it is characteristic of the genre for dancers to avoid precisely duplicating the steps of others. Two basic steps—for reels and, more rarely, for jigs—characterize the building blocks of *sean-nós* dance. The Connemara reel step starts on the third beat of the measure with a flat-footed step (beat "three") followed with a heel brush and a step ("and four") by the other foot. Two more steps follow in succession, with heel brushes on the *off* beats and steps on the *on* beats. The basic jig step in 6/8 time is an alternating right (and)–left–right and left (and)–right–left; with the first step lasting two eighth notes, the second step lasting one eighth note, and the third step lasting three eighth notes. These rhythms can be danced in place or used to travel. In either rhythm, the feet remain close to the floor. It is the improvised variations adopted and adapted by individual dancers that make *sean-nós* dancing so compelling to watch.

The informality of *sean-nós* dance means that while it is sometimes danced on a stage (as in competitions), its primary mode of performance is informal. At an instrumental session at a pub or in a home, someone might jump up and dance just one dance, followed by another person, followed by another; or the first person might dance just

Figure 9.3 *Sean-nós* dancer Annie Devane (accompanied by Seamus Tansey), Connemara

two repetitions of the tune before someone else jumps in. Because all the good *sean-nós* dancers are familiar with the forms of the music, and because most of them have known the local tunes their entire lives, it is a sign of respect to the tradition, together with great skill, for the dancer to physically interpret the tune being played live. For example, a tune with triplets in a particular measure might have that special pattern affirmed by the dancer's feet; similarly, a tune with syncopation, or a repetitive pattern, or some other special characteristic will find its way into the dance. There is a particular sensitivity to the individual tune that links up with the sensitivity and listening skills of the dancer. All of that specificity points to a relationship between dancer and instrumentalist that is much more aurally intimate.

In contrast to step dancing, *sean-nós* and the other dances described below appeal to a distinctly adult sensibility. While children can and do dance *sean-nós* with great skill, much of its appeal to adults is that—as a dance genre—it encourages a relaxed, adult body and a highly individualized form. *Sean-nós* dancing had just begun, by the mid-1990s, to make its way across the Atlantic to North America. In a continent of Irish-Americans dominated by the image of the prepubescent, decorated step dancer (or the image of an adult dressed like one), the contrast with the more adult (and much more sensuous) dancing is particularly striking. In Ireland, too, *sean-nós* dancing has seen a strong upswing in popularity, particularly in the current climate of increased sexual freedom and the loss of social control by the Church.

The major yearly competition for *sean-nós* dance is the Oireachtas or competition that features *sean-nós* singing, not dancing. In other words, while step dancers and others are gathering at their own Oireachtas for step dance, the *sean-nós* dancers gather with the Irish-speaking *sean-nós* singers, reciters, and their enthusiasts! The competition, then, is about celebrating the individuality of *sean-nós* aesthetics, not about costuming or precision in form. Being part of a competition week for singers keeps the value system of *sean-nós* dance more closely related to the older ethos of Gaelic culture, and completely separate from step dance, which is so closely connected to the competitive scene outside of Ireland.

Clothing is always informal except during competitions, where it is one or two steps up from daily wear; women may wear either pants or dresses, and men might wear a brightly colored shirt that emphasizes the chest and allows the arms to stretch easily out from the sides. The idea in both men and women's clothing is to contrast strongly from that used in step dancing. Most dancers wear special shoes for competitions, and many other dancers bring their dancing shoes to parties in case the occasion for a dance should arise. A dancer's shoes are just as important to him or her as a musical instrument is to a musician. The use of taps on the shoes in competitions is controversial; in recent years the use of taps has been forbidden at the (*sean-nós*) Oireachtas, and their use is still debated. Raidió na Gaeltachta ("radio of the Gaeltacht")—an Irish-language branch of RTÉ—broadcasts the *sean-nós* singing and recitation at the Oireachtas. TG4, the national Irish-language television station, broadcasts the *sean-nós* dancing as it happens, and its coverage has helped to further heighten the popularity of the style.

Céilí Dancing

The term *céilí dance* has two meanings. First, a *céilí* dance is an evening of social dancing in which sets and other group dances will likely be danced. In the term's second meaning, *céilí dances* can include specific two-hand and three-hand dances, line dances, circle dances, and other patterns. In the northern part of Ireland, actual *céilí dances* may be a part of the evening, and *céilí dances* have a different origin and style from set dances. The differences between *céilí dances* and set dances is that *céilí dances* are often believed to be entirely indigenous to Ireland, whereas set dances had their origin outside of Ireland. However, the Gaelic League and other organizations of the time had a strong hand in the development and, in fact, the creation of *céilí* dances by the end of the nineteenth century.

> The céilí dances satisfied the revivalist cultural mores of the Gaelic League. The Gaelic League in London first used the term céilí in reference to dance in 1897; it felt that the word céilí—a term in use primarily in Ireland's northern counties to describe a friendly house visit—would impart a homey feeling and attract a crowd to an upcoming league-sponsored dance. The dance repertoire, consisting of 'Sets, Quadrilles, and Waltzes to Irish music,' was carefully conceived that evening to create a strong image of Irish identity.
> (Gedutis 2004: 35)

This establishment, then, of one of several "new traditions" in dance and in Irish culture in general, had the intention of celebrating what the Gaelic League believed to represent an older, better Ireland—not just to the Irish, but to outsiders as well. The *céilí* dances also were intended to replace the popular set dances, which, for all their popularity, were nonetheless foreign and considered impure. In the north, *céilí* dancing has brought with it a host of identity issues—during the worst times of sectarian conflict, even attending a *céilí* was a loud-and-clear statement of politicized affiliation with Catholic Ireland and, by extension, a united Irish island.

Two major patterns are important in *céilí* dancing: "threes" and "sevens." "Threes" are a rocking step in which one foot steps forward, the other foot steps at "home," and the first foot comes back to home for two beats: four beats total. Often the step is repeated on the opposite side, or the dancer may travel to the left or right. Threes may be used to keep dancing during moments when one is in place. "Sevens" are a traveling step to the left or the right. The dancer takes seven steps to the right with the right foot leading; the left foot crosses behind the right to keep up. If the dancer needs to return "home," he or she takes seven steps to the left with the left foot leading and the right foot crossing behind to keep up. Note that "sevens" actually take up eight beats, and "threes" take up four beats. Sevens are often followed by two sets of threes so that the count is uniform: eight beats plus eight beats.

Many *céilí* dances can accommodate as many dancers as there are, because they can simply add more couples to a circle or a line. In the climax of the popular "Waves of Tory" dance from Tory Island (off the northern coast of Donegal), an even number of single couples move under and raise their arms over a long line of other couples, all of whom are clasping hands as they themselves move up the line. The "waves" of the dance's title, then, are created by the graceful up and down movements of the arms. The number of couples is irrelevant; what matters, besides the fact that the dance is great fun for everyone, is that the wave formation appears. In *céilí* dancing it is common to change partners between dances. In addition to the large group dances, many *céilí* dance events feature "two-hand" or couple dancing. These dances are sometimes called "kitchen dances" because they were able to fit into the average Irish kitchen.

Set Dancing

Set dancing developed initially from the French-derived quadrille dances brought by French and English soldiers in the eighteenth and nineteenth centuries. Originally it was a style of country dancing, but it is also popular in urban areas. Pat Murphy argues that this new urban popularity of set dancing has at least something to do with the fact that many urbanites were raised in the country (Murphy 1995: 7). A set dance (not to be confused with solo set dancing, above) features a "set" of eight people (or a half-set of four people) divided into pairs, facing inward with the lady always on the right. The "top" couple has their backs to the music, the "bottom" couple faces the top couple, and the "first side" (to the left of the top) and "second side" (to the right of the top) couples face each other.

Dancing these sets in their original context of barns or houses meant very little room to execute far-reaching moves, so the square of eight people move rather tightly through a set of figures or pattern arrangements. These figures might include a "house around," in which all four couples dance around the square, men starting with the left foot, women starting with the right, stepping one–two–three and one–two–three while pivoting around each other, coming back to "home." Most figures are well known to experienced set dancers. In addition, dancers add special "battering" steps (small, rapid steps drawn from *sean-nós* and step dancing) that add excitement to the dancing of the figures.

Couples in set dancing use several different holds, depending on the figure or the set, or the county that the set comes from as well. The waltz hold features the gent's right hand at the lady's middle of her back, and his left hand holding her right. There can be considerable distance between their bodies in this hold; sometimes, however, a gent might wrap his right arm around the lady's waist to draw her close and shrink the amount of space they take up. The *céilí* hold is much more intimate; the gent and lady grasp left hands, and their right hands reach around each other's waist *inside* the left elbow. This leaves almost no space between the dancers, and gives a very secure hold so that the couple can swing in a clockwise direction. A "lead around" from one region of Ireland allows the couple to dance side-by-side around the square by grasping hands: right with right, left with left. Another region might use a different hold to perform the lead around. Because set dances usually include many more women than men, most ladies can easily switch to the gent's position in a dance, and the terms "lady" and "gent" have become much more about position than about whether one is literally female or male.

Set dancing became, in the twentieth century, the most endangered of all the dance genres because of the determined efforts of the Gaelic League to remove foreign elements from Irish dancing. It had become associated with the bad old days of foreign influences: something that one's grandparents had done, and certainly not something of the present—modern—Ireland. This association developed from a conscious purging of the dances by the Gaelic League, and their replacement by newly-developed *céilí* dances. In the League's expressed goal of weeding out all that was non-native to Ireland, quadrilles and the set dances that evolved from them were strongly discouraged, and they fell almost completely out of popularity and use. Thus by the 1970s, the "invented tradition" of the *céilí* dances came to be perceived as the *most* traditional, the *most* authentic, of the dances. Set dances had receded into the background and many people had forgotten them entirely.

> When one considers that less than twenty years ago [as of 1995] very few sets were danced, or even heard of, outside their own locality, it is amazing to think that for many people of all ages, from all walks of life and diverse social backgrounds, set dancing has become almost a way of life.
>
> (Murphy 1995: 7)

A small revival began shortly after the cultural revival in the 1960s and 1970s, and set dancing evolved into the very popular adult dancing genre it remains today.

"Riverdance" Dancing

The stage production of *Riverdance*, which was filmed and broadcast endlessly in North America on public television stations as part of their fundraising efforts, evolved from a very short dance sequence starring the American dancers Michael Flatley and Jean Butler. It was conceived as the intermission performance in the 1994 Eurovision Song Contest, and its combination of blistering footwork, flamboyant movements, and tightly arranged music—all in just seven minutes—was a show-stopping moment in Irish music and dance history. By the time *Riverdance* had gained momentum as the full-length extravaganza that it eventually became, Ireland was on the verge of legalizing divorce, Mary Robinson had become Ireland's first-ever female president, the priestly scandals had crushed the social and political power of the Catholic Church, the economic boom had started, and the first tentative uses of the term "Celtic Tiger" had found their way into newspapers and magazines. Ireland never looked back.

Produced by Moya Doherty of RTÉ (Ireland's national radio and television corporation), *Riverdance* included mostly Irish-themed (but not entirely traditional) music by composer Bill Whelan and choreography by Michael Flatley and Jean Butler. The production seemed to galvanize public interest in traditional music and dance, even as it infuriated some in the traditional music scene. Irish-American Michael Flatley, whose documented 28 taps per second made it into the Guinness Book of World Records, had been the first American to win the All-World Championship in dance at the age of 17. He was also a winner of the prestigious National Heritage Fellowship from the (American) National Endowment for the Arts in 1988. Flatley later went on to form a more hybridized dance show called *Lord of the Dance*, followed by several hybrid variants titled *Feet of Flames* and *Celtic Tiger*.

Riverdance dancing forms a separate category here because of several elements. For one thing, Michael Flatley and the successive gents that followed him after he left to form *Lord of the Dance* grinned, raised their arms out to the sides, and engaged with the audience visually, instead of keeping a still face and pinning their arms to their sides with their eyes modestly lowered. The almost flirty audience engagement was startling to the observers, and the audience fell apart in adulation. While step dance is repeated right and left in eight-bar sequences, *Riverdance* tends to feature half-patterns, traveling to one side without mirror-like duplication on the other. One of the show's most dazzling visual elements is the great crowd of hard-shoe step dancers in unison, stretched all the way across the stage and from the front to the rear of the stage, like an Irish version of the stage dancing Rockettes from 1930s America. With further uniformity in glamorous costuming, hairstyle and length, and steps, the effect is no less than breathtaking. It is also quite far removed from anything "normal" in terms of the intimacy of Irish solo or group dance.

> [T]his was Irish dance as it had never been seen before: an unashamedly spectacular display which, for once, accepted the sexual undertones of the dance and reveled in its power. The sound was magnified to a volcanic rumble by the combined power of the dancers' feet … The result was electrifying. Ireland was agog. The familiar had been utterly transformed.
>
> (Brennan 1999: 155)

Riverdance features newly-composed choral singing in Irish, Russian dancing, African-American gospel and tap dance, flamenco, hard- and soft-shoe step dancing, set dancing, *céilí* dancing, instrumental music (most notably for foreign audiences, the unfamiliar sight and sound of *uilleann* piping), and solo singing.

Instead of seeing *Riverdance* as some simple and radical departure or break with tradition, therefore, we should view it in terms of an internationalized

Irishness, an identity forged between the 'local' and the 'global' that reverberates with both past and contemporary dance forms.

(Wilson and Donnan 2006: 95)

First in Ireland, then abroad, then divided into three touring companies—each named after an Irish river—traversing the world (see Wulff 2005, for a deeper discussion of this), *Riverdance* has raked in millions of dollars. It has also provided, for the first time, fulltime employment for hundreds of dancers and dance teachers. It has also provided much of the impetus for those 50,000 Americans spending each weekend at step dance competitions across the country.

Every revivalist movement has its purists, its detractors, its developers, and its legions of critics. Traditional Irish dance is no exception. Some people argue that only *céilí* dances (rather than set dances) should be performed for social dance; others say that women "don't look good" doing *sean-nós* dance, and that it should be reserved for men only. The Oireachtas is the place for some of the most heated discussions about what is appropriate in *sean-nós* dance, while the Irish Dancing World Championships invites endless discussion about proper form (and much fretting about those curly wigs) in modern step dance. Enough people, however, simply dance because they love to do it, are skilled in it, and know people who feel the same way they do about it that there appears to be room for every dancer of every style.

The Irish dancing body—whether doing *sean-nós*, old-style, step dance, or hip hop (see below)—tells a story that is simultaneously personal and national. On an international scale, one sees elements of Irish dance in Shania Twain's 1999 music video ("Don't Be Stupid"), in ice skater Jason Brown's routine for the 2014 U.S. National Championships (which used music from *Riverdance*), as party choreography for the below-deck scene in the film *Titanic* (1997), and in various other places. It is as firmly fixed in the American popular imagination as the song "Danny Boy," but it evokes images of joy and high energy rather than grief and loss.

Staging Tradition: The Revival(s) and Beyond

Focusing attention on a "revival" of something is an indication that it has gone moribund; it has died, or has been consigned to stilted artificiality on some musty backwater stage somewhere. Ireland's performing arts have been revived again and again, successfully, to the point that it is undergoing not so much a continuous revival as a continuous surge of waves. Some of that music (and theater, and dance) has ended up onstage, but not all of it. The fact that there have been plenty of *non-staged* Irish traditional performing arts over the decades is a sign of their endurance. The staging of traditional (and revived) music, dance, and theater, then, has been an aspect of the twentieth and twenty-first centuries, but it does not represent the whole.

The first revival of Irish traditional music took place before the turn of the twentieth century with the foundation of the Gaelic League and the National Literary Movement (see Chapter 3). In the first couple of decades of the twentieth century in the United States, Francis and James O'Neill were notating tunes, and the first recordings by the great Sligo fiddlers were making their way back across the Atlantic from the United States to influence the players at home. Concerns about loss of tradition in Ireland were a driving force behind the nineteenth-century urge to preserve and collect, and the exciting developments afforded by new recording technologies in the early twentieth century brought players together who had been divided both by distance and by stylistic conventions.

The next revival occurred with the 1951 founding of Comhaltas Ceoltóirí Éireann, which held its first *fleadh cheoil* the following year. CCÉ is Ireland's most important organization for the promotion and dissemination of traditional music and dance. In the 1950s and 1960s, local branches of CCÉ were established, a constitution was drawn up, and the organization fought hard against "the indifference, dismissiveness, criticisms of 'inferiority' and hostility that unaffiliated musicians in many parts of the island were obliged to face in their everyday lives" (Vallely 2011: 148) during what is widely regarded as a rather dark time for Irish traditional music. The competitions and classes sponsored by CCÉ had a strong and positive impact on the number of young people who play traditional music. For decades, CCÉ (usually referred to as Comhaltas, pronounced "KOL-tas") has taken a very active role in documenting the playing and singing of musicians. Their website, http://comhaltas.ie/music/archive/C62, features a dazzling array of video clips organized by tune (jigs, reels, songs, polkas, slides, etc.), instruments (concertinas, fiddles, pipes, etc.) and venues (competitions, concerts, classes, etc.).

Céilí bands were an important part of the music scene in the 1950s and 1960s; comprising groups of up to a dozen (or so) musicians, these bands were formed to accompany dances. Many of the bands included the bare bones of what would now be considered a "traditional" group: button ("box") accordion, fiddles, flutes, and banjo. Others included pianos and horns. These groups toured all over Ireland, participated in competitions, and traveled abroad as well. Hundreds of *céilí* bands played for dances across Ireland, and many of them made recordings for limited distribution or performed on the radio. Their names (Ballinakill Céilí Band, Tulla Céilí Band, Castle Céilí Band, Kilfenora Céilí Band, and many others) are often still spoken with reverence and admiration by younger players.

In 1968, a group of *uilleann* pipers established Na Píobairí Uilleann ("the *uilleann* pipers") as a separate organization from Comhaltas. All full members are required to be pipers themselves; similar to Comhaltas but specific to pipes, the aims of the NPU are to promote playing and to disseminate knowledge about pipers and piping. Hundreds of pipers are registered members, and pipers and enthusiasts attend competitions, classes, and festivals in Ireland and abroad. An annual *tionól* ("assembly") gathers pipers from all over; separate gatherings are held in Ireland and in North America and Australia. The magazine, *An Píobaire*, is archived online at the extensive NPU website (www.pipers.ie).

The presence of these organizations has sometimes been in opposition to the musicians who have continued to simply play music for the fun of it. The "traditionalists" and "revivalists" sometimes clash, and that difference of opinion (on what is correct, authentic, or real—all of which are powerful buzzwords in various performing communities) is part of the tension and excitement in competitions, performances, sessions, and conversations. The supergroups of the 1960s and 1970s—the next revival—brought those issues to the fore, because in some cases their own membership represented multiple points of opinion.

The Chieftains, formed in 1963 out of Ceoltóirí Chualann (an ad-hoc group of players gathered for a Dublin play performance in the late 1950s), were the first Irish supergroup. Seán Ó Riada developed performance-quality arrangements and compositions for Ceoltóirí Chualann, who then performed and recorded with Gael-Linn Records in the 1960s. Concurrently with Ceoltóirí Chualann, several members of the group formed the Chieftains, which far outlasted its sibling group. Still performing and touring the world (albeit with different members as the decades have passed), the Chieftains can be said to have brought Irish music to worldwide fame. Their many recordings and performances featured careful arrangements of traditional tunes and songs. They also have interacted musically with many players from other nations, including Spain, China, and elsewhere. They sometimes invite a local group to open for them, which is a courteous gesture as well as a guaranteed audience draw. The very fact that they created complicated arrangements and developed both a stage presence and public personae in regard to a ticket-buying audience had a strong influence on the supergroups that followed.

In the late 1960s and 1970s, recordings and concerts by the Clancy Brothers and the Dubliners marked many North Americans' first encounter with Irish music. The Clancy Brothers and the Dubliners were an Irish response to the folk music revival of Britain and North America; they presented themselves as balladeers offering a very different taste of Irish musical culture than the Irish-American fare of the past, and the folk revival audiences of America were very receptive to this combination of new and old. The two groups differed, however, in repertoire: whereas the Clancy Brothers wore cream-colored Aran sweaters and charmed audiences with their presentation of a cleaned-up Irish folk repertoire, the Dubliners located their songs securely in a gritty urban milieu that insisted that Dublin, too, was part of Ireland. Both groups offered an explicitly politicized sensibility, again in response to the civil rights movement of the United States as well as the heating up of the Troubles in the north.

The 1970s saw the formation of a constellation of Irish supergroups that served to define the popular side of Irish traditional music for the next several decades. With the Chieftains (and Ceoltóirí Chualann), the Clancy Brothers, and the Dubliners as their backdrop and impetus, several new supergroups took the idea of tune arrangement and innovation and carried it further. The golden age of the Irish supergroups began with Sweeney's Men (formed in 1966), and continued with Planxty (formed in 1972), The Bothy Band, and Dé Danann (both formed in 1974). These supergroups incorporated the new-to-Ireland bouzouki (pioneered by Johnny Moynihan, Alec Finn, and Dónal Lunny) and the use of DADGAD ("open") guitar tuning to simultaneously provide a powerful rhythmic drive to the music as well as an entirely different set of harmonic colors underlying the melodies of the tunes and songs. World-class fiddlers such as Frankie Gavin, Kevin Burke, Tommy Peoples, Paddy Glackin, and others were members of these groups, and box players Joe Burke, James Keane, and Jackie Daly saw many requests for their participation in sessions and concerts. Pipers Liam O'Flynn and Paddy Keenan were essential players in Planxty and the Bothy Band, respectively, and the *bodhrán*—in the hands of Dónal Lunny and others—became much more common after appearing on so many seminal recordings of this period.

These revival groups (and especially their recordings) were the primary reason that so many non-Irish people were attracted to and inspired by Irish music in the 1970s. Not only in North America, but all over Europe (especially France, Germany, and Scandinavia), parts of Asia, and in Australia and New Zealand, musicians (including the author of this book and many of her friends and academic colleagues) began trying to play Irish tunes on their own instruments, to locate tunebooks and obscure recordings, and to travel to Ireland for the first time. The recordings also helped to activate local music revivals across Northern Europe (and to spur sales of the bouzouki—see Chapter 6!).

Contemporary Music and the Recording Industry

While companies that support the recording and dissemination of Irish traditional music still exist, the ability to produce a decent recording has all become quite localized, with its own do-it-yourself ethos. It is now possible, with a computer and some relatively inexpensive equipment, to make one's own recordings, put them up on a website hosted in Ireland or elsewhere, and use the connections of one's webpage and social media to secure gigs, advertise upcoming events, and allow enthusiasts to download songs. The relative quiet of the Irish countryside does not require perfect studio-quality isolation, so musicians who cannot afford (or simply do not want to pay for) the state-of-the-art studios and production values available in Dublin and elsewhere can simply locate a friend with the equipment, make a recording, and make it available online. In this way, hundreds of Irish artists have broken into a hitherto relatively closed scene, and the market for Irish music recordings has expanded in ways that no one in the recording industry could have predicted in the 1950s (or 1990s). The increasing availability of Voice Over Internet Protocol service also allows, for example, a fiddler in New Zealand to take private, real-time lessons over the Internet with fiddler James Kelly in Florida. In fact, the gorgeous air that James recorded for the accompanying online soundtrack for this textbook was done especially for this book in the privacy of his own home, directly onto his computer's hard drive.

One of the major changes to occur in recent years—starting in the public sessions and reinforced by the recording industry—has been a differentiation between music played for dancing and music played for pleasure. In the *sean-nós* dance section, above, you read about the ways in which a relationship develops between the instrumentalist(s) and the dancer so that each can respond to the other. The tempo must be slow enough (and the instrumentalists attentive enough) to accommodate the dancer's steps. As step dancing (particularly in competition) has shifted toward recorded accompaniment to allow all dancers to practice at an identical tempo, instrumentalists have shifted to participation in Irish traditional music primarily through public performance: at pubs, in homes, and at festivals held primarily in celebration of instrumental music, not dance or song. Without the need to be in musical relationship to one or more dancers, the tempos of the instrumental forms have increased, in some cases leaving behind the instrumentalists accustomed to playing primarily for dancers (Ó hAllmhuráin 1998: 178).

In the 1980s and 1990s the economic boom brought significantly more interaction between Ireland's major players and their audiences abroad, through radio airplay (particularly college radio stations and the United States' National Public Radio), widespread distribution of compact discs, and international tours. By the turn of the twenty-first century Altan, Clannad, Lúnasa, Dervish, Solas, Enya, Afro-Celt Sound System, (Canadian) Loreena McKennitt, and others were household names. The approaches to traditional music taken by each group or singer have resulted in very distinctive sounds, depending on whether a group uses pipes, or a singer, or bass, or drums. Like the other supergroups from the late twentieth-century revival onward, the concerts and recordings of the current supergroups reveal careful thought about arrangements, combinations of instruments, and a clear understanding of the advantages and limitations of the studio and the sound system onstage. The resulting sounds of Altan, Lúnasa, Dervish, and Solas are spontaneous, as if they (and the audience) got together for an evening of live, local performance. Many traditionalist groups such as these occasionally borrow tunes and rhythms from Galicia, Brittany, Scotland, Eastern Europe, and North America, with no perceived loss of "Irishness."

Clannad (formed in 1970) comprises several members of a Donegal family whose overall sound reveals recording technology to be a major contributor to the sound in its own right for the changes it creates; Clannad preceded the electronic sounds and vocal modifications inherent in the recordings of Enya (who is herself a family member of Clannad, but with her own career). The sound of Enya's voice was a surprise to many listeners, not only in Ireland but abroad. But much more than her voice, it was the lush orchestration and combination of synthesized and acoustic accompaniment that were the real revelation. In the early 1990s, an animated music video featuring images of Enya, a masted sailing ship, blooming flowers, and flying birds was released at the same time as Enya's "Orinoco Flow (Sail Away")" recording featured in the video. In the recording itself, Enya's voice was recorded and mixed in dozens of layers to sound like a very large choir. The song was the first New Age hit from Ireland, but it wasn't the last.

Coming at the same time as all the other changes spurring Ireland's economic development, Enya's multi-million-selling recordings—and by extension, the whole array of Celtic-themed New Age recordings—seemed tailor-made to respond to a CD market rich in hyperbole: "echoing with wonder, cloaked in mysticism, steeped in tradition, Celtic music has journeyed through the ages from the old world to the new" (Melhuish 1998: 178). The current upswing of interest in unadorned jigs and reels, sean-nós singing, and set dancing may come as something of a relief to any traditional musician who has been asked if he or she can "play any Enya."

Loreena McKennitt, a Canadian of Irish and Scottish descent, joins a number of performing artists who draw from other areas of the world in creating a blend of musical materials. In building on her theme of pan-Celticism, McKennitt has brought into her recordings and concerts musical elements from Galicia, Brittany, and well into the Middle East. Her work tends to reach roughly the same market as Enya, with the addition of those interested in a particular literary element from which she draws some of her lyrics (Sullivan 1999: 119). McKennitt's status as a North American performer of Irish- and Scottish-themed music gives her, on the one hand, carte blanche in terms of the openness of her influences; she is not limited by Irish (or Scottish) cultural expectations to keep her work within any particular tradition. On the other hand, her fan base is drawn largely from those who enjoy music marketed as "Celtic." Just like all of the fusion artists, she walks a fine line.

The two contemporary groups *Celtic Thunder* and *Celtic Woman* owe at least some of their success to both *Riverdance* and the general interest in "Celtic fusion" music. *Celtic Thunder* (formed in 2007), comprising five young singers from Ireland and Scotland, performs traditional and newly-composed songs in English, many of them love songs, arranged for solo and combined voices, with accompaniment in varied arrangements. An essential element of their sound is the same lush stringed and synthesized accompaniment that has characterized Enya's recordings. *Celtic Woman* (formed in 2004) follows more specifically in Enya's footsteps in that its performers—six women—make much more direct use of atmospheric background accompaniment, vocal effects, and their own physical appearance. Much of their promotional material references their description (in a review) as "Riverdance for the voice." Both groups were formed within the last several years, and have been heavily promoted in Ireland as well as on public broadcasting stations in North America. And while their primary repertoire is in English, their concerts often include one or more songs in Irish.

Irish Punk

Irish and Irish-American hard rock and punk bands have continually appealed to a particular college-age (and older) demographic while referencing Irish or Irish-American materials and sometimes using Irish traditional instruments. Like many punk bands elsewhere in the world, they are very political in their orientation and outspoken about important international issues, particularly the wars in Iraq and Afghanistan, civil rights, and the problems facing the working class.

> Traditional Irish music ... traveled to Appalachia, went back to Ireland in the form of country and western music, mixed it up with rock and roll, and spawned offshoots, including the crossover Celtic rock bands like Black 47.
> (Dezell 2000: 207)

The first real Irish punk band—the Pogues—arose in London in the early 1980s; their name is short for *póg mo thóin* ("kiss my arse" in Irish). They set a particular standard that all other bands have fallen into, even as they can all be clearly differentiated. The group Black 47 (named after the worst year of the Famine, 1847) followed in 1989; they were formed in New York City. Blood or Whiskey is a Kildare band that was created in 1993, Dropkick Murphys (Boston) followed in 1996, and Flogging Molly (Los Angeles) in 1997. Each of these (and the other punk groups) has a fiercely loyal following, often tied to a place; Dropkick Murphys, for example, will *always* be a Boston Band. The typical Irish punk sound is a combination of the hard drumming and distorted guitars of British and American punk *with* Irish traditional instruments such as button accordion, tin whistle, and fiddle. The addition of rough (semi-shouted) vocals and singable choruses is standard punk fare. However, the point that sets Irish punk apart from the rest of the world is its periodic use of triple meter: jigs, slip jigs, and hornpipe rhythms are just as common as high-speed songs in 4/4. Furthermore, Irish punk bands often slip sections of traditional tunes in between verses. A punk CD with an occasionally gentle tune (fingerstyle guitar, vibrato-laden voice, poignant lyrics, and fiddle or tin whistle) is no rarity in this genre.

This kind of re-creation of Irishness to fit twenty-first-century needs and musical interests follows an older pattern of shaping and reshaping not only what it means to be Irish, but also what it means to express Irish identity through music. Considering the primacy accorded to Irish traditional music in the current volume, it might be easy to dismiss some contemporary groups as non-traditional (and certainly they *are* non-traditional). However, to do so would be to ignore the power of multi-platinum album sales, and how those sales translate to financial support for certain musicians over others. Mass marketing and consumption are an essential part of Irish music today, whether it touches the local scene, or paves the way for more "Celtic" productions (Stokes and Bohlman 2003: 16). Just as in the older days of bardic patronage, the very big stage presence of the famous performers brings attention to their public personalities, while their sound often serves to define Irish music for outsiders. Rather than being daunted by the idea of multi-platinum album sales crushing the local players, however, it might be helpful to remember that—at least in its current format—the Internet, together with live, local performances, can be an exceptionally powerful force for the inspiration of musicians of newer generations, as well as for equality of musical access.

Country and Irish

Connected in many ways to American country music, "country and Irish" (sometimes called "country Irish") is music created by Irish performers that sounds distinctly American but with lyrics often specific to Ireland and Irish experiences. The genre developed in the 1960s with singers doing American country music for tourists and locals both, and has surged in popularity since the turn of the twenty-first century, proving to be particularly popular in the rural middle and northern parts of the island. Some of the early country and Irish bands were offshoots of céilí dance bands, including keyboards and horns; for example, Big Tom and the Mainliners used to be the Fincairn Céilí Band. The presence of a singer has been a key element in their collective success. Among the most popular country and Irish singers are Philomena Begley, Declan Nerney, Susan McCann, Daniel O'Donnell, Lisa McHugh, Nathan Carter, Mike Denver, and many others; all of these singers can be found on Internet videos.

Themes of contemporary country and Irish songs include many of the same ones common to American country music: family, place, work, nostalgia, and love. Many country and Irish singers use American Nashville-style accents in performance and on recordings, but some of the older singers use their own accents. Similarly, many country and Irish singers do covers of American country hits, such as Bob Dylan and Ketch Secor's "Wagon Wheel" and John Denver's "Country Roads, Take Me Home." The Irish Country Music Awards ceremony, hosted by Raidió Teilifís Éireann (Ireland's national public radio and television broadcaster), is a popular annual event watched by hundreds of thousands of people, and has been the flagship event of the Irish Country Music Association since the show's inaugural broadcast in 2016.

Irish-American country musician (and one of the world's best-selling artists of all time) Garth Brooks first performed in Ireland in 1997, at the height of the Celtic Tiger years. Popular media and Brooks' own publicity engine suggested that he was a man of both nations, and his popularity continued unabated well beyond his temporary withdrawal from the public eye in 2001. After a tremendous buildup of publicity in advance of his big comeback show scheduled for February 2014 in Dublin, Brooks canceled all of his sold-out concerts at Dublin's Croke Park when local authorities insisted that he perform for just two nights rather than five. The fact that the tour cancelation was a very big deal in Ireland reveals the extent not just of his fan base, but of the importance of country music in Ireland. In connecting directly with fans of American country music *and* country and Irish, Brooks focused public attention on the interests of many in Ireland's middle class.

> the middle class now outnumbers those above and below it, and country music is seen now as their soundtrack, what is often called in Ireland 'middle of the road' music. Such music is cast by its fans and marketers as in step with mainstream values not understood by the educated and privileged.
>
> (McGlynn 2006: 212)

Irish radio and television stations tend to support at least one show that features country and Irish; at any given time, it is relatively easy to locate a country station. Not all songs are in English, however; among many options, the popular *Opry an Iúir* show is hosted by Daniel O'Donnell, and includes songs in Irish as well. The use of the word "Opry," as in Nashville's Grand Ol' Opry, is a clear indication of the connection between American country and Irish country. The genre's strong popularity among rural listeners—and the themes brought up in the lyrics—resonate deeply with a segment of the population that is emphatically not attracted to the traditional music scenes more popular in the southern and western parts of the Republic. Where there are performers and audiences, festivals tend to follow.

Irish Hip Hop

All North American popular musical trends are alive and well in Ireland, from rhythm and blues to indie rock to boy bands to hip hop. Hip hop culture has been thriving worldwide for decades; it appears in recordings and onstage everywhere, including China, Nigeria, Costa Rica, Native North America, Lebanon, and... Ireland. Rappers use whatever languages they wish in order to engage the urgent issues of their specific region and group, and Ireland is no exception. Some of Ireland's rappers perform in Irish (or both Irish and English), while others perform exclusively in English. Language usage can change the rhythm of a performance because Irish and English emphasize different syllables, but one language is not inherently better or worse for use in hip hop (or for singing in general). Performing in Irish doesn't make anyone more "authentic," nor does performing in English make the person a sell-out. Anthony McCann and Lillis Ó Laoire note this in regard to songs in the two languages:

> Such thinking [about the idea of two separate song traditions] leads, on the one hand, to the conceptual closure of a Gaelic song tradition as the paragon of authenticity and Irish identity and, on the other, to a barely developed conceptualization of an English song tradition that is defined within the binary opposition as the degenerate Other of the Gaelic tradition, if not omitted from analyses altogether.
>
> (McCann and Ó Laoire 2003: 248)

Irish hip hop has been around since the 1980s; it is mostly a male genre. The Irish hip hop group Marxman (two Irishmen, two Englishmen) formed in London at the end of the 1980s, and were the first group to combine elements of hip hop with Irish traditional sounds. They highlighted social justice issues, including domestic violence and the legacies of colonialism and slavery. Their 1993 track, "Ship Ahoy," featuring both a tin whistle and the voice of Sinéad O'Connor (singing, not rapping), offers a harrowing narrative connecting the arrival of colonial powers on ships, slavery, the gig economy, and more.

Because Ireland and North America are so deeply intertwined, culturally and historically, it is no surprise that hip hop has had its share of covers and crossovers. The Los Angeles group House of Pain had an international hit with "Jump Around" (1992), which featured significant Irish (and Scottish) imagery such as bagpipers, Irish sweaters, and "Kiss Me, I'm Irish" buttons. The song was then picked up by comedian Des Bishop (born in New York but living in Ireland since the age of 14), who turned their "Jump Around" into "Léim Thart" ("Jump Around"). He created a "hip hop opera" titled "Rap Éire," and was on an Irish-language reality show titled *In the Name of the Fada*. The title itself was a play on the Irish movie, *In the Name of the Father*, the New York-accented "Fada" for "father," and using the *fada* or accent mark to indicate that it was a show about learning to speak Irish.

The Coláiste Lurgan (an independent summer school in County Galway) hosts a program for urban high school kids to improve their Irish language skills. As part of their work, staff members translate and teach students to perform Irish-language covers of popular English-language songs such as "Hello" by Adele, "When the Party's Over" by Billie Eilish, and many others. Their YouTube channel, TG Lurgan, is rich with covers and has over a hundred thousand subscribers, many of whom post comments about "saving the Irish language through music." Some of the items on their channel are covers of popular rap tracks. One to locate, though, is Macklemore's "Can't Hold Us" (type in the title and the words "as Gaeilge").

What does it mean to be an Irish rapper? Is it the urbanite with the splashy videos, or the child of an immigrant with brown skin, or someone whose lyrics are exclusive to Irish experiences? Does Irish rap have to be in one language or another? The Belfast group Kneecap is political in their message, use the Irish language unapologetically, and sometimes use the medium to make statements about, for example, what it is like to be on the wrong side of the Northern Irish police force as in their satirical hit, "C.E.A.R.T.A." ("R.I.G.H.T."). "C.E.A.R.T.A." was banned from RTÉ (Irish public media) for its cursing and references to drug use, but like many hip hop tracks the layers of access to meaning and the references to elements of Irish (or American) culture add complications.

Rap artists in Ireland—whether immigrants or Irish-born—regard hip hop as their own; the members of NUXSENSE (born in Brazil, the Philippines, Romania, Nigeria, etc., but raised in Dublin) don't bring a particularly Irish sound to their work, but are instead focused outward. However, in much the same way that Irish traditional music is having a moment of focus and brilliance, groups such as Kneecap represent a moment in which Irish hip hop (along with rapping with an Irish accent) has become part of the mainstream of Irish popular music. That so many Irish people enjoy word play (from songs to poetry to proverbs to puns) means that hip hop is fertile ground for a living, vibrant musical language such as this one.

Conclusions

Several conclusions arise in considering Irish traditional music and dance in the twenty-first century. Clearly, Irish traditional music is not just one sound. It is solo harping, rowdy pub session playing, bilingual singing, solo fiddle music, lilting, piping, and much more. Dance steps, rhythms, and history are also intimately involved in the manifestation of much of the instrumental music. We also know that Irish cultural history has, in large part, determined the overall sounds that we hear today. From their suppression under colonialism, their enthusiastically supported regulation under the Gaelic League, their decline during a period of economic stagnation, and their extraordinary current popularity, the songs, tunes, dance steps, and even concepts about music and dance have been subject to multiple, competing forces at home and abroad. Irish traditional music belongs *not* to just one era: the bottomless past. Instead, the music includes newly created melodies that fit vividly and seamlessly with tunes of several hundred years ago; all are responsive to the vicissitudes of regional, national, and international popularity.

> When a tradition suddenly becomes wildly popular—as has Irish traditional music—many will immediately and understandably assume that it has been changed to suit modern sensibilities, and will suspect that the tradition has somehow been damaged in the process. The impulse to preserve traditional Irish music and the need for the music—like all human expression—to change in order to reflect the conditions of people who play it, discuss it, and transmit it to the next generation frequently bring such tensions to the fore.
>
> (Smith 2001: 111)

That the music changes is not in question; of course it does. New instruments (from the flute to the accordion to the bouzouki) have been added; a second language (English) found its way into the tradition long ago; and new technologies have had an impact, from the regulators of the *uilleann* pipes to the ProTools recording and mixing equipment in a fifth-story Dublin flat (or a small stone cottage in Cork). Whether these changes radically shift either the sound or the ethos surrounding Irish music is up for perpetual debate. If the changes are, as Scott Reiss describes them, "simply signs of a healthy tradition adapting to novel socioeconomic conditions" (Reiss 2003: 153), then the ongoing debate about tradition and innovation is a healthy one. It is worth remembering as well that tradition and innovation are not inherently oppositional.

Perhaps Irish traditional music is best viewed through layers of lenses: history, language, politics, religion, gender, pedagogy, generations, finances, technology, and laws. These lenses have all contributed to how and why we hear the particular array of Irish traditional musics available to us right now, and why their sound is so immediately recognizable to its practitioners and its enthusiasts alike. In its current manifestation, what people say matters most to the community of Irish instrumental musicians is not so much one's outer category (gender, race, class, nationality, physical ability/disability, etc.) but whether one knows one's instrument, knows some tunes, and plays well with others. As was pointed out in Chapter 1, however, those "outer" categories can have an impact on how one is assessed, dismissed, or welcomed.

Chapters 7 and 8 point to the importance of the individual, the long process of learning a song well enough to make it one's own, and the relationship between the song and the singer. *Sean-nós* songs do not necessarily come cheaply or easily to those encountering them for the first time. Just as a violinist unfamiliar with Irish music can play the notes and printed rhythms of a jig without the resulting tune sounding even remotely like a jig, a singer unfamiliar with *sean-nós* could potentially slog through a *sean-nós* song without a sense of the story, its local implications, how each verse fits in to the whole, and how the song fits in with the rest of the repertoire. It might be a song in Irish, but it wouldn't be *sean-nós*.

It is a little too easy to use the word "tradition" in connection with Irish music, including in the relatively safe context of a textbook intended primarily for college students. What has the word conveyed to you that other words either cannot or have not? Does it mean things? Tunes? Ideas? Practices? The ethnomusicologist and musician Christopher Smith describes "tradition" not as a set of objects, but rather a set of procedures.

> There are 'traditional' modes of transmission, participation, pedagogy, preservation *and innovation*. Thus, it is entirely possible to be 'innovative' within the tradition, but in order to do so, the 'innovator' must have a grasp of the *tradition's* modes for accomplishing this—rather than imposing "innovative methods" from outside the tradition.
>
> (Christopher Smith, personal communication)

People invent traditions all the time, including in Ireland, and they also contribute new works to older, more established repertoires. New composition in Irish traditional music includes a continuous infusion of new jigs, reels, hornpipes, slides, and other dance tunes, along with airs and new songs. Some of the composers are Irish, while others are not Irish by heritage but bring passion and understanding to their compositional work. On the online soundtrack for this textbook, the tune called "The Sturgeon" (which appears just after "The Hag's Purse" on the track by Fingal) was composed by Randal Bays, an American with no Irish heritage but years of experience being steeped in Irish music. Irish-American Chicago fiddler Liz Carroll has written dozens of tunes, many of which have become "traditional" in that they are played by Irish musicians in traditional and contemporary settings all over the world. This is the essence of a living tradition, not a tradition that has been preserved in formaldehyde under glass in a museum.

The chapters of this book have constituted not so much a journey—from the past to the present and from the global to the local—as a dialogue. The spectrum of Irish traditional music—from the crowds of international players at the Willie Clancy Week to the solo singer at home—demands sensitivity to context and intention as much as musicianship for appropriateness of performance. From this perspective, not all of it is an international language; launching into a Kerry tune in Donegal might win you blank stares from the other players, and singing a *sean-nós* song such as "Currachaí na Trá Baine" in North America might lead to a request like "Can't you sing an *Irish* song?" The "imagined community" (Anderson 1991) of Irish music and musicians is a constantly shifting kaleidoscope, redrawing its borders from within and without: to incorporate, to exclude, to redefine. That Irish traditional music has drawn in so many enthusiastic participants to its many communities is remarkable. Its fluid adaptability in the context of great social change attests to its enduring ability to create meaning in the lives of its players and audience members, both local and global.

Discussion Questions

1. Should a musical style always be performed in the same way in order to preserve a sense of continuity and authenticity? How much difference does it make if that musical style is perceived to be endangered?
2. Why would dancing in public be considered a threat to morality by the Church?
3. Where should a group of people draw the line in terms of supporting what they believe to be the best of their cultural products (music and dance among those products), and purging what they believe to be foreign influences, without devolving into chaos?
4. Is it better to learn to know a place by listening to its music, or by playing and singing its music? What benefits and distractions does each effort confer on the listener, player, or singer?
5. Do new compositions in this style of music count as traditional? At what point does a new composition become "traditional"?

Glossary

Aeolian   one of the ancient Greek modes (A B C D E F G)
aisling   ("*ash*-ling") vision song
alalá   ("a-la-*la*") short religious chant of Galicia
amhrán   ("*ow*-rawn") song
bagad (pl. bagadou)   pipe and double reed ensemble from Brittany
barndance   musical form
Bealtaine   ("*bel*-tinna") the eve of 1 May, the first day of summer
biniou   bagpipes of Brittany
bodhrán   frame drum
bombarde   double reed folk oboe in Brittany and Cornwall
bombo   large bass drum of Galicia
bones   a pair of bones or sticks used in one hand for percussion
bouzouki   a long-necked plucked lute with four double courses of strings
brehon   the earliest type of law-giver
Breizh   the local name for the language of Brittany
Breton   the language of Brittany
canntaireachd   Scottish theme and variations, performed vocally to train pipers
caoineadh   ("*kuee*-nyah") lament ("keen" in English)
céilí   ("*kay*-lee") dance and music party, neighborly visits
Celtic   language family comprising two categories: Irish-Gaelic, Scottish-Gaelic, and
    Manx (the Goidelic branch), and Welsh, Cornish, Breton (the Brythonic branch)
ceol   ("kyoel") music
cerdd   ("kairth") Welsh song or tune
chanter   the fingered part of a bagpipe that determines the actual notes played
cláirseach   ("*klar*-shokh") harp
Cornish   the language of Cornwall, currently undergoing a revival
craic   ("crack") good times, conversation, laughter, music ("crack" in English)
crowd   Cornish fiddle

crowdy crawn Cornish frame drum
crwth ("crowd") Welsh bowed lyre
Cymru the local name for the language of Wales
diaspora, Irish the Irish abroad
Dorian one of the ancient Greek modes (D E F G A B C)
eisteddfod Welsh competitive music and dance festival
feadóg ("*fah*-doeg") pennywhistle
feis ("fesh") festival with a competitive element
fest noz Breton music and dance party
fleadh ("flah") festival
Gaeilge ("*guail*-i-gya") the local name for the language of Ireland
Gaeltacht ("*guail*-takht") Irish-speaking districts within Ireland
gaita ("gy-ta") mouth-blown bagpipe of Galicia
Galego the language spoken in Galicia (northwest Spain)
Galltacht ("*gall*-takht") English-speaking districts within Ireland
geantraighe harp music for laughter
goltraighe harp music for mourning
gwerz narrative singing of Brittany
heterophony similar voices; similar melodic lines occurring simultaneously
highland instrumental music form
hornpipe instrumental music form in 4/4, played with a dotted rhythm
Imbolc ("*im*-bolk") the eve of 1 February, the first day of spring
Ionian one of the ancient Greek modes (C D E F G A B)
jig, double instrumental music form in 6/8
jig, slip instrumental music form in 9/8
kan ha diskan two-person responsorial singing of Brittany
kantig religious singing of Brittany
Locrian one of the ancient Greek modes (B C D E F G A)
Lúghnasa ("*lu*-nassa") the eve of 1 August, the first day of autumn
Lydian one of the ancient Greek modes (F G A B C D E)
macaronic song bilingual song (in an Irish context, usually Irish and English)
march instrumental music form in a moderate 4/4 tempo
minstrelsy an early nineteenth-century type of musical theater, sometimes but not always including blackface performers
Mixolydian one of the ancient Greek modes (G A B C D E F)
monophony one voice; a single melody line (vocal or instrumental)
muiñeira Galician dance in 6/8
nosen lawen Welsh music and dance party
noze looan Cornish music and dance party
oireachtas ("*er*-akh-tas") competition in singing, dancing, and recitation
old-time or old-timey fiddle and banjo music of the southern US mountains
Phrygian one of the ancient Greek modes (E F G A B C D)
pìob mhòr Scottish highland bagpipes
piobaireachd Scottish theme and variations, performed on the highland pipes
pitu double reed instrument of Galicia
planxty instrumental music form primarily performed on the harp, in praise of a patron
polka instrumental music form in a moderate 2/4 tempo
polyphony many voices; contrasting musical lines occurring simultaneously
puirt-a-beul ("pwirsht-a-byull") Scottish mouth music
punteiro the chanter on a Galician *gaita* (bagpipe)

pyba ("*pi*-ba") bagpipe of Cornwall

pybeu ("*pi*-ba") bagpipe of Wales

reacaire ("reckara") professional reciter during the bardic era

reel instrumental music form in 4/4, primarily comprising eighth notes

regulators the parts of *uilleann* pipes that provide chordal accompaniment

requinta transverse flute of Galicia

Samhain ("*sow*-in") the eve of 1 November, the first day of winter/New Year's Day

Scotch-Irish lowland Scots who moved to Ulster, then to North America in the eighteenth century

sean-nós ("shan-nos") old style singing and/or dancing

seisiún session, spelled in Irish

session a gathering of musicians for the purpose of playing Irish instrumental music

slide instrumental music form in 12/8, primarily comprising eighth notes

smallpipes bellows-blown pipes of Northumbria and Scotland

son lighthearted lyric songs of Brittany

strathspey instrumental music form in 4/4, with the characteristic sound of an eighth note followed by a dotted quarter note (the "Scottish snap")

suantraighe harp music for sleeping and lovemaking

tamboril snare drum of Galicia

telenn harp of Brittany

telyn ("*tell*-in") harp of Wales and Cornwall

treujenn-gaol clarinet of Brittany

troyl Cornish music and dance party

tuath ("*tu*-wa") small kingdom of early Irish history

údar ("*oo*-dar") the explanation of a song

uilleann pipes ("*ill*-en") Irish bagpipes (*uilleánn* = elbow)

ùrlar the "ground" or theme in Scottish *pìobeareachd*

variety mid-to-late nineteenth-century non-narrative theater form, including acrobats, jugglers, and equestrians in addition to music and dance

vaudeville late nineteenth- and early twentieth-century musical theater, often performed in a hall associated with a chain of halls in different cities

Additional Resources

Further Reading

Thousands of books and articles have been written by outsiders about the many different aspects of Ireland: its history, legal systems, literature, religious ideas and practices, arts, philosophies, politics, languages, etc. In addition, the prolific Irish have themselves written countless nonfiction works about these topics, as well as brilliant novels, short stories, and poetry. Irish film is rich with themes that reveal so much about Irish ways of seeing the world. Yet there is no one "Irish way" of seeing the world; Ireland has as many viewpoints as there are Irish people, and those viewpoints are moving targets at all times. You could arm yourself with ten different history books and discover a completely different Irish history in each one.

The Encyclopedia of Ireland (Lalor 2003) and *The Encyclopedia of the Irish in America* (Glazier 1999) are fascinating sources of information and ideas ready for browsing. Edited volumes with competing and complementary notions of Irish culture can offer you a full array of opinions, citations, and resources. Rather than frustrate yourself too much with the onion-like layers of Irish culture, my next suggestion is for you to browse the References section of this book. Look for titles and subjects that interest you, and once you have checked out the book or article in question, peruse its bibliography. The bibliographies will reveal more resources, and can take you in new and exciting directions. There is still no substitute, though, for actual travel to Ireland, and for meeting enough Irish people at home and abroad that you have a sense of its diversity.

Books on Irish music

Books about music in Ireland fall roughly into several categories: one person's musical adventures; one region's music; the "great man/great woman" biography of a particular musician; and—rather like this textbook—one person's attempt to be all things to all readers when it comes to Irish music. Each type of book offers some kind of musical coverage, and each style of writing appeals to a particular reader. I recommend that you browse through these offerings for something that matches your interests; you will certainly learn something from each of them. Fintan Vallely's 2011 *The Companion to Irish Traditional Music, 2nd edition* is a very impressive first-stop encyclopedia that solidly guides the reader with just the right balance of "big picture" and detail. Similarly, the two-volume *Encyclopedia of Music in Ireland* (White and Boydell 2013), published only in Ireland, is comprehensive and includes works by (and about) almost every scholar of Irish music in addition to various musical topics.

A handful of books serve to introduce the reader to a particular writer/musician's adventures in Ireland. These include *Ireland, a Bicycle and a Tin Whistle* (Wilson 1995), *In Search of the Craic: One Man's Pub Crawl Through Irish Music* (Irwin 2003), *Last Night's Fun: In and Out of Time with Irish Music* (Carson 1996), and *And As I Rode by Granard Moat* (Kiely 1996). A typical blurb reads "Cycling around Ireland in search of traditional music, a tin whistle in his saddlebag, David Wilson follows the coastline (… and …) takes us on a journey across wild open spaces and through crowded pubs and festivals that pulse with energy and life" (back cover copy for *Ireland, A Bicycle and a Tin Whistle*). These books are fun to read and reveal much about the writer's take on Irish music and culture, but also focus attention quite effectively on specific encounters with individual musicians and musical contexts rather than give a sense of the larger picture of Irish music.

Other books cover a specific region within Ireland. These include, for example, *Stone Mad for Music: The Sliabh Luachra Story* (Hickey 1999), *On a Rock in the Middle of the Ocean: Songs and Singers in Tory Island, Ireland* (Ó Laoire 2005), *Flowing Tides: History and Memory in an Irish Soundscape* (Ó hAllmhuráin 2016), *A Hidden Ulster: People, Songs, and Traditions of Oriel* (Ní Uallacháin 2003), *The Musical Traditions of Northern Ireland and its Diaspora* (Cooper, 2009), *Music, Emotion and Identity in Ulster Marching* Bands (Ramsey 2011), and *Ceol na hOileán* ("Music of the Islands") by Tomás Ó Ceallaigh. These offer a picture of one region of Irish music, and can be very helpful when examining area-specific studies or attempting to understand what lies at the heart of a particular group of people's relationship to music.

A third set includes mostly annotated song lyrics, such as *The Stone Fiddle: My Way to Traditional Song* (Tunney 1981), *Rich and Rare: A Book of Ireland* (McMahon 1984), *The Gold Sun of Irish Freedom: 1798 in Song and Story* (Doyle and Folan 1998), and *Songs of Irish Rebellion: Irish Political Street Ballads and Rebel Songs, 1780–1900* (Zimmerman 1967). There are many more books of this kind in the Irish language, and they can be outstanding resources for singers.

Biographies of individual musicians abound, such as *The Songs of Elizabeth Cronin* (Ó Cróinín 2000), *Seosamh Ó hÉanaí: Nár Fhágha Mé Bás Choíche* (Mac Con Iomaire 2007), *Bright Star of the West: Joe Heaney, Irish Song Man* (Williams and Ó Laoire 2012), *Carolan: the Life, Times and Music of an Irish Harper* (Ó Sullivan 2005), *The Masses of Seán and Peadar Ó Riada* (O'Keeffe 2017), *Seán Ó Riada: His Life and Work* (Ó Canainn 2003), *Going to the Well for Water: The Séamus Ennis Field Diary 1942–1946* (Uí Ógáin 2009), and *A Song for Ireland* (O'Hara 1983). Some present fascinating glimpses into individuals while they play or sing, such as Fintan Vallely and Charlie Pigott's book of photographs, *Blooming Meadows: The World of Irish Traditional Musicians*. In conversations among musicians and singers, people tend to celebrate the major players and singers of the past as a way of drawing musical and social connections, cementing one's own reputation, and celebrating those who deserve continuing respect and honor.

General introductions to Irish traditional music include an array of books written by academics. Helen O'Shea's *The Making of Irish Traditional Music* (2008) explores the sessions of County Clare as a way to understand identity, authenticity, and nationalism. Adam Kaul's *Turning the Tune: Traditional Music, Tourism, and Social Change in an Irish Village* (2009) considers the same musical region through the lenses of anthropology and tourism. Tes Slominski's *Trad Nation: Gender, Sexuality and Race in Irish Traditional Music* (2020) is an exciting new work that takes Irish music well beyond issues of ethnic nationalism. Martin Dowling's *Traditional Music and Irish Society: Historical Perspectives* (2014) focuses on the connection of traditional music to modernity in the press, in literature, and in politics. Susan Motherway's *The Globalization of Irish Traditional Song Performance* (2013) is about the ways in which the global and the local cross paths through performance practice. As mentioned above, Fintan Vallely's *The Companion to Irish Traditional Music, 2nd edition* (2011) is an encyclopedia with a wealth of information. Dora Hast and Stan Scott's *Music in Ireland: Experiencing Music, Expressing Culture* (2004) is a case study textbook that offers first-person accounts and encounters with contemporary performers and performances. James Cowdery's *The Melodic Tradition of Ireland* (1990) analyzes issues of tune families, individual performance practice, and the nature of the Irish melody. Gearóid Ó hAllmhuráin's *O'Brien Pocket History of Irish Traditional Music* (1998) offers an intimate view of Irish musical history in both instrumental music and song. Tomás Ó Canainn's *Traditional Music in Ireland* (1978) focuses on the fiddle, *uilleann* pipes, and *sean-nós* singing.

Books on the Irish Diaspora in Music

Two important books explore song lyrics of the Irish and Irish-Americans: Mick Moloney's *Far from the Shamrock Shore: The Story of Irish-American Immigration through Song* (2002) includes a CD and song lyrics, together with important historical moments for the Irish in America. William H. Williams's 2006 book *'Twas Only an Irishman's Dream: The Image of Ireland and the Irish in American Popular Song Lyrics, 1800–1920* is a good way to understand why Americans have viewed the Irish the way they have. Sean Campbell's 2011 *Irish Blood, English Heart: Second Generation Irish Musicians in England* wrestles with issues such as identity, intersections with popular culture, caricatures, and marginalization.

Books on Irish Dance

In Irish dance, the collective works of Helena Wulff and Helen Brennan stand out. Helen Brennan's *The Story of Irish Dance* (Brennan 2001) includes both individual personalities in Irish dance as well as an introduction to the regions, and a more general history of dance in Ireland. Helena Wulff's *Dancing at the Crossroads* (Wulff 2007) uses Irish dance to engage contemporary Ireland's "dance" with modernity and new identities, even as it retains aspects of tradition. Frank Whelan's *The Complete Guide to Irish Dance* (Whelan 2001) includes instructions on step dancing.

Journals

The Journal of Music in Ireland, Ethnomusicology Ireland, The New Hibernia Review, An Phíobaire, the *Journal of American Folklore,* the *Canadian Journal for Traditional Music,* the *International Journal for Traditional Music,* the *Ethnomusicology Journal, Ethnomusicology Forum,* and *The World of Music* are all good resources.

Combing the Web

Many performers of Irish music and dance have their own websites, and it is easy to locate endless YouTube clips of individual performers and tunes. In addition, all the recording companies maintain websites; these can be excellent sources from which to purchase CDs, as not every Irish musician has a contract with iTunes! The websites on this list, then, are likely to endure longer than the latest boom or bust in technology. Be sure to also consult the Routledge website for this book, which will include some specific sites. Check also www.tradlessons.com for tunes played both slowly and up to speed, Alan Ng's tunography (both www.alan-ng.net/irish/learning/ and www.irish-tune.info), and the Ceolas website (www.ceolas.org/tunes/).

Comhaltas Ceoltóirí Éireann is a worldwide organization of Irish music enthusiasts. Their website, http://comhaltas.ie, features audio and video archives, sheet music to download, events, a variety of other resources, and includes a video clip of the day. The Irish Traditional Music Archives (www.itma.ie) is a Dublin non-profit reference center for the research on, and preservation of, Irish song, instrumental music, and dance. Professor Christopher Smith's site (www.coyotebanjo.com/music.html) offers instructional ideas, essays, and some downloadable tunes.

One of the best apps for locating tune identities—you hear a tune and wish to know its title—is Tunepal. You let it record part of a tune and it will match what it records with other recordings and offer you a set of possible tune titles. Another, if you are learning tunes, is The Amazing Slowdowner, which will slow down any recording to a learnable speed without sacrificing the pitch. You can now find plenty of Irish music stations online as well.

Discussion Groups

Assume that any discussion group has its preferences and internal quarrels. Like attending a live session of Irish traditional music, just remember that it's appropriate to listen (or lurk) before announcing your presence (musically or otherwise), and that the longstanding relationships between the musicians or—in this case—the discussion group posters predate your arrival. Both www.mustrad.org.uk and www.thesession.org feature a core group of insiders, and both can offer comments that can be helpful, accurate, and sometimes dead wrong! www.mustrad.org includes discussions about recordings, artists, songs, and tunes, while www.thesession.org features transcriptions of many instrumental tunes in both standard and abc notations, with every possible tune title.

Instruments

Each instrument has its own set of sites hosting forums and discussion groups, which often include good information, articles, or links to articles.

- www.pipers.ie
- www.irishfiddle.com
- www.harp.net
- www.bouzouki.com
- www.concertina.net
- www.irish-banjo.com
- www.chiffandfipple.com/indexbo.html

This is just a sample of what is available! The plethora of sites offering song lyrics and downloads prevents listing all of them; many of them belong to particular singers and feature their own songs.

Irish Music on Radio and Television

If you go to www.rte.ie/radio/index.html, you will find the radio page of Raidió Teilifís Éireann, Ireland's version of PBS. For television, RTÉ also allows you to watch some shows at www.rte.ie/tv/index.html. In either case, you can listen to live streaming radio or watch selected television programs. Other radio resources online include, depending on what you seek:

www.liveireland.com
www.listenlive.eu/ireland.html
www.clarefm.ie
www.midwestradio.ie/mwir/index.php

Another television resource (particularly for Irish language television) includes www.tg4.ie/bearla/scei/beo.asp. For those with a particular interest in music of the Travellers, the Irish Traditional Music Archives has a collection that includes some Traveller musicians and singers:

www.itma.ie/features/playlists/carroll-mackenzie

Keep in mind, however, that online resources change frequently, and that sometimes your computer needs to have special capabilities.

Listening Guide

This book includes an online soundtrack featuring recordings intended to clarify and offer examples of the major points of discussion. The description of each track includes a timeline that enables listeners to follow the tunes precisely (in a minutes:seconds format). Most performers have a (listed) website that readers may peruse for further information about the performer's history, other recordings, or upcoming concert dates. Most of the original recordings from which these tracks originated may be found through www.cdbaby.com, www.ossianusa.com, www.amazon.com, www.cic.ie, or the performers' websites. In addition, any tune, instrument, or performer mentioned in this book can usually be found on YouTube. Once you've found one tune, seek out more versions of the same tune for variations, individual stylistic twists, and even hearing how the tunes sound on different instruments or in different settings.

Some of the tracks have been transcribed in Chapters 6, 7, and 8. Page numbers are listed for the relevant transcriptions, though all notation in this book is prescriptive, rather than precisely descriptive. As a result, some of the notes and phrases may be different, depending on the individual taste, instrument, and choices of the performers. All of the performers selected for inclusion in this CD were very gracious and kindly responsive in allowing their tracks to be used, and deserve special thanks.

Track 1 (transcription on p. 65)

Genre: harp tune (ABCB), 4/4
Track title: "Carolan's Farewell to Music"
Performers: Laoise Kelly, harp. Laoise's first name is pronounced "*Lee*-sha"
Source: Laoise Kelly, *Just Harp*. LK001. laoisekelly.ie

The luxury of playing a solo instrument is that it allows the performer to vary the tempo, the number and types of ornaments on the melody, and (in this case) aspects of harmony as well. This famous piece—called by different names, including "O'Carolan's Farewell to Music" and just "Farewell to Music"—was alleged to have been composed by O'Carolan shortly before his death (though that claim is still under debate). Some scholars refer to him as O'Carolan; others simply write Carolan. We all reference the same person, regardless. Many of his compositions lean rather heavily on influences from composers of the Italian baroque; "Farewell to Music" is much closer in both its melodic and ornamental materials to some of the song types from the early eighteenth century that he might have heard in his travels around Ireland. As you listen to Laoise Kelly's playing, notice that she uses a variable tempo reminiscent of breathing, or even singing. You can hear other samples of her playing on her LaoiseKelly.ie page.

Timeline for "Carolan's Farewell to Music"

0:00–0:32	start of "Carolan's Farewell to Music," A section
0:33–0:59	B section
1:01–1:46	C section
1:47–2:13	reiteration of B section
2:14–2:45	A section
2:47–3:13	B section
3:15–4:00	C section
4:02–4:34	B section

Track 2 (transcription on p. 162)

Genre: hornpipe (AABB), 4/4
Track title: "Moran's Fancy (hornpipe) / The Garden of Daisies (set dance)"
Performers: Tim Collins, concertina
Source: Tim Collins, *Dancing on Silver.* Cróisín Music CM001

The concertina is closely associated with the hornpipe, both of them having entered Ireland through England. However, concertinas play every kind of Irish music (reels, slides, airs), and play for dancing as well as for listening. One of the most enjoyable aspects of this set of tunes, besides Tim Collins's masterful playing, is the way in which they both shift between Ionian (major) and Mixolydian mode. Played in the key of D (which uses a C# when it's a major scale), sometimes the C is played as a C#, sometimes as a C natural. "Moran's Fancy" is a hornpipe, and "The Garden of Daisies" is a set dance. A set dance is a type of instrumental tune (in this case, a hornpipe) used for a specific solo dance composition. Other well-known set dance tunes are "The Blackbird" and "King of the Fairies." Tim Collins is an ethnomusicologist who plays with the influential Kilfenora Céilí Band; he also records, teaches, and performs on his own. His background as a musician from Sliabh Luachra on the Cork/Kerry border has led him to bring slides and polkas from the area into the Kilfenora Céilí Band repertoire and thence to a larger audience. Tim's website is www.timcollins-concertina.com.

Timeline for "Moran's Fancy / The Garden of Daisies"

0:00–0:11	start of "Moran's Fancy," A section
0:12–0:22	reiteration of A section
0:23–0:32	B section
0:33–0:43	reiteration of B section
0:44–0:53	full repetition of "Moran's Fancy," A section
0:54–1:04	reiteration of A section
1:05–1:14	B section
1:15–1:25	reiteration of B section
1:26–1:35	start of "The Garden of Daisies," A section
1:36–1:46	reiteration of A section
1:46–1:56	B section
1:57–2:06	reiteration of B section
2:07–2:17	full repetition of "the Garden of Daisies," A section
2:18–2:27	reiteration of A section
2:28–2:38	B section
2:38–2:52	reiteration of B section

Track 3 (transcription on p. 119)

Genre: reel/barndance (AABB), 4/4
Track title: "Benton's Dream / Mike in the Wilderness"
Performers: Anthea Lawrence, fiddle; Audra Poor, *uilleann* pipes; Lawson Dumbeck, clawhammer banjo
Source: Fiddlehead, *Over the Straits*. Self-produced CD

This track is an example of the connections between old-time music of the southern mountains of the United States and Irish—and Scots-Irish—instrumental music. The three musicians are Americans in the group Fiddlehead, and combine *uilleann* pipes, fiddle, and clawhammer banjo to bridge the gap. "Benton's Dream" is an old-time tune composed by American fiddler Benton Flippen (b. 1920), certainly worthy of the many dozens of repetitions it receives in sessions of old-time playing. "Mike in the Wilderness" is closely related in melodic material (particularly in the A sections of both tunes), but is an Irish barndance. Notice that the sections of "Mike in the Wilderness" are quite brief, and that the C section is played three times through each time it appears on this recording. In addition, "Mike in the Wilderness" includes more quarter notes than one would normally hear in a reel, and those quarter notes are the hallmarks of 4/4 barndances. "Benton's Dream" is played four times before shifting to the next tune, while "Mike in the Wilderness" is played three times in its entirety. Fiddlehead's CDs are available through www.cdbaby.com.

Timeline for "Benton's Dream / Mike in the Wilderness"

0:00–0:09	start of "Benton's Dream," A section: pipes and banjo only
0:10–0:17	reiteration of A section
0:18–0:26	B section
0:27–0:36	reiteration of B section
0:36–0:45	full repetition of "Benton's Dream," A section (addition of fiddle)
0:46–0:54	reiteration of A section
0:55–1:03	B section
1:04–1:12	reiteration of B section
1:13–1:21	full repetition of "Benton's Dream," A section
1:22–1:30	reiteration of A section
1:31–1:39	B section
1:40–1:49	reiteration of B section
1:50–1:58	full repetition of "Benton's Dream," A section
1:59–2:07	reiteration of A section
2:08–2:16	B section
2:17–2:25	reiteration of B section (with stops)
2:26–2:30	start of "Mike in the Wilderness," A section
2:30–2:34	reiteration of A section
2:35–2:39	B section
2:39–2:43	reiteration of B section
2:44–2:48	C section
2:49–2:53	reiteration of C section
2:54–2:58	reiteration of C section
2:58–3:02	full repetition of "Mike in the Wilderness," A section
3:02–3:06	reiteration of A section
3:07–3:11	B section
3:11–3:15	reiteration of B section
3:16–3:20	C section
3:20–3:24	reiteration of C section
3:25–3:29	reiteration of C section
3:29–3:34	full repetition of "Mike in the Wilderness," A section
3:34–3:38	reiteration of A section
3:39–3:43	B section
3:44–3:47	reiteration of B section
3:48–3:52	C section
3:52–3:56	reiteration of C section
3:57–4:08	reiteration of C section

Track 4 (transcription on p. 185)

Genre: sean-nós singing in Donegal style
Track title: "Ag an Phobal Dé Domhnaigh" ("At the Congregation on Sunday"—pronounced "egg unn fubbel jey dow-nee")
Performers: Lillis Ó Laoire, solo voice
Source: Daigan: Traditional Singing from Brittany, Ireland, Scotland and Wales. Fflach Tradd. CD183H

In Chapter 7 you read about *sean-nós* singing, and the differences between the three areas of Donegal, Connemara, and Munster. In this particular Donegal example (notated and discussed in Chapter 7), you can hear a subtle and flexible 3/4-time pulse supporting the melody. In addition, the singer's variations from verse to verse, his expression of the lyrics, and the overall shape of the melody give the song great musical interest. Lillis Ó Laoire is a native Irish speaker from Gortahork in Donegal (in the northwest of Ireland). He also is a two-time winner of the Corn Uí Riada, the premier award for *sean-nós* singing, and professor of Irish Studies at the National University of Ireland in Galway.

Timeline for "Ag an Phobal Dé Domhnaigh"

0:00–0:58   first verse:

Ag an phobal Dé Domhnaigh thug mé mórchion don chailín
At the congregation on Sunday I gave great affection to the girl

Sí ba deise is ba bhreácha dar tógadh riamh i mbaile
She was the prettiest and the finest that was ever reared in any townland

Bhí a béilín mar bheadh an rós ann is bhí a caoinchom mar bheadh an sneachta
Her little mouth was like roses and her gentle waist like snow

'S a Rí nach bhfuil mo lóistín san áit a gcoiríonn sí a leabaidh.
And God I wish my lodging was where she dresses her bed.

0:59–1:53   second verse:

Tá an rógaire 'o mo mhealladh is tá'n peacadh a dhéanamh
The rogue is seducing me and the sin is being committed

Tharraing sé mo chroí istigh agus bhí sé arís a shéanadh
He drew my heart inside and denied it thereafter

Ach má tá do bhean sa bhaile agat nó do leanbán le bréagadh
But if you have your wife at home and your little child to coax

Pill arís uirthi a shladaí 's cha bhíonn roinnt agam féin leat.
Return again to them, you wrecker, and I'll have nothing to do with you.

1:55–2:52   third verse:

Dá mbíodh a fhios ag mo dheartháir mo leatrom ba trua leis
If my brother knew my oppression he would pity me

Dá mbíodh a fhios go dearfa bheadh air imní agus buaireamh
Indeed if he knew he would be worried and upset

Fá mo chéad searc bheith mo thréigean is an créatúr bocht a lua liom
Because my first love was deserting me and the poor creature being engaged to me

'S tú m'ansacht ar fhearaibh Éireann a's in do dhiaidh atá mé buartha.
You are my beloved of the men of Ireland and after you I am sorrowful.

2:54–3:46   fourth verse:

Dá mbíodh péire glan sciathán as mo chliatháin féin anuas liom
If I had a smooth pair of wings down by my sides

Dá mbíodh fhios go dearfa go rachainn ón buachaill
Indeed if I had I would go from the boy

D'éireochainn féin in airde mar bheadh an éanlaith fá na cuanta
I would rise up like the birds by the sea bays

Nó go n-insínn mo ghearán do mo leannán ar an uaigneas.
To tell my story in solitude to my lover.

3:48–4:44   fifth verse:

Bliain agus daichead dá mairfeá thusa a bhuachaill
A year and forty if you lived, my boy

Do ghrása cha dtabharfainn do éinneach ar an domhan
Your love I'd never give to anyone in the world

Ach nuair nach bhfuil na buaibh agam ná na buaraigh lena gceangal
But since we haven't cattle or the spancels to tie them with

Seo mo chúig bheannacht déag duit is beimid araon ag goil 'na bhaile.
My blessings upon you and let us each of us go home.

Track 5 (transcription on p. 160)

Genre: jigs (AABB / AABBCC / AABB), 6/8
Track title: "The Hag's Purse / The Sturgeon / The Ten Penny Bit"
Performers: Randal Bays, fiddle; James Keane, button accordion; Dáithí Sproule,
     guitar
Source: Fingal, *Traditional Irish Tunes and Songs.* New Folk Records NFR 0502

While reels are often more popular than jigs for large public sessions, jigs remain a favorite for many musicians. This set of three jigs includes a newly-composed tune in three parts, "The Sturgeon," by fiddler Randal Bays; "The Hag's Purse" and "The Ten Penny Bit" are classics. New tunes enter the repertoire all the time if they're good ones, and some of the best tunes have been composed by musicians alive today. Fingal is a new trio based in the United States, comprising fiddle, button accordion, and guitar. Randal Bays is an American fiddler who has played and taught Irish music for decades; he lives in the Pacific Northwest. James Keane (currently living in Queens, New York) has studied from and played with many of the great masters of Irish traditional music (and has long since become one himself); he performed with the famed Castle Céilí

Band. Dáithí Sproule has performed as both a solo and ensemble artist for many years, starting with the influential Skara Brae and currently including the supergroup Altan. Each of the three musicians has a website: www.randalbays.com; www.daithisproule.com; and www.jameskeane.com, the last of which has a nice video clip of the three men playing reels.

Timeline for "The Hag's Purse / The Sturgeon / The Ten Penny Bit"

0:00–0:07	start of "The Hag's Purse," A section
0:08–0:15	reiteration of A section
0:15–0:22	B section
0:23–0:30	reiteration of B section
0:31–0:37	full repetition of "The Hag's Purse," A section
0:38–0:45	reiteration of A section
0:45–0:52	B section
0:53–1:00	reiteration of B section
1:00–1:04	start of "The Sturgeon," A section
1:04–1:08	reiteration of A section
1:08–1:12	B section
1:12–1:15	reiteration of B section
1:16–1:19	C section
1:20–1:23	reiteration of C section
1:24–1:28	full repetition of "The Sturgeon," A section
1:28–1:31	reiteration of A section
1:32–1:35	B section
1:35–1:39	reiteration of B section
1:39–1:42	C section
1:43–1:47	reiteration of C section
1:47–1:50	full repetition of "The Sturgeon," A section
1:51–1:54	reiteration of A section
1:55–1:58	B section
1:59–2:02	reiteration of B section
2:03–2:06	C section
2:06–2:10	reiteration of C section
2:11–2:17	start of "The Ten Penny Bit," A section
2:18–2:25	reiteration of A section
2:26–2:33	B section
2:34–2:41	reiteration of B section
2:41–2:48	full repetition of "The Ten Penny Bit," A section
2:49–2:56	reiteration of A section
2:57–3:04	B section
3:06–3:12	reiteration of B section
3:13–3:19	full repetition of "The Ten Penny Bit," A section
3:20–3:27	reiteration of A section
3:28–3:35	B section
3:35–3:48	reiteration of B section

Track 6 (transcription on p. 160)

Genre: reels (AABB form), 4/4
Track title: "Charlie Mulvihill's / The Conspiracy"
Performers: Joanie Madden, tin whistle; Jimmy Higgins, *bodhrán*
Source: Song of the Irish Whistle, volume 2. Hearts O'Space 11090-2

The tin whistle player Joanie Madden (best known for her work with the all-female group Cherish the Ladies) takes full advantage of the spare *bodhrán* accompaniment on this track to allow room for rich variation. Each of these two reels is played twice through; generally, the first time through each section has less variation than the second (or third, or fourth) time through. As each section on this track is played four times (twice each time the tune is completed), a player can (and is expected to) vary the performance somewhat from the previous iteration. You can learn more about Joanie (and the other members of Cherish the Ladies) at www.cherishtheladies.com/index.htm.

Timeline for "Charlie Mulvihill's / The Conspiracy"

0:00–0:08	entry of *bodhrán* (frame drum)
0:09–0:17	start of "Charlie Mulvihill's," A section
0:18–0:26	reiteration of A section
0:27–0:35	B section
0:36–0:44	reiteration of B section
0:45–0:53	full repetition of "Charlie Mulvihill's," A section
0:54–1:02	reiteration of A section
1:03–1:11	B section
1:12–1:20	reiteration of B section
1:21–1:29	start of "The Conspiracy," A section
1:30–1:38	reiteration of A section
1:38–1:46	B section
1:47–1:55	reiteration of B section
1:56–2:04	full repetition of "The Conspiracy," A section
2:05–2:13	reiteration of A section
2:14–2:21	B section
2:22–2:34	reiteration of B section, with slight slowdown at the end of the tune.

Track 7 (transcription on p. 211)

Genre: Traditional song in English
Track title: "Adieu, Lovely Nancy"
Performers: Karan Casey, voice; John Doyle, guitar and mando-cello; Séamus Egan, flute and low whistle; John Williams, concertina; Winifred Horan, fiddle
Source: Solas, *Sunny Spells and Scattered Showers.* Shanachie CD78010

People who specialize in singing in English are often referred to as "traditional singers," while those who specialize in Irish-language singing are called *sean-nós* singers. As it turns out, all the singers on the compact disc included with this textbook have sung and recorded in both languages. Karan Casey sings "Adieu, Lovely Nancy," a common ballad featuring a lovers' dialogue: he prepares to go off to sea, she begs to accompany him, he tells her why she can't come. He thinks about her while he's abroad and offers to marry her, but he's too late: she has died of a broken heart. This song, like many ballads, ends with a warning never to trust a sailor/ploughboy/soldier/rover/young man. Karan's website is www.karancasey.com.

Timeline for "Adieu Lovely Nancy"

0:00–0:29   first verse:
"Adieu, lovely Nancy, for now I must leave you
For the far-off West Indies, I'm bound for to sail
But let my long journey be of no trouble to you
For my love, I'll return in the course of the year."

0:35–1:02   guitar enters; second verse:
"Talk not of leaving me here, lovely Jimmy
Talk not of leaving me here on the shore
You know very well your long absence will grieve me
As you sail the wild ocean where the wild billows roar."

1:07–1:34   third verse:
"I'll cut off my ringlets all curly and yellow
I'll dress in the coats of a young cabin boy
And when we are out on that dark, rolling ocean
I will always be near you, my pride and my joy."

1:39–2:07   fiddle enters; fourth verse:
"Your lily-white hands, they could not handle the cables
Your lily-white feet to the topmast could not go
And the cold winter storms, well, you could not endure them
Stay at home, lovely Nancy, where the wild winds won't blow."

2:08–2:27   instrumental break (fiddle solo)
2:28–2:55   guitar only; fifth verse:
As Jimmy set a-sailing, lovely Nancy stood a-wailing
The tears from her eyes in great torrents did a-flow
As she stood on the beach, oh, her hands she was wringing
Crying, "Oh and alas, will I e'er see you more?"

3:00–3:26   flute and concertina enter; sixth verse:
As Jimmy was a-walking on the quays of Philadelphia
The thoughts of his true love, they filled him with pride
He said "Nancy, lovely Nancy, if I had you here, love
How happy I'd be for to make you my bride."

3:32–3:58   tin whistle and concertina; seventh verse:
So Jimmy wrote a letter to his own lovely Nancy
Saying "If you have proved constant, well, I will prove true"
Oh but Nancy was dying, for her poor heart was broken
Oh the day that he left her, forever he'd rue.

4:03–4:44   all instruments; eighth verse:
Come all of you maidens, I pray, take a warning
And don't trust a sailor boy or any of his kind
For first they will court you and then they'll deceive you
For their love, it is tempestuous as the wavering wind.

Track 8 (no transcription)

Genre: reels (AABBCCDDEE / AABBCCDDEE / AABB), 4/4
Track title: "Patrick Kelly's (The Foxhunter's Reel / The Bucks of Oranmore / Rakish Paddy"
Performers: James Keane, button accordion; Mick O'Connor, flute; Seán Keane, fiddle;
    Garry O'Briain, guitar; Kevin Conneff, *bodhrán*
Source: James Keane and Friends, *Live in Dublin.* Lavalla Records, LA01

This live recording, from November 10, 1998, in Dublin, represents both the energy and the instrumental diversity of a live session. The first reel, "The Foxhunter's," was rescued from obscurity by Seán Keane's recording of Patrick Kelly. In five parts, it certainly counts as one of the "mighty tunes." As you listen to it, listen for the sounds of the blowing horns and animals (horses, dogs, running fox). I learned this tune at the Friday Harbor Irish Music Camp, and just at the point when the fiddle class had learned it and was playing it, a red fox dashed past the window (to shouts of "Run! Run!" by the class)! You can watch multiple versions of this tune on YouTube (type in "Foxhunter Reel") on several different instruments. "The Bucks of Oranmore" is sometimes referred to as the "national anthem of Irish instrumental music" (including by James Keane himself) because of its enduring popularity; it, too, is a five-part tune. "The Rakish Paddy" is one of the important "hits" of the genre. It is rare to hear two five-part tunes played one after the other, and adding the third tune onto the first two is a bonus of this high-energy live performance. On James Keane's website (www.jameskeane.com) you can view some close-ups of James playing the box with the group Fingal, as well as first-rate photographs of the button accordion designed especially for him and named after him.

Timeline for "The Foxhunter's Reel / The Bucks of Oranmore / Rakish Paddy"

0:00–0:05	start of "The Foxhunter's Reel," A section
0:06–0:09	reiteration of A section
0:10–0:13	B section
0:14–0:17	reiteration of B section
0:18–0:21	C section
0:22–0:25	reiteration of C section
0:26–0:29	D section
0:30–0:33	reiteration of D section
0:34–0:37	E section
0:38–0:41	reiteration of E section
0:41–0:45	full repetition of "The Foxhunter's Reel," A section
0:45–0:48	reiteration of A section
0:49–0:52	B section
0:53–0:56	reiteration of B section
0:57–1:00	C section
1:01–1:04	reiteration of C section
1:05–1:08	D section
1:09–1:12	reiteration of D section
1:13–1:16	E section
1:17–1:20	reiteration of E section
1:20–1:24	full repetition of "The Foxhunter's Reel," A section
1:25–1:27	reiteration of A section
1:28–1:31	B section
1:32–1:35	reiteration of B section
1:36–1:39	C section
1:40–1:43	reiteration of C section
1:44–1:47	D section
1:48–1:51	reiteration of D section
1:52–1:55	E section
1:56–1:59	reiteration of E section
2:00–2:03	start of "The Bucks of Oranmore," A section
2:04–2:07	reiteration of A section
2:08–2:11	B section
2:12–2:15	reiteration of B section
2:16–2:19	C section
2:20–2:22	reiteration of C section
2:23–2:26	D section
2:27–2:30	reiteration of D section
2:31–2:34	E section
2:35–2:38	reiteration of E section
2:39–2:42	full repetition of "The Bucks of Oranmore," A section
2:43–2:46	reiteration of A section
2:47–2:50	B section

2:50–2:54	reiteration of B section
2:54–2:58	C section
2:58–3:02	reiteration of C section
3:03–3:05	D section
3:06–3:09	reiteration of D section
3:10–3:13	E section
3:14–3:17	reiteration of E section
3:18–3:21	full repetition of "The Bucks of Oranmore," A section
3:22–3:25	reiteration of A section
3:26–3:29	B section
3:30–3:32	reiteration of B section
3:33–3:36	C section
3:37–3:40	reiteration of C section
3:41–3:44	D section
3:45–3:48	reiteration of D section
3:49–3:52	E section
3:53–3:56	reiteration of E section
3:56–4:03	start of "The Rakish Paddy," A section
4:04–4:11	reiteration of A section
4:12–4:19	B section
4:20–4:27	reiteration of B section
4:27–4:35	full repetition of "The Rakish Paddy," A section
4:35–4:42	reiteration of A section
4:43–4:50	B section
4:51–4:58	reiteration of B section
4:59–5:06	full repetition of "The Rakish Paddy," A section
5:06–5:13	reiteration of A section
5:14–5:21	B section
5:22–5:35	reiteration of B section, with final held note at the end of the tune.

Track 9 (transcription on p. 207)

Genre: Traditional song in English, 3/4
Track title: "The Lass of Aughrim"
Performers: Susan McKeown, voice; Dana Lyn, fiddle; Eamon O'Leary, guitar
Source: "The Lass of Aughrim" (traditional, arranged by Susan McKeown/IMRO/ ASCAP). Performed by Susan McKeown, vocals; Eamon O'Leary, guitar; Dana Lyn, fiddle. © Hibernian Music, ℗ World Village

In Chapter 8, both the text and the transcribed melody of "The Lass of Aughrim" differ from this version, which was learned from the singing of the late tenor Frank Patterson in the film version of James Joyce's short story, "The Dead." In this version, we know only that the narrator apparently does not recognize the young woman holding a baby in front of him in the rain, and that she has come to him in desperation. Chapter 8 fills out the story more completely, but this version includes enough of the bones of the story that its message is clear: don't trust a nobleman! Chapter 8's version of the story would suggest that one shouldn't trust a nobleman's mother. Susan's website is www.susanmckeown.com.

Timeline for "The Lass of Aughrim"

0:00–0:29	instrumental introduction featuring guitar and fiddle, playing one verse
0:30–1:00	first verse:

If you be the lass of Aughrim, as I take it you mean to be
Tell me the first token that passed between you and me.

1:01–1:30	second verse:

Oh don't you remember that night on yon lean hill
When we were together, which I'm sorry now to tell.

1:31–2:00	third verse:

Oh the rain falls on my heavy locks, and the dew wets my skin
My babe lies cold within my arms, and none will let me in.

2:03–2:30	instrumental solo (fiddle), playing one verse
2:33–3:07	fourth verse:

If you be the lass of Aughrim, as I take it you mean to be
Tell me the first token that passed between you and me.

Track 10 (transcription on p. 161)

Genre: slip jigs (AABB form), 9/8
Track title: "Elizabeth Kelly's Favourite / Follow Me Down to Limerick"
Performers: Catherine McEvoy, wooden flute; Steve Cooney, guitars
Source: Catherine McEvoy, *The Home Ruler.* Cló Iar-Chonnachta CICD 172

Catherine McEvoy plays these slip jigs three times through each. Notice, as you listen, that "Elizabeth Kelly's Favourite" flows easily and seamlessly into "Follow Me Down to Limerick." One distinguishing feature that separates the two is their tonality: the first tune is in G minor (or possibly Dorian, but the tune lacks the sixth degree of the scale), and the second is in F Mixolydian with shifts into F major. Whereas the first tune has an AABB form, the second tune has an AABBCC form. While the first tune is played four times, the second tune lasts slightly longer because each of the three times through includes the two extra lines (the C section).

Timeline for "Elizabeth Kelly's Favourite / Follow Me Down to Limerick"

0:00–0:07	start of "Elizabeth Kelly's Favourite," A section
0:08–0:14	reiteration of A section
0:15–0:21	B section
0:22–0:28	reiteration of B section
0:29–0:35	full repetition of "Elizabeth Kelly's Favourite," A section
0:36–0:43	reiteration of A section
0:44–0:50	B section
0:51–0:57	reiteration of B section
0:58–1:04	full repetition of "Elizabeth Kelly's Favourite," A section
1:05–1:11	reiteration of A section
1:12–1:18	B section
1:19–1:26	reiteration of B section
1:27–1:33	full repetition of "Elizabeth Kelly's Favourite," A section
1:34–1:40	reiteration of A section
1:41–1:47	B section
1:48–1:54	reiteration of B section
1:55–2:02	start of "Follow Me Down to Limerick," A section
2:03–2:09	reiteration of A section
2:10–2:16	B section
2:17–2:23	reiteration of B section
2:24–2:30	start of C section
2:31–2:38	reiteration of C section
2:39–2:44	full repetition of "Follow Me Down to Limerick," A section
2:45–2:52	reiteration of A section
2:53–2:59	B section
3:00–3:06	reiteration of B section
3:07–3:13	C section
3:14–3:20	reiteration of C section
3:21–3:28	full repetition of "Follow Me Down to Limerick," A section
3:28–3:35	reiteration of A section
3:35–3:42	B section
3:43–3:49	reiteration of B section
3:50–3:56	C section
3:57–4:10	reiteration of C section, with slight slowdown at the end.

Track 11 (transcription on p. 163)

Genre: slides (AABB), 12/8
Track title: "Rathawaun / The Hare in the Corn"
Performers: Caoimhín Ó Raghallaigh, fiddle; Mick O'Brien, *uilleann* pipes. Caoimhín's name is pronounced "*kwee*-veen oh *ra*-hilly"
Source: Mick O'Brien and Caoimhín Ó Raghallaigh, *Kitty Lie Over.* ACM Records, CD 102

Slides and polkas are most closely associated with the Sliabh Luachra region on the Cork/Kerry border (in the southwest), but they are also played in other parts of Ireland.

In addition, musicians of the region play plenty of jigs and reels, like everyone else. As you listen to this selection, try to hear the way in which each phrase of the tune(s) extends through *four* triplet groups rather than just two, as in a double jig. Slides are in 12/8, with each measure grouped into four triplets; this is intended to give a sense of the melody's phrasing, but—like every instrumental form except the airs—it also has to do with a particular dance rhythm. One of the fun parts of this cut is the way that Mick sometimes matches Caoimhín's pitch, and sometimes plays an octave below him. Can you tell when he does this? Caoimhín Ó Raghallaigh and Mick O'Brien are both from Dublin; you can listen to them and watch them on YouTube. Caoimhín's website is www.caoimhinoraghallaigh.com.

Timeline for "Rathawaun / The Hare in the Corn"

0:00–0:10	start of "Rathawaun," A section
0:11–0:18	reiteration of A section
0:18–0:26	B section
0:26–0:34	reiteration of B section
0:34–0:42	full repetition of "Rathawaun," A section
0:42–0:49	reiteration of A section
0:50–0:57	B section
0:58–1:05	reiteration of B section
1:05–1:13	full repetition of "Rathawaun," A section
1:13–1:20	reiteration of A section
1:21–1:29	B section
1:29–1:36	reiteration of B section
1:37–1:44	start of "The Hare in the Corn," A section
1:45–1:52	reiteration of A section
1:53–2:00	B section
2:00–2:07	reiteration of B section
2:08–2:15	full repetition of "The Hare in the Corn," A section
2:16–2:23	reiteration of A section
2:24–2:31	B section
2:32–2:38	reiteration of B section
2:39–2:46	full repetition of "The Hare in the Corn," A section
2:47–2:54	reiteration of A section
2:55–3:01	B section
3:02–3:14	reiteration of B section, with final held note at the end of the tune.

Track 12 (transcription on p. 130)

Genre: Irish-American song
Track title: "No Irish Need Apply"
Performers: Mick Moloney, vocals and guitar
Source: CD accompanying *Far From the Shamrock Shore: The Story of Irish-American Immigration Through Song* (New York: Crown)

Hundreds of songs have been written about Irish experiences in America. Mick Moloney, a musician, scholar, and professor of folklore and ethnomusicology at New

York University, has made studying Irish-American music one of his lifelong projects. His 2002 book, *Far From the Shamrock Shore*, is a fascinating compendium of songs, stories, and important ideas about emigration, immigration, and assimilation. This track is from the CD that accompanies the book; the song itself highlights one of the darker aspects of the way many Irish were received upon their arrival in North America. It also emphasizes the famous temper of the Irish, and the narrator gets his revenge on the "dirty *spailpín*" (a *spailpín* is a common laborer with the reputation of having a less-than-stellar character) by beating him to a pulp. The song is upbeat, and affirms pride in being Irish through the lyrics of the chorus, as well as the fifth verse. Mick's website is www.mickmoloney.com.

Timeline for "No Irish Need Apply"

0:00–0:20   first verse:
I'm a decent boy just come from Ballyfad
Oh I want a situation and I want it mighty bad
A position I saw advertised, 'tis the thing for me, say I
But the dirty *spáilpín* ended with "No Irish Need Apply."

0:21–0:32   couplet:
Oh says I, "But that's an insult, but to get this place I'll try"
So I went to see that blackguard with No Irish Need Apply

0:33–0:44   chorus:
Well some may think it a misfortune to be christened Pat or Dan
But to me it is an honor to be born an Irishman.

0:45–0:49   concertina "turnaround" (playing the last line of the chorus)
0:50–1:11   second verse:
I started out to find the house and found it mighty soon
He was seated in the corner, he was reading the Tribune
When I told him what I came for he in a rage did fly
And he says, "you are a Paddy and no Irish need apply"

1:12–1:23   couplet:
Then I felt my dander rising and I'd like to black his eye
To tell an dacent gentleman "No Irish Need Apply"

1:24–1:35   chorus:
Well some may think it a misfortune to be christened Pat or Dan
But to me it is an honor to be born an Irishman.

1:36–1:56   third verse:
Well I couldn't stand his nonsense so ahold of him I took

And I gave him such a beatin' as he'd get in Donnybrook
And he hollered "Milia murther!" and to get away did try
And swore he'd never write again "No Irish Need Apply."

1:57–2:07   couplet:
He made a big apology and I bid him then goodbye
Saying when next you want a beatin' write "No Irish Need Apply"

2:08–2:19   chorus:
Well some may think it a misfortune to be christened Pat or Dan
But to me it is an honor to be born an Irishman.

2:26–2:46   fourth verse:
Sure I've heard that in America it always is the plan
That an Irishman is just as good as any other man
Now home and hospitality they never will deny
To strangers here, or ever say "No Irish Need Apply."

2:47–2:58   couplet:
Ah, but some black sheep are in the flock, a dirty lot, says I
A decent man will never write "No Irish Need Apply"

2:59–3:12   chorus:
Well some may think it a misfortune to be christened Pat or Dan
But to me it is an honor to be born an Irishman.

3:13–3:35   fifth verse:
Now old Ireland on the battlefield a lasting fame was made
To all who heard of Meagher's Men and Corcoran's Brigade
Though fools may flout and bigots rage, "Fanatics!" they may cry
But when they want good fightin' men, the Irish may apply.

3:36–3:47   couplet:
And when for freedom and for rights they raise the battle cry
Those rebel ranks will surely think "No Irish Need Apply"

3:48–4:00   chorus:
Well some may think it a misfortune to be christened Pat or Dan
But to me it is an honor to be born an Irishman.

4:01–4:14   concertina "turnaround" (playing the last line of the chorus)

Track 13 (transcription on p. 163)

Genre: march (AABB), 6/8
Track title: "March of the Kings of Laois" (pronounced "leesh")
Performers: Philip Boulding, harp and tin whistle; Pam Boulding, hammered dulcimer;
  Denny Hall, *uilleann* pipes
Source: Magical Strings, *Good People All.* Flying Fish Records, FF70604

An ensemble performance of the harp and hammered dulcimer—both of which can
be notoriously difficult to tune—is featured on this track. The hammered dulcimer is
a trapezoidal box zither struck with light, flexible sticks; though its roots are in what is
now Iran (where it is called the *santur*) it is found in China and Mongolia, and is also
featured in some American folk music groups. Magical Strings is a family band from
the Pacific Northwest of the United States. This is a non-standard arrangement of a
popular march, in that it includes harmony playing by the tin whistle beginning at 2:09.

Timeline for "March of the Kings of Laois"

0:00–0:31	start of "March of the Kings of Laois," A section
0:32–0:57	reiteration of A section
0:58–1:20	B section
1:21–1:43	reiteration of B section
1:44–2:09	full repetition of "March of the Kings of Laois," A section (entrance of tin whistle)
2:10–2:36	reiteration of A section
2:37–2:59	B section
3:00–3:21	reiteration of B section
3:22–3:48	repeating final line to the end

Track 14 (transcription on p. 164)

Genre: polkas (AABB), 2/4
Track title: "Dan O'Connell's Favourite / The Race Classic / The Gullane"
Performers: The members of the group Líadan include Sarah Jane Woods, flute and
  vocals; Elaine Cormican, vocals and whistle; Síle Denvir, vocals and harp; Deirdre
  Chawke, piano accordion; Claire Dolan, fiddle, strings, and vocals; and Valerie
  Casey, vocals, fiddle, and strings. The piano accordion player, Deirdre Chawke, is
  featured on this track
Source: Líadan, *Traditional Irish Music and Song.* Self-produced CD

The separation of Irish instrumental music from dancing is a relatively recent phenomenon. Polkas, when played for dancers, tend to be much slower than when they are
played just for listening. Notice how very fast these musicians are playing! One could
dance to these polkas, but it would be challenging. The six women of Líadan formed a

band while they were students at the University of Limerick's Irish World Academy of Music and Dance. In listening to Deirdre's playing, think of how easily the piano accordion could be heard in the midst of a noisy crowd (either of dancers or listeners), and how the piano accordion could have become such an essential and welcome element in Irish instrumental music. Its strength of "voice," portability (compared to a piano), and ability to adapt to Irish music has made it indispensable. The group's website is www.liadan.ie (note that Irish websites use the tag ".ie" instead of ".com").

Timeline for "Dan O'Connell's Favourite / The Race Classic / The Gullane"

0:00–0:05	start of "Dan O'Connell's Favourite," A section
0:06–0:12	reiteration of A section
0:12–0:18	B section
0:19–0:24	reiteration of B section
0:25–0:30	full repetition of "Dan O'Connell's Favourite," A section
0:31–0:36	reiteration of A section
0:37–0:42	B section
0:43–0:49	reiteration of B section
0:50–0:55	start of "The Race Classic," A section
0:56–1:01	reiteration of A section
1:02–1:07	B section
1:08–1:13	reiteration of B section
1:14–1:19	full repetition of "The Race Classic," A section
1:20–1:26	reiteration of A section
1:27–1:32	B section
1:33–1:39	reiteration of B section
1:40–1:45	full repetition of "The Race Classic," A section
1:46–1:51	reiteration of A section
1:52–1:57	B section
1:58–2:04	reiteration of B section
2:05–2:10	start of "The Gullane," A section
2:11–2:16	reiteration of A section
2:17–2:23	B section
2:24–2:30	reiteration of B section
2:30–2:36	full repetition of "The Gullane," A section
2:37–2:43	reiteration of A section
2:43–2:49	B section
2:50–2:56	reiteration of B section
2:57–3:02	full repetition of "The Gullane," A section
3:03–3:09	reiteration of A section
3:10–3:16	B section
3:17–3:27	reiteration of B section, with slight slowdown at the end of the tune.

Track 15 (transcription on p. 191)

Genre: sean-nós singing in Munster style

Track title: "Cois Abhann na Séad: ("By the River of Gems"—pronounced "kush aw-in nuh sheyd")

Performers: Eilís Ní Shúilleabháin, voice; Peadar Ó Riada, organ. Eilís's name is pronounced "*Ay*-leesh Nee *Hoo*-la-wawn"

Source: Eilís Ní Shúilleabháin, *Cois Abhann na Séad: Amhráin ar an Sean-Nós ó Mhúscraí*. (By the River of Jewels: Sean-Nós Songs from Muskerry). Cló Iar-Chonnachta CICD132

Sean-nós songs from Munster are often called "big songs." They often have long phrases and tend to build to a soaring third line in each verse. In "Cois Abhann na Séad" ("By the River of Jewels") notice that each phrase is rich in lyric content, and that the third line rises to a climax in pitch. Eilís Ní Shúilleabháin comes from the Cúil Aodha district in Muskerry Gaeltacht, a region in the southwest well known for its great singers and strong storytelling tradition. This recording includes only the first three out of five verses. Eilís is a well-known award-winning singer who has taught and performed both in Ireland and abroad.

Timeline for "Cois Abhann na Séad"

0:00–0:04	organ begins with chords
0:05–1:50	first verse:

Cois abhann na séad ar uair bhig a' lae, 's mé ag imeacht fé dhéin mo shláinte
> By the river of jewels at the small hour of day; I progressing for the sake of my health

Mar a mbídís caora 's cnó buí ar ghéaga 's mil bheach 'na shlaod ar bhánta
> Where [red] berries and yellow nuts were on branches and honey flowing on the meadows

Do labhradar na h-éin, do lasadar na spéartha, bhí an fharraige 'na caor-luisne lán suas
> The birds sang, the skies lit up, the sea was full with a blinding red light

Do nhúscail an ghrian a bhí le sealad mór fé chiach agus d'érigh an t-iasc 'na lán rith
> The sun, which had been occluded for so long, awoke and the fish rose up in a full run.

1:52–3:37	second verse:

Ansúd ar dtúis ar imeallaibh ciúise coille cumhra do tharla
There at first at the edge of the fragrant forest I encountered

An fhinne-bhean fhionn gur bhinne liom a tiúin ná an fidil, an fliúit ná 'n cláirseach
The fairest of fair women whose music I found sweeter than fiddle, than flute, than harp

Ba bhreá deas a súil, a mala caol cumtha, a leaca bhí mar chumhar na trá
Her fine pretty eye, her slender well-formed brow, her cheeks like foam on the shore

Ba ghile í ar a píb ná an eala ar a' linn is do líon mo chroí le grá dhí.
Her neck was whiter than the swan on the lake and my heart filled with love for her.

3:40–5:27   third verse:
Nuair a dhearcas í ansúd mar a bhí—an ainnir ba chaoine 's ba bhreátha
When I saw her there as she was—the maiden most gentle and fine

Bhí scáil na gcaor 'na leacain réidh agus fátha bhí 'na gáire
The sheen of berries lit up her smooth cheeks and a smile played on her laugh

Dob é an chom slim do lagaigh mé im chroí le taithneamh dá cló 's dá gáire
It was the slim waist that weakened my heart with pleasure at her shape and her laughter

Ó bhaitheas go bonn bhí a ciabh leí go trom is a cúl buí go casta fáinneach.
From her forehead to her soles her tresses fell heavily and her luxuriant twisting ringlets.

Track 16 (transcription on p. 166)

Genre: highlands (AABB), 4/4
Track title: "Casey's Pig / Dúlamán na Binne Buídhe" ("Seaweed of the Yellow Cliffs"—pronounced "doo-la-mawn nuh binnya bwee")
Performers: Róisín McGrory, fiddle; Damien Harrigan, fiddle
Source: The Fiddle Music of Donegal, volume 2. Cairdeas Records CNF 002

Brother-sister duo Róisín McGrory (née Harrigan) and Damien Harrigan of Donegal play fiddles in this example of highlands. Highlands are related to Scottish strathspeys and flings, and are often characterized by the "Scottish snap" of a short beat followed by a long beat. You can hear this immediately in the first few measures of "Casey's Pig," the first tune on this track. Rather than long–short, long–short, long–short (as in a hornpipe), the snap starts out as short–long, then continues with even eighth notes, and often occurs at the beginning of a measure. By the time the second tune begins, the snap pattern is less pronounced but still evident. Another key feature of their fine playing, besides the fact that their bowing matches so well, is that they use almost all single-stroke bowing, rather than the slurs that characterize so much of the playing of, say, County Clare. Notice how clear each note is; this clarity is not simply because Róisín and Damien have played together for so long (though it surely helps). It is the clarity of—for the most part—up–down–up–down bowing that works here. Compare the sound of this pair of tunes (and players) to "Rathawaun / The Hare in the Corn" and "The Hag's Purse / The Sturgeon / The Ten Penny Bit": Sliabh Luachra style for the former, West Clare style for the latter.

Timeline for "Casey's Pig / Dúlamán na Binne Buídhe"

0:00–0:07	start of "Casey's Pig," A section
0:07–0:12	reiteration of A section
0:13–0:18	B section
0:19–0:23	reiteration of B section
0:24–0:29	full repetition of "Casey's Pig," A section
0:30–0:35	reiteration of A section
0:35–0:40	B section
0:40–0:45	reiteration of B section
0:46–0:50	start of "Dúlamán na Binne Buídhe," A section
0:51–0:55	reiteration of A section
0:56–1:01	B section
1:01–1:06	reiteration of B section
1:06–1:11	full repetition of "Dúlamán na Binne Buídhe," A section
1:12–1:16	reiteration of A section
1:17–1:21	B section
1:22–1:26	reiteration of B section
1:27–1:32	full repetition of "Dúlamán na Binne Buídhe," A section
1:32–1:37	reiteration of A section
1:38–1:41	B section
1:42–1:47	reiteration of B section
1:47–1:52	full repetition of "Dúlamán na Binne Buídhe," A section
1:52–1:57	reiteration of A section
1:58–2:02	B section
2:03–2:09	reiteration of B section, with final held note at the end of the tune.

Track 17 (transcription on p. 182)

Genre: sean-nós singing from Connemara
Track title: "Úna Bhán" ("Fair Úna"—pronounced "oona wawn")
Performers: Joe Heaney, solo voice
Source: Joe Heaney, *From My Tradition*, Shanachie 34019

Joe Heaney was born and raised in Carna, in the western part of Ireland known as Connemara. He moved to the United States and spent the last decade of his life working as a visiting artist in several American ethnomusicology departments. He is widely acknowledged as one of the best of the *sean-nós* singers, and is justly famous for the ways in which he ornamented his songs. This song is discussed and transcribed in Chapter 7; as you listen to this recording, however, compare his vocal timbre to that of the other singers on the recording. Some *sean-nós* singers have a nasality to their singing, while others have a full, rich tone, a very thin, reedy tone, or vibrato, or great articulation, or some other characteristic. A particular timbre is not a requirement for good singing. Instead, one's understanding of the song and its story, together with the feeling one is able to impart, is very important.

Timeline for "Úna Bhán"

0:00–0:56   first verse:
Is a Úna Bhán nach gránna an luí sin ort
Fair Úna, ugly do you lie there

I do leaba chaol chláir imeasc na ndáinte corp
In your bed of planks among a host of corpses

Mar dtige tú le fóir orm a ghrá a bhí ariamh gan locht
If you don't come and succour me, oh love that was ever without fault

Ní thiocfaidh mé chun t-áras go brách ach an oíche anocht.
I'll not come to your place again, save tonight.

0:57–1:48   second verse:
Is a Úna Bhán ba rós i ngairdín thú
Oh Fair Úna, you were a rose in the garden

Ba cláirseach a'cheoil romham sa mbóthar thú
You were a harp playing music before me in the road

Ba chéiliúr is ba cheolmhar ag dul an bhealaigh seo romham thú
Melodious and musical you were going on the road before me

Seo mo chreach mhaidhne bhrónach nár pósadh le do ghrá geal thú.
It is my utter ruin that you were not married to me.

1:50–2:38   third verse:
Tá an sneachta seo ar a' lár is é dearg le fuil
The snow is on the ground and it is red with blood

Ach samhail mo ghrá ní fhaca mé in áit ar bith
But the likeness of my love I never saw anyplace at all

Féachaíse a mhná cé b'fhearr ná an t-óchón sin
Is it a better choice to hear the women keening

Aon ghlaoch amháin a' ghabháil Áth na Donóige.
Or to let out just one call toward the Ford of Donoghue?

2:39–3:19   fourth verse:
Dá mbeadh píopa fada cailce agam is tobac a bheith ann
If I had a long clay pipe at me and tobacco being in it

Tharrangóinn amach é is chaithfinn de mo sháith
I'd draw it out and smoke my fill

Is maith a d'insioinnse dhíbhse cé gcónaíonn Úna Bhán
It's good to hear from you where Fair Úna lived

I gCill Bhríde is gCrích Mha Chill 'mo chreach is mo chrá.
In Cill Bhríde and Crich Mha Chill is my ruin and my sorrow.

3:21–4:06   fifth verse:
'S mo scrúdadh thú Úna Mhic Diarmada óig
You try me severely, Young Úna Mac Dermott

An chéad scoth do na mná buartha agus Brianach óg
All the best to the sorrowful women and young Brianach

Do bhéal mar a bhfuil siúcra mar an leamhnacht 's an fion ar bord
Your mouth is as sugar, as the new milk and the wine on the table

Do chois lúfar a shiúlfadh go fíor i mbróig.
Your agile feet walking well in shoes.

Track 18 (no transcription)

Genre: air (form), free meter
Track title: "Cath Chéim an Fhia" ("The Battle of Deer's Leap"—pronounced "kah
    kheym unn ee-a")
Performers: James Kelly, fiddle
Source: original recording for this disc

James Kelly is one of Ireland's great fiddlers; he emigrated to the United States in the 1970s and now lives in Florida. He kindly offered to make an original recording of an air for this project, and selected the beautiful *sean-nós* song "Cath Chéim an Fhia" ("The Battle of Deer's Leap") to record instrumentally. The poet Máire Bhuí Ní Laoghaire (1774–1849) wrote this song to describe a battle between local people and landlords. The song's verses are included, with many thanks to Eilís Ní Shúilleabháin for both the lyrics and their translation. Notice the variation that James performs from verse to verse, as would a singer; he understands the song's meaning and can give it the *blás* or tasteful feeling that it deserves. Even though James is *playing*, not singing the lyrics, they give a sense of the trajectory of the original song and the feeling that a sensitive instrumentalist can impart. One particular *sean-nós* singer, Níoclas Tóibín, recorded seven verses of this song. James's website is www.jameskellymusic.com.

Timeline for "Cath Chéim an Fhia"

0:00–1:50   first verse:
Cois abhann Ghleanna an Chéama in Uíbh Laoghaire 'sea bhímse
By the river of the glen of the high road in Uíbh Laoghaire they were

Mar a dtéann an fia san oíche, chun síor-chodladh sóghail
Where the deer goes at night to seek quiet refreshing sleep

A' machnamh séal liom féinig 's a déanamh mo smaointe
I was meditating to myself

Ag éisteacht i gcoillte le binn-ghuth na n-eon
Listening in the woods to the sweet voices of the birds.

Nuair a chuala an chath a' teacht aniar, is glór na neach a' teacht le sians'
When I heard the battle coming from the west and the sound of the horses coming

Le fuaim a n-airm do chrith an Sliabh 's níor bhéinn liom a nglór
The mountain shook to the sound of their weapons and I didn't find their sounds sweet

Thángadar go námhadmhar mar a thiocfadh gárda de chonaibh nímhe
They came with enmity like a guard of poisonous hounds coming

Agus cumha mo chroí, na sár-fhir, d'fhagadar gan treoir.
And sadness of my heart, the great men lay scattered.

1:51–3:34   second verse:
Níor fhan fear, bean ná páiste im mbun áitribh ná tí ann
Neither man, woman nor child stayed in their houses there

Na gártha goil do bhí 'ca is na mílte ologon
The crying shouts that were at them, and the lamenting

Ag féachaint ar an ngárda bhí go láidir 'na dtimpeall
Looking at this army that was around them in strength

Ag lámhach is ag líonadh 's ag scaoileadh 'na dtreo
Shooting and reloading and shooting in their direction

An liú gur leath i bhfad i gcian, 'sé dúirt gach flaith gur mhaith leis triall
The shout went up, spread far and wide, all the noblemen wanted to go with them

Gluaisíg go mear, tá 'n cath dá riar is téimís 'na chomhair
March quickly, the battle is on, let us go toward it.

Thángadar na sár-fhir, guim áthas ar chlanna Gael
The great men came, I wish joy to the Irish clan

Is chomaineadar na páinthig le fánaig ar seol.
And they drove the big-bellied people away.

3:35–4:53   third verse:
Níorbh fhada dhúinn go dtáinig lámh-láidir 'nár dtimpeall
It wasn't long before violence came around us

Agus scaipeadar ár ndaoine ar gach maoilinn faoin gceo
And they scattered our people on every hill under the fog

Bhí an Barrach 'na bhumbáille 'ca Barnet agus Beecher
Mr Barry the leader of them, Barnett and Beecher

Hedges agus Sweet, is na mílte eile leo
Hedges and Sweet and thousands more

A Rí na bhFeart go leagaigh iad, gan chlú, gan mheas, gan rath, gan séan
King of Deeds, may you knock them down without reputation, respect, luck, or happiness

Go teintibh meara imeasc na bpian, gan faoiseamh go deo
To quick great fires among the pains, without relief ever

Ach céad moladh mór le h-Íosa nár dhíolamar as an gcóir
But a hundred praises to Jesus that we didn't fall for it

Ach bheith a' déanamh grin de 's á insint ar sógh.
But we made fun of it while sitting around the fire.

Appendix 1: Key Dates in Irish History

c. 10,000 BCE	Evidence of Paleolithic people
c. 8,000 BCE	Evidence of Mesolithic people
c. 4,000–2,000 BCE	Neolithic people create megaliths: standing stones, dolmens, stone circles
c. 2,000 BCE–400 CE	Copper >> Bronze >> Iron Age development
c. 500 BCE	Arrival of Celtic people from mainland Europe
c. 200 BCE	La Tène style of art incorporated into pottery, metalwork, and stonework
35 BCE	First mention of bagpipes in Ireland
400 CE	Christianity becomes established
500	Development of monastic settlements and appearance of many local saints
795	Arrival of the Vikings
c. 800	*The Book of Kells* created
1014	Battle of Clontarf; Brian Ború defeats the Vikings
1170–1171	Anglo-Norman invasion; Henry II declares himself to be king of Ireland
1366	Statutes of Kilkenny passed; Anglo-Normans required to be more English
1536–1541	Dissolution of the Monasteries; Henry VIII took over all monastic lands
1542	The Crown of Ireland Act appoints Henry VIII as Ireland's ruler
1558–1603	Queen Elizabeth I is in power as Queen of England and Ireland
1601	Battle of Kinsale, final battle in England's efforts to conquer Ireland
1607	Flight of the Earls; collapse of the native Irish aristocracy

1607–1920	Penal Laws discriminating against Catholics and, later, Presbyterians
1609	The Plantation of Ulster begins; Scottish Presbyterians settle in the North
1632–1636	Irish-language medieval history *Annals of the Four Masters* created
1649–1653	Oliver Cromwell leads English campaign in Ireland
1670–1738	Turlough O'Carolan, composer, harper, and singer
1690	Battle of the Boyne lost to William of Orange, ensuring Protestant rule
1742	Premiere of Handel's *Messiah* oratorio in Dublin
1792	Belfast Harp Festival
1798	Rebellion led by the United Irishmen, both Protestants and Catholics
1800s	Many instruments enter Irish music: fiddles, accordions, flutes, etc.
1800–1801	Acts of Union, uniting Ireland with England
1808–1834	Thomas Moore's *Irish Melodies* published
1845–1850	The Great Hunger–*an Gorta Mór*–Ireland's population is cut in half
1850	Devotional Revolution: strong re-Catholicization of Irish beliefs
1897	First Oireachtas na Gaeilge (competition of Irish traditional arts)
1916	Easter Rising; Proclamation of Independence issued in Dublin
1919–1921	War of Independence from England
1921	Anglo-Irish Treaty creates partition: Northern Ireland and Irish Free State
1922–1923	Irish Civil War (pro-Treaty vs. anti-Treaty)
1931–1971	Seán Ó Riada, composer and performer
1937	The Irish Free State becomes Ireland, per its new constitution
1949	Ireland becomes the Republic of Ireland
1969	The "Troubles" begin in Northern Ireland
1973	Ireland joins the European Community (later, the European Union)
1973	Law prohibiting married women from earning pay is struck down
1981	Political prisoners in Belfast go on hunger strike; ten men die
1985	Birth control is legalized
1990	President Mary Robinson (first female Irish president) elected
1994	*Riverdance* (short version) performed during the Eurovision Song Contest
1995–2007	Celtic Tiger period of economic prosperity
1996	Divorce is legalized
1998	Good Friday Accords signed, effectively ending the worst of the Troubles
2015	Marriage Equality referendum passes
2016–2020	Brexit debates revive discussion of a hard Republic/Northern Irish border
2018	Abortion is legalized

Appendix 2: Celebrating an Irish Meal

It is easy to halve the potato where there is love.

The Ethnomusicologists' Cookbook (Routledge 2006), together with volume 2 (Routledge 2015) is a compilation of recipes and essays about many different areas of the world. The Ireland chapter of volume 1 is reproduced here for your perusal and, ideally, culinary pleasure. Each entry in those cookbooks is intended to serve a complete meal for six people. Enjoy!

Menu: *Beef Stew with Guinness, Champ with Spring Onions, Steamed Kale, Brown Bread, Apple Cake.* Serve with water or black tea with milk and sugar.
Preparation Time: 3 hours
Cooking process: Start the stew first; while it is simmering, prepare the brown bread and the apple cake. 45 minutes before eating, prepare the champ and the kale. Serves six people.

Recipes

Beef Stew with Guinness

2 lbs. beef for stewing
1/2 c. flour
2 T vegetable oil
2 medium yellow onions
1/2 c. tomato sauce
1 pint Guinness or other stout beer
3 carrots

salt
pepper

Cut 2 lbs. beef into bite-sized pieces. In a plastic bag, pour 1/2 c. flour, 2 t. salt, 1 t. black pepper. Place the meat inside the bag and shake until thoroughly coated; brush off excess flour. Heat 2 T oil in a Dutch oven or large, solidly-built pan. Quickly brown the meat, stirring and turning the pieces. Peel and chop 2 medium onions; add to the pot with 1/2 c. tomato sauce. Stir until the onions start to look translucent. Pour in 1 pint of Guinness and 3 chopped carrots. Cover and simmer slowly for several hours until the meat is very tender. Season to taste.

If stew is too watery, add the remaining flour that you used to coat the meat.

Champ with Spring Onions

6 potatoes
1 bunch spring onions or scallions
1 c. milk
6 T butter
salt
pepper

Peel and cut 4 potatoes into large chunks. Boil them with just enough water to cover until they are soft (about 20 minutes). While the potatoes are boiling, chop 1 bunch of spring onions (including the white parts) and bring to a low simmer in 1 c. milk. Remove from heat. When potatoes appear done, drain the water and mash with 4 T butter, then add the milk/onion mix. Add salt and pepper to taste. Serve with more butter.

Steamed or Boiled Kale

1 large bunch of dark green kale
2 T butter

Wash and stem 1 bunch of dark green kale. Gather all the leaves together and slice horizontally across all of them in 1/4" slices. Steam or boil for 5 minutes; toss with 2 T melted butter. Add salt and pepper to taste.

Brown Bread

2 c. whole oats
2 c. buttermilk
1 t. baking soda
2-1/2 c. wholemeal (if available) or all-purpose flour
salt

Soak 2 c. whole oats in 2 c. buttermilk on the counter overnight. The next morning, mix 1 t. salt and 1 t. baking soda with 2-1/2 c. flour. Shape into a round loaf in the middle of a non-sticking baking sheet (coat lightly with butter if necessary) and cut a cross in the bread right through it, keeping the shape intact. Bake at 350° for one hour. Cut into slices and slather with butter.

Apple Cake

2 large apples
1/4 c. sugar
2-1/2 c. flour
1/2 t. baking powder
1/4 lb. butter
1 egg
1/2 c. milk
1 c. whipping cream

Peel, core, and chop up 2 large apples. Mix them with 1/4 c. sugar and set aside. Whisk 2-1/2 c. flour with 1/2 t. baking powder. Cut in 1 stick butter. Add 1/2 c. sugar. In a separate bowl, beat together 1 egg and 1/2 c. milk. Pour into the center of the dry ingredients and mix gently. Divide into two halves; the first half goes into the bottom of a lightly greased cake or pie pan (dough will be quite sticky, so use your fingers to shape it into the pan). Place the chopped apples on top, then stretch out the second half of the dough with your fingers and cover the apples with it, sealing the sides if possible. Cut a couple of slashes across the top and brush with beaten egg. Bake for 35-40 minutes at 350° and serve with whipped cream if desired.

Tea with Singing and a Pint at the Session

Ireland, once known popularly as "The Land of Song," has a long history of its inhabitants singing or playing away the darkness of rain and winter in the comfortable confines of a cottage kitchen, near a turf fire. Songs lasting up to 15 minutes were interspersed with equally lengthy stories, serving to entertain friends and families during the cold winter months. In the summers, dances might take place at crossroads and other outdoor locations. Ireland has a much more recent history of playing host to instrumental music sessions in pubs. This newer custom had its roots in the immigrant Irish of England, the United States, and Australia needing a place to go and socialize, because the urban tenements were not hospitable to song and music sessions.

Between the time that instrumental music became associated with pubs and the recent and emphatic entry of women into the public areas of the pubs (as opposed to quietly gathering with other women in the "snug"—a private room in back), a dichotomy developed between those who sang at home—usually women, usually in the presence of children and guests—and those who played instrumental music at pubs—usually men. The beverage of choice at home was tea, and the beverage of choice at the pub was a pint of beer (often a stout beer such as Guinness). Together with the abrupt economic upswing of the 1990s, the gender-based divisions between home and pub have diminished significantly. Pub life has been increasingly dominated by the presence of televisions, and home life has been dominated by competing work schedules, leaving significantly less leisure time. The combination of laws being changed to allow married women to enter the workforce with the sudden availability of jobs has resulted in less time for music making, storytelling, and dancing.

Ireland's rapidly changing economic situation has not diminished the enjoyment of food, however. Indeed, Irish food has undergone a radical makeover since the 1990s. The economic boom spurred by Ireland's entry into the European Union brought a renewed interest in fresh local foods, including smoked wild salmon, dark greens, artisan breads and cheeses, and, of course, the potato. The Great Hunger of the 1840s, the bleak result of the Irish people's forced dependence on the potato, continues to have a powerful impact on the way people eat. A single meal at a restaurant today might include four separate potato preparations (boiled, mashed, fried, and baked) in addition to a meat dish and a green vegetable. Hand in hand with the new interest in food has come an explosive growth of restaurants catering not only to wealthy tourists, but to the newly wealthy Irish themselves. While one would expect the growth of good-quality eateries to be limited primarily to the big cities of Dublin, Belfast to the north, and Galway to the west, small villages scattered throughout Ireland are increasingly home to restaurants specializing in fresh local food. One can now find organic goods in local shops.

Because tourism is one of the primary sources of Ireland's wealth, hotels and some pubs, particularly in the popular tourist havens of Dublin and Killarney, have worked hard to accommodate the unceasing need for a "roots experience" by hosting traditional music sessions. Sometimes these sessions are held on stages with full sound systems (like an Irish cabaret), and the musicians intersperse their jigs and reels with popular Irish-American hits like "When Irish Eyes are Smiling" or "Danny Boy." Other contexts for food and music outside the home include pubs that serve a limited number of dishes (bacon and cabbage, lamb stew or beef and Guinness stew, roast chicken, "chips" or fried potatoes, etc.). Locals and visitors alike might enjoy this food and pints of beer or cups of tea while three or four musicians play jigs and reels in the background. In this context, the musicians face each other, ignoring the "audience," and the audience members chat quietly among themselves. At pub sessions, singers are expected to sing only when asked, and only to give the instrumentalists a break late in the evening. Otherwise, the place for song remains in the kitchen with the tea, brown bread with butter and marmalade, and occasional soda bread (usually served as a dessert rather than as the staple).

While beer was once the almost exclusive drink of the average Irishman (Irish whiskies and *poitín*—"moonshine"—more rarely), imported wines are affordable and easily accessible today at all the major shops. Wine drinking has become popular in many middle-class homes, and an upwardly mobile interest in all things culinary has led to a spate of cooking classes and restaurants specializing in foreign cuisines. In addition, "hard lemonade," fortified caffeine drinks, and mixed drinks using vodka or rum are popular favorites in the urban dance scene. It is not too far of a stretch to see the ways that this experimentation with new cuisines has led some Irish people back to exploring traditional methods of cooking. People on the coasts used seaweeds, for example, as food, medicine, and fertilizer for centuries. It is no longer out of the question to see a sweetened seaweed-based dessert on the menu of a gourmet restaurant, or a soup that includes nettles.

The overwhelming sense of shame once associated with "traditional" ways of being (speaking the Irish language, singing in the old style, playing pipes and fiddles, eating wild plants and seaweed and shellfish) is no longer an automatic reaction among the Irish of the twenty-first century. Irish-language schools, for example, have grown dramatically in popularity, and more young people are enthusiastically exploring traditional music-making in ways that would have shocked their elders in the 1950s. Even today, however, certain foods and musical styles invoke in some Irish a deep disdain and resentment over the dark experiences of the past. Aidan Carl Mathews wrote a poem titled "The Death of Irish," speaking of language loss in the late twentieth century:

> The tide gone out for good
> *Thirty one words for seaweed*
> *Whiten on the foreshore.*

This concise but exceptionally revealing poem (from Mathews' 1983 collection *Minding Ruth*) may no longer apply to the Ireland of the twenty-first century. Indeed, Mathews himself recommends that one take the poem "with a grain of salt"! One can now study Irish through online tutorials, program jigs into one's cell phone ringer, and listen to live streaming broadcasts of old-style singing competitions from around the globe. And anyone halfway across the world can enjoy a hearty meal of beef and Guinness stew with champ, kale, brown bread, and apple cake. Just don't forget to sing afterwards in the kitchen.

Recommended listening:

Classic Irish groups from the 1970s include the Bothy Band, Planxty, The Chieftains, Clannad, and others, while contemporary groups Altan, Solas, Lúnasa, and Danu represent the modern face of traditional music. All these recordings feature carefully arranged pieces interspersed with songs. In some cases, the groups have experimented with rock, jazz, punk, and world music. Many individual singers and instrumentalists have made a splash on the scene, and so many brilliant CDs have appeared in the past ten years that it would be impossible to single out one or two without slighting all the others. Look for solo singers, fiddlers, pipers, harpers, "box" (button accordion) players, flutists, and pennywhistle players. Most importantly, support live music by attending a concert or session, or just sing in your car, your kitchen, or your child's bedroom at night.

References

Anderson, Benedict. *Imagined Communities: Reflections on the Origin and Spread of Nationalism.* London: Verso, 1991.

Andrews, J. H. "A Geographer's View of Irish History." In *The Course of Irish History*, edited by T. W. Moody and F. X. Martin, pp. 17–29, Boulder, CO: Roberts Rinehart, 1995.

Badone, Ellen. "Ethnicity, Folklore, and Local Identity in Rural Brittany." *Journal of American Folklore* 100, no. 396 (1987): 161–190.

Bazin, Fenella. "Manx Traditional Music." In *The Companion to Irish Traditional Music*, edited by Fintan Vallely, pp. 226–228. Cork: Cork University Press, 1999.

Bergin, Osborne. "An Introduction to Bardic Poetry" (1913). In *Irish Bardic Poetry*, edited by David Greene and Fergus Kelly, pp. 3–5. Dublin: Dublin Institute for Advanced Studies, 1984.

Bevil, J. Marshall. "The Welsh Crwth, Its History, and Its Genealogy." *Unpublished Master's thesis in Musicology.* Denton, TX: University of North Texas, 1973.

Bourke, Angela. "Songs in English from the Conamara Gaeltacht." In *Dear Far-Voiced Veteran: Essays in Honour of Tom Munnelly*, edited by Anne Clune, pp. 43–58. Miltown Malbay, Ireland: The Old Kilfarboy Society, 2007.

Bowen, Robyn Huw. CD Liner Notes from *Telyn Berseiniol Fy Ngwlad—The Sweet Harp of My Land.* Chicago, IL: Flying Fish Records, FF70610, 1991.

Boydell, Barra and Harry White. *The Encyclopedia of Irish Music*, vol. 1 & 2. Dublin: UCD Press, 2016.

Brannon, Patrick. "The Search for the Celtic Rite: The TCD Sarum Divine Office Mss. Reassessed." In *Irish Musical Studies 2: Music and the Church*, edited by Gerard Gillen and Harry White, pp. 13–40. Dublin: Irish Academic Press, 1993.

Breathnach, Breandán. *Ceol Rince na hÉireann* (Dance Music of Ireland), four volumes. Dublin: An Gúm, 1963.

Breathnach, Breandán. *Folk Music and Dances of Ireland.* Cork: Mercier Press, 1971.

Brennan, Helen. *The Story of Irish Dance.* Dingle, Ireland: Mount Eagle Publications, 1999.

Bunting, Edward. *The Ancient Music of Ireland: The Bunting Collections.* Dublin: Walton Manufacturing Ltd, 2002 [1796, 1809, 1840].

Byrne, F. J. "Early Irish History (1st–9th Century)." In *The Course of Irish History*, edited by T. W. Moody and F. X. Martin, pp. 43–60. Boulder, CO: Roberts Rinehart, 1995.

Campbell, Sean. *Irish Blood, English Heart: Second Generation Irish Musicians in England*. Cork: Cork University Press, 2011.

Carson, Ciaran. *Irish Traditional Music*. Belfast: Appletree Press, 1986.

Carson, Ciaran. *Last Night's Fun: In and Out of Time with Irish Music*. London: North Point Press, 1996.

Carson, Ciaran. *The Táin*. Translated from the Old Irish Epic *Táin Bó Cuailnge*. London: Penguin, 2007.

Casey, Natasha. "The Best Kept Secret in Retail: Selling Irishness in Contemporary America." In *The Irish in Us: Irishness, Performativity, and Popular Culture*, edited by Diane Negra. Durham, NC: Duke University Press, 2006.

Child, Francis James. *The English and Scottish Popular Ballads*. Boston, MA: Forgotten Books, 1882–89.

Clarke, Austin. "The Colonisation of Ulster and the Rebellion of 1641." In *The Course of Irish History*, edited by T. W. Moody and F. X. Martin, pp. 189–203. Boulder, CO: Roberts Rinehart, 1995.

Collins, Kevin. *The Cultural Conquest of Ireland*. Minneapolis, MN: Irish Books and Media, 1990.

Cooke, Peter. *The Fiddle Tradition of the Shetland Isles*. Cambridge: Cambridge University Press, 1986.

Cooper, David. *The Musical Traditions of Northern Ireland and Its Diaspora*. Burlington, VT: Ashgate, 2009.

Corkery, Daniel. *The Hidden Ireland*. Dublin: Gill and Macmillan, 1924.

Cowdery, James R. *The Melodic Tradition of Ireland*. Kent, OH: Kent State University Press, 1990.

Crawford, Barbara E., ed. *The 'Papar' in the North Atlantic*. St. Andrews, Scotland: St. John's House, Papers no. 10, 2002.

Cronin, Mike. *A History of Ireland*. Basingstoke and New York: Palgrave, 2001.

Cunningham, Eric. "Bodhrán." In *The Companion to Irish Traditional Music*, edited by Fintan Vallely, pp. 28–32. Cork: Cork University Press, 1999.

Davis, Leith. *Music, Postcolonialism, and Gender: The Construction of Irish National Identity, 1724–1874*. Notre Dame, IN: University of Notre Dame Press, 2006.

de Paor, Liam. "The Age of the Viking Wars (9th and 10th Centuries)." In *The Course of Irish History*, edited by T. W. Moody and F. X. Martin, pp. 91–106. Boulder, CO: Roberts Rinehart, 1995.

Dezell, Maureen. *Irish America Coming into Clover: The Evolution of a People and a Culture*. New York: Doubleday, 2000.

Dowling, Martin. *Traditional Music and Irish Society: Historial Perspectives*. Burlington, VT: Ashgate, 2014.

Doyle, Danny and Terence Folan. *The Gold Sun of Irish Freedom: 1798 in Song and Story*. Cork: Mercier Press, 1998.

Doyle, David N. "Scots Irish or Scotch-Irish." In *The Encyclopedia of the Irish in America*, edited by Michael Glazier, pp. 842–851. Notre Dame, IN: University of Notre Dame Press, 1999.

Ellis, Peter. Beresford. *Eyewitness to Irish History*. Hoboken, NJ: John Wiley & Sons, 2004.

Feintuch, Burt. "Introduction." CD Liner Notes for *Northumberland Rant: Traditional Music from the Edge of England*. Washington, DC: Smithsonian Folkways Recordings SFWCD 40473, 1999.

Flanagan, Laurence. *Ancient Ireland: Life Before the Celts*. Dublin: Gill and Macmillan, 2000.

Flower, Robin. *The Irish Tradition*. Oxford: Clarendon Press, 1947.

Foley, Catherine. "Step Dance." In *The Companion to Irish Traditional Music*, edited by Fintan Vallely, pp. 380–381. Cork: Cork University Press, 1999.

Fulton, Cheryl Ann. CD Liner Notes from *The Airs of Wales*. Koch International Classics 3-7071-2 H1, 1991.

Gammon, Vic. "England." In *The Garland Encyclopedia of World Music*, vol. 9: *Europe*, edited by Timothy Rice and James Porter, pp. 326–341. New York: Routledge Publishing, 2000.

Gedutis, Susan. *See You at the Hall: Boston's Golden Era of Irish Music and Dance.* Boston, MA: Northeastern University Press, 2004.

Glazier, Michael. "St. Patrick's Day Parade." In *The Encyclopedia of the Irish in America*, edited by Michael Glazier, pp. 821–822. Notre Dame, IN: University of Notre Dame Press, 1999.

Hamilton, Colin "Hammy." "The Flute in Irish Music." In *The Companion to Irish Traditional Music*, edited by Fintan Vallely, p. 137. Cork: Cork University Press, 1999.

Hamm, Charles. "'Erin, the Tear and the Smile in Thine Eyes': Or, Thomas Moore's *Irish Melodies* in America." In *Yesterdays: Popular Song in America*, edited by Charles Hamm, pp. 42–61. New York and London: W.W. Norton and Company, 1983.

Harding, Paul and Joe Bindloss. *Iceland*, 5th ed. London: Lonely Planet, 2004.

Harris, Ruth-Anne M. "Introduction." In *The Great Famine and the Irish Diaspora in America*, edited by Arthur Gribben, pp. 1–20. Amherst, MA: University of Massachusetts Press, 1999.

Hast, Dorothea and Stanley Scott. *Music in Ireland: Experiencing Music, Expressing Culture.* New York: Oxford University Press, 2004.

Hastings, Gary. *With Fife and Drum: Music, Memories and Customs of an Irish Tradition.* Belfast: Blackstaff Press Ltd, 2003.

Heymann, Ann. "Harp." In *The Companion to Irish Traditional Music*, edited by Fintan Vallely, pp. 170–173. Cork: Cork University Press, 1999.

Hickey, Donal. *Stone Mad for Music: The Sliabh Luachra Story.* Dublin: Marino, 1999.

Hyde, Douglas. *A Literary History of Ireland from Earliest Times to the Present Day.* London and Leipzig: T. Fisher Unwin, 1910.

Ignatiev, Noel. *How the Irish Became White.* New York: Routledge, 1995.

Irwin, Colin. *In Search of the Craic: One Man's Pub Crawl Through Irish Music.* London: André Deutsch, 2003.

Jarman, Neil. "For God and Ulster: Blood and Thunder Bands and Loyalist Political Culture." In *The Irish Parading Tradition: Following the Drum*, edited by T. G. Fraser, pp. 158–172. New York: St. Martin's Press, 2000.

Jones, Alan. "Northumbrian Traditional Music." CD Liner Notes for *Spirit of the Border: Northumbrian Traditional Music*. Monmouth, UK: Nimbus Records NI5615, 1999.

Kaul, Adam R. "The Anthropologist as Barman and Tour-Guide: Reflections on Fieldwork in a Touristed Destination." *Durham Anthropology Journal* 12, no. 1 (2004): 22–36.

Kaul, Adam R. *Turning the Tune: Traditional Music, Tourism, and Social Change in an Irish Village.* New York: Bergahn Books, 2009.

Kiely, Benedict. *And As I Rode by Granard Moat.* Dublin: Lilliput Press, 1996.

Kinney, Phyllis. "Wales." In *The Garland Encyclopedia of World Music*, vol. 8: *Europe*, edited by Timothy Rice and James Porter, pp. 342–359. New York: Routledge, 2000.

Krassen, Miles. *O'Neill's Music of Ireland.* New York: Oak Publications, 1976.

Kuter, Lois. "Brittany." In *The Garland Encyclopedia of World Music*, vol. 8: *Europe*, edited by Timothy Rice and James Porter, pp. 558–565. New York: Routledge, 2000.

Kuter, Lois. "Celtic Musics." In *The Garland Encyclopedia of World Music*, vol. 9: *Europe*, edited by Timothy Rice and James Porter, pp. 319–323. New York: Routledge, 2000.

Lalor, Brian, ed. *The Encyclopedia of Ireland.* New Haven, CT: Yale University Press, 2003.

Léger, Devon. "Gay Traditions: Talking with Stepdancer and Trad Singer Nic Gareiss." https://www.nodepression.com/gay-traditions-talking-with-stepdancer-and-trad-singer-nic-gareiss/ (accessed 07/17/2019), 2012.

Leyburn, James G. *The Scotch-Irish: A Social History.* Chapel Hill, NC: University of North Carolina Press, 1962.

Lhuyd, Edward. *Archaeologia Brittanica*, vol. I: *Giving Some Account Additional to What Has Been hitherto publish'd, of the Languages, Histories and Customs of the Original Inhabitants of Great Britain.* Oxford: Ashmolean Museum, 1707.

Lott, Eric. *Love and Theft: Blackface Minstrelsy and the American Working Class*. New York: Oxford University Press, 1993.

Mac Con Iomaire, Liam. "Sean-nós." In *The Companion to Irish Traditional Music*, edited by Fintan Vallely, pp. 336–338. Cork: Cork University Press, 1999.

Mac Con Iomaire, Liam. *Seosamh Ó hÉanaí: Nár Fhágha Mé Bás Choíche*. Indreabhán, Ireland: Cló-Iar Chonnachta, 2007.

MacKillop, James. *Dictionary of Celtic Mythology*. New York: Oxford University Press, 1998.

Marshall, Erynn. *Music in the Air Somewhere: The Shifting Borders of West Virginia's Fiddle and Song Traditions*. Morgantown, WV: West Virginia University Press, 2006.

Mathews, Ceri. "Wales." In *The Companion to Irish Traditional Music*, edited by Fintan Vallely, pp. 424–425. Cork: Cork University Press, 1999.

McCaffrey, Carmel and Leo Eaton. *In Search of Ancient Ireland: The Origins of the Irish from Neolithic Times to the Coming of the English*. Chicago: New Amsterdam Books, 2002.

McCann, Anthony and Lillis Ó Laoire. "'Raising One Higher than the Other': The Hierarchy of Tradition in Representations of Gaelic- and English-Language Song in Ireland." In *Global Pop, Local Language*, edited by Harris M. Berger and Michael Thomas Carroll. New York: Routledge, pp. 233–265, 2003.

McCarthy, James and Euan Hague. "Race, Nation, and Nature: The Cultural Politics of 'Celtic' Identification in the American West." *Annals of the Association of American Geographers* 94, no. 2 (2004): 387–408.

McCloskey, Robert. *Make Way for Ducklings*. New York: The Viking Press, 1941.

McCullough, Lawrence. "Style in Traditional Irish Music." *Ethnomusicology* 21, no. 1 (1977): 85–97.

McDonagh, Rosaleen "Why Minority Ethnic Status Matters: A Traveller View." The Irish Times. https://www.irishtimes.com/opinion/why-minority-ethnic-status-matters-a-traveller-view-1.2994178 (accessed 07/19/19), 2017.

McDonald, Forrest. "Prologue." In *Cracker Culture: Celtic Ways in the Old South*, edited by Grady McWhiney, pp. xxi–xliii. Tuscaloosa, AL: The University of Alabama Press, 1998.

McGlynn, Mary. "Garth Brooks in Ireland or, Play That Country Music, Whiteboys." In *The Irish in Us: Irishness, Performativity, and Popular Culture*, edited by Diane Negra. Durham, NC and London: Duke University Press, 2006.

McKittrick, David and David McVea. *Making Sense of the Troubles: The Story of the Conflict in Northern Ireland*. Chicago: New Amsterdam Books, 2002.

McNamara, Brian. "Uilleann Pipes." In *The Companion to Irish Traditional Music*, edited by Fintan Vallely, pp. 410–414. Cork: Cork University Press, 1999.

Melhuish, Martin. *Celtic Tides: Traditional Music in a New Age*. Kingston, ON: Quarry Music Books, 1998.

Mercier, Mel. "Bones." In *The Companion to Irish Traditional Music*, edited by Fintan Vallely, pp. 33–35. Cork: Cork University Press, 1999.

Moloney, Mick. "USA." In *The Companion to Irish Traditional Music*, edited by Fintan Vallely, pp. 414–416. Cork: Cork University Press, 1999.

Moloney, Mick. *Far from the Shamrock Shore: The Story of Irish-American Immigration Through Song*. New York: Crown Publishers, 2002.

Motherway, Susan H. *The Globalization of Irish Traditional Song Performance*. Bulrington, VT: Ashgate, 2013.

Mulcrone, Mick. "The Famine and Collective Memory: The Role of the Irish-American Press in the Early Twentieth Century." In *The Great Famine and the Irish Diaspora in America*, edited by Arthur Gribben, pp. 219–238. Amherst, MA: University of Massachusetts Press, 1999.

Murphy, Pat. *Toss the Feathers: Irish Set Dancing*. Cork: Mercier Press, 1995.

Negra, Diane. *The Irish in Us: Irishness, Performativity, and Popular Culture*. Durham, NC: Duke University Press, 2006.

Ní Chathasaigh, Máire. "Mode." In *The Companion to Irish Traditional Music*, edited by Fintan Vallely, pp. 243–244. Cork: Cork University Press, 1999.

Ní Riain, Nóirín. "The Nature and Classification of Traditional Religious Songs in Irish: With a Survey of Printed and Oral Sources." In *Irish Musical Studies 2: Music and the Church*, edited by Gerard Gillen and Harry White, pp. 190–253. Dublin: Irish Academic Press, 1993.

O'Boyle, Sean. *The Irish Song Tradition*. Cork: Ossian Publications, 1976.

O'Brien, Sharon. *The Family Silver: A Memoir of Depression and Inheritance*. Chicago, IL: University of Chicago Press, 2004.

Ó Canainn, Tomás. *Traditional Music in Ireland*. Cork: Ossian Publications, 1978.

Ó Canainn, Tomás. *Seán Ó Riada: His Life and Work*. Cork: The Collins Press, 2003.

O'Connor, Jennifer J. "The Irish Origins and Variations of the Ballad 'Molly Bawn'." *The Canadian Journal for Traditional Music* 14 (1986): 10–18.

O'Driscoll, Robert and Lorna Reynolds, eds. *The Untold Story: The Irish in Canada* (2 vol. set). Toronto: Celtic Arts of Canada, 1988.

Ó hAllmhuráin, Gearóid. *O'Brien Pocket History of Irish Traditional Music*. Dublin: The O'Brien Press, 1998.

Ó hAllmhuráin, Gearóid. "The Great Famine: A Catalyst in Irish Traditional Music Making." In *The Great Famine and the Irish Diaspora in America*, edited by Arthur Gribben, pp. 104–132. Amherst, MA: University of Massachusetts Press, 1999.

Ó hAllmhuráin, Gearóid. *Flowing Tides: History and Memory in an Irish Soundscape*. New York: Oxford University Press, 2016.

O'Keeffe, John. *The Masses of Seán and Peadar Ó Riada: Explorations in Vernacular Chant*. Cork: Cork University Press, 2017.

Ó Laoire, Lillis. "Níl Sí Doiligh a Iompar! / No Load to Carry: A Personal Response to the Current Situation of Irish." In *Who Needs Irish? Reflections on the Importance of the Irish Language Today*, edited by Ciarán Mac Murchaidh, pp. 46–63. Dublin: Veritas Publications, 2004.

Ó Muirithe, Diarmuid. "Song, Macaronic." In *The Companion to Irish Traditional Music*, edited by Fintan Vallely, pp. 354–356. Cork: Cork University Press, 1999.

O'Neill, Francis James. *Irish Minstrels and Musicians: The Story of Irish Music*. Cork and Dublin: The Mercier Press, 1987 [1913].

O'Shea, Helen. "Getting to the Heart of the Music: Idealizing Musical Community and Irish Traditional Music Sessions." *Journal of the Society for Musicology in Ireland* 2 (2006–7): 1–18.

O'Shea, Helen. *The Making of Irish Traditional Music*. Cork: Cork University Press, 2008.

Ó Tuama, Seán. *An Grá in Amhráin na nDaoine*, reprinted in *Repossessions* (1995). Cork: Cork University Press, 1960.

Pettit, Lance. *Screening Ireland: Film and Television Representation*. Manchester: Manchester University Press, 2000.

Porter, James. "Introduction: Locating Celtic Music (and Song)." *Western Folklore* 57, no. 4 (1998): 205–224.

Porter, James. "Scotland." In *The Garland Encyclopedia of World Music*, vol. 9: *Europe*, edited by Timothy Rice and James Porter, pp. 360–377. New York: Routledge Publishing, 2000.

Pramaggiore, Maria. "'Papa Don't Preach': Pregnancy and Performance in Irish Contemporary Cinema." In *The Irish in Us: Irishness, Performativity, and Popular Culture*, edited by Diane Negra, pp. 110–129. Durham, NC: Duke University Press, 2006.

Quinn, Bob. "Sean-nós, Speculative Origins." In *The Companion to Irish Traditional Music*, edited by Fintan Vallely, pp. 339–345. Cork: Cork University Press, 1999.

Quinn, Sean. "Piano accordion." In *The Companion to Irish Traditional Music*, edited by Fintan Vallely, pp. 5–6. Cork: Cork University Press, 1999.

Raftery, Barry. *Pagan Celtic Ireland: The Enigma of the Irish Iron Age*. London: Thames and Hudson, 1994.

Ralls-MacLeod, Karen. *Music and the Celtic Otherworld: From Ireland to Iona*. New York: St. Martin's, 2000.

Ramsey, Gordon. *Music, Emotion and Identity in Ulster Marching Bands: Flutes, Drums, and Loyal Sons*. Bern, Switzerland: Peter Lang, 2011.

Rees, Stephen. "Wales: Crwth." In *The Companion to Irish Traditional Music*, edited by Fintan Vallely, pp. 425. Cork: Cork University Press, 1999.

Reiss, Scott. "Tradition and Imaginary: Irish Traditional Music and the Celtic Phenomenon." In *Celtic Modern: Music at the Global Fringe*, edited by Martin Stokes and Philip V. Bohlman, pp. 145–169. Lanham, MD: Scarecrow Press, 2003.

Rimmer, Joan. *The Irish Harp/Cláirseach na hÉireann*, 2nd edn. Cork: Mercier Press, 1977.

Ritchie, Jean. *Folk Songs of the Southern Appalachians as Sung by Jean Ritchie*. New York: Oak Publications, 1965.

Roediger, David R. *The Wages of Whiteness: Race and the Making of the American Working Class*. New York: Verso, 1991.

Saer, D. Roy, ed. *Caneuon Llafar Gwlad* (Songs from Oral Tradition), vol. 1. Cardiff: The National Museum of Wales, 1974.

Sargent, Helen Child and George Lyman Kittredge, eds. *English and Scottish Popular Ballads, Edited from the Collection of Francis James Child*. Boston and New York: Houghton Mifflin Company, 1904.

Schiller, Rina. *The Lambeg and the Bodhrán: Drums of Ireland*. Belfast: The Institute of Irish Studies, 2001.

Shields, Hugh. *Narrative Singing in Ireland: Lays, Ballads, Come-All-Yes and Other Songs*. Dublin: Irish Academic Press, 1993.

Slominski, Tes. "'Pretty Young Artistes' and 'The Queen of Irish Fiddlers': Intelligibility, Gender, and the Irish Nationalist Imagination." *Ethnomusicology Ireland* 2, no. 3 (2013): 1–21.

Slominski, Tes. "Queer as Trad: LGBTQ Performers and Irish Traditional Music in the United States." In *The Oxford Handbook of Music and Queerness*, edited by Fred Everett Maus and Sheila Whiteley. New York: Oxford University Press, 2018.

Slominski, Tes. *Trad Nation: Gender, Sexuality, and Race in Irish Traditional Music*. Middletown, CT: Wesleyan University Press, 2020.

Smith, Christopher J. "The Celtic Guitar: Crossing Cultural Boundaries in the 20th Century." In *The Cambridge Companion to the Guitar*, edited by Victor Anand Coelho, pp. 33–43. Cambridge: Cambridge University Press, 2003.

Smith, Christopher J. "Blacks, Irish, and the Antebellum Creole World of William Sidney Mount." *Unpublished Paper Presented at the 2008 Annual Conference of the Society for Ethnomusicology*. Middletown, CT, 2009.

Smith, Sally K. Sommers. "Irish Traditional Music in a Modern World." *New Hibernia Review* 5, no. 2 (2001): 111–125.

Stivers, Richard. *Hair of the Dog: Irish Drinking and Its American Stereotype*. New York: Continuum Press, 2000.

Stokes, Martin and Philip V. Bohlman. "Introduction." In *Celtic Modern: Music at the Global Fringe*, edited by Martin Stokes and Philip V. Bohlman, pp. 1–26. Lanham, MD: Scarecrow Press, 2003.

Strang, Jillian and Joyce Toomre. "Alexis Soyer and the Irish Famine: 'Splendid Promises and Abortive Measures'." In *The Great Famine and the Irish Diaspora in America*, edited by Arthur Gribben, pp. 66–84. Amherst, MA: University of Massachusetts Press, 1999.

Suggett, Richard. "Vagabonds and Minstrels in Sixteenth-Century Wales." In *The Spoken Word: Oral Culture in Britain, 1500–1850*, edited by Adam Fox and Daniel Woolf, pp. 138–172. Manchester: Manchester University Press, 2003.

Sullivan, Mairéid. *Celtic Women in Music: A Celebration of Beauty and Sovereignty*. Kingston, ON: Quarry Music Books, 1999.

Sykes, Bryan. *Saxons, Vikings, and Celts: The Genetic Roots of Britain and Ireland*. New York: W.W. Norton and Co, 2006.

Teitelbaum, Benjamin R. *Lions of the North: Sounds of the New Nordic Radical Nationalism*. New York: Oxford University Press, 2017.

Trend, J. B. "Music in Spanish Galicia." *Music and Letters* 5, no. 1 (1924): 15–32.

Trew, Johanne. "Canada." In *The Companion to Irish Traditional Music*, edited by Fintan Vallely, pp. 50–51. Cork: Cork University Press, 1999.

Tunney, Paddy. *Where Songs Do Thunder*. Belfast: Appletree Press, 1991.

Tuohy, David and Mícheál Ó hAodha. *Postcolonial Artist: Johnny Doran and Irish Traveller Tradition*. Newcastle, United Kingdom: Cambridge Scholars, 2008.

Twain, Mark. *The Adventures of Huckleberry Finn*. North Chemford, MA: Courier Dover Publications, 1884.

Uí Ógáin, Ríonach. *Going to the Well for Water: The Séamus Ennis Field Diary 1942-1946*. Cork: Cork University Press, 2009.

Vallely, Fintan, ed. *The Companion to Irish Traditional Music*, 2nd ed. Cork: Cork University Press, 2011.

Waters, Mary C. *Ethnic Options: Choosing Identities in America*. Berkeley, CA: University of California Press, 1990.

Whelan, Frank. *The Complete Guide to Irish Dance*. Belfast: Appletree Press, 2000.

White, Harry. *The Keeper's Recital: Music and Cultural History in Ireland, 1770–1970*. Notre Dame, IN: University of Notre Dame Press, 1998.

Wilkinson, Desi. "Brittany." In *The Companion to Irish Traditional Music*, edited by Fintan Vallely, pp. 40–43. Cork: Cork University Press, 1999.

Wilkinson, Desi. "'Celtitude,' Professionalism, and the *Fest Noz* in Traditional Music of Brittany." In *Celtic Modern: Music at the Global Fringe*, edited by Martin Stokes and Philip V. Bohlman, pp. 219–256. Lanham, MD: Scarecrow Press, 2003.

Williams, Sean. "Irish Music and the Experience of Nostalgia in Japan." *Asian Music* 37, no. 1 (2006a): 101–119.

Williams, Sean. "Ireland." In *The Ethnomusicologists' Cookbook*, edited by Sean Williams, pp. 267–272. New York: Routledge, 2006b.

Williams, William H. A. *'Twas Only an Irishman's Dream: The Image of Ireland and the Irish in American Popular Song Lyrics, 1800–1920*. Urbana, IL: University of Illinois Press, 1996.

Wilson, David A. *Ireland: A Bicycle and a Tin Whistle*. Montreal: McGill-Queen's University Press, 1995.

Wilson, Thomas M. and Hastings Donnan. *The Anthropology of Ireland*. New York: Berg, 2006.

Wulff, Helena. "Memories in Motion: The Irish Dancing Body." *Body and Society* 11, no. 4 (2005): 56–62.

Wulff, Helena. *Dancing at the Crossroads: Memory and Mobility in Ireland*. New York: Berghahn Books, 2008.

Zimmerman, Georges Denis. *Songs of Irish Rebellion: Irish Political Street Ballads and Rebel Songs, 1780–1900*. Dublin: Four Courts History Classics, 2002.

About the Author

Sean Williams, PhD is Professor of Ethnomusicology at The Evergreen State College in Olympia, Washington, where she has taught since 1991. She was drawn to Irish music and musicians in the San Francisco Bay Area as an undergraduate at UC Berkeley. In graduate school she was fortunate to work closely with Joe Heaney, the great singer from Connemara, and she has studied and performed Irish music ever since. At The Evergreen State College she regularly teaches a year-long, full-time program in Irish Studies ("Ireland in History and Memory"), leading students from the Pacific Northwest of the U.S. to the Atlantic Northwest of Ireland.

Williams earned both her MA and PhD degrees in ethnomusicology from the University of Washington, Seattle. Her master's degree focused on Irish *sean-nós* ("old style") singing, and her PhD examined the sung poetry of West Java, Indonesia. She sings in Irish, English, Indonesian, and Sundanese, and plays the Irish fiddle, classical guitar, banjo, and many other instruments. Her books include: *The Sound of the Ancestral Ship: Highland Music of West Java* (Oxford, 2001); *The Ethnomusicologists' Cookbook, volumes I* and *II* (Routledge, 2006 and 2015); *The Garland Handbook of Southeast Asian Music*, with Terry E. Miller (Routledge, 2008); *Bright Star of the West: Joe Heaney, Irish Song Man*, with Lillis Ó Laoire (Oxford, 2011); and *English Grammar: 100 Tragically Common Mistakes (and How to Correct Them)* (Zephyros Press, 2019).

Index

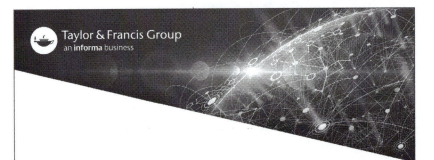